DESIRE AND DOMESTIC FICTION

Desire and Domestic Fiction

A POLITICAL HISTORY
OF THE NOVEL

Nancy Armstrong

OXFORD UNIVERSITY PRESS
New York   Oxford

Oxford University Press

Oxford New York Toronto
Delhi Bombay Calcutta Madras Karachi
Petaling Jaya Singapore Hong Kong Tokyo
Nairobi Dar es Salaam Cape Town
Melbourne Auckland

and associated companies in
Berlin Ibadan

First published in 1987 by Oxford University Press, Inc.,
200 Madison Avenue, New York, New York 10016

First issued as an Oxford University Press paperback, 1989

Oxford is a registered trademark of Oxford University Press

Library of Congress Cataloging-in-Publication Data
Armstrong, Nancy.
Desire and domestic fiction.

Includes index.
1. Domestic fiction, English—History and criticism.
2. English fiction—Women authors—History and criticism.
3. Feminism and literature—Great Britain. 4. Women
and literature—Great Britain. 5. Women in literature.
6. Sex role in literature. 7. Home in literature.
8. Family in literature. I. Title.
PR830.D65A7 1987 823'.009 86-16482
ISBN 0-19-504179-8 (alk. paper)
ISBN 0-19-506160-8 (pbk.)

12 14 16 15 13
Printed in the United States of America

For L.T.

Acknowledgments

This project was supported by grants from the American Council of Learned Societies, the American Association of University Women, and the Josephine Nevins Keal research fund of Wayne State University. I am grateful to the Fawcett Museum and particularly to its assistant director, David Doughan, for giving me access to the educational literature for women described in Chapters 2 and 3. A section of Chapter 1 appeared under the title of "The Rise of Feminine Authority in the Novel" (in *Novel*, 15, no. 2 [1982], 127–45), and I would like to thank the editor Mark Spilka for his kind attention to my work. My book owes much to William Sisler and Marion Osmun of Oxford University Press whose expertise and good humor saw it through publication.

I could never have written this book without the personal encouragement and professional support given to me through the years by Homer Obed Brown, Jerome J. McGann, Marjorie Perloff, Thomas A. Sebeok, Wendy Steiner, and Jane P. Tompkins. I owe just as much to those who read this manuscript at various stages of its production and who helped to make it say what I wanted it to say: Susan Kirkpatrick, John Kucich, Vassilis Lambropoulos, and Clifford Siskin. I am especially grateful to Michael Davidson, Juliet MacCannell, John Maynard, and William Tay for their knowledgeable readings of the completed manuscript. Each stage of my argument was vigorously contested and revised in graduate seminars at the State University of New York at Buffalo (spring 1984) and the University of California, San Diego (fall 1984). To the students in those seminars I extend my gratitude for making the whole project far more complicated and pleasurable than I had any reason to expect. Allon White read the completed manuscript for Oxford University Press, and his expert suggestions guided its revision. He has my enduring affection.

Much as my book has intellectualized the middle-class family, I cannot allow the contributions of certain members of my own family to go unacknowledged. I wish to thank my mother Jeanne Bowes for providing an example of domesticity that was more arduous to realize than an academic career; my brother John Bowes for redeeming certain moments of family life with irony; and my three sons, Scott, Mark, and John Armstrong, for finding amusement in my deviation from most of the domestic norms. Finally, in tracing the history of domestic fiction, I am most indebted to Len Tennenhouse, Kathy Ashley, Homer Brown, and Don Wayne—old friends whose convictions at crucial turns of the process seemed indistinguishable from my own and whose thinking has shaped the places of this argument in which I take greatest satisfaction.

Solana Beach, California   N.A.
July 1986

Contents

DESIRE AND DOMESTIC FICTION

Introduction:
The Politics of Domesticating
Culture, Then and Now

Thus towards the end of the eighteenth century a change came about which, if I were rewriting history, I should describe more fully and think of greater importance than the Crusades or the Wars of the Roses. The middle-class woman began to write.

VIRGINIA WOOLF, *A Room of One's Own*

From the beginning, domestic fiction actively sought to disentangle the language of sexual relations from the language of politics and, in so doing, to introduce a new form of political power. This power emerged with the rise of the domestic woman and established its hold over British culture through her dominance over all those objects and practices we associate with private life. To her went authority over the household, leisure time, courtship procedures, and kinship relations, and under her jurisdiction the most basic qualities of human identity were supposed to develop.

To consider the rise of the domestic woman as a major event in political history is not, as it may seem, to present a contradiction in terms, but to identify the paradox that shapes modern culture. It is also to trace the history of a specifically modern form of desire that, during the early eighteenth century, changed the criteria for determining what was most important in a female. In countless educational treatises and works of fiction that were supposedly written for women, this form of desire came into being along with a new kind of woman. And by representing life with such a woman as not only desirable but also available to virtually anyone, this ideal eventually reached beyond the beliefs of region, faction, and religious sect to unify the interests of those groups who were neither extremely powerful nor very poor. During the eighteenth century, one author after another discovered that the customary way of understanding

3

social experience actually misrepresented human value. In place of the intricate status system that had long dominated British thinking, these authors began to represent an individual's value in terms of his, but more often in terms of *her,* essential qualities of mind. Literature devoted to producing the domestic woman thus appeared to ignore the political world run by men. Of the female alone did it presume to say that neither birth nor the accoutrements of title and status accurately represented the individual; only the more subtle nuances of behavior indicated what one was really worth. In this way, writing for and about the female introduced a whole new vocabulary for social relations, terms that attached precise moral value to certain qualities of mind.

It was at first only women who were defined in terms of their emotional natures. Men generally retained their political identity in writing that developed the qualities of female subjectivity and made subjectivity a female domain. It is fair to say that Sterne's heroes, like Fielding's Joseph Andrews, clearly declared themselves anomalous when they inverted the model and, as males, experienced life as a sequence of events that elicited sentimental responses. In this respect, they came to the reader in a form considered more appropriate for representing a female's experience than that of a male. In nineteenth century fiction, however, men were no longer political creatures so much as they were products of desire and producers of domestic life. As gender came to mark the most important difference among individuals, men were still men and women still women, of course, but the difference between male and female was understood in terms of their respective qualities of mind. Their psychological differences made men political and women domestic rather than the other way around, and both therefore acquired identity on the basis of personal qualities that had formerly determined female nature alone. During the course of *Wuthering Heights,* for example, one can see Heathcliff undergo a transformation that strips away the features of a Gypsy from Liverpool at the turn of the century and attributes all his behavior to sexual desire. By a similar process, Rochester loses his aristocratic bearing by the end of *Jane Eyre* to assume a role within a purely emotional network of relationships overseen by a woman. It is only by thus subordinating all social differences to those based on gender that these novels bring order to social relationships. Granting all this, one may conclude that the power of the middle classes had everything to do with that of middle-class love. And if this contention holds true, one must also agree that middle-class authority rested in large part upon the authority that novels attributed to women and in this way designated as specifically female.

In demonstrating that the rise of the novel hinged upon a struggle to say what made a woman desirable, then, I will be arguing that much more was at stake. I will consider this redefinition of desire as a decisive step in producing the densely interwoven fabric of common sense and sentimentality that even today ensures the ubiquity of middle-class power. It is my contention that narratives which seemed to be concerned solely with matters of courtship and marriage in fact seized the authority to say what was female, and that they did so in order to contest the reigning notion of kinship relations that attached most power and privilege to certain family lines. This struggle to represent sexuality took the form of a struggle to individuate wherever there was a collective body, to attach psychological motives to what had been the openly political behavior of contending groups, and to evaluate these according to a set of moral norms that exalted the domestic woman over and above her aristocratic counterpart. I am saying the female was the figure, above all else, on whom depended the outcome of the struggle among competing ideologies.

For no other reason than this could Samuel Richardson's novel *Pamela* represent a landowner's assault upon the chastity of an otherwise undistinguished servant girl as a major threat to our world as well as to hers. And Richardson could have Pamela resist such an assault only by confronting and then overthrowing the reigning notion of sexuality as articulated by Mr. B's subservient housekeeper. Scoffing at Pamela's claim that "to rob a person of her virtue is worse than cutting her throat," the housekeeper regards Mr. B's assaults as perfectly natural and states, "how strangely you talk! Are not the two sexes made for one another? And is it not natural for a gentleman to love a pretty woman? And suppose he can obtain his desires, is that so bad as cutting her throat?"[1] Clearly representing a minority position, Pamela prevails nevertheless through the novel's most harrowing scene where her master, with the help of the housekeeper, slips into bed and pins her naked body beneath him. Rather than yielding up even momentary satisfaction, this scene constitutes one of the least erotic bedroom encounters between male and female in literature:

> he kissed me with frightful vehemence; and then his voice broke upon me like a clap of thunder. Now, Pamela, said he, is the dreadful time of reckoning come, that I have threatened—I screamed out in such a manner, as never anybody heard the like. But there was nobody to help me: and both hands were secured, as I said. Sure never poor soul was in such agonies as I. Wicked man! said I; O God! my God! this *time!* this one *time!* deliver me from this distress! or strike me dead this moment! (p. 213)

Pamela escapes with her virtue as she becomes a creature of words (she protests) and of silence (she swoons). Mr. B's attempt to penetrate a servant girl's material body magically transforms that body into one of language and emotion, into a metaphysical object that can be acquired only through her consent and his willingness to adhere to the procedures of modern love. That this is indeed the Pamela Mr. B eventually desires calls into question the whole notion of sexuality on which the housekeeper's common sense had been based.

In opening the argument of this book, I can only suggest how such a transformation occurred on a mass basis and how it revised the entire surface of social life. The nature and extent of its historical impact is only implicit in the one scene from *Pamela* that does seem genuinely erotic. In this scene, we may observe the transfer of erotic desire from Pamela's body to her words. When Richardson at last allows Mr. B to have his way with the girl, erotic desire makes its brief reappearance in the novel, not on their wedding night, but at the climax of their courtship, as Mr. B forcibly takes possession of Pamela's letters:

> Artful slut! said he, What's this to my question?—Are they [the letters] not *about* you?—If, said I, I must pluck them out of my hiding-place behind the wainscot, won't you see me?—Still more and more artful! said he—Is this an answer to my question?—I have searched every place above, and in your closet, for them, and cannot find them; so I *will* know where they are. Now, said he, it is my opinion they are about you; and I never undressed a girl in my life; but I will now begin to strip my pretty Pamela. (p. 245)

As he proceeds to probe her garters for a few more precious words, Pamela capitulates and, in a shower of tears, delivers up what he desires. Thus having displaced the conventionally desirable woman onto a written one, Richardson infuses the new body with erotic appeal. The pleasure she now offers is the pleasure of the text rather than those forms of pleasure that derive from mastering her body.

However inadequate this substitution may seem to us today, readers remain thoroughly enchanted by narratives in which a woman's virtue alone overcomes sexual aggression and transforms male desire into middle-class love, the stuff that modern families are made of. As the heirs to a novelistic culture, we are not very likely to question the whole enterprise. We are more likely to feel that the success of repeated pressures to coax and nudge sexual desire into conformity with the norms of heterosexual monogamy affords a fine way of closing a novel and provides a satisfactory goal for a text to achieve. Novels do not encourage us to doubt whether sexual desire already existed before the strategies were devised to domesticate it. Nor do novels often question the premise that such desire, if it is not so domesticated, constitutes the gravest danger—

and root of all other threats—to society. And I know of no major criticism of the novel which does not at some point capitulate to the idea that sexual desire exists in some form prior to its representation and remains there as something for us to recover or liberate. It is this dominant theory of desire, I believe, that authorizes domestic fiction and yet conceals the role such fiction played in modern history. More to the point, in ignoring the historical dimension of desire, this theory—at once psychological and literary—has left us no way of explaining why, at the inception of modern culture, the literate classes in England suddenly developed an unprecedented taste for writing for, about, and by women.

I know of no history of the English novel that can explain why women began to write respectable fiction near the end of the eighteenth century, became prominent novelists during the nineteenth century, and on this basis achieved the status of artists during the modern period. Yet that they suddenly began writing and were recognized as women writers strikes me as a central event in the history of the novel. Ian Watt's classic study *The Rise of the Novel* ties the popularity of such writers as Defoe and Richardson to an economic individualism and Puritan ethic they shared with a substantial portion of the new reading public. But Watt's historical explanation fails to consider why "the majority of eighteenth-century novels" were written by women. When it comes time to account for Jane Austen, historical explanations elude him, and he falls back on a commonplace claim: "the feminine sensibility was in some ways better equipped to reveal the intricacies of personal relationships and was therefore at a real advantage in the realm of the novel."[2] Of late, it seems particularly apparent that such attempts to explain the history of the novel fail because—to a man—history is represented as the history of male institutions. Where women writers are concerned, this understanding of history leaves all the truly interesting questions unasked: Why the "female sensibility"? How "better equipped"? What "intricacies"? Whose "personal relationships"? Why an "advantage in the realm of the novel"? And, finally, how did all this become commonplace?

As if in response, Sandra Gilbert and Susan Gubar's *The Madwoman in the Attic* at least attempts to account for a tradition of female writers. While Watt is concerned with just how fiction played to the interests of a changing readership, Gilbert and Gubar concentrate on the authors themselves and the conditions under which they wrote. They argue that women authors, in contrast with their male counterparts, had to manage the difficult task of simultaneously subverting and conforming to patriarchal standards.[3] But when understood within this gendered frame of reference, the conditions for women's writing appear to remain relatively constant throughout history because the authors in question were women and because the conditions under which they wrote were largely determined by men. Thus, like Watt, Gilbert and Gubar virtually ignore the historical conditions that women have confronted as writers, and in so doing they ignore the place of women's writing in history. For Gilbert and Gubar, too, history takes place not in and through those areas of culture over which women may have held sway, but in institutions dominated by men. Because both these definitive histories of the novel presuppose a social world divided according to the principle of gender, neither of them can possibly consider how such a world came into being and what part the novel played in its formation. Yet these are the very questions we must consider if we want to explain why women became prominent authors of fiction during the nineteenth century in England. So long as we assume that gender transcends history, we have no hope of understanding what role women played—for better or worse—in shaping the world we presently inhabit.

To describe the history of domestic fiction, then, I will argue several points at once: first, that sexuality is a cultural construct and as such has a history; second, that written representations of the self allowed the modern individual to become an economic and psychological reality; and third, that the modern individual was first and foremost a woman. My argument traces the development of a specific female ideal in eighteenth and nineteenth century conduct books and educational treatises for women, as well as in domestic fiction, all of which often were written by women. I will insist that one cannot distinguish the production of the new female ideal either from the rise of the novel or from the rise of the new middle classes in England. At first, I will demonstrate, writing about the domestic woman afforded a means of contesting the dominant notion of sexuality that understood desirability in terms of the woman's claims to fortune and family name. But then, by the early decades of the nineteenth century, middle-class writers and intellectuals can be seen to take the virtues embodied by the domestic woman and to pit them against working-class culture. It took nothing less than the destruction of a much older concept of the household for industrialization to overcome working-class resistance. In time, following the example of fiction, new kinds of writing—sociological studies of factory and city, as well as new theories of natural history and political economy—established modern domesticity as the only haven from the trials of a heartless economic world. By the 1840s, norms inscribed in the domestic woman had already cut across the categories of status that maintained an earlier, patriarchal model of social relations.[4] The entire surface of social experience had come to mirror those kinds of writing—the novel prominent among them—which represented the existing field of social information as contrasting masculine and feminine spheres.[5]

This book, which links the history of British fiction to the empowering of the middle classes in England through the dissemination of a new female ideal, necessarily challenges existing histories of the novel. For one thing, it insists that the history of the novel cannot be understood apart from the history of sexuality. In dissolving the boundary between those texts that today are considered literature and those that, like the conduct books, are not, my study shows that the distinction between literary and nonliterary was imposed retrospectively by the modern literary institution upon anomalous works of fiction. It shows as well that the domestic novel antedated—was indeed necessarily antecedent to—the way of life it represented. Rather than refer to individuals who already existed as such and who carried on relationships according to novelistic conventions, domestic fiction took great care to distinguish itself from the kinds of fiction that predominated in the eighteenth and nineteenth centuries. Most fiction, which represented identity in terms of region, sect, or faction, could not very well affirm the universality of any particular form of desire. In contrast, domestic fiction unfolded the operations of human desire as if they were independent of political history. And this helped to create the illusion that desire was entirely subjective and therefore essentially different from the politically encodable forms of behavior to which desire gave rise.

At the same time and on the same theoretical grounds, my study of the novel challenges traditional histories of nineteenth century England by questioning the practice of writing separate histories for political and cultural events. Rather than see the rise of the new middle class in terms of the economic changes that solidified its hold over the culture, my reading of materials for and about women shows that the formation of the modern political state—in England at least—was accomplished largely through cultural hegemony. New strategies of representation not only revised the way in which an individual's identity could be understood, but in presuming to discover what was only natural in the self, they also removed subjective experience and sexual practices from their place in history. Our education does much the same thing when it allows us to assume that modern consciousness is a constant of human experience and teaches us to understand modern history in economic terms, even though history itself was not understood in those terms until the beginning of the nineteenth century. We are taught to divide the political world in two and to detach the practices that belong to a female domain from those that govern the marketplace. In this way, we compulsively replicate the symbolic behavior that constituted a private domain of the individual outside and apart from social history.

In actuality, however, the changes that allowed diverse groups of people to make sense of social experience as these mutually exclusive worlds of information constitute a major event in the history of the modern individual. It follows, then, that only those histories that account for the formation of separate spheres—masculine and feminine, political and domestic, social and cultural—can allow us to see what this semiotic behavior had to do with the economic triumph of the new middle classes. In effect, I am arguing, political events cannot be understood apart from women's history, from the history of women's literature, or from changing representations of the household. Nor can a history of the novel be historical if it fails to take into account the history of sexuality. For such a history remains, by definition, locked into categories replicating the semiotic behavior that empowered the middle class in the first place.

It is one thing to call for a study that considers the rise of the novel and the emergence of a coherent middle-class ethos as being one and the same as the formation of a highly elaborated form of female. It is quite another to account for phenomena such as writings for, by, and about women that have so far steadfastly resisted every effort of literary theory to explain their production and relevance to a moment in history. I have drawn upon the work of Michel Foucault—relying, in particular, on *The History of Sexuality, Volume I*, as well as *Discipline and Punish*—to identify the problem inherent in all but a few discussions of sexuality in literature. Foucauldian histories break up the traditional modes of historical causality in order to focus our attention on the place of language and particularly writing in the history of modern culture, as well as on the very real political interests that are served when certain areas of culture—those I am calling sexuality—remain impervious to historical investigation. I want to stress the relationship between the sexual and the political. I want to isolate some major historical changes in this relationship because—as the studies of Watt and of Gilbert and Gubar demonstrate particularly well—it is very possible to situate women's writing in history without showing the political interests that such writing served, just as it is very possible to show the politics of women's writing without acknowledging how those interests changed radically with the passage of time. Foucault, on the other hand, makes it possible to consider sexual relations as the site for changing power relations between classes and cultures as well as between genders and generations.

He offers a way out of the problem plaguing the studies of Watt and

Gilbert and Gubar—the inability to historicize sexuality—by means of a double conceptual move. The first volume of his *History of Sexuality* makes sex a function of sexuality and considers sexuality as a purely semiotic process. Sexuality includes not only all those representations of sex that appear to be sex itself—in modern culture, for example, the gendered body—but also those myriad representations that are meaningful in relation to sex, namely, all the various masculine or feminine attributes that saturate our world of objects. Sexuality is, in other words, the cultural dimension of sex, which, to my way of thinking, includes as its most essential and powerful component the form of representation we take to be nature itself.[6] Thus we can regard gender as one function of sexuality that must have a history. My study of the novel will demonstrate that, with the formation of a modern institutional culture, gender differences—though one of many possible functions of sexuality—came to dominate the functions of generation and genealogy, which organized an earlier culture.

Most studies of the British novel more or less consciously acknowledge the difference between sex and sexuality, referent and representation. With almost flawless consistency, however, criticism of the novel has made this distinction only to imbed a modern truth in the referent. I find it difficult to think of a single study of the novel that does not posit an opposition between writing and desire in which desire, when written, loses at least some of its individuality, truth, purity, or power, which is nevertheless there for critics to recover. But Foucault does not accept this opposition. He asks us to think of modern desire as something that depends on language and particularly on writing. It is on this ground that his *History of Sexuality* assaults the tradition of thinking that sees modern sexuality as logically prior to its written representation. And, I should add, Gilbert and Gubar's approach to the novel resembles Watt's by positing a specific form of sexuality as natural, that is, as sex. Both studies assume this prior and essential form of sexuality is what authors subsequently represent or misrepresent (it is all the same) in fiction. It is as if their opposing accounts of the production of fiction have agreed to disagree on the relatively minor issue of whether writing operates on the side of culture to repress nature or, alternatively, brings us closer to the truth of nature. Either way sex is situated historically prior to sexuality. According to Foucault, however, sex neither was nor is already there to be dealt with in one way or another by sexuality. Instead, its representation determines what one knows to be sex, the particular form sex assumes in one age as opposed to another, and the political interests these various forms may have served.

Any representation of sex as something that has been misunderstood and must be known, something that has been repressed and must be liberated, Foucault would argue, itself operates as a component of sexuality. More than that, such representations give modern sexuality its particular political thrust, which produces rather than represses a specific form of sexuality. During the eighteenth and nineteenth centuries, as Foucault has observed, the discovery of the fact of desire hidden within the individual prompted an extensive process of verbalization that effectively displaced an eroticism that had been located on the surface of the body. The discourse of sexuality saw such forms of pleasure as a substitution for some more primary, natural, and yet phantasmagorical desire. The discovery of this repressed sexuality thus provided justification for reading and interpreting sexual behavior wherever one found it, always with the Enlightenment motive of discovering truth and producing freedom, always consequently with the very different result of enclosing sex within an individual's subjectivity.

"The notion of repressed sex is not, therefore, only a theoretical matter," Foucault insists.

> The affirmation of a sexuality that has never been more rigorously subjugated than during the age of the hypocritical, bustling, and responsible bourgeoisie is coupled with the grandiloquence of a discourse purporting to reveal the truth about sex, modify its economy with reality, subvert the law that governs it, and change its future.[7]

It is not to wag the finger at middle-class hypocrisy that Foucault represents modern sexuality as behaving in this apparently contradictory way. Instead, he would have us see how the modern tendency that opposes desire to its verbal representation reproduces the figure of repressed sexuality. Any attempt to verbalize a form of sexuality that supposedly has been repressed in fact reproduces the distinction between essential human nature and the aspects of individual identity that have been imposed upon us by culture. This distinction does not allow us to examine culture and nature as two mutually dependent constructs that are together a political function of culture. Foucault alone shifts the investigation of sexuality away from the nature of desire to its political uses. He rejects the opposition between desire and writing in order to consider modern desire as something that depends on writing. "The question I would like to pose," Foucault explains,

> is not, Why are we repressed? but rather, Why do we say, with so much passion and so much resentment against our most recent past, against our present, and against ourselves, that we are repressed? By what spiral did

we come to affirm that sex is negated? What led us to show, ostentatiously, that sex is something we hide, to say it is something we silence? (pp. 8–9)

Foucault asks us, in other words, to understand repression at once as a rhetorical figure and as a means of producing desire. According to the same way of thinking, writing actively conceals the history of sexuality by turning repression into a narrative form. The history so produced constitutes a myth of progressive enlightenment. According to the Foucauldian hypothesis, however, our thinking is most completely inscribed within middle-class sexuality when we indulge in this fantasy, for the repressive hypothesis ensures that we imagine freedom in terms of repression, without questioning the truth or necessity of what we become with the lifting of bans. When, on the other hand, we abandon the practice of putting knowledge in a domain of nature outside of and prior to representation, we stand a chance of avoiding the tautology inherent in the notion of repression. No longer assuming that, when written, desire loses some of its individuality, truth, purity, or power, we may no longer feel strangely compelled to discover the truth about desire. Instead, we may understand desire as inseparable from its representation and understand its representation, in turn, as part of political history. In Foucault's account of the triumph of middle-class culture, the discovery of sexual repression provides an entirely new basis for understanding the relationship between one individual and another. Following his example, we can say that modern sexuality (for example, the middle-class idea that desirable femaleness was femininity) gave rise to a new understanding of sex (as the female was defined first by Darwin and then by Freud). We can also say that the representation of the individual as most essentially a sexual subject preceded the economic changes that made it possible to represent English history as the narrative unfolding of capitalism. Thus what began chiefly as writing that situated the individual within the poles of nature and culture, self and society, sex and sexuality only later became a psychological reality, and not the other way around. Foucault makes us mindful of this inversion of the normal relationship between forms of desire and the writing that represents them when he refers to the whole apparatus for producing modern individualism as "the discourse of sexuality."

But in order to describe the formation and behavior of such a discourse of sexuality in England, one must, I believe, refine Foucault's productive hypothesis to include the issue of gender. A semiotic capable of explaining virtually any form of human behavior in fact depended above all else on the creation of modern gender distinctions. These came into being with the development of a strictly female field of knowledge, and it was within this field that novels had to situate themselves if they were to have cultural authority. Even where poetry was concerned, the female ceased to represent the writers' muse and, with the Romantics, became instead a function of imagination that provided figurative language with a psychological source of meaning. And if a single cultural reflex could identify what was Victorian about Victorianism, and thus could isolate the moment when the new class system that distinguished landowner from capitalist and these from the laboring classes was securely entrenched, it was the insistence that a form of authority whose wellsprings were the passions of the human heart ultimately authorized writing. Therefore, while strategies of gender differentiation play little role in Foucault's writing, they must be considered paramount in a study that considers the history of the British novel as the history of sexuality.

My point is that language, which once represented the history of the individual as well as the history of the state in terms of kinship relations, was dismantled to form the masculine and feminine spheres that characterize modern culture. I want to show that a modern, gendered form of subjectivity developed first as a feminine discourse in certain literature for women before it provided the semiotic of nineteenth century poetry and psychological theory. It was through this gendered discourse, more surely than by means of the epistemological debate of the eighteenth century, that the discourse of sexuality made its way into common sense and determined how people understood themselves and what they desired in others. The gendering of human identity provided the metaphysical girders of modern culture—its reigning mythology. The popular concepts of subjectivity and sensibility resembled Locke's theory that human understanding developed through an exchange between the individual mind and the world of objects, an exchange that was mediated by language. But instead of a "soul"—Locke's word for what exists before the process of self-development begins—the essential self was commonly understood in terms of gender.[8] Conduct books for women, as well as fiction in the tradition of Richardson, worked within the same framework as Locke, but they constructed a more specialized and less material form of subjectivity, which they designated as female. If the Lockean subject began as a white sheet of paper on which objects could be understood in sets of spatial relations, then pedagogical literature for women mapped out a field of knowledge that would produce a specifically female form of subjectivity. To gender this field, things within the field itself had to be gendered. Masculine objects were understood in terms of their relative economic and political qualities, while feminine objects were recognized by their relative emotional qualities. At the site of the household, family life, and all that was hallowed as female, this gendered field of information contested a dominant political order which depended, among other things, on representing women as economic and political objects.

Such a modification of Foucault allows one to see that sexuality has a history that is inseparable from the political history of England. To introduce their highly influential *Practical Education* in 1801, for example, Maria Edgeworth and her father Robert announce their departure from the curriculum that reinforced traditional political differences: "On religion and politics we have been silent because we have no ambition to gain partisans, or to make proselytes, and because we do not address ourselves to any sect or party."[9] In virtually the same breath, they assure readers: "With respect to what is commonly called the education of the heart, we have endeavored to suggest the easiest means of inducing useful and agreeable habits, well regulated sympathy and benevolent affections" (p. viii). Thus their proposal substitutes the terms of emotion and behavior for those of one's specific sociopolitical identity. Basing identity on the same subjective qualities that had previously appeared only in the curricula designed for educating women, the Edgeworths' program gives priority to the schoolroom and parlor over the church and courts in regulating all human behavior. In doing so, their educational program promises to suppress the political signs of identity. But, of course, to render insignificant the traditional way of naming and ranking individuals is a powerful political gesture in its own right. Perfectly aware of the political force to be exercised through education, the Edgeworths justify their program for cultivating the heart on the political grounds that it constituted a new and more effective method of policing. In their words, "It is the business of education to prevent crimes, and to prevent all those habitual propensities which necessarily lead to their commission" (p. 354).

To accomplish their ambitious political goal, the Edgeworths invoke an economy of pleasure in which the novel has been implicated since its inception in the late seventeenth century, an economy that cannot in fact be understood apart from the novel or from the criticism that grew up around the new fiction to censor and foster it simultaneously. To begin with, the Edgeworths accept the view that prevailed during the eighteenth century, which said fiction behaved subversively and misled female desire:

> With respect to sentimental stories, and books of mere entertainment, we must remark, that they should be sparingly used, especially in the education of girls. This species of reading cultivates what is called the heart

prematurely, lowers the tone of the mind, and induces indifference for those common pleasures and occupations which, however trivial in themselves, constitute by far the greatest portion of our daily happiness. (p. 105)

But the same turn of mind recognizes the practical value of pleasure when it is harnessed and aimed at the right goals. Convinced that the "pleasures of literature" acted upon the reader in much the same way as the child's "taste for sugar-plums" (p. 80), the Edgeworths along with other forward-thinking educators began to endorse the reading of fiction that made social conformity seem necessary, if not entirely desirable. Although they name *Robinson Crusoe* as capable of leading immature minds astray, the Edge-worths also grant the book practical value. But they grant the book more value, curiously enough, for the very readers whom fiction most endangered: "To girls this species of reading cannot be as dangerous as it is to boys: girls must soon perceive the impossibility of their rambling about the world in quest of adventures" (p. 111). This is one of many statements that suggest how socialization was fixed to gender. It considers *Robinson Crusoe* educational for the expressed reason that women would never imagine undertaking Crusoe's economic adventures. There is also a strong possibility that early educational theorists recommended *Crusoe* over De-foe's other works because they thought women were likely to learn to desire what Crusoe accomplished, a totally self-enclosed and functional domain where money did not really matter. It was no doubt because Cru-soe was more female, according to the nineteenth century understanding of gender, than either Roxana or Moll that educators found his story more suitable reading for girls than for boys of an impressionable age.

If the reading of fiction came to play an indispensable role in directing desire at certain objects in the world, it was not because such narratives as *Robinson Crusoe* administered a particularly useful dose of didacti-cism. Instead, I would like to pose the possibility that moral hegemony triumphed in nineteenth century England largely through consent rather than coercion; it was precisely because they were leisure-time reading that such books as *Robinson Crusoe* were important to the political struggle between the ruling classes and the laboring poor. In his study of the im-pact of Sunday schools on working-class culture during the nineteenth century, Thomas Walter Laqueur contends that it was through their man-ner of inculcating literacy and a hunger for books, not through their overt promotion of certain behavioral norms, that English Sunday schools en-sured docility in regions where we would expect to find violent resistance to industrialization.[10] But these new forms of literacy seemed to intrude upon the cultural stage brandishing a double-edged sword. Education did not necessarily make newly impoverished laborers safe for an industrializing world; it could in fact have made them extremely dangerous. If education helped to produce a more tractable working class, working-class radicalism was predicated on literacy too—that is, on political pamphlets, on alternative programs for education, and even on a literature that spoke to their needs and desires rather than to those of their employers. Thus, Laqueur concludes, literacy did not simply indoctrinate the poor in the values and practices that would make them fit to inhabit an industrial world. More importantly, the total appropriation of the time during which the poor carried on traditional collective activities was essential in disarming the subversive potential of working-class literacy. Laqueur reasons that Sunday schools became an effective means of socialization not because they taught the necessity of self-sacrifice and respect for authority, but because they offered recreational programs that occupied many of the idle hours when people gathered in their customary fashion and when political plans might otherwise have been hatched.

The same principle extends, I believe, to the reading of fiction. As education became the preferred instrument of social control, fiction could accomplish much the same purpose as the various forms of recreation promoted by Sunday schools. The period following 1750 saw a new effort to regulate the free time of children and, by extension, the free time of their parents. Removing the stigma from novel reading no doubt conspired with activities promoted by Sunday schools to combat historically earlier notions of self, of family, and of pleasure. To unregulated time and pleasure was attributed the possibility of undermining the political order, as if, in the words of one concerned citizen, idleness alone could "fill the land with villains, render property insecure, crowd our jails with felons, and bring poverty, distress and ruin upon families."[11] But chief among the practices that the new cast of educators sought to criminalize and then to suppress were drinking, violent sport, and profligacy. The reformist policies were particularly effective in controlling the discontented laborer because those aspects of working-class culture that, in purely moral terms, most threatened the laborer's hope for salvation were also the practices that best fostered political resistance.[12]

Allon White has argued persuasively that the successful effort to push carnival and popular culture to the margins of social life was related to the victorious emergence of specifically bourgeois practices and languages, which were reinflected within a framework where they indicated an individual's degree of socialization.[13] And the novel is implicated in this process. If the production of a specifically female curriculum was an important moment in our cultural history, then the inclusion of novels within the female curriculum was also significant. Until well into the

eighteenth century the reading of fiction was considered tantamount to
seduction, but in the last decades of that century, certain novels were
found fit to occupy the idle hours of women, children, and servants. At
that point, the novel provided a means of displacing and containing longstanding symbolic practices—especially those games, festivities, and other
material practices of the body that maintained a sense of collective identity. Certain novels in particular transformed all they contained into the
materials of a gendered universe. And once they did so transform the
signs of political identity, such signs could, as the Brontës' madwomen
demonstrate, include forms of desire that challenged the norms distinguishing gender. Reading such works of fiction would still have the desirable effect of inducing a specific form of political unconscious.[14]

In formulating a theory of mass education in which fiction had a de-
ceptively marginal role to play, the Edgeworths and their colleagues were
adopting a rhetoric that earlier reformers had used to level charges of
violence and corruption against the old aristocracy. They placed themselves in an old tradition of radical Protestant dissent, which argued that
political authority should be based on moral superiority. At issue in the
way that sexual relations were represented, according to Jacques Donzelot, "was the transition from a government of families to a government
through the family."[15] Sexual relations so often provided the terms of
argument that no representation of the household could be considered
politically neutral. To contest the notion of a state that depended on inherited power, Puritan treatises on marriage and household governance
represented the family as a self-enclosed social unit in whose affairs the
state could not intervene. Against genealogy the treatises posited domesticity.[16] But in claiming sovereignty for the father over his home, they
were not proposing a new form of political organization. According to
Kathleen M. Davis, the Puritan doctrine of equality insisted only upon
the difference of sexual roles in which the female was certainly subordinate to the male, and not upon the equality of the woman in kind. "The
result of this partnership," Davis explains, "was a definition of mutual
and complementary duties and characteristics." Gender was so clearly
understood in oppositional terms that it could be graphically represented
as such:[17]

Husband	Wife
Get goods	Gather them together and save them
Travel, seek a living	Keep the house
Get money and provisions	Do not vainly spend it
Deal with many men	Talk with few

Husband	Wife
Be "entertaining"	Be solitary and withdrawn
Be skillful in talk	Boast of silence
Be a giver	Be a saver
Apparel yourself as you may	Apparel yourself as it becomes you
Dispatch all things outdoors	Oversee and give order within

In representing the family as the opposition of complementary genders, Puritan tracts enclosed the domestic unit. If they wanted to cut it off from the genealogical tree of state and so use it to authorize the household as an independent and self-generated source of power, their moment had not yet arrived. The hegemonic potential of the model had yet to be realized at that point in time. For the Puritan household consisted of a male and female who were stucturally identical, positive and negative versions of the same attributes. The female did not offer a competing form of political thinking.

Unlike the Puritan authors, the educational reformers of the nineteenth century could look back on a substantial body of writing that had represented the domestic woman in a way that authorized such a political alternative. Before it provided a common ideal for individuals who would otherwise see themselves in competition or else without any relationship at all, the household had to be governed by a form of power that was essentially female—that is, essentially different from that of the male and yet a positive force in its own right. Although certainly subject to political force, the domestic woman exercised a form of power that appeared to have no political force at all because it seemed forceful only when it was desired. It was the power of domestic surveillance. The husband who met the standards listed above passed into oblivion well before the aristocratic male ceased to dominate British political consciousness, but the domestic woman enjoyed a contrary fate. In the centuries intervening between our own day and that of the Puritan revolution, she was inscribed with values that addressed a whole range of competing interest groups and, through her, these groups gained authority over domestic relations and personal life. In this way, furthermore, they established the need for the kind of surveillance upon which modern institutions are based.

Indeed, the last two decades of the seventeenth century saw an explosion of writing that proposed to educate the daughters of numerous aspiring social groups.[18] The new curriculum promised to make these women desirable to men of a superior rank and in fact more desirable than women who had only their own rank and fortune to recommend them. The curriculum aimed at producing a woman whose value resided chiefly in her femaleness rather than in traditional signs of status, a woman who possessed psychological depth rather than a physically attractive surface, one who, in other words, excelled in the qualities that differentiated her from the male. As femaleness was redefined in these terms, the woman exalted by an aristocratic tradition of letters ceased to appear so desirable. In becoming the other side of this new sexual coin, the aristocratic woman represented surface instead of depth, embodied material instead of moral value, and displayed idle sensuality instead of constant vigilance and tireless concern for the well-being of others. Such a woman was not truly female.

But it was not until the mid-nineteenth century that the project of gendering subjectivity began to acquire the immense political influence it still exercises today. Around the 1830s, one can see the discourse of sexuality lose interest in its critique of the aristocracy as the newly organizing working classes became the more obvious target of moral reform. Authors suddenly took notice of social groups who had hardly mattered before. Reformers and men of letters discovered that politically aggressive artisans and urban laborers lacked the kind of motivation that characterized middle-class individuals. Numerous authors sought out the causes of poverty, illiteracy, and demographic change, not in the rapidly changing economic circumstances that had impoverished whole groups of people and torn their families asunder, but within those individuals themselves whose behavior was found to be at once promiscuous and insufficiently gendered. In analyzing the condition of the working classes, authors commonly portrayed women as masculine and men as effeminate and childlike. By representing the working class in terms of these personal deficiencies, middle-class intellectuals effectively translated the overwhelming political problem caused by rapid industrialization into a sexual scandal brought about by the worker's lack of personal development and self-restraint. Reformers could then step forward and offer themselves, their technology, their supervisory skills, and their institutions of education and social welfare as the appropriate remedy for growing political resistance.

In all fairness, as Foucault notes, the middle classes rarely imposed institutional constraints upon others without first trying them out on themselves. When creating a national curriculum, the government officials and educators in charge adopted one modeled on the educational theory that grew up around the Edgeworths and their intellectual circle, which can be considered the heir to the dissenting tradition.[19] It was basically the same curriculum proposed by eighteenth century pedagogues and reformers as the best way of producing a marriageable daughter. For one thing, the new curriculum drew upon the female model in requiring familiarity with British literature. By the end of the eighteenth century, the Edgeworths were among those who had already determined that the program aimed at producing the domestic woman offered a form of social control that could apply to boys just as well as to girls. And by the mid-nineteenth century, the government was figuring out how to administer much the same program on a mass basis. In forming the conceptual foundation upon which the national curriculum was based, a particular idea of the self thus became commonplace, and as gendered forms of identity determined more and more how people learned to think of themselves as well as of others, that self became the dominant social reality.

Such an abbreviated history cannot do justice to the fierce controversies punctuating the institution of a standard curriculum in England. I simply want to locate a few sites where political history obviously converged with the history of sexuality as well as with that of the novel to produce a specific kind of individual, and I do so to suggest the political implications of representing these histories as separate narratives. As it began to deny its political and religious bias and present itself instead as a moral and psychological truth, the rhetoric of reform obviously severed its ties with an aristocratic past and took up a new role in history. It no longer constituted a form of resistance but distinguished itself from political matters to establish a specialized domain of culture where apolitical truths could be told. The novel's literary status hinged upon this event. Fiction began to deny the political basis for its meaning and referred instead to the private regions of the self or to the specialized world of art, but never to the use of words that created and still maintains these primary divisions within the culture. Favored among kinds of fiction were the novels which best performed the operations of division and self-containment that turned political information into the discourse of sexuality. These novels made the novel respectable, and it is significant that they so often were entitled with female names such as Pamela, Evelina, or Jane Eyre. With this transformation of cultural information came widespread suspicion of political literacy, and with it, too, a mass forgetfulness that there was a history of sexuality to tell.

In this way, the emergence and domination of a system of gender differences over and against a long tradition of overtly political signs of social identity helped to usher in a new form of state power. This power—the power of representation over the thing represented—wrested authority from the old aristocracy on grounds that a government was morally obliged to rehabilitate degenerate individuals rather than to maintain their subjection through force. After the Peterloo Massacre of 1819, it was clear that the state's capacity for violence had become a source of embarrassment. Overt displays of force worked against legitimate authority just as they did against subversive factions. If acts of open rebellion had justified intervention into areas of society that the government had never had to deal with before, then the use of force on the part of the government gave credence to the workers' charges of oppression. The power of surveillance came into dominance at this moment, displacing the traditional uses of force. Like the form of vigilance that maintained an orderly household, this power did not create equality so much as trivialize the material signs of difference by translating all such signs into differences in the quality, intensity, direction, and self-regulatory capability of an individual's desire.

One could easily regard this history as yet another "just so" story were it not for the way it implicates literature and literacy in political history. Foucault's preoccupation with the power of "discourse" distinguishes his narrative from those of Marx and Freud, but the real targets of his anti-disciplinary strategies are the traditional historians who ignore the hegemony of which modern literature is only one function. It is certainly possible to take issue with the way in which he collapses such categories as "history," "power," "discourse," and "sexuality." It is also right to be troubled by his failure to mention those topics that seem most germane to his argument. In the case of "sexuality," for example, there is his virtual disregard for a mode of gender differentiation that enables one sex to dominate the other, just as, in his epic study of "discipline," we must ask where is there mention of ideology or of the collective activities that resisted it? Even though he explains the formation of institutions that exercise power through knowledge, and even though he takes steps to call those institutions into question by making the political power of writing visible as such, the history Foucault tells is nevertheless a partial one.

No history of an institution—whether that of prison, hospital, and schoolroom, as Foucault describes them, or of courts, houses of parliament, and marketplace, as more conventional historians prefer—can avoid the political behavior of the disciplinary model because these histories necessarily diminish the role of the subject in authorizing the forces that govern him. Moreover, such histories tend to ignore the degree to which forms of resistance themselves determine the strategies of domination. Thus we find, in Foucault's *Discipline and Punish,* that the dismembered body of the subject composing half the scene on the scaffold disappears as the modern penal institution closes around it. The same can be said of the body of the plague victim in Foucault's account of "the birth of the clinic."[20] The history of domination over the subject's material body seems to come to an end as the state begins to control individuals through strategies of discourse rather than by means of physical violence. But to say that this body is no longer important to the history of domination does not mean that other cultural formations disappear. The panopticon, Foucault's most completely articulated figure of power, is incomplete in itself as a model of culture. It requires something on the order of "carnival," Mikhail Bahktin's figure for all the practices that, with the growth of disciplinary institutions, were entirely cast out of the domain of culture.[21]

I think we need to create other ways of talking about resistance as well, for literary criticism too easily translates carnival—and all the material practices of the body that are tolerated within its framework—into the simple absence or inversion of normative structures. If one could allow for such heterogeneity—the overlapping of competing versions of reality within the same moment of time—the past would elude the linear pattern of a developmental narrative. In the model I am proposing, culture appears as a struggle among various political factions to possess its most valued signs and symbols.[22] The reality that dominates in any given situation appears to be just that, the reality that dominates. As such, the material composition of a particular text would have more to do with the forms of representation it overcame—in the case of domestic fiction, with its defiance of an aristocratic tradition of letters and, later on, with its repudiation of working-class culture—than with the internal composition of the text per se. I would pursue this line of thought one step further and say that the internal composition of a given text is nothing more or less than the history of its struggle with contrary forms of representation for the authority to control semiosis. In this respect, there is no inside to the text as opposed to the outside, no text/context distinction at all, though we must make such distinctions for purposes of copyright laws and traditional literary analyses.

The chapters that follow demonstrate this point by constructing a history of the domestic woman as she was represented, not only in the great domestic novels, but also in texts that never developed such literary pretensions. In reading these materials, I aim neither to discover forms of repression nor to perform acts of liberation, although my argument has a definite political goal. Rather, I am committed to a productive hypothesis. I want to show how the discourse of sexuality is implicated in shaping the novel, and to show as well how domestic fiction helped to produce a subject who understood herself in the psychological terms that had shaped fiction. I regard fiction, in other words, both as the document and as the agency of cultural history. I believe it helped to formulate the ordered space we now recognize as the household, made that space totally functional, and used it as the context for representing normal behavior. In so doing, fiction contested and finally suppressed alternative bases for human relationships. In realizing this, one cannot—I think—ignore the fact that fiction did a great deal to relegate vast areas of culture to the status of aberrance and noise. As the history of this female domain is articulated, then, it will outline boldly the telling cultural move upon which, I believe, the supremacy of middle-class culture has rested. Such a history will reenact the moment when writing invaded, revised, and contained the household by means of strategies that distinguished private from social life and thus detached sexuality from political history. On the domestic front, perhaps even more so than in the courts and the marketplace, the middle-class struggle for dominance was fought and won.

While others have isolated rhetorical strategies that naturalize the subordination of female to male, no one has thoroughly examined the figure, or turn of cultural logic, that both differentiates the sexes and links them together by the magic of sexual desire. And if we simply assume that gender differentiation is the root of human identity, we can understand neither the totalizing power of this figure nor the very real interests such power inevitably serves. So basic are the terms "male" and "female" to the semiotics of modern life that no one can use them without to some degree performing the very reifying gesture whose operations we would like to understand and whose power we want to historicize. Whenever we cast our political lot in the dyadic formation of gender, we place ourselves in a classic double bind, which confines us to alternatives that are not really alternatives at all. That is to say, any political position founded primarily on sexual identity ultimately confirms the limited choices offered by such a dyadic model.[23] Once one thinks within such a structure, sexual relationships appear as the model for all power relationships. This makes it possible to see the female as representative of all subjection and to use her subjectivity as if it were a form of resistance. By inscribing social conflict within a domestic configuration, however, one loses sight of all the various and contrary political affiliations for which any given individual provides the site. This power of sexuality to appropriate the voice of the victim works as surely through inversion as by strict adherence to the internal organization of the model. It was doubtless because such a form of transgression affirmed their normative structure that middle-class intellectuals were the first to produce an extensive vocabulary of sexual crimes and perversions.

Still, there is a way in which this book owes everything to the very academic feminism it often seems to critique, for if reading women's texts as women's texts were not now a professionally advantageous thing to do, there would be no call to write a history of this area of culture. However, in view of the fact that women writers have been included in the *Norton Anthology* as part of the standard survey of British literature and also as a collection by themselves, and in view of the fact that we now have male feminists straining to hop on the bandwagon, it is time to take stock. It is time to consider why the literary institution feels so comfortable with a kind of criticism that began as a critique of the traditional canon and the interpretive procedures the canon called forth. I can only conclude that in concerning itself with writing by and representations of women, literary criticism has not destabilized successfully the reigning metaphysics of sexuality. Clearly, by generating still more words on the subject, it has invigorated the discourse that sustains such a metaphysics. And yet I am convinced that one cannot tell the history of the British novel without, at the same time, considering the history of gender formation. I know this means that in the end I will have reified the themes whose reifying behavior it is my purpose to examine; I will have turned sex into sexuality too. But recognizing this, and with a view toward demonstrating how, at crucial points in its history, the novel used a thematics of gender to appropriate political resistance, I feel it is well worth the risk to compromise theory and erode the Olympian perspective on culture that such procedures as Foucault's occasionally allow one to enjoy. To remove oneself from the field under consideration is finally impossible, and attempting to do so does little to show how we might use the sexual clichés of this culture to imagine some other economy of pleasure, some genuinely subversive end.

If my study of the novel clarifies only one point, then, I would like it to demonstrate the degree to which modern culture depends on a form of power that works through language—and particularly the printed word—to constitute subjectivity. According to this premise, as purveyors of a specialized form of literacy, we invariably perpetuate the hegemony I have been describing. That we do so is especially true when we make novels into literary texts where psychosexual themes control the meaning of cultural information that might otherwise represent some contrary political viewpoint. When that happens, our interpretive procedures not only conceal the process by which the novels themselves reproduce modern forms of subjectivity. Our procedures also conceal the degree to which we think and write novelistically in order to make sense of the past and of cultures different from our own. In fact, we render ourselves unconscious of the political power we ourselves exercise whenever we represent sexuality as existing prior to its representation. Grounded on a metaphysics that is yet to be widely recognized as such, and working through a highly sophisticated network of strategies by which the humanities and social sciences ground themselves on that rockbed of truth— human nature itself—sexuality continues to conceal the politics of writing subjectivity.

To avoid the female strategy of self-authorization, I will be describing the behavior of an emergent class from a historically later position which that class has empowered—from a position within that class and supported by it. I say this as a way of insisting that in constructing a history of female forms of power, I do not mean to appropriate a form of resistance but rather to reveal the operations of a class sexuality by which I have often found myself defined. At the risk of appearing dogmatic, I have at moments overstated my case and so violated the pluralistic ideology espoused by the best liberal element within my profession. I have adopted this tactic as a means of countering those who would emphasize woman's powerlessness—and we are certainly rendered powerless in specifically female ways—and therefore as a means of identifying for critical consideration that middle-class power which does not appear to be power because it behaves in specifically female ways. I will insist that those cultural functions which we automatically attribute to and embody as women—those, for example, of mother, nurse, teacher, social worker, and general overseer of service institutions—have been just as instrumental in bringing the new middle classes into power and maintaining their dominance as all the economic take-offs and political breakthroughs we automatically attribute to men. I am not, in other words, constructing a woman's history from the viewpoint of an oppressed or silent minority, for that would falsify what I do and what I am. In constructing a history of the modern woman, I want to consider the ways in which gender collaborates with class to contain forms of political resistance within liberal discourse. I want to use my power as a woman of the dominant class and as a middle-class intellectual to name what power I use as a form of power rather than to disguise it as the powerlessness of others.

To write an adequate history of domestic fiction, then, it seems to me that one must modify permanently what literary historians can say about history as well as about literature. Such scholars and critics collaborate with other historians, as well as with those who make it their business to appreciate high culture, when they locate political power primarily in the official institutions of state. For then they proceed as if there is no political history of the whole domain over which our culture grants women authority: the use of leisure time, the ordinary care of the body, courtship practices, the operations of desire, the forms of pleasure, gender differences, and family relations. As the official interpreters of the cultural past, we are trained, it appears, to deny the degree to which writing has concealed the very power it has granted this female domain. It is no doubt because each of us lives out such a paradox that we seem powerless to explain in so many words how our political institutions came to depend on the socializing practices of household and schoolroom. Yet, I contend, the historical record of this process is readily available in paperback. We call it fiction.

With this in mind, I have tried to defamiliarize the division of discourse that makes it so difficult to see the relationship between the finer nuances of women's feelings and the vicissitudes of a capitalist economy run mainly by men. My study identifies several places in cultural history where the one cannot be fully understood without the other. But I would still consider such an effort to be a frivolous demonstration of literary scholarship if it were not for the other people who are attempting to open new areas of culture to historical investigation and to provide some understanding of our own status as products and agents of the hegemony I am describing. In adopting various critical strategies, I have made no effort to be faithful to any particular theory. To my mind, such academic distinctions offer neither a trustworthy basis for making intellectual affiliations nor a solid basis for mounting an argument that concerns our own history. Rather than distinguish theory from interpretation and feminism from Marxism, deconstructionism, or formalism, I care mainly about those scholars and critics who have helped me to discover traces of the history of the present in several eighteenth and nineteenth century texts and to understand my own insights as part of the larger project now going on within those disciplines where individuals have undertaken the work of creating a new political literacy.

1

The Rise of Female
Authority in the Novel

Orlando sipped the wine and the Archduke knelt and kissed her hand.
In short, they acted the parts of man and woman for ten minutes
with great vigour and then fell into natural discourse.

VIRGINIA WOOLF, *Orlando*

This chapter will consider the domestic novel as the agent and product
of a cultural change that attached gender to certain kinds of writing. Female writing—writing that was considered appropriate for or could be
written by women—in fact designated itself as feminine, which meant
that other writing, by implication, was understood as male. But female
writing was not only responsible for the gendering of discourse; it was
also responsible for representing sexual relations as something entirely
removed from politics. As such, gender provided the true basis of human
identity. By adopting the voices of women, such authors as Defoe and
Richardson deliberately renounced what Walter Ong has described as "a
sexually specialized language used almost exclusively for communication
between male and male." Until well into the nineteenth century, he points
out, "learning Latin took on the characteristics of a puberty rite, a *rite
de passage*, or initiation rite: it involved the isolation from the family,
the achievement of identity in a totally male group (the social), the learning of a body of relatively abstract tribal lore inaccessible to those outside
the group."[1] Men who lacked this specialized language were automatically placed outside the dominant class whenever they wrote. In assuming
the guise of a woman, however, an author could avoid overtly disclosing
his position as royalist or dissident. The female view was simply different
from that of an aristocratic male and not likely to be critical of the dominant view. Fielding's uncouth heroes may generate a sense of political
innocence by virtue of the gap between their education and the one their
urbane author clearly possesses, but the explicitly female narrators of *Pa-*

mela, Evelina, or *The Mysteries of Udolpho* are more effective in launching a political critique because their gender identifies them as having no claim to political power. As women, furthermore, these protagonists understand social experience as a series of sexual encounters. Although characteristically naive, their responses are far from simple. Indeed, they constitute a sophisticated range of sensations, emotional nuances, and moral judgements. Novelists could make a woman's response as flattering or caustic as they wished if the woman in question interpreted behavior on the basis of sexual rather than political or economic motivations. Domestic fiction mapped out a new domain of discourse as it invested common forms of social behavior with the emotional values of women. Consequently, these stories of courtship and marriage offered their readers a way of indulging, with a kind of impunity, in fantasies of political power that were the more acceptable because they were played out within a domestic framework where legitimate monogamy—and thus the subordination of female to male—would ultimately be affirmed. In this way, domestic fiction could represent an alternative form of political power without appearing to contest the distribution of power that it represented as historically given.

This was the difference between *Robinson Crusoe* and *Pamela,* then. Even Defoe could not write a successful sequel to his novel, and inasmuch as his masculine form of heroism could not be reproduced by other authors, we cannot say *Crusoe* inaugurated the tradition of the novel as we know it. By way of contrast, Richardson's story of relentless sexual pursuit and the triumph of female virtue proved infinitely reproducible. The differences between the political order Crusoe establishes in his solitary circumstances and the forces that drove him to the island in the first place have generated endless debate over Defoe's political beliefs. Not so with *Pamela.* The contradiction between her way of running the household and the way of the outside world was no doubt all too apparent at the time the novel was written. Fielding was not alone in accusing Richardson of playing fast and loose with social reality. He thought Richardson insulted the intelligence of readers by asking them to believe that a servant could dissuade a man of Mr. B's position from having his way with her. Fielding found it ludicrous to think that a man of such station would so overvalue the virginity of a woman who was not particularly well born. But despite the fact that Richardson's representation of the individual inspired Fielding to write two novels in rebuttal, literary criticism has not seen fit to dwell on the political implications of the discrepancy between Mr. B's extraordinary desire for Pamela and the principles that apparently ruled behavior in Richardson's society.

From the nineteenth century on, critics have much preferred to regard *Pamela* as representing an enclosed and gendered self rather than a form of writing that helped to create this concept of the individual. As if this self alone of all things cultural were not subject to historical change, critics tend to read Pamela's sexual encounters as psychological rather than political events. Thus they can pass off the ideological conflict shaping the text as the difference between a man and a woman rather than between a person of station and a person of low rank. Writing apparently gained a certain authority as it transformed political differences into those rooted in gender. To the authority that came with concealing the politics of writing in this way we can attribute the development of a distinctively female form of writing. Despite charges of sentimentality and despite unsuccessful attempts such as Fielding's to place the novel in a masculine tradition of letters, novels early on assumed the distinctive features of a specialized language for women. A novel might claim a female source for its words, concentrate on a woman's experience, bear a woman's name for its title, address an audience of young ladies, and even find itself criticized by female reviewers.[2] Although concerned mainly with the vicissitudes of courtship and marriage, and fictional courtships and marriages at that, fiction that represented gender from this gendered viewpoint exerted a form of political authority.

The Logic of the Social Contract

Domestic fiction represented sexual relationships according to an idea of the social contract that empowered certain qualities of an individual's mind over membership in a particular group or faction. From the seventeenth century on, the contract was used as a strategy for legitimizing various claims to power. In Enlightenment discourse, however, the contract acquired new status. It provided the trope of enlightenment that organized narratives of individual growth and development. To see how the novel might have played a role in history, one must first understand the rhetorical power of this figure. If, during the course of the eighteenth century, the contract appeared to lose credibility as a model for political relationships, it was because the logical contradictions inherent in the figure, and thus in the purely rhetorical nature of the contract itself, were relatively easy to see.[3] When it took the form of domestic fiction rather than political theory, however, the contract enjoyed a different fate. The contradictions inherent in theory eventually changed the way people understood sexual relationships. It could be said that the social contract lives on as a sexual contract even today. To demonstrate how fiction carried on the work of an earlier political theory by invoking the sexual contract, I would like to turn briefly to Rousseau's *The Social Contract* (1762) and explain the rhetorical transformations he achieved through the logic of contractual exchange.

The contract requires that there be two different parties for the enactment of a mutually beneficial exchange. Even though the two parties must be different, they cannot be adversaries, for that would require a third and external form of authority to regulate the relationship between the two parties. In order to avoid such a situation, which would produce a society founded on force, Rousseau devises a fiction. Like Defoe, he invents a world originating outside of political history. Also like Defoe, he accomplishes this by creating an individual who exists prior to the formation of any political group. But here is a paradox: only when the individual is already so individuated can the ideal society develop; in contrast with the world that actually existed for Rousseau, the model society could have no factional interests. Louis Althusser, for one, has explained the rhetorical sleight of hand by which this fictional society avoids reproducing the problems afflicting the pre-revolutionary France in which Rousseau lived. According to Althusser, the power of the contract depended not so much on the logic of exchange as on the figurative power of the contract to constitute the very parties it proposed to regulate.[4] According to the logic of the contract, each of the two parties must exist prior to the enactment of an exchange. As a figure, however, the contract creates the two parties who supposedly enter into the exchange. Rousseau uses the fiction of an original contract to create an individual who exists independent of social relationships. In unfolding his narrative of the origin of the state, Rousseau makes the first person, an unsocialized individual, into the second person, or social body, through an act of voluntary submission. Under these special circumstances alone, the authority to whom one submits in entering into society is actually oneself, and the state, in turn, "being formed of the individuals that compose it, neither has nor can have any interest contrary to theirs."[5]

Now let us return to the logical requirements of the contract and the rhetorical transformation they effect. If it is necessary that two parties be essentially the same before the contract can bring them together in a mutually empowering relationship, it is also necessary that the two be differentiated by the exchange. As he enters into a relationship with the state, then, Rousseau's individual undergoes a transformation by volunteering to curb his acquisitive appetite so that he might secure his property and live in peace with others. This transformation does not repress, but rather extends and perfects, his individuality. "Although in this state, he is deprived of many advantages that he derives from nature," Rousseau contends, an individual "acquires great ones in return; his faculties are exercised and developed; his ideas are expanded; his feeling ennobled; his whole soul is exalted" (p. 22). Displacing entirely the material necessities that initially inspired Rousseau's model individual to enter into a contract with the state, self-perfection miraculously becomes an end in itself; personal growth and development motivate him to grow and develop. Thus reinflected within the framework of the individual, his desire becomes an exclusively psychological force.

It is obviously crucial to Rousseau's whole project that no other political affiliations mediate between his individual and the state. Indeed, whenever it represents individual motivation in terms of the interests of property, Rousseau's narrative threatens to revert to a situation where socialization comes about through repression rather than as the means of self-fulfillment. When power is based on an uneven distribution of wealth, the ideal state inevitably loses its vital difference from the dismal state Rousseau envisioned in his earlier *Discourse on the Origin of Inequality* (1754). Under such conditions, a political faction will rule. A few will eventually dominate the majority at the cost of repressing the essential qualities of the individual subject: "In proportion as he becomes sociable and a slave to others," Rousseau writes in the *Discourse,* the subject "becomes weak, fearful, mean-spirited, and his soft and effeminate way of living at once completes the enervation of his strength and of his courage" (p. 184).

In *The Social Contract,* Rousseau admits that a system of voluntary consent, in order to become a reality, depends on education. "For the mechanism to carry out its function properly," as Althusser explains, Rousseau must add the condition that " 'The people must have adequate information,' i.e., there must be enlightenment" (p. 150). Thus of the public, Rousseau says, "It must be made to see objects as they are, sometimes as they ought to appear." Desire must be directed toward these objects in the right way. Not only must the public be "shown the good path it is seeking," but it must "be guarded from the seductions of private interests" as well (p. 41). To fulfill these imperatives, curiously enough, Rousseau's enlightened public must be "without any communication among the citizens." For still pursuing the logic of the contract, he reasons that the unrestricted circulation of information would produce some "partial association, whose will becomes general in reference to its members, and particular with reference to the state" (p. 31). If allowed to represent objects in terms of a particular interest, individuals would revert to their political identity. They would understand themselves as a faction.

On the one hand, for the contract to be a true alternative to government based upon force, Rousseau must represent that power as an extension of each individual, which requires individuals to exist as individuals prior to the society that controls them. But, on the other hand, to imagine the second party of the contract as a state composed of enlightened individuals who desire nothing so much as the common good, Rousseau must install a social force prior to the individual. Something must be there from the beginning to individuate and direct each man's desire toward the common good. Pushed to this conclusion by the logical demands of the contract, Rousseau imagines a form of authority that comes into being through a mutually beneficial exchange. The authority rises neither from the individual nor from the state. It is an invisible power—the power of education, indeed of language itself. Such power appears to be simply a natural desire, but in fact it creates the fiction that such desire has a basis in nature. Rousseau imagines such manipulation of desire as the alternative and antidote to a state based on force. He creates an individual capable of transforming his own historical circumstances through the production of laws that are at once the extension and containment of his desires. As the figurative operations of the contract suggest, this representation of power had the power to individuate people and to aim their desires at a common goal. And it is entirely reasonable to say that such power eventually transformed the historical conditions under which Rousseau wrote. In saying this, I am not supporting the preposterous hypothesis that Rousseau was somehow responsible for the events of 1789. To the contrary, I am suggesting that Rousseau, along with numerous other writers and intellectuals in England and on the Continent, ushered in an age dominated by the power of discourse rather than force, by cultural hegemony rather than political revolution.

It can be argued that the contract provides the central trope of Enlightenment discourse, which always creates what it seems to organize and individuates what it claims to unify. If Rousseau made any mistake in his version of the social contract, it was simply to make the political motives underlying his logic too obvious. More than a decade before *The Social Contract* was published, British philosophers had already discounted the idea of a state founded on voluntary consent. In his essay "Of the Original Contract" (1748), David Hume claims to have encountered only one case in all the documents of antiquity where the "obligation to government is ascribed to a promise, . . . in Plato's *Crito:* where Socrates refuses to escape from prison, because he had tacitly promised to obey the laws."[6] According to Hume, power resides not so much in the consent of the people as in their belief in the fiction that such a promise has indeed been made. In other words, the power of consent derives from the fiction of an original contract and not from the fact of its enactment. Only the sheer force of tradition founded on belief in this fiction makes people adhere to the law. On this basis, Hume rejects both alternatives of earlier political debate concerning the legitimate source of state authority. To say that the monarch manifests either the divine will of God or the voluntary consent of the individual is equally false in his view. The true nature of political authority resides not on superior force, but on laws, not on consent, but on opinion: "So great is the force of laws, and of particular forms of government, and so little dependence have they on the humours and tempers of men, that consequences almost as great and certain may sometimes be deduced from them, as any which the mathematical sciences can afford us."[7] Hume appears to reject Rousseau's theory entirely. In arguing against the notion of an original contract, however, he actually employs the same logic. Even in disclosing the fictional nature of the contract, Hume imagines the state as one based on a form of power which perpetuates itself through a similar fiction of history that authorizes certain traditions. In distinguishing "tradition" from fiction, he makes the two appear to be much the same thing. For him, to put it simply, history is the fiction that people have long regarded as truth.

To demonstrate the novel's implication in the larger historical process that brought the new middle classes into power, I have initially drawn from the works of Rousseau and Hume to suggest how they transformed the themes of an earlier, aristocratic culture by arguing for the claims of the individual over those of an elite political group. These works also suggest that such a transformation—the representation of society as composed of individuals rather than groups—exerted a form of political authority in its own right. But it took Jeremy Bentham's *The Theory of Fictions* to explain how the power of the social contract was nothing other than the power of fiction. In this, his last work, long viewed as the product of his dotage, the arch utilitarian calls into question the epistemological basis for the state that he put forth in his earlier writing. Published in part in 1812 but not in its entirety until 1929–32, *The Theory of Fictions* argues that one understands most of physical life in terms of fictions of right, obligation, truth, or justice. "In theory," Bentham contends, these purely fictional entities "were assumed for axioms; and in practice they were observed as rules."[8] In saying this, he is simply claiming that the actual distribution of power depends largely on the terms in which we agree to represent it. No social order can be said to exist without the invisible element of language. Less real, in his view, than the objects it represents, language is all the more powerful for not being among them. As a thing made chiefly of language, then, the state does not simply regulate the world of objects in the manner of earlier governments. The state Bentham came to imagine is one that exerts the power of words over things. Understanding perhaps better than anyone else the power that is inherent in the word, he proclaims, in the chapter entitled "The Fiction of an Original Contract," that "the season of *Fiction* is now over: insomuch that what formerly might have been tolerated and countenanced under the name, would, if now attempted to be set on foot, be censured and stigmatized under the harsher appellations of *encroachment* or *imposture*" (p. 122). If knowledge is to become power, then, it cannot appear to be so. Above all, it cannot appear to operate in the interests of a political group. The form of knowledge that will appear to operate in everyone's interest is the one that appears to reside in things themselves. In this case, knowledge has no particular political location. It becomes a ubiquitous presence that lends objects value and regulates as it defines them.

I have made this brief foray into extraliterary territory as part of an effort to suggest how fiction might have worked in concert with other, very different kinds of writing to produce a new form of political power. Whenever the rhetorical operations of the contract became apparent, as they did to some extent in Hume's essay but even more so in Bentham's *The Theory of Fictions*, the power that could be exercised through fictions of personal development also became apparent as such. If Rousseau's version of the contract implied that fictions are necessary for the individual to think of himself as a particular kind of self, then Hume's critique of the orginal contract implied that fictions ensure that various individuals will see themselves in relation to the same form of political authority. Bentham argued simply that fiction itself was the only thing that had held people in subjection to one kind of state and could, if properly understood, allow them to take charge over another. Given that a sophisticated theory of fiction appears to have developed alongside the novel, and given that novels characteristically identify themselves as fiction and yet presume to be more faithful to life than earlier fictions, we might expect the history of the novel to provide the record of the power that helped to determine how people understood themselves as individuals and what they thought it meant to be happy and free. In other words, if fiction did in fact play such a role in cultural history, we should be able to read the history of the novel as the formation of the individual who proved fit to inhabit a world based on the twin powers of supervision and information control, a world, in short, like ours. But such a historical understanding of the novel was not to be, for the power fiction would come to exercise depended entirely on denying the inherently political aim of fictions of personal development; the production of the modern individual required above all else a specific form of political unconscious.

Within Rousseau's career, the rhetoric of repression came first. The repressed individual of his *Discourse on the Origin of Inequality* required a particular form of liberation: a form of self-fulfillment that came with the disappearance of political identity. Thus we can regard the notion of repression as the necessary "other" side of enlightenment. Such a notion confined the possibilities for human identity between the poles of political subjection, on the one hand, and apolitical subjectivity on the other. This way of thinking about one's relationship to the state assumed that the interests of any one group were pursued at the expense of another's. The only good political motive was therefore a defensive one, made on behalf of a group that had been repressed. And the only way to remedy such a situation without becoming repressive in turn was to rescue individual members of a repressed group. Shaped by this logic, the social contract characteristically offered a private solution for problems that were inherently political. In so doing, it necessarily obscured the political identity of a faction and the claims that could be made on behalf of such a group.

As it gave rise to modern liberal discourse, the social contract produced a contradiction on which the rise of the novel depended. The novel developed sophisticated strategies for transforming political information into any one of several recognizable psychological conditions, and it did so in a way that concealed the power exercised by discourse itself in carrying out this transformation on a mass scale. As if to acknowledge the degree to which the social contract was primarily a linguistic contract that concealed what was really at stake in any struggle to control meaning, Rousseau abandoned his attempt to write either political theory or fables of education like *Émile*. In exile after 1762, he turned to writing strange autobiographical narratives—the *Dialogues* and *Reveries of a Solitary Walker,* as well as the *Confessions*—where thinking might proceed uninhibited by history and where writing itself appeared to rise from sources within the individual that were independent of the political world.

The Logic of the Sexual Contract

I have emphasized the degree to which *The Social Contract,* in all its manifestations, was a fictional construct, a fact that appears to have been recognized in its day. The idea of free individuals voluntarily entering into a contract with one another was obviously impossible to realize in a state where people were already born into different classes and status groups that denied them an opportunity to make the kind of choice which the contract specified as necessary for its success. But my main concern is with the rhetorical operation of the contract as it passed into the British domestic novel. I am not suggesting that we identify popular culture, instead of the philosophic tradition, as the source of the information that actually saturated human experience, although such is likely the case. Although I will draw contrasts between Rousseau's theory and the less lofty domain of fiction, I am concerned with the rhetorical behavior they had in common. I will argue that, on this basis, certain fiction shared an ideological position with Enlightenment philosophy, and I will proceed according to the Foucauldian hypothesis that various kinds of writing worked together in an unwitting conspiracy that would eventually authorize modern institutional procedures. In fiction, the contract created a language for social relationships that was immensely useful for purposes of an emergent capitalism. This language provided one way of justifying the ideological destruction of fixed status positions. Freeing the identities of various groups of individuals in this way was probably instrumental in producing wage labor. Although at that time the contract represented a minority view, it took the form of a self-authorizing strategy that eventually empowered the emergent classes.

Historical studies of the novel represent early novels and romances as a rather unsavory lot. In fact, there is good reason to believe that novels did not become literary works until the twentieth century. By the late eighteenth century, however, certain novels such as those by Burney and other lady novelists were certainly considered polite.[9] This was the moment in history when people began to understand social relations in terms of the modern class society, and when political affiliations were understood, not as a function of loyalties to those above and below one in a chain of economic dependency, but in relation to those who derived their economic livelihood from similar sources in labor, land, service, or capital. Not only was this the time when sexual behavior emerged as a common standard for identifying and evaluating individuals from all reaches of the social world, it was also the period during which the entire tradition of the novel was being established. In 1809–10, Walter Scott put together the first collected edition of what he called *The Novels of Daniel Defoe*, which excluded *Roxana* and *Moll Flanders*. In the same year, 1810, Mrs. Barbauld's *The British Novelists; with an Essay; and Prefaces Biographical and Critical* appeared in fifty volumes. This was followed by Mudford's *British Novelists* (1810–17) and later by perhaps the most influential of all such collections, *Ballantyne's Novelist's Library*, edited in

1821–24 by Walter Scott.[10] From these beginnings, a history of the novel based on a radically narrow selection of eighteenth century fiction developed backward in time.

In his illuminating essay "The Institution of the English Novel," Homer Obed Brown explains how the nineteenth century novel, as defined by Scott, Barbauld, and others, determined which works of earlier fiction would constitute the novelistic tradition. To explain the essentially ahistorical procedures that govern most histories of the novel, Brown writes:

> To put matters crudely, I am going to argue that the English novel was invented or instituted around the beginning of the 19th century, not in the early 18th . . . and the history of its "rise," now widely accepted, the one that begins with Defoe, did not become institutional until the middle of our own century. There should not be anything shocking or surprising about this. All histories are, of course, necessarily reconstructions, and the histories of the origins of institutions are peculiar versions of this truism in that they require our forgetting that they are reconstructions. This peculiarity is carried, in fact, in the word institution (a word that has its own interesting history) because it means both a thing—an organization or set of practices—and the act of a specific moment of founding or originating the thing, organization, or set of practices. Moreover, as a verb or verbal, it implies orginating with a plan, a purpose, a design—an intentional act. When we think of a literary genre as an institution, as the novel has so often been thought of, the compulsion to repress the fact that the instituting act is a reconstruction becomes multiplied in power.[11]

Granting Brown's thesis, one cannot say that Defoe and Fielding, as well as Richardson if we credit his own account, were faced with a set of expectations that had to be met in writing a novel.[12] On the other hand, when Austen and the Brontës sat down to write novels, they apparently knew they were writing novels, and they knew what a novel was. They even knew that in order to be novelists in the best sense of the word, they had to distinguish their work from other novels by asserting that they were telling the truth where others had written mere fiction.

For by then it had been established that novels were supposed to rewrite political history as personal histories that elaborated on the courtship procedures ensuring a happy domestic life. That novels ultimately seemed to steer clear of politics held as true for the more masculine fiction of Fielding and Scott as it did for the domestic fiction of Richardson and Austen. But fiction was particularly good at picking up the fragments of an agrarian and artisan culture when it recast them as gender differences and contained them within a domestic framework. It seems to me that the novels which best exemplify the genre for us today are indeed those which translated the social contract into a sexual exchange. By representing social conflict as personal histories, gothic tales of sensibility, and stories of courtship and marriage, a relatively few eighteenth century authors were allowed to displace an entire body of fiction in which political conflict was not so thoroughly transformed by middle-class love. My description of a few early nineteenth century novels will show that this subtle power of transformation was not peculiar to domestic fiction or to novels in general, much less to literature. It was a political strategy in its own right that certain novels shared with other kinds of writing characterizing the age.

I am emphasizing the similarities between the social and sexual contracts, even though they gave shape to two very different kinds of writing. I do so in order to prepare the way for explaining how a critique of the state could prove all the more effective when the political nature of that critique was concealed. In the writing of John Stuart Mill, for example, one can see how the social contract was taken up and concealed within sexual relationships. Cast in this form, the contract was so thoroughly confused with nature itself by the mid-nineteenth century that Mill launched his famous argument for women's enfranchisement by invoking the very principle that ratified their subjection. No harm can come of giving them the vote, he assures the recalcitrant reader, "for the law already gives it to women in the most important of all cases to themselves: for the choice of the man who is to govern a woman to the end of her life, is always supposed to be voluntarily made by herself."[13] In this statement, Mill clearly uses the sexual contract to cancel out the political one. Thinking in the best liberal terms, he assumes that a woman's destiny depends on her desire for a mate, in exchange for which she will readily relinquish a political identity of her own. On this basis, he concludes that "the majority of women of any class are not likely to differ in political opinion from the majority of men" (p. 37). He believes, in other words, that the sexual contract regulates social relationships so firmly that political change—the enfranchisement of women—cannot in fact change the political order.

We can see the same figure of the sexual contract at work in natural history as Charles Darwin uses it to grant women power with one hand while taking it away from them with the other. Strangely compelled to supplement his *Origin of the Species* with the companion piece *The Descent of Man, and Natural Selection in Relation to Sex*, Darwin draws upon a contractual model to identify the female's contribution to the triumph of the human species:

> The sexual struggle is of two kinds; in the one it is between individuals of
> the same sex, generally the males, in order to drive away or kill their rivals,

the females remaining passive, whilst in the other, the struggle is likewise between individuals of the same sex, in order to excite or charm those of the opposite sex, generally the females, which no longer remain passive, but select the more agreeable partners.[14]

It is only by this curious twist in the law of heredity that competitive features are virtually absent in the female, making it necessary for her to depend for survival on the mate she selects. A sexual exchange—where he fights with competing members of his species for her, and she in return domesticates him—does more than simply bring male and female together. It also differentiates individuals within a given species according, first and foremost, to gender. It is on this basis that Mill and Darwin exempt women from political relations and detach domestic life, by definition, from the competitive practices that are supposed to characterize men.

It has not been difficult for us to understand how women were handicapped by social applications of this model, even though the model purports to empower them, and even though nineteenth century women apparently found it easy to see distinct advantages in a life without labor. What is not so clear and therefore remains a far more interesting problem is how this particular representation of female power might have served the interests of a readership made up of both men and women and how, in so doing, it authorized women writers. Fredric Rowton's preface to his anthology of women's poetry, *The Female Poets of Great Britain* (1848), offers a clear example of the cultural sleight of hand that both granted women the authority to write and denied them the power to make political statements. To justify his selection of poetry exclusively written by women, Rowton draws on the same contractual model that Mill tried unsuccessfully to challenge and that Darwin would make into a science. Rowton writes that

> I am quite prepared to grant that the mental constitutions of the sexes is *different;* but I am not at all prepared to say that "difference" means "inferiority." It is easy enough to understand that the sphere of woman's duty requires powers altogether dissimilar from those which are needed by the male; but that this is any proof of a smaller development of mind, I beg leave to deny. Woman's qualities may be less conspicuous, but they are quite as influential. Man has to bear outward, tangible rule; and his faculties are necessarily of an authoritative, evident, external commanding order. Woman has to bear invisible sway over the hidden mechanism of the heart; and her endowments are of a meek, persuasive, quiet, and subjective kind. Man rules the mind of the world; woman its heart.[15]

As its smugness suggests, this designation of power as either feminine or masculine in nature is not the least bit original. Rowton nevertheless does us a service because, by composing the statement entirely of middle-class commonplaces written and taken to heart by the literate classes, he conveniently illustrates how a model of sexual exchange created a gendered form of power peculiar to a society that was undergoing industrialization.[16] According to the middle-class ideal of love, or what Lawrence Stone has called "the companionate marriage," the female relinquishes political control to the male in order to acquire exclusive authority over domestic life, emotions, taste, and morality.[17] We have no grounds for assuming that such an exchange was intended primarily to keep women in line. In distinguishing male from female authority, this representation of social relationships sought to break down the prerogatives that traditionally belonged to a male aristocracy. The next chapter will consider the political consequences of this symbolic transformation, but for my present purposes, I want to focus on the rhetoric of the sexual contract itself.

Rowton's preface implies that the social differences between male and female depend on a form of subjectivity that in turn depends on gender differences. His unquestioned belief in the essential difference between the minds of a man and a woman provides the rationale for his publishing *The Female Poets of Great Britain.* If nature decrees women to write "not as the rivals" but as the "partners" of men, it follows that women's writing will complement that of men and never be able to engage male writing in a critical manner. A debate between the sexes becomes especially difficult to imagine if genres are rooted in gender. Thus Rowton identifies feminine discourse as personal and subjective rather than political or philosophical in character. By way of proof he invites one to observe, "In all the Poems in this volume, it would be difficult to find a passage written to accelerate man's political advancement; whilst every page will display some effort to stimulate his moral progress."[18] One finds it easy indeed to discover these categories at work in the very writing that helped to produce them. But we might ask instead how the female's lack of access to economic and political power authorized certain forms of writing. This authority, as I will demonstrate, was not a matter of biological gender, for any use of language was considered essentially female if sufficiently detached from the contentious ways of the marketplace and rooted instead in the values of the heart and home.

These conditions for reception were an extension of the themes organizing the novel, and they testify to its power to transform a readership's understanding of social relationships. Respectable fiction, I will argue, was that which represented political conflict in terms of sexual differences that upheld a peculiarly middle-class notion of love. It is no accident, then, that novels by such major authors as Dickens and Thackeray move toward fulfillment of the sexual contract with all the consistency of novels by Austen, the Brontës, and Gaskell. The division and balance of authority that Rowton describes was obviously understood as the only way to resolve a conventional plot. Particularly when brought about through the efforts of a female protagonist, a successful conclusion could be none other than a life free of physical labor and secured by the patronage of a benevolent man. The idea that one could gain authority through such dependency undoubtedly served manifold interests in justifying the exclusion of women from business and politics. But the belief that domestic life and moral sensibility constituted a female domain was much more than a sop to the woman. Although it did not seem to be political or economic on the surface, female authority was nevertheless real, for the language of sexual relations itself was considered acceptable feminine writing. By virtue of their apparent disregard for matters that were supposed to concern men, plots turning on the sexual contract offered the means of passing off ideology as the product of purely human concern. I would argue that the sexual contract is still in fact instrumental in regulating social relationships; it does much the same work that Rousseau imagined the social contract would perform.

The Sexual Contract as Narrative Paradigm

In opening *Pride and Prejudice,* Jane Austen identifies herself by invoking a model of sexual exchange to which she could not have personally subscribed: "It is a truth universally acknowledged that a single man in possession of a good fortune must be in want of a wife."[19] This asseveration establishes historically specific relations between Austen's work and a readership. She situates herself as a writer with knowledge of sexual relations and the intention, however ironic, of demonstrating the truth of the sexual contract. Thirty years later, however, Charlotte Brontë begins the fictional autobiography *Jane Eyre* in the voice of a woman who seems to be empowered by her speech alone. With neither money, nor status, nor good looks, nor charm to recommend her, Jane Eyre begins her rise to a secure position within the dominant class in a remarkably forthright manner:

> *Speak* I must; I had been trodden on severely, and *must* turn: but how? What strength had I to dart retaliation at my antagonist? I gathered my energies and launched them in this blunt sentence: "I am not deceitful: if I were, I should say I loved you; but I declare I do not love you: I declare I dislike you the worst of anyone in the world."[20]

Evidently Brontë's readership acknowledged the authority of language that had little else behind it but the force of female emotions. If Brontë could simply assume this common ground with her readership, one for which Austen had to stake out a claim, then it was because such authors as Austen had helped to establish the woman's authority over a specific domain of knowledge—that of the emotions.

Writing more than twenty years later, George Eliot begins *Middlemarch* with a historical reference to a woman's self-sacrifice, an example she recalls on grounds that it should be an essential part of her readers' cultural knowledge: "Who that cares much to know the history of man, and how the mysterious mixture behaves under the varying experiments of Time, has not dwelt, at least briefly, on the life of Saint Theresa."[21] Eliot calls attention to this heroine only to show in the fiction that follows how a much more important contribution by women goes unrecognized in the annals of conventional history. Not only does she ask us to understand women's history as something outside and essentially different from that of men, but in concluding the novel, she also asks us to acknowledge the fact that human experience is profoundly affected by those whose work takes place in a domain outside the political sphere. What is true for women's history, she implies, holds true for the novelist's craft as well: "the growing good of the world is partly dependent on unhistoric acts; and that things are not so ill with you and me as they might have been, is half owing to the number who lived faithfully a hidden life, and rest in unvisited tombs" (p. 578).

These works demonstrate the degree to which the sexual contract authorized women writers as it governed the form of the novel. Moving one step further, however, Emily Brontë's *Wuthering Heights* uses the contract as the means of giving a woman's knowledge precedence over that of a man in explaining social relationships. Mr. Lockwood may transcribe the Earnshaw family history that constitutes the plot of the novel. But even though his classical education, foreign travel, and novel-reading experience certainly qualify him to write this history, he cannot do so without the family retainer Nelly Dean, who has access to the knowledge that makes sense of family relationships. She alone combines the knowledge contained in the "master's library" with lore garnered from "country folk," with the gossip relayed between various households, and with a memory that has recorded events in terms of the emotions they generate. The radical changes in the distribution of political power within the family over the years make little sense without Nelly's historical account of the desires that have brought such changes about. And although Lockwood is the one to solicit the tale and put it in writing, he cannot provide the source of its meaning. That even in all its worldliness the male point of view proves inadequate is dramatized by the number of readers who have felt inspired to do the work of interpreting Lockwood. They seek out within this narrator the sources of his peculiar fascination with the Earnshaw family, of his ensuing illness, as well as of the tale that apparently cures him. Something about the novel compels one, in other words, to create a private emotional basis for meaning, if not in Lockwood, the putative author, then in an author presumed to be Emily Brontë herself.

We might even go so far as to see the "Puppet Master" of *Vanity Fair* or the "story-weaver at his loom" who steps forth in the afterword to *Our Mutual Friend* as further proof that the viewpoint of male novelists was bound by the same imperative to draw authority from the female domain of knowledge. Thackeray's concern for Napoleonic history notwithstanding, the author's perspective in *Vanity Fair* is certainly neither on the grand scope of political events in Europe nor on the fortunes of men in love and war. His is the record of the small shockwaves felt on the homefront by two women who endeavor to keep themselves well supported by men. Nor was Dickens exempt from the rule that separated moral authority from political authority on the grounds that each sprang from separate, gendered spheres of knowledge. As George Ford has demonstrated, Dickens' violation of this rule caused him to lose the support of the Victorian readership. "According to the reviewer in the *Westminster:* 'In all his tales there is a latent desire to improve and strengthen the charities of life, raise the trampled upon, soften intolerance, diffuse knowledge, promote happiness.'" Yet, Ford notes, "Oddly enough, twenty-two years later, in 1864, the *Westminster* reversed its verdict. 'We believe him to have been the main instrument in the change which has perverted the novel from a work of art to a platform for discussion and argument.'"[22] With a genre whose language was supposed to display female behavior ("*improve* and *strengthen the charities* of life, *raise* the trampled upon, *soften* intolerance, *diffuse* knowledge, and *promote happiness*"), Dickens dared enter into political debate. The reviewers obviously took this as an intrusion of the male into female territory, a form of rudeness that apparently undermined a novelist's authority.

More telling perhaps than transgressions of the sexual division of discourse is the insistence by women writers that gender differences should be maintained. Mary Shelley's preface to the 1831 edition of *Frankenstein* testifies to the fact that the novel was nothing other than "my waking dream."[23] Thus she claims for this writing an unmediated source in the female imagination, her own. Her husband's tinkering with the manuscript, she assures us (placing him in much the same relation to herself as Brontë placed Lockwood to Nelly), extended only to superficial matters of style. Similarly, it is with this protest that a worldly-wise Mrs. Gaskell introduces *Mary Barton,* her "tale of Manchester Life," to a readership who had just survived the turbulent 1840s: "I know nothing of Political Economy, or of the theories of trade."[24] But it is wrong for us to imagine that her claim to know only the ways of the heart is a humble statement, for if nothing else, her novels prove that love can resolve even the most violent political conflicts. According to her, the sexual contract overrules the social contract, and love is the most powerful "regulating law between two parties" (p. 460).

It was Charlotte Brontë who turned the demonstration of emotional power into an aesthetic imperative when she criticized Jane Austen for failing to plumb the depths of her characters. Brontë once described Austen as "a lady, but certainly no woman" since her "business" as author "is not half so much with the human heart as with the human eyes, mouth, hands, and feet."[25] From this statement, one might infer that Charlotte wholeheartedly approved of her sister Emily's novel in which the emotions run roughshod over the well-polished behavior displayed within Austen's fictional parlors. That was not the case, however. Charlotte took her sister's writing to task for an entirely different kind of deficiency that made Emily fall short of the female standard. Charlotte's preface to the 1850 edition of *Wuthering Heights* claims that Emily's "will was not very flexible, and it generally opposed her interest, her temper was magnanimous, but warm and sudden; her spirit altogether unbending."[26] Such imperious qualities manifest themselves in writing that Charlotte describes in terms of masculine features—"the rough, strong utterance, the harshly manifested passions, the unbridled aversions, and headlong partialities of unlettered moorland hinds and rugged moorland squires" (p. 9). Such fiction seems honest but so terribly "unlettered," according to Charlotte, that in going to the opposite extreme from Austen's genteel style, it undermines the authority of female writing just as surely.

Charlotte's preface and "biographical notice" were written in response to the very skeptical reviewers of the novel's original 1847 edition. While conceding that *Wuthering Heights* was, among other things, "unlettered," she was nevertheless arguing that it was not in fact "strange," "coarse and loathsome," or an example of an author's "power thrown away," as the reviewers had claimed.[27] She warded off these charges by characterizing the author of *Wuthering Heights* as someone who possessed the genius of the Romantic poet, but who was actually more of an ingenue. Furthermore, the novel's 1850 edition dropped the masculine pseudonym that had been used in the original publication and, in appearing under

Emily's real name, it came to the public as the product of a culturally marginal and mortally ailing woman. "Under an unsophisticated culture, inartificial tastes, and an unpretending outside," Charlotte writes of her sister, "lay a secret power and fire that might have informed the brain and kindled the veins of a hero; but she had no worldly wisdom" (p. 8). This representation of the author effectively explains away her apparent lapses in decorum by regarding them as signs of innocence and, given their lack of masculine power, as signs of an authentic female nature. Consequently, Charlotte's preface removes *Wuthering Heights* from the contemporary world where the novel's representation of sexual relationships, which so clearly challenge certain features of the contractual model, would have to be viewed as subversive. Encouraging readers to locate the meaning of Emily's fiction in the secret recesses of her emotional life, the preface dismisses such violations of the sexual contract as mere symptoms of imperfect gender definition. But in doing so, of course, the preface brings the norms of gender to bear on the fiction in question and effectively feminizes, or removes that fiction from, political controversy. J. Hillis Miller reveals the assumption on which this strategy for feminizing fiction relies when he claims, "The validity of Emily Brontë's visions depends upon their being kept private. Their purpose is to create an inner world excluding other people and the real world."[28]

Charlotte Brontë presumably meant to suggest that somewhere between the excesses of Austen's inauthentically feminine prose and Emily Brontë's aggressively female style, there is an ideal style of fiction. She anticipates that such an ideal would have been realized in Emily's work had her sister's imagination been allowed to develop completely. "Had she but lived," according to Charlotte, "her mind would of itself have grown like a strong tree, loftier, straighter, wider-spreading, and its matured fruits would have attained a mellower ripeness and sunnier bloom" (p. 11). This lofty, fruit-bearing tree provides Charlotte with a metaphor for a female style that is neither so aggressive as her sister's nor as withholding as Austen's. We can, I think, regard *Jane Eyre* as a dramatization of the limits and privileges that female authority ideally allows. It is fair to say that in developing the character of a heroine who acquires the power to author her own history, Brontë identifies the source of her own authority as a writer as well. To achieve a position from which to speak with authority, Jane must abdicate roles within the economic, religious, and educational institutions of her society. She must become an institution in her own right. Other institutions create cul-de-sacs that fix the heroine's authority to a place. By relinquishing positions in the public sphere, it turns out, she gains happiness without any threat to her reason or self-restraint.

By focusing on the issue of the heroine's authority over the emotions, *Jane Eyre* allows us to slip past a crucial detail that brings the story to a state of emotional gratification. More so perhaps than her virtue or passion, it is an endowment from Jane's wealthy uncle that makes her happiness possible. This money serves as one link in a causal chain that takes Jane from orphanhood to a position of social respectability. But more importantly, Jane's inheritance allows her to fulfill a cultural formula that is virtually inseparable from the novel's form—the exchange between male and female. Initially, the money allows Jane to get out from under her obligation to her cousin St. John Rivers. Then, with economic autonomy, she acquires the power to pursue sexual desires that magically claim priority over any social duty: "I broke from St. John, who had followed and would have detained me. It was *my* time to assume ascendancy. *My* powers were in play, and in force" (p. 370). Jane breaks off her impending alliance with her cousin St. John, not because he has offered her a life of poverty and self-denial, but because he has refused— in exchange for controlling her economic circumstances—to grant her sovereignty over his heart. On the other hand, earlier in the novel, Jane's alliance with Rochester was disallowed on very different grounds, not because he was already married (for all Jane knows when she decides to return to him, that contract is still in existence), but because she had no economic power to relinquish. Rochester was her employer. Only when she no longer needs his money can she become the mistress of his heart, and it is in this role, not as a governess, that she takes her rightful place of dominion over his home. It is worth noting that with this exchange female authority takes the form of linguistic authority—the supervision of information. Jane describes her role in relation to the blind Rochester as a combination of nursemaid and interpreter: "He saw nature—he saw books through me; and never did I weary of gazing for his behalf, and of putting into words the effect of field, tree, town, river, cloud, sunbeam . . . and impressing by sound on his ear what light could no longer stamp on his eye" (p. 397). Relinquishing her economic identity thus empowers Jane to rewrite the material conditions under which sexual relationships ideally occur. Cast in her words, her context becomes a thoroughly domesticated text that has been filtered through a woman's perception and infused with her emotional response.

By representing this transaction as either a moral or an emotional imperative rather than as an economic necessity, *Jane Eyre* takes part in the larger cultural strategy underlying middle-class sexuality itself. As the novel detaches both desire and the need for its constraint from the principles governing the marketplace, it sustains the illusion of Jane's autonomy and therefore the illusion that she controls her personal experience.

The good marriage concluding fiction of this kind, where characters achieve prosperity without compromising their domestic virtue, could be used to resolve another order of conflict, the conflict between an agrarian gentry and urban industrialists, for one, or between labor and capital, for another. By enclosing such conflict within a domestic sphere, certain novels demonstrated that despite the vast inequities of the age virtually anyone could find gratification within this private framework. As it became the woman's sphere, then, the household appeared to detach itself from the political world and to provide the complement and antidote to it. And in this way, novels helped to transform the household into what might be called the "counterimage" of the modern marketplace, an apolitical realm of culture within the culture as a whole.[29]

The Sexual Contract as Narrative Process

To make a tradition of such relatively homebound authors as Burney, Radcliffe, Austen, Gaskell, the Brontës, Eliot, and Woolf thus strikes me as similar to adopting the complacent manner of Rowton, the Victorian editor, when he declared men the engineers of history, the creators of ideology, and the forgers of political conscience. This is not to say we should disregard what these authors tell us about the working of the female imagination and the social circumstances affecting it. One may argue that many women's novels indeed signal the reader to regard fiction as a major source of information about the condition of women. The more closely nineteenth century fiction asks us to focus on domestic life and the personal experience of women, however, the more it will also insist that the information at hand is natural and universal and hence removed from political history. Unless we regard representations of personal life and domestic relations as a cultural strategy arising from specific historical conditions and serving definite political ends, our observations will simply reify a nineteenth century model of sexual exchange. To describe the novel under such circumstances is not to get at female nature or even at female culture, in my opinion, but rather to reproduce pure ideology as if it were one or the other. I am not discounting the possibility of determining what is specifically female about this kind of writing. To the contrary, I am suggesting that only by determining what is sexuality in the Foucauldian sense of the word can we possibly isolate sex from the other power relations operating under its cloak. For now, we can evade the trap of understanding sexual differences as a universal condition or a static paradigm simply by considering how, in a few important examples, the sexual contract developed along with the changing conditions for literary reception.

The degree to which the gender of representation is in fact bound not to the author's sex, but to the institution of the novel as well as to changing social attitudes becomes evident when one draws some comparisons between the major women novelists of the period and a few of their more illustrious male contemporaries. For men, too, the model of sexual exchange organized stories about power relationships in a way that allowed readers to deny the political basis of their pleasure. When acted out by a woman, aggressive individualism folded back into paternalism upon her marriage to a man of higher station. While she might gain superiority over men in moral terms, even the most ambitious woman desired nothing more than economic dependency upon the man who valued her for her qualities of mind. Richardson's *Pamela* provides one of the clearest examples of the political contradiction contained within this exchange. Couched as the diary of a virtuous servant girl, the story of her abuse at the hands of an unscrupulous master makes Pamela's resistance seem admirable, if not very true to life in Richardson's day. When her persecutor undergoes a moral conversion and asks her to marry him, we are supposed to regard this as an act of contrition on his part rather than presumption on hers. As Ian Watt has observed, "these struggles . . . mirror larger contemporary conflicts between the two classes and their way of life."[30] At the same time, such conflicts can be allowed much freer rein through a female protagonist because her power is ultimately subject to the authority of a man. Competing class interests are therefore represented as a struggle between the sexes that can be completely resolved in terms of the sexual contract.

Perhaps more telling in this respect are those instances when sexuality does not conceal the clash between political interests. Moll Flanders offers an obvious case in point. Whenever she is seduced, as she is on several occasions, there is no denying that she provides a site for Defoe to represent political conflicts. Furthermore, once Moll has surmounted the social barriers that separate her from the leisure classes, she takes on a new name and condemns her most advantageous moves up the ladder. In other words, she takes a position opposing her original social identity. Contradictions in the political world produce such dissonances, which become all the more disturbing when they govern a woman's personal history and make her appear deceptive. For this reason, no doubt, *Moll Flanders* and *Roxana* had to wait until our own century before they could be classified as novels. And no doubt these narratives required something on the order of psychoanalysis to explain away obvious discontinuities occurring within the female rather than between her and some male.

Pursuing this line of thinking still further, we must consider it possible that a novel like *Pride and Prejudice* operates according to the same broadly based political strategy simply because it seems to concern itself exclusively with the problem of marrying off a number of daughters. Around the time Austen wrote, the novel was being defined by Scott, Barbauld, and others in a way that gave meaning to such narratives whose resolution depended on marriage. The novel was identified with fiction that authorized a particular form of domestic relations. But if Austen could not vary the form and still write a respectable novel, she could modify the content and thus the nature of the social conflict that marriage appeared to resolve.

In fact, her modifications of the Richardsonian model are notably subtle. *Pride and Prejudice* presents the reader with a group of women who are daughters of polite country gentlemen and who compete among themselves in a matchmaking game. They require husbands with money and status and in return offer themselves, their manners, and their qualities of mind. The game of love decides which female virtues are the most advantageous in a woman aspiring to live the good country life. As a result, such traditional female attributes as chastity, wit, practicality, duty, manners, imagination, sympathy, generosity, beauty, and kindness are pitted against each other in the competition among the Bennet sisters and their friends. Jane, the Richardsonian sister, languishes for want of a husband until the very end of the novel, but Austen does not allow Lydia, who acts the part of the adventuress, to do very much better. What is more, in capturing a husband, Lydia jeopardizes the family's reputation and thus limits her sisters' possibilities for marriage. In this way, the novel makes the reader consider what enables the heroine, Elizabeth Bennet, to attract a man who not only saves her family's estate but also elevates their social position. While excelling in none of the traditionally feminine qualities represented by her competitors, Elizabeth surpasses them on an entirely different plane. Her particular assets are the traditionally masculine qualities of rational intelligence, honesty, self-possession, and especially a command of the language, all of which at first seem to impede a good marriage.

From the beginning, Elizabeth's father distinguishes her from his other daughters even though, as Mrs. Bennet puts it, "'she is not half so handsome as Jane, nor half so good humoured as Lydia. . . .' 'They have none of them much to recommend them,' replied he; 'they are all silly and ignorant like other girls; but Lizzy has something more of quickness than her sisters'" (p. 2). In the end, the most eligible male in the novel confirms this alternative basis for desirability. When asked why he chose to marry Elizabeth, Darcy tells her, "'For the liveliness of your mind, I did.'" In a characteristic act of verbal aggression, Elizabeth challenges his power to define her and answers the question herself: "'The fact is, that you were sick of civility, of deference, of officious attention. You were disgusted with women who were always speaking and looking, and thinking for *your* approbation alone. I roused, and interested you, because I was so unlike *them*'" (p. 262). Although she wins Darcy's heart on the basis of what amounts to a direct violation of the female ideal, Elizabeth renounces all her pertness the instant she agrees to marry him. Her "liveliness of mind" loses its cutting edge, and from then on she will exert a softening influence in the world projectd at the end of the novel. But what might appear to be a discontinuity within her character in fact demonstrates this novel's reliance on the figure of sexual exchange. As this figure takes over, the novel redistributes authority between Darcy and Elizabeth in a manner that clearly demonstrates its ability to translate political conflict into psychological terms. Their union miraculously transforms all social differences into gender differences and gender differences into qualities of mind:

> It was a union that must have been to the advantage of both; by her ease and liveliness, his mind might have been softened, his manners improved, and from his judgement, information, and knowledge of the world, she must have received benefit of greater importance. (p. 214)

It is important to notice exactly how such a representation creates personal fulfillment where there had been internal conflict and social unity where there had been competing class interests. By attributing political and emotional authority to the male and female respectively, the figure inscribes the political within the male character and then contains both within heart and home.

Novels rewarding self-assertion on the part of those in an inferior position undoubtedly provided the middle-class readership with a fable for their own emergence. Especially when acted out as the options of a female protagonist, social competition could be sexualized and therefore suppressed even while it was being experienced. But once the blight of expanding industrial cities and the threat of popular uprising changed the background against which people read such works of fiction, middle-class supremacy became less an utopian fantasy and more a fact to be justified and defended. With the publication of the People's Charter in 1837, the logic of the contract was used to support workers' demands for self-government.[31] Under such conditions, novelists had to change their strategies of self-authorization or else run the risk of authorizing claims that were opposed to their own interests.

This change in the conditions for writing is particularly apparent in the difference between Austen's characteristic strategy for representing social conflict and the strategy more typical of the 1830s and 1840s. Like Dickens' *Oliver Twist* and Thackeray's *Vanity Fair*, for example, *Wuthering Heights* and *Jane Eyre* were composed during the turbulent period between the Reform Bill of 1832 and the onset of mid-century prosperity. These novels share a fantasy of upward mobility in which a protagonist of inferior status enters into the leisure classes. They share this fantasy with earlier fiction too. Like Dickens and Thackeray, however, the Brontës feel compelled to change the consequences of acting out the fantasy, and they make this change in similar ways. Heathcliff cannot penetrate the old squirarchy without dismantling it. The same can be said of Becky Sharp and less obviously of Oliver, who ruptures the bonds among his distinguished forefathers at the moment of his conception. The social climbers of the 1840s invariably threaten to become intruders, if not tyrants in their own right, by pursuing individualistic goals. Rather than justify the form of power that comes into being on such a basis, novels that were written against the ominous background of swelling industrial centers and Chartist rebellions represent any kind of competition as a disruptive force.

By turning the figure of sexual exchange against itself, fiction no longer provided a fantasy in which one could enjoy watching class lines dissolve within marriage. Instead, it began marking boundaries that it had formerly felt free to cross. In this regard, it is worth recalling that in *Oliver Twist*, Fagin's true villainous nature is initially cloaked behind a maternal exterior of sizzling sausages, schoolroom games, and terms of endearment. But his simulation of benign authority disintegrates as the profit motive comes into conflict with his feminine virtues and cancels them out. Together with Oliver's sinister stepbrother, Fagin prevents Oliver from discovering his mother's identity, and through Sikes, he brings about the murder of Nancy the prostitute. In many respects, *Wuthering Heights* might seem to offer an unlikely comparison to *Oliver Twist*. Even so, Heathcliff's features change in a way remarkably similar to Fagin's as his romantic qualities give way in the second half of the novel to the "besetting sin" of "avarice." Here, too, aggression toward the established form of authority proves ultimately self-defeating, and value comes to be located in the ghost of Catherine Earnshaw, a female power that preserves the family line, excludes intruders who have wandered into the country, and in this way rids the family of forms of competition that rule the world of money. A second generation of characters, notably domesticated in comparison with their prototypes in the first half of the novel, comes to dominate through inherited rights rather than through economic competition or marriage.[32] A similar ambivalence toward female authority as manifest in earlier fiction makes itself felt in the dual heroines of *Vanity Fair*. One trusts in emotional constancy and moral restraint, the other relies upon unscrupulous instincts and pure opportunism. The reader discovers soon enough that one woman prospers at the expense of the other. Thackeray's is not a political reality in which everyone prospers from the success of a few. Thus with Becky's ascendancy, the author's sympathies shift to the sentimental heroine, Amelia, only to represent her passivity as tiresome. Even so, he feels compelled to neutralize Becky, whose aggressive individualism threatens the very class of people who have already risen to power by similar means.

The same ambivalence seems to qualify the ending of Brontë's *Jane Eyre*. Despite the machinery of contractual relations, something obviously gets out of hand in this novel. Too many readers have seen Jane's ascendancy in the final chapters, not as a mutually enhancing exchange, but as the symbolic castration of Rochester. And they feel this no less because he still has his title and fortune—the signs of masculine authority. The sense of imbalance in the relationship between the sexes seems to derive from fiction's disruption of the traditional hierarchy that granted the male dominance over the female. It is as if the female, far from representing the interests of the literate classes, actually threatens the tranquility of private life at all levels of the social world when she challenges class lines. For the sexual contract no longer aims to make the aggressive female desirable or to reward female desire, but rather to provide women with security in exchange for their submission to a traditional role. It is not only in the Brontës' novels that extraordinary violence accompanies a shift to something resembling a matrilineal order. As with the intrusion of Catherine's ghost and the blinding of Rochester, female authority comes into being with the executions that conclude *Oliver Twist* and the plunge of the knife that may well have hastened Joseph Sedley's death in *Vanity Fair*. Their power over the male sometimes resembles the demonic force—manifest in the madwoman—that would define these women as anti-heroines and undesirable wives.

At the beginning of the nineteenth century, Austen felt obliged to close *Pride and Prejudice* by relocating political authority at Pemberley, Darcy's ancestral home, and at considerable distance from the town where the Bennets' embarrassing relatives live. With such a geographical shift, the novel maintains the continuity of traditional political authority while appearing to broaden its social base by granting Elizabeth authority of a strictly female kind. In contrast, novels written near the middle of the century stress the disruptive effects of any redistribution of authority. We see the social gap between male and female widen in *Wuthering Heights* and *Jane Eyre*, as well as in *Vanity Fair*. The distance closes only when one of the contending parties has been eliminated or otherwise clearly subordinated. From this it is reasonable to conclude that the contract underlying sexual relationships had to change with the entrenchment of middle-class power.

In converting traditionally male prerogatives into forms of female authority, these mid-century novels tend to represent the female in a menacing light. Her ascendancy over the household produces discontinuities that are never quite resolved through a traditional sexual exchange despite a novelist's gesture toward closure. One cannot help but feel relief when Heathcliff's power dies out as he surrenders to Catherine Earnshaw's spell, but as he explains to Nelly, the loss of his destructive energy itself takes on sinister overtones: "'Nelly, there is a strange change approaching— I'm in its shadow at present. I take so little interest in my daily life, that I hardly remember to eat, and drink'" (p. 255). In removing Heathcliff, this change restores the ancestral home of the Earnshaws to the "ancient stock and lawful master." Again, however, the process has its sinister side because it is motivated by a woman, in this instance, Catherine's daughter. In transforming the Earnshaw heir from a servant into a gentleman, the second Catherine displays the overbearing features of her mother: "she changed her behaviour, and became incapable of letting him alone: talking at him; commenting on his stupidity and idleness; expressing her wonder how he could endure the life he lived—how he could sit a whole evening staring into the fire, and dozing" (p. 245). Where there had always been wild brambles around Wuthering Heights, Catherine has Hareton put in "her choice of a flower bed in the midst of them" (p. 250). The disruptive effect of feminization is finally accomplished when the family—or what remains of it—abandons the Heights for the more modern and effeminate surroundings of Thrushcross Grange. A similar act of dislocation occurs in *Jane Eyre* where it is possible for the lovers to unite only after Thornfield Hall has burned to the ground and the family, again reduced, has moved to a bungalow on the outskirts of the family estate. As Jane approaches the site of her reunion with Rochester, Brontë describes the place in terms that should remind us of the enshrouded castle in the stories of Sleeping Beauty and Briar Rose: "the trees thinned a little; presently I beheld a railing, then the house—scarce, by this dim light, distinguishable from the trees; so dank and green were its decaying walls" (p. 379). An obvious inversion of the fairy tale pattern, this place contains a male who will be kissed back to life by a female. Rather than behaving as complementary halves of the same political structure, then, male and female so clearly represent competing forces in the mid-century novels that a contractual exchange empowers the female at the expense of exhausting the male.

To close a description of what is actually a continuing process, I would like to provide a few examples that show how the sexual contract changed during the second half of the century. It is worth noting, first of all, that while Charlotte Brontë could allow Jane Eyre a degree of sexual freedom and social mobility that obviously went beyond the author's own experience, the same does not hold true for Lucy Snowe, the spinster schoolteacher of Brontë's later novel *Villette*. Nor does George Eliot, also writing after the mid-century mark, grant her protagonists nearly so much room to exercise their desire as Eliot herself was able to enjoy. It is remarkable, furthermore, that the mere thought of sexual initiative on the part of Louisa Gradgrind, an otherwise unnoteworthy bourgeoise, overshadows the far more momentous issues that surface in Dickens' *Hard Times*. In a novel rumbling with labor unrest and crises within the educational system, Dickens pursues the sexual theme with perfect aplomb, as if he knew that in fiction at least these volatile political issues could be resolved simply by subjugating the female. It is significant, then, that he cannot allow a figure like Austen's Darcy or Brontë's Rochester to gain authority over Louisa. These males are earlier embodiments of political authority that by the mid-nineteenth century had been banished from the domain of polite fiction. Adopting instead a strategy that is meant to cancel out the power of female desire, Dickens returns Louisa to her father in a state of infantile dependency. The domestic world assumes a more traditional form in the novel only when she gives herself over to Sissy Jupe, a circus girl who desires, before anything else, to find her lost father.

Dickens clearly breaks down the character of the self-possessed woman into those two familiar Victorian stereotypes, the virgin and the adventuress. His resolution provides no mediation of the two, for it depends on exalting the passive woman and ridding the world of all active female desire. In Eliot's *Mill on the Floss,* the locus classicus for Maggie Tulliver's dilemma is the medieval trial for witchcraft. This Victorian version of the double bind condemns a woman for having demonic power if she swims and celebrates her innocence if she drowns. The dynamics of sexual exchange are apparently such that the female gains authority only by redeeming the male, not by pursuing her own desires. Fiction written after the mid-century mark severely punishes women if they resist the established forms of political authority, no matter how ineffectual their resistance turns out to be. The same fiction rewards female characters when they steadfastly oppose the competitive behavior that resembles the heartless warfare mapped out in Darwin's biology.

At about the time the sexual contract was turning against itself in this way, Rowton's anthology of female poetry appeared. His preface makes clear that the figure of the contract could no longer be used to inject an element of individualism into the system. Instead, female desire must be turned to the rhetorical work of transforming the male from a competitive brute into a benevolent father. Rowton's female anthology and feminine poetics spring from this political imperative. The collection can be considered an attempt to contain female authority by maintaining its detachment from writing produced by men. Given the fact that Victorian women had little direct access to economic or political power, however, one has to wonder why the Victorian novel suddenly found it necessary to render women passive and exclude them from the masculine sphere.

Once again, I would like to stress the rhetorical dimension of the obsession with sexual purity. More than anything else, this obsession demonstrates how the literate classes sought to revise the way in which people talked, wrote, and thought about themselves in relation to others. I would further argue that this effort was part of a much more profound revision of the contract and its various features, including the kinds of maleness and femaleness it could contain, the basis on which the two were distinguished, and the conditions for a good marriage. This change brought with it a shift in moral emphasis from the claims of the individual asserted through female desire to those of the community, which required such desire to submit to rational control. With the ascendancy of the middle classes, it would no longer do for the ideal woman to represent an emergent form of power. We find that fiction positions her outside a now openly competitive system where she is "different," rather than on the inside where she might clamber up. But once cultural territory had been mapped out and found meaningful in one way as opposed to another, this meaning could not be transformed at an author's will. The novelist's authority was still identified with that of the female. The voice of late nineteenth century authors gains authority from detachment, by coming to us from outside the social world rather than from its center. To this separation of powers within the culture one can probably attribute the growing number of critics and reviewers as well as editors on the order of Rowton. The belief that essential differences distinguished men from women and gave each powers that the other did not possess provided the basis, as Elaine Showalter has explained, on which a feminine subculture sought to extend women's power.[33]

As if to demonstrate that no area of culture—and especially not sexuality—remains stable through time and repeated usage, modernist writers like Virginia Woolf and Jean Rhys deliberately abandoned the feminine aesthetic. A post-Freudian culture apparently gave them what their predecessors lacked, a language for articulating the gaps and silences of earlier domestic fiction. Or perhaps it is more accurate to say that the new and more specialized language of the self provided by psychoanalysis—along with changes in the sciences, philosophy, and the sister arts, including literary criticism—allowed them to represent depths in the female subject that were beyond the limits of an earlier discourse to imagine. In Woolf's *Mrs. Dalloway,* the polite exchanges of a language at once sexual and political degenerates into the language of women, an empty discourse dramatizing the absence of both communication and community. In its place, Woolf offers a language of the true self, which is fluid, neither male nor female, but capable of containing within the self the figure of an exchange that once had organized social relations. The figure comes to us as a voice that cannot be female because it represents what is both male and female, always from a position that alienates the reader from the past and from the sexual norms that circumscribe consciousness. This, according to Woolf, is how the modern Clarissa understands herself as a gendered person:

> She had the oddest sense of being herself invisible; unseen; unknown; there being no more marrying, no more having of children now, but only this astonishing and rather solemn progress with the rest of them, up Bond Street, this being Mrs. Dalloway, not even Clarissa any more; this being Mrs. Richard Dalloway.[34]

It is perhaps more appropriate to look to *Orlando*—my own favorite—which Woolf so much as said was written by other novels and whose protagonist changes sex and status along with the requirements of history s/he encounters, always with the intention of concealing his or her true identity. A brief example from this metahistory of subjectivity will have to do: "Orlando sipped the wine and the Archduke knelt and kissed her hand. In short, they acted the parts of man and woman for ten minutes with great vigour and then fell into natural discourse."[35] I should add that "natural discourse" is for Orlando and the Archduke a history of the various transformations required to keep the truth of his or her desire concealed and Orlando thus one step ahead of his or her suitors, which as with all fiction, Woolf seems to say, leaves us with the skins of old selves as the substance of human identity. Jean Rhys's *Wide Sargasso Sea* provides another rewriting of the domestic novel.[36] It retells the story of *Jane Eyre* from the perspective of the madwoman in the attic, this time stressing the cultural otherness of the female and representing the femininity of an earlier age as the projection of male desires upon the past and upon another culture, as well as upon a woman. In this framework, the madness of Rochester's first wife can be considered a form of resistance.

The real self is presumably elsewhere in these novels, while the sexual self is subject to economic interests and encumbered by historical necessity. But again we find that male authors such as Joyce and Lawrence share with their female contemporaries a notion of sexuality that breaks down the distinctions between masculine and feminine discourse maintained by earlier novels. Such a transgression of sexual boundaries became, then, not a feminist or even a female response to the model of sexual exchange so much as a rhetorical strategy by which certain authors placed themselves outside the reigning categories of their culture and, in this way, identified themselves as an elite intellectual minority. However, it can also be argued that in positing themselves a world apart from their moment in history modernist authors carried on the nineteenth century project that used fiction to distinguish politics from sexuality.

2

The Rise of the
Domestic Woman

It is only by seeing women in their own homes, among their own
set, just as they always are, that you can form any just judgement.
Short of that, it is all guess and luck—and will generally be ill-luck.
How many a man has committed himself on a short acquaintance,
and rued it all the rest of his life!

JANE AUSTEN, *Emma*

In their effort to make young women desirable to men of a good social
position, countless conduct books and works of instruction for women
represented a specific configuration of sexual features as those of the only
appropriate woman for men at all levels of society to want as a wife. At
the same time, such writing provided people from diverse social groups
with a basis for imagining economic interests in common.[1] Thus it was
the new domestic woman rather than her counterpart, the new economic
man, who first encroached upon aristocratic culture and seized authority
from it. This writing assumed that an education ideally made a woman
desire to be what a prosperous man desires, which is above all else a
female. She therefore had to lack the competitive desires and worldly
ambitions that consequently belonged—as if by some natural principle—
to the male. For such a man, her desirability hinged upon an education
in frugal domestic practices. She was supposed to complement his role
as an earner and producer with hers as a wise spender and tasteful consumer. Such an ideal relationship presupposed a woman whose desires
were not of necessity attracted to material things. But because a woman's
desire could in fact be manipulated by signs of wealth and position, she
required an education.

In assuming this, eighteenth century conduct books and educational
treatises for women forced open a contradiction within the existing cul-

tural territory that had been marked out for representing the female. These authors portrayed aristocratic women along with those who harbored aristocratic pretensions as the very embodiments of corrupted desire, namely, desire that sought its gratification in economic and political terms. The books all took care to explain how this form of desire destroyed the very virtues essential to a wife and mother. Narratives of her ideal development would come later. The educational handbooks for women simply mapped out a new field of knowledge as specifically female. In doing so, they declared their intention to recover and preserve a woman's true (sexual) identity in a world run according to other (political and economic) measures of men. With this as its justification, the writing devoted to defining the female wrought an important change in the understanding of power. It severed the language of kinship from that of political relations, producing a culture divided into the respective domains of domestic woman and economic man.

After reading several dozen or more conduct books, one is struck with a sense of their emptiness—a lack of what we today consider "real" information about the female subject and the object world that she is supposed to occupy. Under the sheer force of repetition, however, one does see a figure emerge from the categories that organize these manuals. A figure of female subjectivity, a grammar really, awaited the substance that the novel and its readers, as well as the countless individuals educated according to the model of the new woman, would eventually provide. In such books one can see a culture in the process of rethinking at the most basic level the dominant (aristocratic) rules for sexual exchange. Because they appeared to have no political bias, these rules took on the power of natural law, and as a result, they presented—in actuality, still present—readers with ideology in its most powerful form.

With this in mind, I describe the field of information as represented by eighteenth century conduct books for women, knowing that the historical importance of the formation of such a field can be understood neither as a psychology nor as a set of rules designed to restrict female behavior. As they revised the sexual contract, authors and readers—men and women both—used the same rules to formulate a new mode of economic thinking, even though they represented that thinking as pertaining only to women. To see the sexual contract once again as an economic contract is the only way, then, to treat modern sexuality as the political language it happens to be. The following discussion argues that, by virtue of its apparent insignificance, a body of writing concerned with devising a special kind of education for women in fact played a crucial role in the rise of the new middle classes in England.

The Book of Class Sexuality

Until sometime around the end of the seventeenth century, the great majority of conduct books were devoted mainly to representing the male of the dominant class.[2] For purposes of my argument, it does not really matter whether or not aristocrats were actually the ones to take such instruction seriously. What does matter is what the literate public considered to be the dominant social ideal. Ruth Kelso and Suzanne Hull have shown that during the sixteenth and seventeenth centuries there were relatively few books for instructing women as compared to those available to men. Their research also shows that books addressing a readership with humbler aspirations increased in popularity during the seventeenth century.[3] Although by mid-century they outnumbered conduct books that exalted the attributes of aristocratic women, the distinctively Puritan flavor of some marriage manuals and books on household governance made it quite clear that they were not endorsing the preferred cultural norms.[4] But neither was their advice for women supposed to challenge the aristocratic ideal. Whatever their political attitude toward the aristocracy, these books did not presume to represent a more desirable woman but simply outlined domestic procedures that were practical for people of less means and prestige. An exclusive concern for the practical matters of running a household classified certain handbooks for women as domestic economies, which meant they belonged to an entirely different genre than conduct books that aspired to be courtesy literature. Although some books argued that domestic economy should be part of an ideal gentlewoman's education, they did not come into their own until the last decade of the seventeenth century.[5] Until then, different levels of society held recognizably different ideas about what made a woman marriageable. During the first decades of the eighteenth century, however, categories that had apparently remained fairly constant for centuries underwent rapid transformation.

The distinction between conduct books and domestic economies changed so that each reached out to the other's reader. So popular did these books become that by the second half of the eighteenth century virtually everyone knew the ideal of womanhood they proposed. Joyce Hemlow considers this writing the purest expression of the same interest in manners that one finds in Burney: "the problem of the conduct of the young lady was investigated so thoroughly that the lifetime of Fanny Burney, or more accurately the years 1760–1820, which saw also the rise of the novel of manners, might be called the age of courtesy books for women."[6] To this I would add an important qualification. While the lifetime of Burney—

and, one might note, of Austen as well—should indeed be seen as the high point of a tradition of conduct books for women, it would be misleading to suggest that the two kinds of writing—women's courtesy books and novels of manners—sprang into being and passed out of currency together. The production of conduct books long preceded novels of manners and in fact virtually exploded during the period following the failure to renew the licensing act in 1695, thus preceding the novel of manners by several decades.[7] And although today we find authors neither designing curricula to educate young women at home nor writing fiction to demonstrate the proprieties of feminine conduct, the conduct book is still alive and well. Besides all the books and advice columns telling women how to catch and keep a man, and besides numerous magazines imaging the beautiful home, there are also home economics courses that most women must take before graduating from high school. Perhaps because their most basic tenets became social facts with the formation of the national curriculum that included male and female pupils, conduct books have grown more specialized during our own century—concentrating now on thin thighs, on the manners of a business woman, and with equal frequency on such specific domestic skills as French cooking or English gardening, which men are supposed to learn as well as women.

It is safe to say that by the mid-eighteenth century the number of books specifying the qualities of a new kind of woman had well outstripped the number of those devoted to describing the aristocratic male.[8] The growth of this body of writing thus coincided with the rise of the popular press, itself a part of the larger process that Raymond Williams has aptly named "the long revolution."[9] Lord Halifax's *Advice to a Daughter* first appeared in 1688 and ran through two dozen editions, winning great popularity for nearly a century until Dr. Gregory's *Father's Legacy to his Daughters* and Hester Chapone's *Letters on the Improvement of the Mind* supplanted it. John Mason's study of courtesy literature shows that the number and variety of ladies' conduct books began to increase with the publication of such books as *The Ladies Dictionary* (1694) and *The Whole Duty of Women* (1695).[10] Where men are concerned, his study shows that by mid-century the form gradually mutated into other forms—satire, for example—once the production of the ideal social leader who dominated Renaissance treatises was no longer imagined as its primary goal. Meanwhile, the conduct book for women enjoyed a different fate. Educational literature that addressed a female readership quickly became very popular once it broke free from the aristocratic model, and despite a falling off after the 1820s, many books remained in print well into the nineteenth century.

Throughout this period, countless female conduct books, ladies magazines, and books of instruction for children all posited a similar feminine ideal and tended toward the same objective of ensuring a happy household. Indeed, the end of the eighteenth century saw not only the publication of proposals for institutions devoted to educating women, but also the development of programs designed to instruct women at home. Erasmus Darwin's *A Plan for the Conduct of Female Education in Boarding Schools* (1798) and the Edgeworths' *Practical Education* (1801) are only two of the more famous efforts at institutionalizing the curriculum proposed by conduct-book literature. In representing the household as a world with its own form of social relations, a distinctively feminine discourse, this body of literature revised the semiotic of culture at its most basic level and enabled a coherent idea of the middle class to take shape. That the relative number of conduct books appeared to decrease as the eighteenth century came to an end was not because the female ideal they represented passed out of vogue. To the contrary, there is every reason to think that by this time the ideal had passed into the domain of common sense where it provided the frame of reference for other kinds of writing, among them the novel. The next chapter will show that Richardson's tediously protracted description of the household in *Pamela* can be supplanted by Austen's minimalist representation precisely because the rules governing sexual relations laid out in the conduct books could be taken for granted. Austen could simply allude where Richardson, in defiance of an earlier notion of sexual relations, had to elaborate for hundreds of pages. More than that, Austen knew perfectly well her readers had identified those rules not only with common sense, if not always with nature, but also with the form of the novel itself.

Conduct books addressed a readership comprising various levels and sources of income and included virtually all people who distinguished themselves from the aristocracy, on the one hand, and from the laboring poor on the other. Although written in various regional, professional, and political voices, each with the specific concerns of a local readership foremost in mind, the conduct books written during the first decades of the eighteenth century nevertheless proposed an ideal that was reappearing with wonderful regularity. Their evident popularity therefore suggests we might detect the presence of a "middle class," as we mean it today, much earlier than other writing from that time in history indicates. Even if we use Hemlow's later dates of 1760–1820 to mark the high point of the writing of manners, we must still confront a historical paradox. Conduct books imply the presence of a unified middle class at a time when other representations of the social world suggest that no such class yet existed.

Most other writing in fact suggests that the eighteenth century Englishman saw himself within a static and hierarchical society, radically different from the dynamic struggle of landlords, capitalists, and laboring poor that would accompany the rise of the middle class during the early decades of the nineteenth century. Harold Perkin provides this encapsulated view of how social relationships were understood in eighteenth century England: "The old society then was a finely graded hierarchy of great subtlety and discrimination, in which men were acutely aware of their exact relation to those immediately above and below them, but only vaguely conscious except at the very top of their connection with those on their own level."[11] These men apparently felt allegiance only to those immediately above and below them in economic chains, and they probably harbored antagonism toward those who occupied similar positions in other chains of dependency. According to Perkin, the absence of anything resembling a modern middle class is particularly apparent in England, where there was no word for *bourgeoisie* "until the nineteenth century," because "the thing itself did not exist, in the sense of a permanent, self-conscious urban class in opposition to the landed aristocracy" (p. 61). The English view of society proved to be incorrigibly vertical, he continues, for no sooner did one generation of townsmen succeed in business or trade than they sought to raise their social status by becoming country gentlemen.

If conduct books addressed a fairly wide readership with fairly consistent social objectives, then they present us with a historical contradiction of major proportions—a middle class that was not actually there. It was no mystery who occupied the top of the social ladder as well as the bottom, but there are only the most irregular and diverse data concerning those in the middle. Reviewing his information concerning the period from 1688 to 1803, Perkin describes what he calls "the middle ranks" of the "old society":

> The middle ranks were distinguished at the top from the gentry and nobility not so much by lower incomes as by the necessity of earning their living, and at the bottom from the labouring poor not so much by higher incomes as by the property, however small, represented by stock in trade, livestock, tools, or the educational investment of skill or expertise. (p. 23)

We should note that Perkin organizes this field of information negatively in that his description accounts for those people who were neither aristocracy nor laboring poor. Everywhere within this field there were hierarchies—professional and economic—marked by "an infinity of graduated statuses." By the same token, he claims, every occupation was marked "by internal differences of status greater than any which separated it from those outside" (p. 24). This is not to say that Perkin's map of eighteenth century society is any less a representation than that which can be extrapolated from the conduct books of an earlier time. I am simply suggesting that during the early eighteenth century most authors regarded differences of status as the only accurate way of identifying individuals within the middle ranks of their society. They did not, in other words, perceive what common interests might have united all those at the same social level. That the female conduct book presupposed horizontal affiliations among the literate public where no such affiliations would exist as a matter of practice for another sixty to a hundred years has obvious bearing on social and literary history alike. It marks a basic change in the public understanding of social relations as well as a change in what constituted good taste in reading. But I should hasten to add that the question raised by this body of discourse is not the same one addressed by Ian Watt or Richard Altick in their studies of the novel-reading public. We cannot ask the conduct book to explain what new social elements had been introduced into the readership that so altered its taste.[12] The available data do not allow us to do so. If changes in socioeconomic categories came after similar changes in the categories governing female education, we must ask instead what the new domestic ideal said to a heterogeneous economic group that ensured this ideal would keep on making sense well into the nineteenth century—after political relationships assumed a modern configuration.

During the eighteenth century, the conduct book for women became such a common phenomenon that many different kinds of writers felt compelled to add their wrinkles to the female character. Besides men like Halifax, Rochester, Swift, and Defoe—all of whom tried their hands at writing conduct books for women—there were also pedagogues such as Timothy Rogers, Thomas Gisborne, and T.S. Arthur, clergymen like Rev. Thomas Broadhurst, Dr. Fordyce, and the darling of Austen's generation, Dr. Gregory, as well as a number of women authors such as Sarah Tyler, Miss Catherine E. Beecher, and the Countess Dowager of Carlisle, all of whom have long since faded from cultural memory. Like Hester Chapone, Hannah More, and Maria Edgeworth, some authors made their reputations by writing conduct books, while other conduct-book authors like Mary Wollstonecraft and Erasmus Darwin were known primarily for writing in more prestigious modes. Even when the author's name is obscure, as most of these names indeed are, one can usually infer a social identity from the female virtues to which the writer grants highest priority, for these virtues are inevitably linked to functions which that writer feels are essential to good household management.

Taken together, these local voices comprise a text displaying obvious distinctions between town and country, between old money and new, among income levels and various occupations, and particularly among the different amounts of leisure time people had to occupy. It is the whole purpose of this chapter to show how such points of difference came to be contained within a framework that was remarkably predictable. By dividing the social world on the basis of sex, this body of writing produced a single ideal of the household. But the domestic ideal did not so much speak to middle-class interests as we now understand them. In fact, it is accurate to say that such writing as the conduct books helped to generate the belief that there was such a thing as a middle class with clearly established affiliations before it actually existed. If there is any truth in this, then it is also reasonable to claim that the modern individual was first and foremost a female.

The handbook that gained such immense popularity in England at the end of the seventeenth century was a hybrid form that combined materials from earlier devotional books and books of manners ostensibly written for aristocratic women, with information from books of maternal advice to daughters, as well as with descriptions of the housewife's practical duties as depicted in humbler handbooks of domestic economy, almanacs, and recipe books. Written by Timothy Rogers, an otherwise unremarkable educator with dissenter's sympathies, *The Character of a Good Woman, both in a Single and Married State* provides a particularly useful example of the genre as it appeared at the beginning of the eighteenth century. The book holds true to its subtitle and represents the ideal female as a bipartite character. Among the qualities of the unmarried woman that the author extolls are modesty, humility, and honesty. In earlier writing, these conspicuously passive virtues were considered the antidote to natural deficiencies that had been the female's heritage ever since the Fall of Man. In keeping with Enlightenment strategies, however, the new mode of instruction declares it will cultivate the inherently female qualities that are most likely to ward off the vanity which contemporary social life instills. Published in 1697, *The Character of a Good Woman* does not represent women as more prone to corruption and thus more in need of redemption than men; it exalts female nature because, as the author claims, women are "generally more serious than men. . . , as far beyond in the lessons of Devotion as in the tuneableness and sweetness of your voice."[13] Here passive virtue is both in keeping with female nature and essential to preserving that nature.

The passive virtue of the unmarried woman constitutes only half of the paradigm that rapidly gained currency during the eighteenth century. To the qualities of the innocent maiden, conduct books appended those of the efficient housewife. As if straight from Renaissance handbooks on domestic economy, these books developed categories that defined the ideal woman in her married state. Her representation was as practical and detailed as the maiden's was abstract and homiletic in style. Except for unqualified obedience to her husband, the virtues of the ideal wife appeared to be active. A list of her duties could have included household management, regulation of servants, supervision of children, planning of entertainment, and concern for the sick. It quickly becomes apparent, however, that the main duty of the new housewife was to supervise the servants who were the ones to take care of these matters. The table of contents for *The Young Ladies Companion or, Beauty's Looking-Glass,* which was written in 1740, demonstrates a typical mix of topics drawn from courtesy literature as well as from the practical handbooks: 1. Religion, 2. Husband, 3. House, Family and Children, 4. Behavior and Conversation, 5. Friendships, 6. Censure, 7. Vanity and Affectation, 8. Pride, 9. Diversions.[14] At this point in history, the social differences implicit in the different materials that went into conduct books have faded. The features of the devout maiden have been bonded to those of the industrious housewife, forming a new but utterly familiar system of signs.

Contained within the framework of gender rather than status, the earlier meaning of traditionally female features—practical duties and abstract virtues alike—changed even while they seemed to pass into the eighteenth century untouched by the individual imagination. Different categories of female identity, which were drawn from quite diverse traditions of writing and aimed at various social groups, formed a single representation. In their combination, contrary notions of taste transformed one another to form a standard capable of reaching across a broad spectrum of social groups. Once the practical duties of the common housewife had been included within the framework of courtesy literature, they became more and more tightly restricted to those tasks that were performed within and for the household alone. In contrast with earlier domestic economies, the eighteenth century conduct books ceased to provide advice for the care of livestock or the concoction of medicinal cures. Producing goods to be consumed by the household was apparently no longer their readers' concern. In this respect, even the eighteenth century instructional literature modeled upon the earlier domestic economies was influenced by courtesy literature. The more practically oriented books still emphasized frugality, for example. But in their instructions for the preparation of food, frugality became a matter of good taste and a way of displaying domestic virtue, not of stretching the resources to meet the needs of the household. In proposing a menu "proper for a frugal as well as a sumptuous table," for example, *The Compleat Housewife or, Accomplished Gentlewoman's Companion* (1734) converted the notion of propriety from an economic norm to a new national standard. A meal commensurate with one's means, in other words, became a meal "suitable to English constitutions and English Palates, wholesome, toothsome, all practical and easy to be performed."[15]

If the female's abstract virtues endowed the duties of the housewife with value, the spiritual virtues honored in earlier courtesy literature became limited in how they might help her perform her practical duties. Once female virtue became so linked to work, conduct books banished from the ideal woman the features that had once seemed desirable because they enhanced the aristocratic woman. In a conduct book of the mid-nineteenth century, T. S. Arthur goes so far as to assault the ideal of cloistered virtue that for centuries had been considered desirable in unmarried aristocratic women. In his view, "What is called the religion of the cloister is no religion at all, but mere selfishness—a retiring from *actual duty in the world,* into an imaginary state of sanctimoniousness" (italics mine).[16] Thomas Broadhurst's *Advice to Young Ladies on the Improvement of the Mind and Conduct of Life* (1810) shows an equally prevalent tendency toward anti-intellectualism directed at women who sought an elite education—once the privilege of well-born women—and the pleasures of intellectual life:

> She who is faithfully employed in discharging the various duties of a wife and daughter, a mother and a friend, is far more usefully occupied than one who, to the culpable neglect of the most important obligations, is daily absorbed by philosophic and literary speculations, or soaring aloft amidst the enchanted regions of fiction and romance.[17]

Such attacks on both religious and intellectual women condemn female virtues associated with the dominant social ideal of earlier culture. In this manner, the conduct books sought to define the practice of secular morality as the woman's natural duty. If certain agrarian and artisan forms of labor were considered unfeminine by virtue of their inclusion in the conduct book, then certain manifestations of aristocratic taste and learning were declared corrupt and opposed to the mental accomplishments of the good wife and mother. In the process, her duties were pared down to those that seem remarkably frivolous but that were—and to some extent still are—considered nonetheless essential to domestic happiness.

I would like to suggest that the peculiar features and extraordinary durability of the domestic ideal had everything to do with its capability to suppress the very conflicts so evident in the bewildering field of dialects comprising this body of writing until the second half of the eighteenth century. The authors of conduct books were acutely sensitive to the subtlest differences in status, and each represented his or her readers' interests in terms of a differential system that opposed country and town, rich and poor, labor and leisure, and no doubt more refined or local socioeconomic interests. Within such a semantic field, the representation of any male role automatically defined a partisan position. In deciding what role a male should ideally fulfill, then, the authors of both fiction and conduct books had to stand on one side or another in a number of these thematic oppositions. And to do so would limit a readership accordingly. The female, in contrast, provided a topic that could bind together precisely those groups who were necessarily divided by other kinds of writing. Virtually no other topic appeared to be so free of bias toward an occupation, political faction, or religious affiliation. In bringing into being a concept of the household on which socially hostile groups felt they could all agree, the domestic ideal helped create the fiction of horizontal affiliations that only a century later could be said to have materialized as an economic reality. As part of an effort to explain how domestic fiction happened to survive and acquire prestige while other forms of writing rose and fell in popularity, the following description demonstrates how formulation of the domestic woman overcame the conflicts and contradictions inherent in most other Enlightenment efforts at rewriting the conditions of history.

A Country House That is Not a Country House

It is relatively easy to distinguish those conduct books meant for rural readers from those addressing people in town. Despite these and all the other signs of competing economic interests that presupposed a politically diverse readership, the eighteenth century books for women nevertheless agreed that the country house should be the site of the ideal household. By this they meant the country house should cease to provide a model of aristocratic culture and should offer instead a model that would be realized in any and all respectable households. This way of representing life in the country house made it possible for competing interest groups to ignore their economic origins and coalesce around a single domestic ideal. The opposition between city and country, which marked a major division between economic and political interests at the time, only enhanced the advantages of the domestic ideal. Urban tradesmen and merchants, for example, ordinarily would have thought they had little in common with independent farmers and grain dealers, and traditional representations of the country house only reinforced this political opposition. The country house of seventeenth century England had encouraged popular belief that those at the very top of the social hierarchy were the ultimate end of production. In such a hierarchical system of relationships, people who were entitled to a privileged position were expected to display their wealth in certain highly prescribed ways.[18] In its most idealized form, the old society appeared to be governed by a patron who distributed wealth and power down a series of hierarchically organized relationships until virtually every client benefited from this generosity. Such, for example, is the form that social authority assumes in the country-house poems of the seventeenth century.[19]

So important were forms of sumptuary display to maintaining the social order during the sixteenth and seventeenth centuries that a series of royal proclamations detailed the permissible forms of aristocratic display. Using wealth to display the signs of high social status was forbidden to those whose birth and title had not qualified them to do so. In her proclamation of 6 July 1597, Queen Elizabeth voiced concern about the "confusion in all places being great where the meanest are as richly appareled as their betters."[20] By "meanest" she was obviously referring to non-aristocrats whose money could disguise a lack of noble origins. To remedy this situation, she reiterated a national dress code which specified, among other things, that "none shall wear in his apparel cloth of gold or silver tissued, silk of color purple under the degree of an earl, except Knights of the Garter in their purple mantles" (p. 176). Besides listing clothing and materials that must be used according to rank, degree, and proximity to the Queen, the proclamation also limited the total amount one could spend each year on clothing. These restrictions extended to women whose body, like that of the male, was an ornamental body representing the family's place in an intricately precise set of kinship relations determined by the metaphysics of blood. The order extended from viscountesses to barons' daughters and wives of barons' eldest sons, from gentlemen of the privy chamber to those who attended duchesses, countesses, and so forth. The list concluded with an order that "no person under the degrees specified shall wear any guard or welt of silk upon any petticoat, cloak or safeguard" (p. 179).

These attempts to regulate aristocratic display were intended to prevent wealth from obscuring kinship rules that maintained the social hierarchy. This political imperative might well have motivated James I to issue proclamations ordering the nobility out of the city and into the countryside where they were supposed to win popular support by displays of hospitality. Leah S. Marcus has argued that James meant these measures to counter political resistance that was gathering in the city but that also appeared to extend into the countryside in 1616 when attempts by landlords to fence in common land brought about rioting.[21] In a speech to the Star Chamber in that same year, James, like Elizabeth before him, represents the city as a place attracting so many people that "all the countrey is gotten into *London;* so as with time, England will onely be *London,* and the whole countrey be left waste."[22] He claimed that wives and daughters, attracted by foreign fashions, forced their husbands and fathers to abandon the country for London where a woman's virtue would inevitably be tarnished. To correct all these abuses, he issued an injunction to "keepe the old fashion of *England:* For it was wont to be the honour and reputation of the English Nobilitie and Gentry, to liue in the countrey, and keepe hospitalitie" (pp. 343–44). James, in other words, saw the good country life as a means of maintaining popular support for the crown. And with this in mind, he saw to it that the aristocratic practices centered in the country house would represent all that was truly British.

Eighteenth century conduct books for women therefore contended with two particularly powerful traditions, one having to do with the rules for displaying the aristocratic body and the other having to do with the practice of hospitality in the countryside. These symbolic practices authorized aristocratic power—power based on birth and title alone—whose site was the country manor house. It is reasonable to assume that, in opposing these traditions, female conduct books changed the ideal of what English life ought to be when they replaced the lavish displays of aristocratic life with the frugal and private practices of the modern gentleman. This was no doubt the primary political aim of such writing and the main reason why it suddenly attracted so many authors and readers. But the new representation of English country life itself depended on another rhetorical strategy that denigrated the ornamental body of the aristocrat to exalt the retiring and yet ever vigilant domestic woman. In challenging the metaphysics of blood, such a representation would eventually hollow out the material body of the woman in order to fill it with the materials of a gender-based self, or female psychology. Subsequent chapters will trace this process, but my purpose in this chapter is to show how the conduct books' definition of the desirable woman first enabled a substantial number of competing interest groups to identify their economic interests with the same domestic ideal.

This strategy for deflecting the political opposition between country and city can be isolated in any number of handbooks. *The Compleat*

Housewife or, Accomplished Gentlewoman's Companion (1734) promises
to give its reader a set of "Directions generally for dressing in the best,
most natural, and wholesome Manner, such Provisions as are the Products
of our Country, and in such a Manner as is most agreeable to English
Palates" (p. 2). How the ideal of a table that was fitting and proper for
any size purse in the realm actually served agrarian interests becomes
apparent when we consider what kind of food the handbook forbids. In
claiming it is "to our Disgrace" that Englishmen have "so fondly admired
the French Tongue, French *modes,* and French Messes" (p. 2), the author
speaks on behalf of agricultural interests. But it is important that he attack
the urban taste for things imported by assaulting the "unwholesome" diet
which supposedly caters to aristocratic taste. Restricted to domestic matters, his political commentary avoids raising the opposition between agricultural interests and those of an increasing number who were importing
goods for urban markets. A few years later, in 1740, *The Young Ladies
Companion or, Beauty's Looking-Glass* similarly lashes out against im-
moderate household expenditures. Using terms that would have been especially meaningful to ambitious townspeople, this author elaborates the
economic disaster that ensues from aping aristocratic standards:

> when usual Presents are made, and an expensive Marriage is solemniz'd,
> gaudy cloaths and Equipage are bought, and perhaps, a London house fur-
> nished, a considerable Part of this Portion will be disburs'd and the forlorn
> Hero of this shewy, noisy farce, will discover too late how much more
> eligible it had been to have marry'd a LADY well born, of a discreet, mod-
> est, and frugal Education, and an agreeable Person with less Money, than
> a haughty Dame with all her Quality Airs about her. (p. 113)

Despite regional differences, the author who writes for readers in town
and the one who addresses a rural readership agree with each other on the
components of the ideal domestic life. Both situate the model household
in opposition to the excesses of aristocratic behavior, and both contest
the prevailing system of status distinctions in order to insist on a discreet
and frugal household with a woman educated in the practices of inconspicuous consumption. They maintain that such behavior is a more accurate indication of good breeding than the traditional distinctions of title
or wealth. *The Young Ladies Companion or, Beauty's Looking-Glass* also
lays out the economic basis for desiring the woman of "discreet, modest,
and frugal Education" over and against one of great fortune who is likely
to be a "haughty Dame with all her Quality Airs about her." The woman
who brings more wealth to the marriage turns out to be a bad investment
in this account. She is described as "the dearest purchase now in England,

. . . not excepting the *South-Sea Stock*" (p. 115), the notorious financial corporation whose stock rose in several months time from £100 to £1000 in 1720 and then plummeted several months after that. By way of contrast to the woman who brings a large dowry but requires an ostentatious style of living, this gentleman considers the frugal wife a solid investment. "For every thousand Pound" the wealthier woman brings, he calculates, her needs will multiply accordingly: "she spends more than the interest of it; for besides her private expence, the gay furniture, the rich Beds, China-Ware, Tea-Table, visiting rooms, rich coach, etc. must be chiefly placed to her Account" (p. 115). To this way of thinking, the woman who feels so obliged to display signs of status—in the manner of aristocratic women—will soon prove too expensive to keep.

It is important to note that the qualities of the desirable woman—her discretion, modesty, and frugality—described the objectives of an educational program in terms that spelled out a coherent set of economic policies for the management of the household. The authors of these educational books for women turned the virtues of the new woman into a language resonating with political meaning. These virtues were simultaneously the categories of a pedagogical theory, the form of subjectivity it engendered, the taste that resulted, and the economy that such taste ensured. In arguing for a new set of qualities to desire in a woman, these books therefore made her capable of authorizing a whole new set of economic practices that directly countered what were supposed to be seen as the excesses of a decadent aristocracy. Under the dominion of such a woman, the country house could no longer authorize a political system that made sumptuary display the ultimate aim of production. Instead, it proposed a world where production was an end in itself rather than a means to such an end.

The frugal domestic economy that these conduct books idealize in their educational program for women was one fueled by interest from investments rather than by labor. It differed in this significant respect from the household represented in the sixteenth and seventeenth century Puritan handbooks, as well as from the country ideal preferred by James I. This modern household did not identify the source of one's income with a certain craft, trade, region, or family; its economy depended on money earned on investments. Such money made the household into a self-enclosed world whose means of support were elsewhere, invisible, removed from the scene. The few statements quoted above, like those in the discussion to follow, strongly suggest that the good country life so depicted no longer revealed one's origins or political allegiances. The negation of traditional differences between those at the very top and those at the bottom of the social scale cleared the cultural ground for a class sexuality that valued people according to intrinsic personal qualities. A group of people consquently came to understand themselves as part of an educated elite who, in Harry Payne's words, prided themselves on "gentility, science, innovation, . . . and economic realism."[23] Such an ideal representation of the ruling class had the advantage—in theory at least—of making available to many in the middle ranks the good country life that had formerly seemed available only to those of title.

Not only did the pleasures of country life actually crown the success of several generations of English businessmen during the course of the nineteenth century, but apparently the lesser gentry and prosperous farmers also took pains to educate their daughters according to the principles of this conduct-book ideal. By 1825, then, one finds a conduct book modeling the exemplary household on that "of a respectable Country Gentleman, with a young family whose Net Income is from £16,000 to £18,000 a year, and whose expences do not exceed £7000."[24] The author nevertheless described this household in the conventional manner to contrast it sharply with the corrupt and extravagant habits attributed to the old aristocracy. At the same time, one can notice that such criticism of the aristocracy had lost most of its political edge. Sexual differences appear to have become much more important than economic differences in defining an individual's place in the world, and conduct books from the early decades of the nineteenth century had already come to see the country house, not as the center of aristocratic (male) power, but as the perfect realization of the domestic woman's (non-aristocratic) character. During the high Victorian age, this model of middle-class domesticity began to determine the way the aristocracy represented themselves as well. Mark Girouard cites a number of instances that testify to this curious loop in British cultural history:

> In the 1870s Lord and Lady Folkstone chose to be painted singing "Home, Sweet Home" with their eldest son. A portrait of Lord Armstrong, the millionaire arms dealer, shows him reading the newspaper in his dining room inglenook at Cragside, over the fireplace of which is inscribed "East or West, Home is Best." An essential part of the new image cultivated by both new and old families was their domesticity; they were anxious to show that their houses, however grand, were also homes and sheltered a happy family life.[25]

In comparing the domestic ideal as represented in conduct books to its appearance on the English countryside, one discovers a gap of more than a century between these written accounts and their social realization.

I call attention to this discontinuity in order to claim importance for representation itself. I want to suggest that by developing a language strictly for relations within the home, conduct books for women inadvertently provided the terms for rethinking relationships in the political world, for this language enabled authors to articulate both worlds while they appeared to represent only one. To this capability we can probably attribute the persistent sense that the conduct book spoke to male readers even while it addressed itself specifically to women. In so doing, the new domestic ideal succeeded where Defoe's island kingdom had failed. It established a private economy apart from the forms of rivalry and dependency that organized the world of men. The new domestic economy derived power from interest-bearing investments, a form of income that effectively destroyed the old agrarian ideal by effacing the whole system of status signs which lent that ideal its value. At the same time, the new country house harked back to an earlier agrarian world where the household was a largely self-contained social unit. In appearing to be logically prior to ideology in this respect, the new language of the household acquired power akin to that of natural law.

Labor That is Not Labor

Conduct books appear to be as sensitive to the difference between labor and leisure as they are to the tension between town and country or to the line separating the rich from the poor. This distinction was always implicit in the number of idle hours it was assumed a woman had to fill. In figuring out a way to convert this time into an ideal program of education, however, the books took labor and leisure off their separate conceptual planes and placed them in a moral continuum. Here a woman was ranked according to the specifically female virtues she possessed rather than to the value of her family name and social connections. But in order to create such a female system of values in the first place, the conduct books represented the domestic woman in opposition to certain practices attributed to women at both extremes of the social scale. A woman was deficient in female qualities if she, like the aristocratic woman, spent her time in idle amusements. As the conduct books represent them, such activities always aimed at putting the body on display, a carry-over from the Renaissance display of aristocratic power. For a woman to display herself in such a manner was the same as saying that she was supposed to be valued for her body and its adornments, not for the virtues she might possess as a woman and wife. By the same token, the conduct books found the laboring woman unfit for domestic duties because she, too, located value in the material body. Conduct books attacked these two traditional notions of the female body in order to suggest that the female had depths far more valuable than her surface. By implying that the essence of the woman lay inside or underneath her surface, the invention of depths in the self entailed making the material body of the woman appear superficial. The invention of depth also provided the rationale for an educational program designed specifically for women, for these programs strove to subordinate the body to a set of mental processes that guaranteed domesticity.

It is important to observe how the conduct books differentiated the new woman from the woman who served as the means of displaying aristocratic power. As if of one mind, they agreed that any woman's value necessarily depreciated as she took up the practice of self-display. "It is true," remarks one book, "that the mere splendour of wealth and title will at all times attract a circle of admirers, as frivolous and uninformed as many of their possessors." Those who aspire to the fashionable world become "low minded satellites of fashion and greatness." They can never equal those whom they endeavor to mirror, the author continues, but "merely flatter themselves that they deserve a brilliancy and consequence from the more dignified body around which they move."[26] Although it appears to speak from an utterly conservative position, one quite in keeping with the ideology that prompted the royal proclamations of Elizabeth and James, this statement is shaped by a revealing contradiction that allows it to serve a set of interests absolutely opposed to those represented by the aristocratic body of Renaissance culture.

According to the logic of this statement, the genuine person of leisure is worth "more" than women who "merely" flatter themselves by virtue of their proximity to aristocratic power, but this is not the distinction that matters most in the author's system of values. While affording a precise way of differentiating members of the fashionable world, "splendour" and "brilliancy" nevertheless fail to provide a reliable way of assessing women. For the author of this conduct book, women who devote themselves to practical matters are less likely to be "frivolous and uninformed" than women who posses "wealth and title." But even though the practical kind "are infinitely to be preferred to that large class of superficial females whose sole ambition it is to be seen and noticed in the circle of gaiety," any outward and visible signs of value, even those of a practical nature, imply some emotional lack in the woman that significantly lowers her value on the marriage market. There is no doubt in the author's mind that "If a woman were only expert in the use of her needle, and properly skilled in domestic economy," she still would not be prepared to meet her domestic obligations.[27] To be completely prepared, she must also have the qualities of mind that ensure her vigilance over the household.

Before abandoning this example, we should take note of the fact that its attack on aristocratic conduct is more than an argument for a certain kind of woman or even for a certain kind of household; it is also an argument against the traditional notion of amusement. What happens to amusement reveals the most characteristic—and indeed powerful—rhetorical strategy of the conduct books. First they negate those practices that had been acceptable or even desirable cultural practices, and then they endow those practices with positive value by placing them within the framework of female subjectivity. It is of equal importance that these books overthrow the tradition going back to the proclamations of Elizabeth and James and, by a second inversion, situate subjectivity prior to the display of the body as the cause of unseemly female behavior. Thus we find the proclivity for self-display among certain woman represented as subjectivity gone awry: "Destitute of all *amusements with herself,* and incapable of perceiving her chief happiness to center at home, in the bosom of her family, a lady of this description daily sallies forth in quest of adventures" (italics mine).[28] The conduct books always use women who pursue amusement as examples to demonstrate why women lacking the conduct-book virtues do not make desirable wives. Such women are "regularly seen in the ballroom or at the card-table, at the opera or in the theatre, among the numberless devotees of dissipation and fashion."[29] That, in a word, is their crime: these women either want to be on display or simply allow themselves to be "seen." It is not that the conduct books disapprove of dancing, enjoying music, playing cards, or even attending theatrical performances when they are enjoyed in the sanctuary of one's parlor. This is a difference that both Austen and Burney scrupulously observe along with conduct-book authors. It is a woman's participation in public spectacle that injures her, for as an object of display, she always loses value as a subject. More than that, these books lump the woman of fashion together with "numberless" others who—in the conduct book's terms—similarly lack the quality of subjectivity that makes a woman desirable; she cannot be "seen" and still be vigilant. As it constitutes the female subject, then, such writing strips the body of the signs of identity that are essential to displaying female value according to aristocratic rules of kinship.

The production of female subjectivity entails the dismantling of the aristocratic body. In fact, the two must be understood as a single rhetorical move. So powerful was the effect of the critique of aristocratic behavior that by the end of the eighteenth century conduct books addressing words of advice to women of noble descent exhibit curious forms of stress and embarrassment. Written in 1806, Elizabeth Hamilton's *Letters: Addressed to the Daughter of a Nobleman on the Formation of Religious and Moral Principle* cannot assume that women of wealth and position also have virtue. She must take pains to argue such virtue back into existence. But even in this she proceeds by defensive strategies as she protests that wealth, beauty, and an elite education do not necessarily cancel out a woman's domestic virtues. On the basis of her familiarity with people of nobility, Mrs. Hamilton insists "that the consciousness of high descent, and elevated rank, and splendid fortune, does not necessarily give birth to pride; no, not even where, in addition to these advantages, nature has bestowed the most transcendent talents, and the charm of every personal attraction!"[30] In contrast to the ordinary run of conduct books, furthermore, this one must abandon the logic that links outward signs of humility with domestic value. Instead, the author resorts to metaphor. Poetry is apparently the only way she can imagine to counter a logic that pits the brilliant features of aristocratic beauty against the inconspicuous features associated with domesticity (and a women who wrote poetry could always be accused of indulging in a form of aristocratic display). So thoroughgoing was the condemnation of aristocratic display that Mrs. Hamilton feels compelled to devise figures linking surface to depth so that the brilliance of the surface will not imply an underlying emptiness. "Such persons are to society," she explains, "not only the brightest ornament, but the most estimable blessing. Their influence, like that of the sun, extends not merely to the surface; it penetrates into the dark and hidden places of the earth" (p. 108). By suggesting that a woman could have depth as well as surface, Mrs. Hamilton argues that a woman could excel in both public and private spheres, that she could be the object of the gaze and still possess the subjective qualities required of a good wife and mother. For all her efforts, however, Mrs. Hamilton's metaphors only direct the reader's attention to what could no longer be stated as truth.

It is a curious thing that even though conduct books represented aristocratic behavior as the very antithesis of the domestic woman, they never once exalted labor. They generally found women who worked for their living to be morally bankrupt too. The governess is an obvious case in point. Because her work was restricted to domestic duties, she belonged to the cast of respectable women, and hers was one of the few professions open to women of the gentry who had to support themselves. At the same time, the governess was commonly represented as a threat to the well-being of the household.[31] Whether she was in fact a person of breeding fallen from economic grace or someone of lower rank who hoped to elevate herself through a genteel education, she was marketing her class and education for money. The governess is particularly useful for purposes of my argument because she combines certain features of the aristocracy with those of the working woman. Yet that was clearly not the reason why authors and readers used her for drawing cultural lines. It was by fulfilling the duties of the domestic woman for money that she blurred a distinction on which the very notion of gender appeared to depend. She seemed to call into question an absolutely rigid distinction between domestic duty and labor that was performed for money, a distinction so deeply engraved upon the public mind that the figure of the prostitute could be freely invoked to describe any woman who dared to labor for money. One sweeping condemnation of female servants claimed that "Half the wretched beings of their sex, who live on the deplorable wages of iniquity, for the short time they live at all, are there being discharged out of service to pride."[32] The motivations of any woman who worked out of a desire for money were automatically in doubt, but it must have been particularly disturbing to think of such a woman supervising the young. The governess' transgression of the line distinguishing labor from domestic duty obviously lies behind such common assaults on her character as this: "Nor can we greatly wonder at the false position which governesses hold, when we consider how often they are induced by merely selfish and sordid motives to seek the employment which they ought to engage in only from a conviction of their fitness, mental and moral, for so important a post."[33]

As conduct books differentiated the woman's ideal role from both labor and amusement, they created a new category of labor. One finds that while these books elaborate all of the tasks that can be called domestic duty, they still represent the woman of the house as apparently having nothing to do. Ideally servants would perform most, if not all, of the work specified for maintaining the household. Yet the difference between the excesses that conduct books attributed to country-house life in an aristocratic culture and the domestic economy they envisioned for their readers has everything to do with the presence of the right kind of woman. To solve the enigma of what essential function this woman performed, I must refer back to the distinction between the woman as subject and the woman as the object of display. It is helpful to recall how the domestic woman comes into being as the notion of amusement is redefined within the framework of her subjectivity. In this way, hers appears to be precisely the power to turn behavior into psychological events. More than that, hers is the power to control and evaluate such events. To exercise this power, according to conduct-book logic, requires a passive and retiring woman. In 1798, the notably liberal thinker Erasmus Darwin held forth this kind of woman as the objective of his educational program:

> The female character should possess the mild and retiring virtues rather than the bold and dazzling ones; great eminence in almost anything is sometimes injurious to a young lady; whose temper and disposition should appear to be pliant rather than robust; to be ready to take impressions rather than to be decidedly marked; as great apparent strength of character, however excellent, is liable to alarm both her own and the other sex; and to create admiration rather than affection.[34]

Contrasting attributes shape each sentence, setting the mild-mannered woman of the conduct books against her flashier counterpart, the woman of high social station. Both characterizations are positive, yet one is definitely to be preferred over the other, and in purely semantic terms the domestic woman seems to be the less positive of the two. In other words, this author gives the traditional concept of female beauty its due in order to declare it obsolete. What he calls for is not a woman who attracts the gaze as she did in an earlier culture, but one who fulfills her role by disappearing into the woodwork to watch over the household. And thus Darwin concludes the introduction to his program for female education with this statement:

> Hence if to softness of manners, complacency of countenance, gentle unhurried motion, with a voice clear and yet tender, the charms which enchant all hearts can be superadded internal strength and activity of mind, capable to transact the business or combat the evils of life, with a due sense of moral and religious obligation, all is attained which education can supply; the female character becomes compleat, excites our love and commands our admiration. (p. 4)

In quoting this passage, I simply want to call attention to the shift in diction that locates power in the mental features of the domestic woman, power that was stripped away from the body in the preceding passage. So "compleat," this new woman commands "admiration" as well as "love" whereas before she deserved only "affection." In this comparison between two desirable women, we are witnessing the fact of cultural change from an earlier form of power based on sumptuary display to a modern form that works through the production of subjectivity.

The domestic woman's capacity to supervise was clearly more important than any other factor in determining the victory of this ardently undazzling creature over all her cultural competitors. For this reason, it appears, the peculiar combination of invisibility and vigilance personified in the domestic woman came to represent the principle of domestic economy itself. From *Thoughts in the Form of Maxims Addressed to Young Ladies on their First Establishment in the World* comes the advice, "Do not attempt to destroy his [the male's] innocent pleasures by pretexts of oeconomy; retrench rather your own expences to promote them."[35] The conduct books demonstrate how a woman who sought to enhance her value through forms of self-display would significantly diminish her family's possibilities for happiness, but more than her restraint from such behavior was required in order for the ideal domestic situation to be realized. The simple absence of domestic virtue would eliminate that possibility too. As one author writes:

> Vain are his [her husband's] labours to accumulate, if she cannot, or will not, expend with discretion. Vain too are his expectations of happiness if economy, order, and regularity, are not to be found at home; and the woman who has no feeling and principle sufficient to regulate her conduct in these concerns, will rarely acquit herself respectable in the more elevated posts of female duty.[36]

If "his" aim is "to accumulate," then "hers" is "to regulate," and on "her conduct in these concerns" depends the success of all "his labours." By implication, female "feeling and principle" increase male earning power by freeing up capital even as it is taken in and consumed by the household. The domestic woman executes her role in the household by regulating her own desire. On her "feeling and principle" depends the economic behavior that alone ensures prosperity. So conceived, self-regulation became a form of labor that was superior to labor. Self-regulation alone gave a woman authority over the field of domestic objects and personnel where her supervision constituted a form of value in its own right and was therefore capable of enhancing the value of other people and things.

Economy That is Not Money

Because it suppressed economic differences, particularly concealing the ever-widening gulf between rich and poor, this new form of value made sense to people with widely varying incomes in the old society. Despite its association with wealth and leisure, the country house also carried with it some of the cultural residue of a self-sufficient economy. True to their roots in the domestic economies of an earlier period, conduct books represented such an economy in opposition to one based on money. The conduct books invariably reformulated this opposition as their way of mounting an attack on what they saw as the excesses of a corrupt aristocracy. The recipes comprising the bulk of *The Compleat Housewife or, Accomplished Gentlewoman's Companion* reveal some rather costly ingredients—partridge and venison, for example—that average Englishmen obviously could not afford to enjoy without becoming either gentlemen or poachers. Insisting nonetheless on their suitability "for a frugal as well as for a sumptuous table," the author does not mean to imply that his is a subsistence diet. His intention is that of a reformer: to combat the evils of the aristocratic standard of taste with an alternative standard that is, by implication, better for all but those of the lower ranks of society. "There are indeed already in the World various books that treat on the Subject and which bear great Names, as Cooks to Kings, Princes, and Noblemen," his preface declares, but "many of them to us are impracticable, others whimsical, others impalatable, unless to depraved Palates" (p. 2). By representing the more privileged table as an object of disgust, such handbooks invest the frugal table with superior value.

Material differences appear to have little to do with determining the quality of life one can enjoy. As the author of *The Compleat Housewife* situates the ideal table in opposition to meals that display wealth and title, he calls attention to qualities of mind he observes in the objects under his consideration, qualities that include practicality, wholesomeness, steadiness, and concern for health. The frugal table nourishes the social body, just as aristocratic taste corrupts it. Unlike that which enforces hierarchical distinctions, the more moderate standard of living extends to a wide spectrum of individuals within the economy. But if the conduct-book rhetoric did not exclude those at the bottom of the economic ladder from the good life, it never suggested the poor could live life as well as those who had plenty of money. Although relatively few felt compelled to say it in so many words, it was always assumed, as one of the more outspoken authors explains, that "where the blessings of independence and fortune are liberally bestowed, sufficient time may easily be found for all the purposes of mental improvement, without neglecting any of the more important and sacred offices of active virtue."[37] Such virtue evidently belonged to the woman who had neither suffered economic scarcity nor indulged in extravagance. As another conduct book explains, one's wife is much more likely to be frugal "if she has always been used to a good style of living in her father's house."[38] This subordination of money to a higher standard of value distinguished the ideal household from family life both at the top and at the bottom of the social ladder where—in each case—people were known for their profligate spending.

All these examples either suggest or openly state that without the domestic woman the entire domestic framework would collapse. From the beginning, her supervisory presence was a necessary component of its cultural logic. The consistency with which such terms as "modesty," "frugality," "regularity," and "discretion" recur cannot be ignored. The more practical conduct books address quite different local readerships concerning the constitution of the household, the nature of its objects, the number and kinds of its servants, the manner of its table, the style of its occupants' dress, and the conduct of their leisure activities, often down to the smallest detail in one category or another. But by the time the eighteenth century was well underway, the general categories of a domestic domain had been established and linked to qualities in the female. She brought these qualities to the sexual contract. At the same time, they were qualities that became demonstrably hers as she ran the household according to the taste that she acquired through a female education. This is to say the female character and that of the home became one and the same as she translated her husband's income into the objects and personnel comprising his household. Such an exchange at once enacted an economic contract and concealed the particular nature of the transaction because it fulfilled the sexual contract.

It must have been a remarkable moment when this way of representing kinship relations took hold. For the first time in history a view was put forth—admittedly a minority view—that appealed to people from radically different backgrounds, with substantially different incomes, and with positions in different chains of social relations. Any number of people in the middle ranks could thus believe that the same ideal of domestic life was available to them. To imagine this was to imagine an order of political relations that was substantially different from the one in force at that moment of history. To explain why the new mode of political thinking depended on the production of a certain kind of woman, I have chosen *The Compleat Servant,* a handbook from 1825, to demonstrate just how precisely codified—and hence reproducible—the sexual contract had become by the time the new middle classes were beginning to assume cultural ascendancy.

Identifying himself as "a servant who had passed time in the homes of the great," the anonymous author of *The Compleat Servant* shows how the principles of domestic economy might be translated into a precise calculus for the good life that could be extended to people of various incomes. Such is the claim of his preface: "As no relations in society are so numerous and universal as those of Masters and Servants—as those of Household Duties and performers of them—so it is proportionately important that they should be well defined and understood."[39] His idea

of how the domestic economy relates to economy per se is so precise he
can graphically represent the conversion of the one into the other:[40]

Net Annual Inc.	Household expense	Servants and equipage	Cloths and extras	Rent and repairs	Reserve
£1000	333	250	250	125	42
£2000	666	500	500	250	84
£3000	1000	750	750	375	375
...	...	...	...	...	...
£10,000	3333	2500	2500	1250	420

Most striking is the way in which this graphic representation translates
the economic contract into a sexual one. The first column, or amount of
income, represents what the male brings to the exchange. Although this
way of designating male value distinguishes one individual from another
according to the amount of money each brings to the household, it is
important to note that the figure of sexual exchange has already translated
the vertical organization of the old society into terms that nearly destroy
its heterogeneity. As a result, the figure behaves much like any other
representation of the social contract; it creates the very differences it proposes to unify. The chart specifies income as an amount rather than as a
form of labor, trade, or service in relation to those whom one serves and
who in turn serve him. Value is cut free from its source in human labor,
and merely quantitative differences replace the qualitative distinctions of
status and rank that held together the old society. In this purely relational
system, income alone has come to represent the male party of the sexual
exchange.

The transformation of male identity is only one half of an exchange
between gender-specific systems of value. The chart cited above records
two separate semiotic moves that together implicitly transform the whole
organization of British society. The first strips the male of his traditional
political identity, which was based on privileges of birth and proximity
to the crown. The second converts income (the left-hand column) into
the categories of the household. If we have to read vertically to gather
the information concerning the male, then the chart requires us to read
horizontally for the female. Under her supervision, income is taken into
the household where it becomes a field of information organized according to the categories of domestic economy. The female operates in this
sexual exchange to transform a given quantity of income into a desirable
quality of life. Her powers of supervision ensure the income will be distributed according to certain proportions designed to meet certain domestic criteria, no matter what the amount of the husband's income may
be. This double translation of one's social value—from a concept of quality based on birth to a quantity of income, which then materializes as a

certain quality of domestic life—creates the economic basis for affiliation among competing interest groups. It creates an ideal exchange in which the female alone can perform the necessary economic transformation. Such a representation implies that people with incomes ranging from £1000 to £10,000 per year could share a world of similar proportions and therefore aspire to the same quality of life. There is also the implication that this world is available to those higher (as indeed the author's exemplary gentleman was) as well as lower on the social ladder, provided they choose to observe the categories comprising the economy of the ideal country life.

But *The Compleat Servant* does not leave it at that. It goes on to elaborate each category of objects, services, and personnel down to the microlevel of the individual item and its value in guineas. So even as this model of good country living has near universal applicability, it also makes quite specific recommendations. To demonstrate how representation can be at once so highly generalized and yet specialized for the individual case, I include the following list, which explains how money should be distributed to personnel:[41]

	Guineas
Housekeeper	24
Female Teacher	30
Lady's Maid	20
Head Nurse	20
Second Ditto	10
Nursery Maid	7
Upper House-Maid	15
Under House-Maid	14
Kitchen Maid	14
Upper Laundry Maid	14
Under Ditto	10
Dairy Maid	8
Second Ditto	7
Still Room Maid	9
Scullion	9
A French Man Cook	80
Butler	50
Coachman	28
Footman	24
Under Ditto	20
Grooms	
Nursery Room Boy	
2 Gameskeepers	
2 Gardeners	

Only a very few of the author's possible readers could hope to meet all the expenses on the list. But in order to create the same household on considerably less, he explains, one need only begin at the top of the list, omit the dittos, and consume in proportion to the amount of one's income. Thus we see why he has included basic housekeepers and childcare personnel at the top of the list, while relegating to the bottom, as least necessary, those servants whom only people of privilege can employ. The vertical system of relationships based on the quantity of the man's income is therefore preserved, but this quantitative standard is also inverted as it is enclosed within a female field of information where qualitative values ideally dominate. The author insists that, even so, anyone can observe the correct proportions and, within proportioning categories, the correct exercise of priorities. In his view, only the exercise of these personal qualities—elsewhere known as "discretion," "modesty," "frugality," and "regularity"—can ensure domestic happiness.

This handbook offers an unusually systematic representation—a grammar, really—of what was by that time in history a common language of objects and domestic personnel. It is fair to say that from the mid-eighteenth century on, every female conduct book presupposed such a grammar just by focusing on one or more of its categories. The principle of translation demonstrated in the above-cited text was at work in most conduct books from the beginning of the eighteenth century. By the early nineteenth century when *The Compleat Servant* appeared, then, this principle had transformed the material surface of social life to the point where such a descriptive grammar could be written. It was not that English homes underwent wholesale redecoration. I think it more likely that the texture of the household changed as people started reading it differently, that is, as people began to regard the household in the terms of a written representation. At least it is quite plausible that domestic life first became an autonomous text when its objects and personnel, which appeared to have little relation to region and the local labor conditions external to them, achieved identity according to an internal force—a psychological principle—that held them all together. By means of this principle of reading, too, the household ceased to display the value of the man's income and instead took on the innermost human qualities of the woman who regulated the domestic economy.

As a world of objects thus invested with meaning, the household could not be invoked and used arbitrarily any more by authors of fiction than by those who wrote conduct books. Domestic fiction proceeded from the assumption that a similar interpretive mechanism could be put in motion merely by representing these objects in language. Such language would be governed by the very same rule that converted material differences into psychological ones, or male values into female norms. Before Richardson wrote *Pamela,* the feminized household was already a familiar field of information, but it had yet to be written as fiction. And by the time Austen's novels appeared, the sophisticated grammar organizing that field evidently had so passed into common knowledge that it could simply be taken for granted. If Austen's writing proceeds with a kind of unprecedented economy and precision, it is at least in part owing to this intertextuality. In her world, one could not only extrapolate a man's net worth from just a few household objects, but could also place his wife on a psychological scale. In *Emma,* for example, Frank Churchill's capricious purchase of a piano for Jane Fairfax represents an intrusion of male values into the exclusively female household of her Aunt Miss Bates. The mere appearance of an object that violates the proportions and priorities of such a household is enough to generate scandalous narratives implying that Jane has given in to seduction. Or Augusta Elton's failure to appreciate Emma's modest style of wedding dress—"Very little white satin, very few lace veils; a most pitiful business!"[42]—is sufficient to brand her own taste as hopelessly bound to materialistic values that contradict the metaphysics of domesticity dominating Austen's ideal community.

Later on, Mrs. Gaskell extended this code of values into the households of the laboring poor. In *Mary Barton,* she describes this scene in order to demonstrate how a woman's devoted application of domestic economy might enhance the value of a man's meager wages:

> In the corner between the window and the fire-side was a cupboard, apparently full of plates and dishes, cups and saucers, and some more nondescript articles, for which one would have fancied their possessors could find no use—such as triangular pieces of glass to save carving knives and forks from dirtying tablecloths.[43]

The Brontës, on the other hand, would carry the same ideal forth into the Yorkshire countryside where the apportionment of space within a house and the objects that fill it always describe the coming into being of this object world and the clash between its values and those of the traditional country house. But Dickens would carry the art of this object language to its logical extreme by creating a totally fetishized world. One need not think only of the junk shops that reappear here and there throughout his fiction, nor even of Wemmick's castle in *Great Expectations,* which Lévi-Strauss took as his example par excellence of bricolage, or a second-hand object language.[44] More important even than these curious set pieces are

Dickensian representations of the household inhabited by new money. Here one watches objects enter into a demonic exchange with their owners whereby things acquire human qualities and the people who live in a relationship with such things become as objects regulated by the very things they have endowed with human value. As Dorothy Van Ghent has noted, this particular form of exchange between subject and object permeates the Dickensian world and generates its distinctive character, which is that of a world all of surface where individuals convey the absence of depth.[45] There is, for instance, the well-known passage from *Our Mutual Friend* where Dickens allows a piece of the Podsnap plate to pass for commentary on the people assembled around it:

> Hideous solidity was the characteristic of the Podsnap plate. Everything was made to look as heavy as it could, and to take up as much room as possible. Everything said boastfully, "Here you have as much of me in my ugliness as if I were only lead; but I am so many ounces of precious metal worth so much an ounce;—wouldn't you like to melt me down?" A corpulent straggling epergne, blotched all over as if it had broken out in an eruption rather than been ornamented, delivered this address from an unsightly silver platform in the centre of the table.[46]

One should note that this critique of Podsnappery aims not at those who fulfill the conduct-book code, but at those who use objects to display wealth and power. Dickens' affection for cultural inversion leaves unmolested the whole idea of the household as a purely relational system of objects that includes people among them. The appearance of this world of objects that is free of labor distinguishes the home from the world of work and binds individuals together by forms of affection rather than by any need for economic survival. To construct and preserve this world without labor requires unflagging concern and vigilance, however, and this is where the female ideally figures in. She and not the male, as Dickens proves better than anyone else, should endow things with her docile features of character.

The Power of Feminization

From the beginning of the eighteenth century, conduct books had always presupposed the existence of a gendered self, a self based on the existence of positive female features rather than on the lack or even the inversion of certain qualities of the male. In writing *The Character of a Good Woman, both in a Single and Married State* (1697), for example, the author feels he should defer to a feminine readership on religious matters despite the fact he is speaking as their religious instructor. "To you we are beholden," he says, speaking both as a male and as a member of the clergy, "for the Devotion and Numerousness of our Assemblies, for you are without flattery, generally more serious than Men, and you helpt to make them so."[47] By the end of the eighteenth century, however, such statements of deference not only represented the essential qualities of female nature, but they did so in a way that endowed this representation with the power of behavioral norms. As conduct books transformed the female into the bearer of moral norms and socializer of men, they also changed the qualities once attributed to her nature and turned them into techniques for regulating desire. These techniques aimed at nothing so clearly as producing gender-differentiated forms of economic behavior. Conduct books of the mid-nineteenth century thus completed a circular process that would also change the economic practices considered most natural and desirable in a male.

Written in the United States in 1853, T.S. Arthur's *Advice to Young Ladies on their Duties and Conduct in Life* extends the principle of female virtue into the rationale for a form of economic behavior that became known as the doctrine of enlightened self-interest. This doctrine represented the principle of female education in a way that made it applicable to men as well as to women, as the author's diction implies:

> We are all lovers of ourselves more than lovers of God, and lovers of the world more than lovers of our neighbors; and it is hard for us to conceive how there is any real pleasure to be found in denying our own selfish desires in order to seek the good of another. A very little experience, however, will make us plainly see that the inward delight arising from the consciousness of having done good to another is the sweetest of all delights we have ever known. (p. 13)

This passage first attacks the Christian notion of self-sacrifice on grounds that it violates the facts of human nature over which self-interest holds sway. The Christian ethos is dismissed by the first sentence, however, only to be slipped back in through the second. Once banished, conventional theological doctrine returns in a thoroughly secularized form, as a quality that is considered by the author to be necessary in a woman and that has universal application as well. If conduct books habitually opposed their feminine ethos to aristocratic self-indulgence, then they did so in order to transform man's acquisitive instincts to serve the general good. They did not try to suppress those instincts. Represented as qualities inherent in sexuality, which were then differentiated according to gender, the two forms of desire—acquisitiveness and altruism—posed no contradiction. The sexual exchange converted male acquisitiveness into objects that diffused gratification throughout the household.

The logic of the contract had so thoroughly reorganized sexual relations by the beginning of the nineteenth century that the principle of domestic duty could be extended, then, beyond the middle-class household to form the basis of a general social policy. The reformist platform of Hannah More and her colleagues was founded on this principle. "Even those who admit of the power of female elegance on the manners of men," she argues, "do not always attend to the influence of female principles on their character."[48] If it is given to women to regulate the desires of men, then domestication constitutes a political force of no meager consequence, according to More. As she explains in the opening to her *Strictures on the Modern System of Female Education,*

> The general state of civilized society depends, more than those are aware who are not accustomed to scrutinize into the springs of human action, on the prevailing sentiments and habits of women, and on the nature of the estimation in which they are held. (p. 313)

Dr. Gregory similarly assures his many readers, "The power of a fine woman over the hearts of men, of men of the finest parts, is even beyond what she conceives."[49] With a kind of relentlessness, nineteenth century authors picked up the language that would identify supervisory skills with a woman's sexual appeal. Written in 1822, *The New Female Instructor or, Young Woman's Guide to Domestic Happiness* cites "instances of the ascendancy with which WOMEN OF SENSE have always gained over men of feeling."[50] Invoking the belief that specific powers adhered to gender, the author promises to elaborate "all those qualities which will enable you to attain the much desired art of pleasing, which will entitle you to the character of a WOMAN OF SENSE, and which will bestow on you all the power of which I have just spoken" (p. 2).

As such writing turned sexual pleasure into a regulatory power, it also endowed the power of surveillance with all the characteristics of a benevolent parent. The new practical curriculum adopted the strategy formulated by conduct-book authors as it set out to produce a self-regulating individual. It would introduce practical mathematics and science into the standard curriculum, to be sure, but throughout the first half of the nineteenth century and well into the second, the educational reformers—reformers of all kinds for that matter—concentrated inordinate energy on controlling the peripheral activities of the individual's leisure rather than on ensuring one's economic survival.[51] Pedagogical concern seemed to fix upon novels, newspapers, and conversation and not upon the seemingly more practical areas of knowledge. The next chapter—and indeed the rest of the book—will focus on this notion of literacy as a form of social control. For now it need only be said that many conduct-book authors seemed to feel a woman's education amounted to little more than instilling good reading habits and cultivating conversational skills. They appeared to feel confident that such an education would establish the basis for her effective management of the home.

This notion of women's work as the regulation of information lies behind a fable included in T.S. Arthur's handbook. It should therefore give us some idea of how the strategies of domestication would be turned into a broad-reaching—and inherently colonial—policy in the States. The fable states that its purpose is to prove that "No matter how many and great may be the disadvantages under which a young girl may labor, she may yet rise, if she will, very much above the point, in external condition, from which she started in life."[52] At the same moment when the popularity of self-help philosophy was peaking,[53] the conduct books declined to show that a working woman could elevate herself socially through industrious labor. To the contrary, we are told,

> Out of the young girls in the work-room where Ann [the heroine of the fable] learned her trade, all with no better advantages than she had possessed, seven married men of low minds and vulgar habits, and never rose above their original condition. Two were more like Ann, and they were sought by young men of a better class. One of them did not marry. (p. 76)

Indeed, the fable shows that as Ann rises above those "of low minds and vulgar habits" through her mastery of the lessons of feminine conduct, she elevates herself socially; she becomes a woman whom "a better class" of men are willing to marry. As far as this story is concerned, all that is necessary for a woman to rise above her "original condition" is to resist the temptations of idleness and become an example of the middle-class norms of femininity. Having established this as the grounds for her sexual appeal to the male, the tale concludes with a description of the reward Ann earns for so nearly embodying the female standard: "And in proportion as she thus rises will she find a higher degree of happiness and be able to do more good than otherwise would have been possible to her" (p. 76). If by internalizing the conduct-book norms, Ann can marry above her station, then altruism is both the reward for this effort of self-regulation and her obligation as the wife of a prosperous man. The tale concludes, in other words, by exalting a form of labor that is no labor at all, but a form of self-regulation that serves as an end in itself.

This principle would be extrapolated from the household and applied to society at large where it offered a way of displaying aristocratic largesse—or benevolent paternalism, as it is more appropriately called—in relation to those groups who had suffered most from the changes brought about by England's industrialization. The political application of this new idea of labor becomes instantly apparent if one observes how the principle organizing the household was extended outward to provide the liberal rhetoric for representing the relationship between one social group and another. In devising a curriculum for a boarding school run by his two illegitimate daughters, Erasmus Darwin tried to think of a way of instilling in women the idea that their work was its own reward. "There should be a plan in schools to promote the habit as well as the principle of benevolence," as he calls it. With this in mind, he suggests that "each lady might occasionally contribute a small sum, on seeing a needy naked child, to purchase flannel or coarse linen for clothes, which they might learn to cut out, and to make up themselves; and thus the practice of industry might be united with that of liberality."[54] In allowing women to produce goods for charity when it was no longer respectable for them to produce goods for their own kin, much less for purposes of trade, the conduct books fostered a certain form of power relations that would flourish later as the welfare institutions of a modern culture developed.

It was their acknowledged aptitude for performing acts of charity that first enabled women to move out of the home and into the political arena. As Martha Vicinus has argued, "The public debate about conditions among the urban poor gave reformers the opening they needed."[55] On the basis of a need for charitable work among these newly impoverished social elements, women began carving out territory for domestic work in the larger social arena. Vicinus offers a particularly telling quote from Frances Power Cobbe, an advocate for celibacy among single women, to illustrate this line of argument:

> "The private and home duties of *such women as have them* are, beyond all doubt, their first concern, and one which, when fully met, must often engross all their time and energies. But it is an absurdity, peculiar to the treatment of women, to go on assuming that all of them *have* home duties, and tacitly treating those who have none as if they were wrongly placed on God's earth, and had nothing whatever to do in it. There must needs be a purpose for the lives of single women in the social order of Providence . . . she has *not* fewer duties than others, but more extended and perhaps laborious ones. Not selfishness—gross to a proverb—but self-sacrifice more entire than belongs to the double life of marriage, is the true law of celibacy." (pp. 13–14)

Translating Cobbe's statement into the terms of this chapter, one can see the notion of charity was inexorably linked to the female role of household overseer. One can see, too, how the same logic that allowed women to carry the skills they possessed as women into the new world of work would eventually provide the liberal rationale for extending the doctrine of self-regulation and, with it, the subtle techniques of domestic surveillance beyond the middle-class home and into the lives of those much lower down on the economic ladder. It was not uncommon for nineteenth century conduct books to put forth a rather explicit theory of social control, as exemplified in the following statement:

> Take a mind at the lowest possible grade, the little outcast of the streets, abandoned by parents from whom even nature's humanizing instincts had disappeared, exposed to every influence of evil, and knowing none for good; the first steps to reclaim, to humanize such a mind, would be to place it in a moral atmosphere, to cultivate and raise its intelligence, and to improve its physical condition.[56]

I simply want to take note of how educational theory places all the stress on psychological rehabilitation. The "physical condition" of the "little outcast of the streets" comes as something of an afterthought.

The sexual division of labor may have begun by allowing two different ways of understanding the social reality to coexist side by side, rather like the Puritan model of marriage. But the insertion of a new idea of work into the field of social information would eventually make the sexual division of labor serve as a way of reconceiving the whole. Because they confined themselves strictly to matters of domestic economy, the conduct books may seem less noteworthy in themselves than the other writing characterizing the eighteenth and nineteenth centuries. But what I have been tracing by circling backwards and forwards in time across this relatively ignored yet utterly familiar body of data is the formation of a specialized language of sexuality. In suppressing chronology, my point has been to show how this language—by circulating between the psychological and the economic, as well as between the individual and the state—separated and reconstituted each in relation to the other and so produced a discourse, a new way of packaging cultural information that changed the entire surface of social life. Such a change could not have occurred in a single moment or through the effort of any particular person, even though some kinds of writing clearly enjoyed more currency than others during this period of time. More likely, the change worked through the persistent use of certain terms, oppositions, or figures until sexual differences acquired the status of truth and no longer needed to be written as such. Taking on the power of a metaphysics, then, these categories had the power to influence not only the way people understood work, but also how they viewed, and thus experienced desire for, the world of objects.

Despite noticeable changes in the stress and terminology of the conduct books, which point us outside the household to the vicissitudes of economic life, to social history and the affairs of men, as well as to the sequence of events that have come to comprise literary history, I have for the most part regarded these quite different texts as a single voice and continuous discourse. My purpose in doing so has been to show how I think domestic culture actually worked as a principle of continuity that pervaded the social surface to provide a stable conceptual framework within which these "outside" changes appear as so many variations on the sexual theme. Although a female genre, often written by women and directed at female readers, conduct books of the eighteenth and nineteenth centuries—or for that matter, earlier female conduct books—were attuned to the economic interests that they designated as the domain of the male. By virtue of its apparent detachment from the larger economy of which it was an instrumental part, domestic economy provided the fables in terms of which economic relations would also be rethought. Furthermore, as I have argued, sexual relations could shape this new master narrative precisely because its power seemed to be so restricted.

As conduct books rewrote the female subject for an eighteenth century audience, they shifted the whole strategic intention of the genre from reproducing the status quo—an aristocratic household—to producing an ever-retreating future. If it preceded the formation of a coherent set of economic policies associated with capitalism, this reformist rhetoric anticipated even the establishment of marriage as a social institution. The conduct books always saw the domestic world as one that ought to be realized. When passage of the Marriage Act of 1754 institutionalized the household and placed it more firmly under state control than ever before, the sense of its futurity did not vanish for authors and readers of conduct books. With the wild demographic shifts of the late eighteenth century and the violent labor disputes of subsequent decades, the sexual division of labor rapidly became a *fait accompli,* but the conduct books preserved their rhetorical edge of a promise yet to be realized. Even today this promise apparently cannot be distinguished from the form itself. Such handbooks still offer the power of self-transformation. The illusion persists that there is a self independent of the material conditions that have produced it and that such a self can transform itself without transforming the social and economic configuration in opposition to which it is constructed. This transformational power still seems to arise from within the self and to affect that self through strategies of self-discipline, the most perfect realization of which is perhaps anorexia nervosa. What we encounter in books of instruction for women, then, is something on the order of Foucault's productive hypothesis that continues to work upon the material body unencumbered by political history because that body is the body of a woman. On grounds that her sexual identity has been suppressed by a class that valued her chiefly for material reasons rather than for herself, the rhetoric of the conduct books produced a subject who in fact had no material body at all. This rhetoric replaced the material body with a metaphysical body made largely of words, albeit words constituting a material form of power in their own right. The modern female body comprised a grammar of subjectivity capable of regulating desire, pleasure, the ordinary care of the body, the conduct of courtship, the division of labor, and the dynamic of family relationships.

As such, the writing of female subjectivity opened a magical space in the culture where ordinary work could find its proper gratification and where the very objects that set men against one another in the competitive marketplace served to bind them together in a community of common domestic values. If the marketplace driven by male labor came to be imagined as a centrifugal force that broke up the vertical chains organizing an earlier notion of society and that scattered individuals willy-nilly across the English landscape, then the household's dynamic was conceived as a centripetal one. The household simultaneously recentered the scattered community at myriad points to form the nuclear family, a social organization with a mother rather than a father as its center. The very fact of its interlocking symmetries suggests that the doubled social world was clearly a myth before it was put into practice, as was indeed the case for almost a century.

3

The Rise of the Novel

Every language has its anomalies, which, though inconvenient, and in themselves once unnecessary, must be tolerated among the imperfections of human things, and which require only to be registered, that they may not be increased, and ascertained, that they may not be confounded: but every language has likewise its improprieties and absurdities, which it is the duty of the lexicographer to correct or proscribe.

SAMUEL JOHNSON, Preface to the *Dictionary*

Definitions could be useful if we didn't use words to make them.

JEAN-JACQUES ROUSSEAU, *Émile*

By the mid-eighteenth century, new forms of writing were contending with those that had long dominated English thinking, each claiming the right to declare what features made a woman most desirable. The sheer volume of print already devoted to the project of redefining the female indicates that by that time a massive ideological struggle was underway. But in addition to conduct books, ladies magazines, and such newspapers as the *Tatler*, whose title was supposedly coined out of deference to its female readership, some authors created their idea of womankind out of the most unpromising material of all, namely, the novel. The novel had a reputation for displaying not only the seamy undersides of English political life, but also sexual behavior of a semi-pornographic nature. On both counts, it was considered a vulgar form of writing.[1] As late as 1810, a well-known conduct-book author could say of his readers, "While cultivating a refined taste for the admirable productions of the classic British authors, I may venture to predict, that you will find neither time nor leisure nor much inclination for writing of *an inferior rank*" (italics mine). By this he means "to include in one undistinguishing censure, all the various productions which come under the name of novels."[2]

In shaping an ideal woman out of the stuff of novels, then, novelists did not appear to be assaulting the dominant culture so much as rescuing both the female and the domestic life she superintended from their fate at the hands of degenerate authors. It was this strategy that Richardson set in motion when, after declaring he was not actually writing a novel, he used fiction for redefining the desirable woman. Such an event helped to change both the terms of cultural conflict and the nature of the victory that would be won. But I want to stress that *Pamela* was not so much about this struggle as quite literally part of it. As I shall demonstrate, the strategies of the larger conflict gave Richardson's first novel its peculiar form. One can observe his strategies with particular clarity in those places that are usually considered clumsy or tedious within the framework of "the art of the novel." To speak of the qualities of the text that resist modern aesthetics, however, is to identify the role of the text in the far more extensive process I call feminization, whereby certain areas of aristocratic culture were appropriated for the emergent social group.[3]

By the end of the eighteenth century, conduct books had settled on one kind of fiction as truly safe for young women to read. This was a non-aristocratic kind of writing that was both polite and particularly suitable for a female readership. It also had the virtue of dramatizing the same principles sketched out in the conduct books. Burney's *Evelina* is only one of the better-known examples of the fiction by lady novelists, as the women who wrote polite novels were called. So well established did this kind of writing become, so thoroughly did the literate classes grant it approval over the other, older, and more prevalent varieties of fiction, that it eventually supplanted everything the novel had formerly been. In this manner, a relatively new form of writing came to define the genre within a remarkably few number of years. Austen could write *Northanger Abbey* and the rest of her fiction knowing full well what a novel had to do in order to be considered a novel. She never pursued the direction in which she began her writing career. Her *Lady Susan* was a work of fiction, to be sure, but it was certainly no novel in the polite sense of the term, for the heroine appeared to be a successful adventuress in the mode of Restoration drama. When by the middle of the nineteenth century the new middle classes were entrenched and the British economy had stabilized, the novel was already known as a female form of writing, and the conflict between fiction and the polite tradition of letters had all but been resolved. By this point, such fictions as Richardson's and Burney's were brought within the realm of the normative, and a continuous tradition of the novel could be written backward as well as forward in time. As the novel was written into a literary history, however, the process of its production disappeared. Only the novels themselves preserved the struggle between writing that only later became known as the novel and another kind of fiction—once referred to as novels or romances—that has since been consigned to the attics and storerooms of cultural history.

Beginning with Richardson's *Pamela*, then, one can observe the process by which novels rose to a position of respectability among the genres of writing. This process created a private domain of culture that was independent of the political world and overseen by a woman. Such a cultural fantasy held forth the promise that individuals could realize a new and more fundamental identity and thus free themselves of the status distinctions organizing the old society. In this respect, the novel provided a mighty weapon in the arsenal of Enlightenment rhetoric, which aimed at liberating individuals from their political chains. Richardson demonstrated how fiction could deploy strategies that reorganized the country house around a woman who had nothing but a gendered form of literacy to offer. But as much as his strategies may have resembled those which Rousseau put to use in writing *The Social Contract*, they nevertheless offered an important variation on familiar Enlightenment themes: they constituted the female subject as she became an object of knowledge in and through her own writing. Richardson was probably only trying to gain the authority to create this woman, and most likely he only sought to control the interpretive strategies that readers brought to bear on her behavior. But fiction itself demonstrates that by the end of the eighteenth century the same strategies which laid claim to the rights of the individual underwent a form of mutation and acquired the power to control the individual on whose behalf they continued to argue. I would now like to read select works of fiction as the history of certain political strategies that first offered the theory and rationale for modern social institutions, but that later came to be used as techniques of social control.

The Battle of the Books

In formulating what we now know as the middle-class household, conduct books displayed a new form of semiotic behavior. Such behavior—namely, the contracts I have identified as tropes of self-production—shifted the entire struggle for political power from the level of physical force to the level of language. This is no secret. Institutional cultures characteristically maintain themselves through the regulation of literacy and the commodification of language. But conduct books are particularly explicit about exactly how the new order of household with a new form of authority at its center was produced through education. As we have seen Rousseau argue, to produce an individual who had no particular political identity required—before anything else—the strict control of information. For Rousseau, the general good had to be embraced as an individual's own personal good, which depended on each individual receiving the same information on an individual basis. Otherwise one would come to understand the general good as that of a specific faction. Not unlike the Rousseau of *Émile*, then, English conduct books sought to promote a gender-based philosophy of education known as "the cultivation of the heart."

If English conduct books began by insisting that women had certain positive qualities deriving from gender, they inevitably stressed the point that femaleness in its natural form offered at best an unsteady socializing force. Femaleness could even be seen as a source of serious political disruption. Thomas Gisborne's *Enquiry into the Duties of the Female Sex* (1789) is one of many conduct books to offer a litany of those destabilizing traits to which women are particularly prone because, ironically enough, such traits are also female virtues:

> The gay vivacity and quickness of imagination, so conspicuous among the qualities in which the superiority of women is acknowledged, have a tendency to lead to unsteadiness of mind; to fondness of novelty; to habits of frivolousness, and trifling employment; to dislike of sober application; to dislike of graver studies, and a too low estimation of their worth; to an unreasonable regard for wit, and striving accomplishments; to a thrift for admiration and applause; to vanity and affectation.[4]

When they prohibited female labor, conduct books made many hours available for women to indulge in "trifling employment." Because of her "gay vivaciousness and quickness of imagination," however, a future wife could never be left to her own devices.

As such, the matter of how to occupy women's idle hours commanded as much attention in conduct books as did her economic behavior. Authors thought out their domestic economy in terms of a cultural imperative to free the woman from labor in order to put her to work as a supervisor. Leaving her with little to do, however, created a situation designed to encourage the very forms of decadence which those books used for purposes of characterizing the old aristocracy. In fact, a common complaint against these educational programs was their tendency to prepare women for a life of uselessness and frivolity.[5] Thus the critics of these programs agreed with the advocates of a gender-based theory of education, which held that a woman's social environment presented her with too many forms of activity that smacked of amusement. And so, renouncing the idea of female labor and yet recognizing the dangers of leisure, authors of conduct books generally insisted that the activities comprising the domestic arts—and therefore a woman's duty—had to be carefully supervised precisely where they seemed the most frivolous. For it was there that a woman's education might revert to the status of those unregulated amusements that were supposed to mislead her desire.

Convinced that a woman's leisure activities required supervision, authors intent upon solving the problem posed by amusement developed a new notion of taste—a specifically non-aristocratic notion—and a new way for women to occupy time. "The Rudiments of Taste," explains Erasmus Darwin,

> should be taught [to women] with some care; since taste enters into their dress, their motions, their manners, as well as into all the fine arts which they have leisure to cultivate, as drawing, painting, modeling, making artificial flowers, embroidery, writing letters, reading, speaking, and into almost every circumstance of life.[6]

Care must be taken, he goes on to explain, that these activities not become means of self-display; they must always provide occasion for "mental" or "moral culture." Supervision presumably made all the difference between amusements that led to corruption and forms of leisure that occupied a woman constructively. The activities comprising her education could be considered educational only if they were supervised, and by the same token, virtually anything could be considered educational if it provided an occasion for supervision. In fact, it appears that the more useless the activity was, the more it lent itself solely to the exercise of supervisory techniques.[7] In learning how to perform these activities, one therefore learned the art of domestic supervision. As the supervision of leisure-time activities provided the means of domesticating the woman, the woman so domesticated acquired mainly the techniques of supervising leisure time. In keeping with this strategic objective, reading was at once the most useful and the most dangerous way to take up a woman's time.

The idea that literacy offered the most efficient means for shaping individuals was the *raison d'etre* of conduct books. This presupposition was inherent in the genre from its beginnings in an earlier age. For purposes of the present argument, then, let me simply assert that behind all pedagogical statements on the matter, and no doubt behind the whole attempt of eighteenth century British philosophy to understand human understanding as well, was the assumption that an individual developed herself through an exchange between subject and object worlds. At the heart of these theories of personal development was the more basic assumption that language could constitute a mutually transforming relationship between the self and an external world of objects. It is not my purpose to address the subtleties of these theories, for I am more interested in isolating the crude theoretical basis for a popular psychology, or common sense, which one can observe in the conduct books.

At the risk of oversimplifying the entire question of Enlightenment epistemology, I would like to suggest how all such theories might have arisen from a specific understanding of the relationship between reading, sexuality, and social control, and how that relationship might have been represented in a way that gave those theories something like the power of myth. Even though I will use only a few examples to illustrate my point, one must assume it took innumerable statements describing the body of female knowledge and its procedures to flesh out a theory that could not even be recognized as such because its power derived from sheer repetition. It was no doubt the fulfillment of this double objective of theory—both to explain and to mystify—that allowed DuBoscq's *La femme heroique ou les heroines comparees avec les heros, en toute sorte de vertus* to cross the channel, survive through reprintings in 1632, 1633, 1634, 1636, 1639–40, 1643, 1658, and after being translated in 1753 as *The Compleat Woman*, to resurface yet again that year as *The Accomplish'd Woman*. DuBoscq offers this explanation of how language mediates the subject and object worlds:

> Be our disposition or Innocence what it will, as Bodies, even without our Assent, take the Qualities of what we feed on; so our Minds, in despite of ourselves, are apt to imbibe I know not what from the Books we read: Our humours alter ere we are aware; we linger with the Gay and Pleasant, we grow dissolute with the Libertine, and we mope with the Melancholy; insomuch, that nothing is more common than to see Persons wholly changed after reading certain Books; they assume new Passions, they lead quite another life.[8]

One should note how the notion of taste—or "you are what you eat"— carries over from the dining table to the scene of reading where the same economy applies to the consumption of information. But good taste in reading is far more important in determining the nature and value of the individual than is the food he or she eats. Invoking one of the two most common figures for the consequences of misreading (seduction is the other), another author claims: "Poisons under due control may act beneficially upon the physical frame, but *moral* poison can seldom be limited in its effect; and the heart and mind once tainted, purity and truth of feeling once injured, the destructive results are, in most cases, sure and overwhelming."[9] Although this theory is couched in universal terms, it has special application to women.

It is by taking in the wrong sort of information that the value of a woman's character is most surely threatened, because such information makes her desire the wrong sort of things. In a statement that reveals his affiliation with an earlier moment in time as well as his relevance to the modern audience, DuBoscq works this variation on the theme of the Fall: "It seems as if the same spirit that deceived the *first woman*, still inspired some of her Daughters with like sentiments, by promising them that their eyes shall be open'd to behold very admirable things."[10] Thus he identifies the "eyes" as portals of entry, "things" as objects of visual consumption, "sentiments" as targets of seductive images, and perception as the conduit of corruption from the outside world to subjectivity. Here and elsewhere the danger posed by bad information—desire for "very admirable things"—is described both as a poison and as a form of seduction. By using the same powerfully suggestive combination of metaphors and lending them a quite literal meaning, such authors meant to create a sense of urgent need for their curriculum designed specifically for women. But DuBoscq's combination of metaphors happens to comprise a figure of pollution.

At stake in the appearance of such a figure is the very principle of group identity.[11] And if this principle applies to eighteenth century British society, then the identity of a group of non-aristocratic but literate people—namely, those who authored and consumed conduct books with increasing avidity—appears to have rested on the formation of female subjectivity. According to DuBoscq, women "have the more need of Reading [than men] to render their Minds commendably fertile and polite; and especially to moderate that Vivacity, which, being left to itself, would sometimes run the hazard of appearing ridiculous and absurd."[12] A later author simply states that "The choice of books is of great importance in the education of children" in order to claim that this principle is particularly true of girls: "The sons will, perhaps, at an early age, be put under the care of tutors, but the formation of the minds of the daughters is the peculiar province of the mothers."[13] Early on, DuBoscq uses sexual reproduction as an analogy for the transmission of knowledge through reading. To talk about the dangers inherent in the reproduction of subjectivity, he simply translates pollution from a physical into a psychological event: "for as Mothers upon viewing Some extraordinary Object, often leave the Marks thereof upon their Infants, why should we not believe that the lascivious Stories in Romances may have the same effect upon our Imagination, and that they always leave behind them Some Spots upon the Soul?"[14] Imbedded within the analogy is a theory of subjectivity that requires the strict regulation of reading for women, for just as they reproduce members of the family, they also reproduce forms of subjectivity. This analogy became the theory underlying the rhetoric of later conduct books as figurative usage assumed the status of factual truth.

Conduct books did not provide the materials for this reading program, although they might include moral fables and occasionally presented themselves in the form of exemplary conversations and letters. But they did go to elaborate lengths to distinguish between good reading and bad, to specify the categories and sometimes the titles of books, and to explain how these materials were to be used. They all insisted that extensive cultivation of the fine arts had a tendency to generate vanity and to call forth the selfish passions. By saying that the fine arts were not within the field of female knowledge, these books distinguished a female education both from that of the male and more importantly from the classical education associated with an aristocratic tradition. By way of contrast, the same books also insisted that the formation of female taste required some familiarity with British classics. An author was only typical in demanding "you must study Milton and Shakespeare"[15] or even in recommending a whole tradition including "Young, Goldsmith, Thomson, Gray, Parnell, Cowper, Campbell, Burns, Wordsworth, Southey; also the ethical parts of Pope's poetry."[16] Frequently appearing among recommended titles were important essays on beauty and the imagination, as well as excerpts from history and a smattering of French and Italian taught by the conversational method. These materials comprised the substance of a curriculum to which later authors would add geography, mathematics, and natural history. It is obvious to me that the point of such curricula—in the beginning at least—was not to restrict women's intellectual activity, but to define such information as female. This was a much more aggressive political proposition than one aimed at subordinating an already subordinate sex. The establishment of a female standard of taste offered a positive alternative to the male standard, which was based on the classical tradition. And if these alternative areas of study for women seem utterly commonplace to us now, it is only because handbooks for educating women, each insignificant in itself, together formulated the basic categories that would later determine the standard Anglo-American curriculum. Modern educational institutions, I am suggesting, continued the project of feminizing the subject as they made what had been a specifically female body of knowledge into a standard for literacy in general.

From various instructions of this kind, one can piece together a precise methodology for reading that could—and eventually would—be extended to virtually every kind of information. Reading history, for example, could be used to offer young women a number of lessons. For one of these lessons, the Reverend Broadhurst defers to Hume. "From history," he writes in a rather self-important manner, "the fair sex may learn that love is not the only, nor always the predominant, principle in the hearts of man."[17] The motive for providing women with this lesson, according to another writer, is to "speak of History as a picture of man in his gradual advancement from the mere fighting, murdering animal of olden times, to the intelligence and intellectual cultivation of the present day." The progress of mankind is supposed to be understood as the product of individual genius, furthermore. The student should not simply be given "isolated facts," but asked "whether she has thought of the difference in the glory pertaining to an Alexander and a Julius Caesar, or to such men as Penn, Jenner, Wattes, and Cooke, with his magnificent application of the powers of Galvanism."[18] To consider which form of power is greater, military force or that of modern technology, readers are required to assume that all western history is the history of men, not a genealogy or story of kinship relations. Wherever history is discussed in these books, as if by some prior agreement among authors, a link is forged between the personal and the political to make the world outside the household arise from great efforts made by individual men. It was not uncommon for authors to propose that women acquire their knowledge of history by reading the memoirs and biographies of famous men in relation to the times that felt their influence. "History," according to one, "should be considered as a skeleton, which is to be filled out by all the collateral information you can procure."[19]

If history provides a corrective to the worst tendencies of the female mind, any use of figurative language is to be approached with extreme caution. Truth, Mrs. Hamilton confesses, "must sometimes permit herself to be arrayed by the hand of fancy. When she appears thus decorated, some care is, however, necessary, lest the attention should be so much engaged by the drapery, as to overlook the symmetry and proportions of the figure which it conceals."[20] One cannot help but notice that the truth to be found in fictional narrative steps forth in this passage as a woman, where the conduct books endow history with the characteristics of great men. In so identifying writing with gender, however, it is not the opposition of fiction to truth that really matters, but rather the strategies of reading that all writing consequently requires. Like that of more fanciful writing, the truth of history lies beneath the surface where it can be discovered by a specific interpretive process that translates it into sexual and ultimately psychological terms.

Representation must, in other words, be regarded as if it had all the qualities of an individual human being. After alerting her reader to the dangers of figurative language, Mrs. Hamilton goes on to say of fictional characters that it actually matters little "when or where they lived, or indeed whether they lived at all. The sole question to be asked is, whether such and such dispositions and opinions would naturally and inevitably lead to such and such conclusions."[21] Moreover, Erasmus Darwin obviously felt he was taking a bold step forward in suggesting that women be instructed in the heathen mythologies. Since, in his words,

> a great part of this mythology consists of personified vices, much care should be taken in female schools, as well as in male ones, to prevent any bad impressions which might be made on the mind by this kind of erudition; this is to be accomplished by explaining the allegorical meaning of many of these supposed actions of heathen deities, and by shewing that they are at present used only as emblems of certain powers, as Minerva of wisdom, and Bellona of war, and thus constitute the language of the painters; and are indeed almost the whole language that art possesses, besides the delineation of visible objects in rest or in action.[22]

Again, it should be emphasized, this statement makes clear how a precise set of interpretive procedures offered strategies that assigned a specific emotion to each of the deities. Darwin could allow his reader to consume almost any kind of information provided that reader knew how to interpret it. For this was to turn any and all information into one kind of truth for which the recommended use of heathen deities offered the paradigm. Despite a tendency to exhibit impolite forms of behavior, he contended, classical mythology could find a place in the female curriculum, whose vocabulary was capable of translating any and all works of art into emotional phenomena, which then became subject to moral evaluation. It was as if Darwin sensed that a vocabulary capable of displacing the historical surface of language was also one that could make virtually any work of high culture available to the ordinary consumer.

These few examples should be sufficient to show how the feminization of certain areas of knowledge entailed a prosaic rendering of various cultural materials as developmental narratives that bear striking resemblance to those works of fiction we now consider novels. Fiction, however, was the one thing that could not be reproduced in female form. Its sense-making behavior—whatever that was, the conduct books were too polite to say—evidently resisted the very procedures for reclassifying cultural information that women readers were supposed to perform. At least conduct books never failed to represent fiction as "other" writing, that is, writing that contained all the falsehoods against which their mode of truth stood rigidly opposed. It was understood that novels were not male writing, for they were often written by women. Yet the mere mention of novels and romances was invariably a prelude to warnings that represented such writing as a form of seduction.[23] Throughout the eighteenth century, educational theory remained absolutely firm on this point; parents and teachers must "Use no Monstrous, Unnatural, or Preposterous Fictions to divert her with, but either ingenious fables, or real histories."[24] In the last decade of that century, however, a sudden shift of categories can be observed. To be sure, there were the same claims that fiction "may give a distaste to more useful knowledge," that it makes one "return to the common duties of life with regret," or that it "blunts the feelings of readers towards real objects of misery."[25] At the same time, one finds abundant evidence to suggest that the classification of fiction had suddenly become more sophisticated. Some novels even conformed to the conduct book's criteria for educational reading, while others provided the means of regulating leisure time. Erasmus Darwin's *A Plan for the Conduct of Female Education at Boarding Schools* classifies novels as serious, humorous, or amorous. While he strictly forbids novels that fall into the last category, he openly endorses those in the first category, especially works by Burney, Brooke, Lennox, Inchbald, and Smith, "all of which," in his words, "I have here introduced by the character given to me of them by a very ingenious lady."[26] Among the serious reading, reading so safe as to be recommended by such an "ingenious lady," Darwin oddly enough includes *Robinson Crusoe*, and just as curiously, in recommending some of the humorous variety for more mature readers, he mentions *Tom Jones* as one novel that does not attempt to inflame the passions so much as to provide an imitation of life.

If it was on the basis of gender that people condemned fiction, I should add, it was also on the basis of gender that fiction received its strongest endorsement. When considering his own tendency to keep his curriculum for women relatively free of the taint of male knowledge, he questions whether this principle should be applied to the novel. How, he asks, "can young women, who are secluded from the other sex from their infancy, form any judgement of men, if they are not to be assisted by such books as delineate manners?" And lest we misunderstand what he means by such books and what he wishes to imply is their function, Darwin resorts to a novelistic strategy. He offers this individual case, for example, to demonstrate that fiction not only provides an appropriate way to occupy leisure but also has educational value for women:

A lady of fortune who was persuaded by her guardian to marry a disagreeable and selfish man, speaking to her friend of the ill humour of her husband, lamented that she had been prohibited from reading novels. "If I had read such books, said she, before I was married, I should have chosen better; I was told that all men were alike except in respect to fortune."[27]

I should hasten to add that in endorsing fiction such conduct books as Darwin's did not really question the established distinction between taste and vulgarity. They simply applied another standard of taste to what women read and wrote, a standard that made this writing available—in theory at least—to virtually everyone.

If a novel were to be put in the hands of women, children, and servants, it had to regulate literacy. A declamation against fiction was no doubt the best inducement to read fiction, for it always assumed that if left to their own devices all of these people would prefer works of fiction. Thus when novel reading became an acceptable practice, we can observe the basis on which good fiction was distinguished from bad. This is the same as asking under what conditions could fiction be read and not poison the female mind. Certainly fiction was supposed to stay in its place. It was never supposed to replace more serious reading. "No pastry can ever be a proper substitute for a solid joint," as one author says, but pastry is very different from poison and in some ways more powerful than meat. Thus "the best novels that ever were written would not be suitable as the *only*, or even the principle study of a young girl." Instead, "novels should be kept as a relaxation from study, or a source of amusement during temporary indisposition. Many are indeed excellent and unobjectionable *as amusements*; and, in the present day especially, we have several writers whose works will at once delight and instruct the reader."[28] To be sure, this is a banal version of the figures of honey and light used by Matthew Arnold to represent high culture, but it is the version that would eventually define the middle-class concept of art.

The novel alone could indeed "delight and instruct" at one time. No doubt for this reason, early in the nineteenth century it became the prerogative of the woman so educated to apply the principle to servants: "In every kitchen there should be a library, for which a judicious selection of books will be requisite, and nothing beyond the comprehension of kitchen readers admitted."[29] By the second half of the nineteenth century, the novel served a far more sophisticated role, but one still consistent with the principle of feminization. In her *Papers for Thoughtful Girls, with Illustrative Sketches of Some Girls' Lives*, Sarah Tyler brings to her program of education a subtle understanding of how reading differentiates individuals according to gender and, in so doing, develops a highly refined hierarchy within the household that ensures its own reproduction. According to this theory, daughters who aspire to assume the position of mothers "must find some definite object in their studies" and learn "Latin to read with a studious elder brother; natural history to engage a younger 'callant'; drawing to occupy a delicate sister; political economy to amaze and amuse papa."[30] Thus the daughter's reading was aimed at differentiating the family according to gender and to hierarchical distinctions within gender, particularly in the case of the male. In requiring her to be all things to all people, I am suggesting, the conduct book made the female the overseer of gender formation.[31] But this noticeably specialized program for reading did include one kind of reading for the domestic woman herself, presumably to develop her facility for defining others psychologically. She should have "penetration into the best novels to lighten the short leisure, relax and soften the somewhat contracted and concentrated sympathies of mama, or one and all to bestow on friends and neighbors."[32]

The novel, in other words, had to observe all the same sense-making procedures as the conduct book. Upon granting this point, however, one encounters a problem. The eighteenth century fiction that made it into literary history was anything but a simple application of the popular theory of reading as a process of self-transformation. At the same time, there does remain a considerable body of writing that deserves to be called a conduct book in fictional form: fables included within conduct books, conduct books cast as dialogues between a girl and her female virtues, stories in ladies magazines, collections of stories for children, or the kind of fictionalized personal letter that Richardson used as his model for *Pamela*. One is bound to find these fictions stuffy, patronizing, and already written, everything, in short, that Austen mocked in *Pride and Prejudice* when she had Mary Bennet speak the conduct-book clichés in all their tiresome perfection.

Strategies of Self-Production: *Pamela*

Richardson has been accused of all the faults for which Austen ridicules Mary Bennet, and not without reason. But it is also because he used the feminizing strategies of conduct-book literature in his first work of fiction that it was received with such acclaim and even recommended from the pulpit in a time when novels were considered morally dangerous. We know that Richardson took great pains to distinguish his "pretty novel" from the "horrid romancing" of others and that he tried to control the interpretation of *Pamela* by calling together ladies for the purpose of discussing his fiction.[33] In addition to making numerous revisions, he drew upon this and his later fiction to compile a book of moral homilies for publication. He even published and revised his correspondence in a compulsive effort to reclassify his fiction as something other than common fiction. But if, as Richardson insisted, *Pamela* is not a novel according to the standards of his day, then neither is it a conduct book. As Richardson obviously knew, conduct books never represented the female body at all, except to mention the particularities of dressing or to recommend a modest bearing when a woman presented herself to the public view. Nor did they value the body as a female body, even in those passages that describe procedures for health and hygiene. Although they frequently declared that fiction would somehow prevent a woman from performing her domestic duties, these books also refused to say what exactly was so threatening about fiction that women had to shun it above all other reading.

In writing *Pamela*, Richardson struck upon a double maneuver that ensured his novel was not a novel in the derogatory sense of the word, even though it was indeed a work of fiction. He deployed the strategies of conduct-book literature within fiction, and he contained the strategies of the most deleterious fiction—a tale of seduction—within the framework of a conduct book. To domesticate fiction, he thematically represented both modes of writing—fiction that aimed at producing the new domestic world and fiction that reinforced the stratifying strategies identified with the old society—as the struggle between a female servant and her aristocratic master. He represented their struggle for possession of the female body in scene after scene of seduction, which he elaborated in minute detail. Thus he provided a local habitation and a name for the very sexual behavior against which the conduct books had pitted their rhetoric. But Richardson also used fiction to enter into a struggle with fiction. And he saw to it that this struggle was one which other fiction would lose, for sexual relations would be contained within the categories of domestic economy. Indeed, the last third of *Pamela* deals with little else but the details of household management, as described in the previous chapter.

Once again, I want to stress the fact that the struggle Pamela wages against the advances of Mr. B does not point to some order of events going on outside of language; it records a struggle that actually took place within fiction. On the outcome of this struggle hinged the right to determine not only what made a female desirable, but also what made her female in the first place. By having Pamela gain the power of self-representation, Richardson enclosed the tale of her seduction within a framework that, like the conduct book, redirected male desire at a woman who

embodied the domestic virtues. Richardson thus carried on the project of
the conduct book, but by doing so in and through fiction, he carried it
into the symbolic heart of the old society—the aristocratic country house—
where it engaged in a mortal dialectic with the dominant political categories. Pamela's successful struggle against the sexual advances of Mr.
B transformed the rules of an earlier model of kinship relations into a
sexual contract that suppressed their difference in station. Rather than that
of a master and servant, then, the relationship between the protagonists
of these competing kinds of fiction may be understood as that of male
and female. There can be no better illustration than this of how the discourse of sexuality worked and of what political goal was achieved as it
suppressed the political categories that until then had dominated writing.

To make my point, let me first recall the relationship between male
and female as it appears in an early seventeenth century Puritan marriage
pamphlet:[34]

Husband	Wife
Get goods	Gather them together and save them
Travel, seek a living	Keep the house
Get money and provisions	Do not vainly spend it
Deal with many men	Talk with few
Be "entertaining"	Be solitary and withdrawn
Be skillful in talk	Boast of silence
Be a giver	Be a saver
Apparel yourself as you may	Apparel yourself as it becomes you
Dispatch all things outdoors	Oversee and give order within

As much as its principle of gender differentiation resembles that organizing modern households, and even though its Puritan heritage certainly
distinguishes British fiction from the fiction of other capitalist nations,
the domestic ideal illustrated above did not pass through the centuries
unmodified. By so enclosing the family, the static and binary model of
Puritan handbooks and sermons sought to establish an alternative basis
for political power and represented the family as a little commonwealth
in whose government the larger state could not interfere. As such, the
domestic unit resisted the dominant notion of kinship relations at two
crucial points. First, it represented the state within the state as independent and as containing relationships that were based on gender rather than
on family or fortune. In thus contesting the dominant notion of power
relations, however, the Puritan household organized the state within the
state in terms of the radically disymmetrical relations of monarch and

subject. As Robert Cleaver explains, the household was a commonwealth made up of two sorts, "The Governor" and "those who must be ruled."[35] This direct assault on the principle of monarchy never succeeded in transforming the political organization of England.

But the Puritan version of the household contained another point of resistance, which came into play later on in the history of the family. Post-Enlightenment versions of the household appeared to leave the political world alone as they avoided the language of government that runs through seventeenth century handbooks of marriage. Eighteenth century conduct books in particular presumed to tamper exclusively with sexual relations and then solely with the female component. At the same time, however, they claimed to represent all households as the natural domain of a woman who was dedicated to making the place into a happy middle-class home. By representing only the household, these later conduct books accomplished what earlier and avowedly political representations of the family had not been able to do. Although theirs was very much a minority view, the conduct books detached the household from the larger political order and made it a world of its own, a world where status distinctions were suspended.

Pamela demonstrates perhaps more clearly than any other single example that to transform one party of the sexual contract effectively transforms the relationship between the two sexes and therefore the contract itself. To explain how *Pamela* turns the minority representation of sexual relations into an instrument of hegemony, I offer below an example from a section of the sexual contract in which Mr. B attempts to negotiate with the servant girl who has steadfastly resisted all his sexual advances. Particularly important is the form in which Richardson presents this contract to his readers. He counterpoints Mr. B's demands with Pamela's responses and inserts them side by side in this paradigmatic fashion about midway through the narrative:[36]

To Mrs. Pamela Andrews.	This is my Answer.
II. I will directly make you a present of 500 *guineas*, for your own use, which you may dispose of to any purpose you please: and will give it absolutely into the hands of any person you shall appoint to receive it; and expect no favour in return, till you are satisfied in the possession of it.	II. As to your second proposal, let the consequence be what it will I reject it with all my soul. Money, sire, is not my chief good: May God Almighty desert me, whenever it is! and whenever, for the sake of that, I can give up my title to that blessed hope which will stand me in stead, at a time when millions of gold will not purchase one happy moment of reflection on a past misspent life!

IV. Now, Pamela, will you see by this, what a value I set upon the free-will of a person *already* in my power; and who, if these proposals are not accepted, shall find, that I have not taken all these pains, and risked my reputation, as I have done, without solving to gratify my passion for you, at all adventures; and if you refuse, without making any terms at all.

IV. I know, sir, by woful experience that I am in your power: I know all the resistance I can make will be poor and weak, and, perhaps, stand me in little stead: I dread your *will* to ruin me is as great as your *power*: yet, sir, will I dare .to tell you, that I will make no free-will offering of my virtue. All that I *can* do, poor as it is, I *will* do, to convince you that your offers shall have no part in my choice; and if I cannot escape the violence of man, I hope, by God's grace, I shall have nothing to reproach myself, for not doing all in my power to avoid my disgrace; and then I can safely appeal to the great God, my only refuge and protector, with this consolation, That my will bore no part in my violation.

Simply by inserting Pamela's voice into the field dominated by Mr. B's contract, Richardson empowers the subject of aristocratic power with speech. In allowing her the grounds for negotiating such a contract, furthermore, he modifies the presupposition of all previous contracts, namely, that the male defined and valorized the female as a form of currency in an exchange among men. This is to say that Richardson's version of consensual exchange empowers the female to give herself in exchange with the male. Although this novel claims to deal only with the sexual contract, doing so in this instance also revises the way in which political relationships are imagined.[37]

The male party of this exchange is a member of the older landed gentry. It is perhaps curious that someone of such high yet untitled status should provide the target of Richardson's reformist rhetoric. Still, one finds it consistently true that—from Richardson's Mr. B to Austen's Mr. Knightley to Brontë's Mr. Rochester—the male of the dominant class, as represented in fiction, is likely to occupy precisely such a social position. He is likely to bear certain features of the ruling class that inhibit the operations of genuine love. To a certain degree, however, domestic fiction remakes this figure in the image of a new ruling class. The gentry was permeable, a class one could enter through marriage, and its features as a group, like those of the manor house, could be remodeled to the specifications of the middle-class family.[38]

It is worth noting that the male of the dominant class, though he may bear certain features of the libertine or of the snob, is capable of going either way socially, but his female counterpart is generally not. Such women as Mr. B's sister Lady Davers, or Darcy's aunt Lady Catherine de Bourgh, or Rochester's fiance Blanche Ingram are hopelessly devoid of feelings and concerned only with displaying their position. They embody the features of the dominant class that, in contrast with a fine pair of eyes or a genteel education, cannot be included among those of the domestic woman. What I am suggesting by making this comparison is that Richardson endows Mr. B with certain political features that can be transformed by the thematics of gender. Within the gendered framework, the male is indeed defined in political terms, for this is precisely what it means to be male. Only those features of the aristocratic woman that testify to her development of certain psychological qualities can go into the making of the new domestic ideal. Through marriage to someone of a lower station, the male but not the female of the upper gentry can be redeemed. I do not mean to imply that this class of people really behaved in so paradoxical a manner as fiction depicted them, but rather that such a representation of the upper gentry offered the rhetorical means for redistributing certain attributes, along with corresponding powers and privileges, according to the principle of gender.

As a man of significantly higher station than his own servant, Mr. B is initially disposed to consider that his offer to grant Pamela economic independence in return for sexual pleasure is a gesture of pure generosity. He could claim such pleasure as his to enjoy without entering into a consensual exchange at all. By virtue of being master of the estate and thus of all the personnel and objects therein, Mr. B already possesses—as he reminds Pamela—the thing he most desires. Had Richardson endowed Pamela with wealth or station, Mr. B would be perfectly within the rules of his caste to marry her, for she would then not only possess an erotic body but an estate and bloodline as well. The fact that Mr. B tries and fails to seduce Pamela on so many occasions tells us that this woman possesses some kind of power other than that inhering in either the body of a servant or in that of a prominent family. By making the female party to the contract, Richardson implies an independent party with whom the male has to negotiate, a female self who exists outside and prior to the relationships under the male's control.

When in the history of writing before *Pamela*, we might ask ourselves, did a female, let alone a female servant, have the authority to define herself so? To understand the power Richardson embodies in the non-aristocratic woman, one need only observe how he endows her with subjective qualities. In her response to Article II of Mr. B's proposition, Pamela asserts an alternative form of value to that of his money and rank. This value is called into being as she rejects what Mr. B offers in exchange for the pleasure of using her body. At all costs, even that of life itself, she resolves to preserve an essential self that the male of the dominant class does not and cannot possess by virtue of his wealth and monopoly on violence. In both Articles II and IV, we can see Richardson counter the power available in the aristocratic tradition by drawing on the language of theological tradition for the terms of Pamela's resistance. "Hope," "reflection," "reproach," as well as "soul" describe the feelings of a woman bent on preserving control over her body in the face of a system that gives license to sexual assault. Richardson does not settle on this language because he is particularly interested in representing the condition of her soul. He uses this terminology to give her value as a partner in marriage.

The term "will" is especially revealing in this respect. By the time Richardson is through with it, it no longer has anything to do with the grand tradition of theological debate. It has everything to do with a new concern for personal motivation.[39] Caught up and redefined within the figure of the contract, the whole idea of will becomes individuated, sexual, and internalized; it becomes, in other words, the volition required before any consensual contract can take place. In acquiring a modern psychological meaning, furthermore, "will" also adheres to a principle of economy. To accept Mr. B's money would cause Pamela to suffer a loss that she describes in spiritual terms but that she also identifies as bad business; if she accepts his money, she will have to look back upon a "misspent" life. To refuse Mr. B on these grounds makes the integrity of the female body, regardless of birth and station, worth more than money and defines that body within a system of values that cannot be translated into economic value per se. Richardson's heroines embody a contrary principle of economy that is founded on the sexual contract or gender relations and that is to be understood as distinct and apart from the social contract or relations among social groups. The female in this exchange is thus constituted as a form of resistance, or "will," which poses an alternative moral economy to that of the dominant class.

Her power *not* to consent redefines the nature of the contract between man and woman as it had been represented by a Puritan tradition, according to which a woman voluntarily entered into master-servant relationship when she consented to marriage. Rather than enter into a sexual contract that replicates the economic contract of master and servant, Pamela holds out for an exchange between parties whose difference is determined only by gender. Ironically enough, in making a romance that sought to unite the extremes of the social hierarchy, Richardson had to erase virtually all socioeconomic markings before the male and female could enter into an exchange. What chance did Richardson have of over-throwing the centuries-old notion of contractual relations that bound one to submit to those of superior rank? Fielding thought Pamela's resistance silly; a man of Mr. B's station would never have been willing to "risk his reputation" (as Mr. B himself explains in the contract quoted above) in order to enjoy such a woman's sexual favors. But simply by intro-ducing the figure of the female with a capacity to say "no" and then providing a basis on which she could find such refusal advantageous, Richardson overthrew the longstanding tradition of thinking about court-ship and kinship relations. Fielding as much as conceded this point when he drew upon these strategies to write fiction that sought to expose Rich-ardson's total misrepresentation of political circumstances. It should be understood that I am using Richardson's name in a strictly rhetorical sense when I say this, for of course Pamela's "no" would have meant very little had she not been speaking with the voice of thousands who by then knew the conduct-book philosophy of reading. Nor, for that matter, would her denial have reverberated through time had it not addressed millions who came to understand themselves as basically the same kind of indi-vidual first described in these female conduct books.

The effect of inserting Pamela's written presence into Mr. B's text as if she were equal to the dominant class is the effect of supplementation. Paired with the words of her master, her response displaces the master-servant relationship onto a battle between the sexes, where the value of the politically subordinate party arises from an alternative source, her gender, rather than from her place in a political hierarchy. While Mr. B offers money in exchange for her body, she maintains that her real value does not derive from her body; she is not, in other words, currency in a system of exchange among men. Saying this, as Pamela does on more than one occasion, only raises the question of why, if Richardson meant to locate value in a site other than the woman's material body, did he produce a long and unremitting tale of seduction. Pamela insists that her identity depends on her sexual purity, for in her words, "to rob a person of her virtue is worse than cutting her throat" (p. 111). If the male's forcible penetration of her body assaults the very life of the non-aristo-cratic woman herself, then the master's exercise of his power over the bodies of those within his household amounts to murder. It destroys their value. Thus with a stroke Richardson forces his reader to condemn the political system that authorizes the exercise of such power.

By rewriting the female body in this fashion, Richardson overturned the basis on which political relationships were understood as natural and right. Whether he meant to do this or not, it is clear that his tale of seduction participates in a much larger cultural project. Pamela fights to possess her body in a world where the necessity of doing so is a minority view. Over and against her claim that sexual penetration of the body is tantamount to murder, Mrs. Jewkes, Pamela's custodian, delivers the verdict of common sense—"how strangely you talk!"—and then proceeds to put her charge through a catechism concerning the laws of sexuality: "Are not the two sexes made for one another? And is it not natural for a gentleman to love a pretty woman? And suppose he can obtain his desires, is that so bad as cutting her throat?" (p. 111). If we turn to one of the two central scenes in the novel where Mr. B succeeds in gaining control over Pamela's body, it soon becomes clear that even without much of a struggle Pamela's own definition of her body triumphs over his common sense. To the woman he has pinned naked on her bed beneath him, Mr. B delivers these lines: "You see now you are in my power!—You cannot get from me, nor help yourself" (p. 213). Rather than possess her in this violent manner, however, he would prefer to release her unmolested upon her consent to exchange her body for money. At the very moment when the terms of that contract seem impossible for the woman to refuse—when it means her submission by force if not by consent— Richardson suddenly changes the terms of sexual relations in the novel. That is, he changes what it is the male must possess in order to possess the woman, for it is not a creature of flesh and blood that Mr. B encounters in the body naked and supine upon the bed, but a proliferation of female words and feelings.

Pamela successfully resists Mr. B's attempts to exercise traditional forms of power—money and force—because she possesses herself through the exertions of her own emotions. She swoons. She returns to consciousness to hear her assailant vow "that he had not offered the least indecency; that he was frightened at the terrible manner I was taken with the fit; that he should desist from his attempt, and begged but to see me easy and quiet, and he would leave me directly, and go to his own bed" (p. 213). Thus Richardson stages a scene of rape that transforms an erotic and permeable body into a self-enclosed body of words. Mr. B's repeated failures suggest that Pamela cannot be raped because she is nothing but words. As such, she demonstrates the productive power of the trope of the contract. Presuming to rescue the pure and original Pamela, Richardson creates a distinction between the Pamela Mr. B desires and the female who exists prior to becoming this object of desire and who can therefore claim the right of first property to herself. By means of a curious splitting of the female, Richardson represents the two of them—male and female—struggling for possession of Pamela: "He came up to me, and took

me by the hand, and said, Whose pretty maiden are you?—I dare say
you are Pamela's *sister*, you are so like her. So neat, so clean, so pretty!
. . . I would not be so free with your sister, you may believe; but I must
kiss *you."* In characteristically Richardsonian style, the splitting that occurs whenever Mr. B tries to possess Pamela has a doubling effect by
producing a subject who can claim possession of herself as an object. "O
sir," she replies, "I am Pamela, indeed I am: indeed I am Pamela, *her
own self"* (p. 53). As it provides occasion for her to resist Mr. B's attempts to possess her body, seduction becomes the means to dislocate
female identity from the body and to define it as a metaphysical object.

Significantly, Pamela's transformation from an object of desire into a
female sensibility also transforms Mr. B. He once desired only the surface of her body and found her resistance annoyingly "saucy" and "pert."
After the rape scene, however, Mr. B comes full circle to desire the same
female qualities that formerly obstructed his advances. His assessment of
these qualities reveals how Richardson uses the figure of sexual exchange
to produce a modern concept of gender:

> You have a good deal of wit, a great deal of penetration, much beyond
> your *years*, and, as I thought, your *opportunities.* You are possessed of
> an open, frank, and generous mind; and a person so lovely, that you excel
> all your sex, in my eyes. All these accomplishments have engaged my
> affection so deeply, that, as I have often said, I cannot live without you;
> and I would divide, with all my soul, my estate with you, to make you
> mine upon my own terms. These you have absolutely rejected; and that,
> though in saucy terms enough, yet in such a manner as makes me admire
> you the more. . . . And I see you so watchful over your virtue, that though
> I hoped to find it otherwise, I cannot but confess my passion for you is
> increased by it. But now, what shall I say farther, Pamela?—I will make
> you, though a party, my adviser in this matter, though not, perhaps, my
> definitive judge. (p. 223)

Even though Mr. B still lacks the language to rationalize marrying someone of a position so far beneath him, a language which Pamela's letters
will eventually supply, the contract has nevertheless done its work effectively.

If we compare this statement to the dialogue between male and female
that Richardson pairs off to dramatize their contractual negotiations, we
find that the dialogue takes on a dialectical force. Even as it dramatizes
the failure of the male party to effect an exchange in economic and political terms, Mr. B's ridiculously protracted seduction of an otherwise
unnoteworthy servant girl redefines the two parties of the contract. At
this moment, Richardson creates the possibility for an exchange that vi-

olates neither the integrity of the female body nor the conditions of female subjectivity. Theirs can no longer be understood as an exchange of his money for erotic pleasure once Mr. B acquires all the qualities of the prosperous male who—as the conduct books promise—desires nothing so much as the female accomplishments that conduct books describe in glowing terms. Upon his transformation, Mr. B enjoys an entirely different form of pleasure from Pamela than he formerly sought: "Said he, I hope my present temper will hold; for I tell you frankly, that I have known in this agreeable hour, more *sincere pleasure* than I have experienced in all the guilty tumults that my desiring soul compelled me into, in the hopes of possessing you in my own terms" (p. 229, italics mine). Now seemingly heedless of his "reputation," or of the violations of his class codes that he might be committing by privileging the abstract virtues of his maid, Mr. B understands the benefits he reaps from his relationship with Pamela in terms that must have sounded a familiar economic note:

> My beloved wants no language, nor sentiments neither; and her charming thoughts, so sweetly expressed, would *grace* any language; and this is a *blessing* almost peculiar to my fairest.—Your so kind acceptance, my Pamela, added he, *repays* the *benefit* with *interest* and leaves me under *obligation* to your *goodness*. (p. 387, italics mine)

Although the dominant discourse now encompasses that of the female, it has been thoroughly infiltrated by a terminology that is utterly hostile to an earlier model of exchange. Accordingly, one finds the terms of Christian theology ("grace," "blessing") mingled with those of nascent capitalism ("benefit," "interest") to form a distinctively modern discourse of sexuality.

It is important to see that what happens in this novel could never happen in a conduct book, much as the two kinds of writing shared a single strategic intention. To be sure, *Pamela* carried on the same struggle to define the female that was being waged wherever writing invoked the need for female education and for the reform of sexual practices. Represented as the struggle between a master and his female servant, *Pamela* contained this struggle first within the household and then within the writing that transformed Pamela herself into a distinctively female form of subjectivity. The differentiation and enclosure of a female self was nothing short of a victory for the modern self over the political system that was authorized by a household which a male governed and sustained by his patronage. If a servant girl could claim possession of herself as her own first property, then virtually any individual must similarly have a self to withhold or give in a modern form of exchange with the state. We know Pamela has such a self only because she acquires the power to withhold it. *Pamela* can dramatize, as no other kind of writing can, the triumph of this sexual self over traditional forms of political identity because the novel arose out of the struggle between modes of writing to define sexuality. To put it quite crudely, this novel is a struggle in which one fiction captures and translates the other into its terms. More than likely, the writing of normal sexuality did not proceed with the intention of dismantling the hierarchical world, or it would not have concentrated so much effort on the female. Nevertheless, Richardson's strategy of enclosing subjectivity and then endowing it with power in its own right was also an aggressive act of reclassification; it was the means by which all manner of political information could be turned into features of gender.

This political dimension to Richardson's sexual theme constantly threatens to overturn the psychological hermeneutics of Pamela's writing and to place the text among the common sort of novels and romances. Against the threat of semiotic inversion, Richardson marshalled not only all manner of extratextual precautions, but also—and more importantly from a historical perspective—the strategies conduct books had devised in their own effort to control meaning. Such strategies shift the struggle for meaning from the level of political force to that of language. *Pamela* reminds us at every turn that we are witnessing a process of writing. Even as she records her emotional responses to a world governed by an unscrupulous man, Pamela worries that the daily record will turn out to be a romance. Mr. B tells her they are making "a pretty story in a romance" (p. 26), and she discovers that his plots have the power to turn her record into "horrid romancing" despite all her attempts to evade them. When he finally hands her the authority to author their history, she exclaims, "my story would furnish out a surprising kind of novel if it was to be well told" (p. 258). It is fair to say the act of writing becomes so obtrusive that the purity of her language seems to matter more than that of her body.

On her language alone depends the power of her resistance. As she puts it, "How then, sir, can I act but by shewing my abhorrence of every step that makes towards my undoing? And what is left me but words?" (p. 220). "Words" are indeed all Pamela has to exert against the coercion of rank and a large fortune, but her "words" prove the more powerful for being the only power she has. The more Mr. B persists in his attempts to possess her, the more he subjects his behavior to Pamela's view, and the deeper she penetrates into the heart of the dominant culture to appropriate its material as the stuff of her own subjectivity. Even before her letters are publicly aired and authorized, Richardson grants them a reformist power that is actually the power to form desire. Mr. B feels compelled to censor the letters lest they damage his reputation, but by confiscating them, he has not really escaped the classificatory power of Pamela's pen. Quite the contrary, he finds himself taken up within and converted to her mode of narration.

It is no ordinary moment in political history when a male novelist imagines a woman whose writing has power to reform the male of the dominant class. Surely, if this had been an ordinary novel, the scene where Richardson situates Mr. B astride Pamela's naked body would qualify as the most erotic scene in a narrative made of his fruitless efforts at surmounting her discourse. But this is hardly the case; Mr. B's attempt to seize pleasure from her body only engenders fear on his part as well as on hers. When he reads Pamela's letters, on the other hand, such male aggression suddenly achieves its traditional objective and gratifies sexual desire. Although he could not penetrate her body, Mr. B has Richardson's permission to pry at will into the secrets of her written self, to spy on her every act of writing, to intercept her letters, and finally to force her to divulge the whereabouts of even more writing. Strange to say, by far the most and perhaps the only genuinely erotic scene in the novel occurs when Mr. B takes possession of a thoroughly self-inscribed Pamela.[40] It is as if, having displaced the conventionally desirable female onto a written one, Richardson at last allows novelistic convention to have its way with this woman:

> Artful slut! said he, What's this to my question?—Are they [Pamela's letters] not *about* you?—If, said I, I must pluck them out of my hiding-place behind the wainscot, won't you see me?—Still more and more artful! said he—Is this an answer to my question?—I have searched every place above, and in your closet, for them, and cannot find them; so I *will* know where they are. Now, said he, it is my opinion they are about you; and I never undressed a girl in my life; but I will now begin to strip my pretty Pamela; and I hope I shall not go far before I find them. (p. 245)

Only by so deflecting eroticism away from the material body and onto writing could Richardson develop procedures for reforming libertine desire. He represented this change as a process of reading.

Such reading provided a new object of pleasure that was supposed to redirect male desire away from the surface of the female body and into its depths. When Mr. B finally removes her dress, he no longer finds an erotic body to be possessed at all, but a body of sentiments having no reality other than words. Pamela's writing, Mr. B admits at last, "has made me desirous of reading all you write; though a great deal of it is against myself" (p. 242). The letters about Pamela's body not only succeed in transforming that body into a body of words, they also offer Mr. B a self that has been represented and evaluated in feminine terms, a purely sexual and psychological phenomenon that challenges the codes of his class. To her he surrenders mastery over sexual relations, which he then allows to dominate the rest of the novel: "There is such a pretty air of romance as you relate them, in your plots, and my plots, that I shall be better directed in what manner to wind up the catastrophe of the pretty novel" (p. 242). Along with the authority to write their story, he hands the regulation of the household over to her, and the novel becomes little more than the conduct book it has passed through so much peril to resemble.

By representing relationships within the traditional country house as a struggle between competing interest groups, Richardson challenged the dominant cultural ideal. By casting this struggle as a sexual relationship, he concealed the politics of such representation. This may, as a number of readers have claimed, be attributed to his personal ambivalence both toward those of higher station in eighteenth century society and toward women.[41] But what retrospectively appears as ambivalence can, I believe, be better explained as the artfulness of the middle-class intellectual reworking certain cultural materials to aim desire away from the aristocratic body and into a world of private gratification that anyone by implication could enjoy. Richardson indicates a more acute consciousness of the politics of writing than we are usually willing to grant someone of his unsubtle psychological understanding. At crucial instances throughout his narrative, he takes pains to connect the struggle over writing, the struggle to control interpretation, with the struggle for political power. I have already referred to the way in which he has Pamela reject Mr. B's generous offer of an economic contract, and I have explained how the narrative of seduction enables Richardson to produce female subjectivity as a form of resistance. But he also uses turns of phrase that openly acknowledge the political dimension of sexual conflict. Mr. B says of Pamela, for example, "the artful *creature* is enough to corrupt a nation by her seeming innocence and simplicity" (p. 169). Because the point is to do away with political categories, however, this potential for interpreting Pamela's behavior as subversion is there chiefly to be contained and transformed within her letters. The language of power must be ever present as an interpretive possibility if Richardson is to dramatize Mr. B's conversion to Pamela's sentimentality.

To understand all the fuss he makes over the morality of fiction—and whether he is writing a novel or not—it is necessary to understand Richardson's writing as a material reality in its own right. He says as much when he wraps Pamela in her letters, replacing the surface of her body with the depths of her private feelings in a scene that reveals the new— and true—object of Mr. B's desire. Cast in this light as quite literally a struggle between two kinds of self-representation, the Richardsonian text is not *about* a struggle between opposing political groups that achieves mediation in and through writing so much as it is a struggle for control of the very terms in which political conflict will be understood and mediation accomplished. This novel concludes not with a marriage of families or fortunes, but with a message that conjoins different modes of subjectivity to produce the gender-divided world of the conduct books. In triumphing over the other languages of the novel, personal letter writing successfully removes domestic relations from all economic and political considerations as it subjects such relations to a woman's moral scrutiny and emotional response.

That this panoptical conception of authority is the same one Bentham would later represent as a political theory is clear. *Pamela* offers a narrative in which the work of the pen is rivaled only by that of the eyes. In fact, it is fair to say that while Pamela is imprisoned on Mr. B's estate the assaults on her body seem neither so frequent nor so perverse as the "watchments" she has to endure. It is to establish the power of observation as superior to that of either money or force that Richardson suddenly breaks into the narrative he has entrusted to Pamela on every other occasion:

> Here it is necessary, the reader should know, that the fair Pamela's trials were not yet over; but the worst were to come, at a time when she thought them at an end; and that she was returning to her father: for when her master found her virtue was not to be subdued, and he had in vain tried to conquer his passion for her, being a gentleman of pleasure and intrigue, he had ordered his Lincolnshire coachman to bring his travelling chariot from thence, . . . he drove her five miles on the way to her father's; and then turning off, crossed the country, and carried her onwards toward his Lincolnshire estate. (p. 91)

If this seems an awkward shifting of rhetorical gears, it is because the change in the direction of Mr. B's coach does indeed effect an abrupt shift in the form of political power that has, up to this point in the narrative, dominated sexual relations. Why else invent another country house if not to have a country house organized according to a new set of rules? In the Lincolnshire estate, Mr. B is significantly invisible in person, but he is omnipresent in the form of vigilant surrogates who do little else but watch Pamela's every move and intercept most of her letters. Pamela, in other words, becomes an object of knowledge. Where he once spied on her undressing from the vantage point of her closet, Mr. B now possesses the means of insinuating himself into the most private recesses of her emotions through reports on her every word and gesture, as well as through the record of her emotional experience contained in her letters. Her isolation and a rigid form of censorship that all but prohibits communication create greater anguish than even the threat of physical assault. For the Lincolnshire estate is represented as a grimly gothic version of the first manor house, replacing, for example, the benign Mrs. Jervis with the malevolent Jewkes and the paternal coachman John with the demonic Colbrand who owes loyalty only to his master. This nightmarish version of the country house leaves no doubt that the threat of self-annihilation intensifies as the assault on Pamela's body becomes more a matter of ocular rape than of physical penetration. Such a shift in the strategy of sexual violation to the violation of psychological depths provides a strategy for discovering more depths within the female to write about, thereby producing more words by which to displace her body.

Pamela wins the struggle to interpret both herself and all domestic relations from the moment the coach swerves off the road to her father's house and delivers her at Mr. B's Lincolnshire estate. The power dominating at the estate is already female power. It is the power of domestic surveillance. The reader of conduct books knows, furthermore, that Mrs. Jewkes will not successfully manage the household because she has "a huge hand, and an arm as thick as my waist," "a hoarse, man-like voice," and many other masculine features (p. 116). The manor house displays a need, the satisfaction of which requires turning the house into the one represented in conduct books. I am not suggesting that having a mannish woman in charge is what makes the house so different. Rather, the difference lies in the fact that sexuality in this household bears little resemblance to the kind of transaction enabled by the other estate. Lincolnshire does not dramatize a bawdy bedroom comedy ruled by desire that aims to possess the female body; it dramatizes instead the operations of female subjectivity. Such a place establishes essentially the same structure of power as the eighteenth century medical theater where anatomies were performed before an audience. In this characteristically modern theater, as at Lincolnshire, power did not reside in the object of the gaze, whose model and emblem was the docile body of the cadaver undergoing dissection. Instead, it operated through the eye of an observer who discovered truth beneath the surface of that body. This, I have been arguing, was the form of power that would sweep aside an earlier form that inhered in the aristocratic body and depended on that body's power to hold the gaze of the people.

At Lincolnshire, Pamela is released from her servile position as a domestic laborer to spend her hours doing little else but telling a story that resembles an instruction book in how to write the feminine emotions. Mr. B has situated her where she can be observed. Because she spends her time not only observing but also representing herself and others, however, it is here that she seizes the power of surveillance as her own. In other words, as soon as the assault on her body has settled into this form of voyeurism, then her victory over such oppression requires only a shift in the direction and dynamics of gazing.[42] This is the function of Pamela's kind of writing. It turns the gaze back upon itself as a critical mirror of power to establish much the same relationship that Richardson himself establishes with "other" fiction. As Mr. B reads her letters aloud to her parents and to his neighbors and sister, he makes public the knowledge she intended to keep strictly between herself and her parents. As he speaks her writing, then, his speech incorporates its own critique—a form of resistance to his codes of social identity. By reading her private communication, then, he internalizes her moral authority, her conscience becomes his, his speech is indistinguishable from her writing, and she has achieved a form of power over him. Every time Mr. B reads one of her letters, he exposes both her innermost thoughts and the innermost secrets of the country house under his supervision. Her letters display her capability for self-regulation and his corresponding need for her supervision. As writing displaces the exercise of force with the force of surveillance, in other words, it also shifts the power of the gaze from the male to the female. The ideal conditions as specified by Pamela in her objection to Mr. B's initial offer of a contract are therefore met. They marry.

Having ensured the power of her gaze through writing, Pamela grows tired, she says, "of their gazing" and retires from public view into the objects and activities of the household under her control (p. 299). And after the marriage is solemnized, events come to the reader as a "journal of all that passes in these first stages of my happiness" (p. 475). Who does not question Richardson's wisdom in furnishing us with almost two hundred pages of this account? All narrative conflict dissolves into catalogues of household duties and lists of do's and do not's for prospective housewives; several of these passages in the novel could have been taken directly from any one of a number of conduct books. As she takes over the text, furthermore, Pamela's writing waxes suddenly stuffy, static, and both patronizing and obsequious, displaying all those qualities, in short, that made conduct books themselves seem so empty and tedious to read once their historical moment had passed. No longer a form of resistance, in other words, the female voice flattens into that of pure ideology. From a historical perspective, however, it makes perfect sense that Richardson should feel compelled to transform his first work of fiction into such a static paradigm. The principle of reading that governed programs for female education also provided him with procedures for rewriting the country house in opposition to an aristocratic tradition of letters.

It is well worth noting how such a reordering of the household uses certain features of the aristocratic country house in order to render the existing mode of kinship relations obsolete. One might remark that Mr. B himself renounces the desire he once found perfectly appropriate for a master to hold for a servant girl, and he does so in terms that put such desire in the past: "O how heartily I despise all my former pursuits, and headstrong appetites! What joys, what true joys, flow from virtuous love! joys which the narrow soul of the libertine cannot take in, nor his thoughts conceive! and which I myself, whilst a libertine, had not the least notion of!" (p. 379). The "joys" of which he speaks have little to do with the pleasures of the flesh as the bedroom that formerly provided a setting for narrative events disappears entirely from the printed page as it comes to occupy a blank space between two of Pamela's journal entries. The more expansive joys to which Mr. B refers are diffused throughout the household as its time and space are reorganized under Pamela's supervision.

Before Pamela assumes control of the household, its organization resembles nothing so much as a paranoid conspiracy. For as Pamela's writing exposes the secrets of life within the aristocratic household, Richardson turns the place into a theater for sexual intrigue. Household personnel are bound only by the principle of satisfying their master's desire. Time as well as space and human labor are devoted to serving this single end. According to the emergent domestic doctrine, however, this principle of order actually produces disorder. As Pamela observes:

> By this we may see . . . of what force example is, and what is in the power of the heads of families to do: And this shews, that evil examples, in superiors, are doubly pernicious, and doubly culpable, because such persons are bad *themselves*, and not only do no good, but much *harm* to others. (pp. 399–400)

When Pamela becomes mistress of the household, on the other hand, the servants are ruled by her moral example rather than by the sheer force of political loyalty and economic power. Because a well-regulated household depends entirely on the moral qualities of the female in charge, it cannot succumb to the double tyranny of male desire and aristocratic whim. As Pamela describes the relationship between the order of the household and her own qualities of mind, they are clearly one and the same:

In short, I will endeavor, as much as I can, that good servants shall find
in me a kind encourager; indifferent ones be made better, by inspiring them
with a laudable emulation; and bad ones, if not too bad in nature, and quite
reclaimable, reformed by kindness, expostulation, and even proper men-
aces, if necessary; but most by a good example. (p. 350)

Those who have defended her honor fall into the first category; those who
have not fall into the third, and nary a one, not even the odious Mrs.
Jewkes, proves to be beyond the power of Pamela's redemptive example.
With this, the place ceases to operate in the manner of a paranoid conspiracy and readily converts to rational order.

Several strategies of this order deserve our attention. These strategies
develop out of the narrative combat between modes of writing. They constitute a process of feminization that the conduct books, by virtue of their
exclusive focus on female matters, do not have to put into force. These
are strategies, in other words, that reorganize the manor house according
to the principles of domestic economy discussed in the previous chapter.
Now a proselytizer of domestic virtue himself, Mr. B explains the reforms that must be effected in a country house such as his. Of women
to the manor born, he says, "they generally act in such a manner, as if
they seemed to think it the privilege of birth and fortune, to turn day into
night, and night into day, and are seldom stirring till it is time to sit down
to dinner; and so all the good old family rules are reversed" (p. 389).
Thus to the woman of his own caste he attributes habits that disrupt the
natural order of things; to the modern woman, on the other hand, he
grants the power to restore order by inverting the patterns established by
the idleness and amusement of the aristocratic woman. Even though it is
no longer permissible for Pamela to labor, her hours are now more rigidly
regulated than before, the principle being that, as Mr. B explains, "man
is as frail a piece of machinery as any clock-work whatever; and, by
irregularity, is as subject to be disordered" (p. 390). Indeed each hour of
the day well into the evening is accounted for mostly in this way: "You
will then have several useful hours more to employ yourself in, as you
shall best like; and I would generally go to supper by eight" (pp. 389–
90). This dramatizes nothing else so much as the total reorganization of
leisure time toward which the conduct books also aspired.

Curiously enough, such reorganization is accomplished in the name of
the old aristocratic ideal of hospitality. If Pamela keeps to a routine, Mr.
B explains, then "whomsoever I bring home with me to my table, you'll
be in readiness to receive them; and will not want to make those foolish
apologies to unexpected visitors, that carry with them reflection on the
conduct of those who make them" (p. 389). The well-ordered house will,

in short, be the more able to extend the tradition of hospitality to any and all who require it. But the failure to extend hospitality, we should note, does not point to a man's lack of position and wealth so much as to his wife's lack of domestic virtue; such lapses "carry with them reflection on the conduct of those who make them." The same principle dictates Pamela's appearance. She is not to display herself for guests, but always to exhibit "that sweet ease in your dress or behavior, which you are so happy mistress of" (p. 389). What most clearly distinguishes Mr. B's dress code from that issued by royal proclamation during the Renaissance is the careful attention to facial expression, for there the true qualities of the woman, as opposed to her rank, may be noted.

> I expect from you, whoever comes to my house, that you accustom your-self to one even, uniform complaisance: That no frown take place on your brow: That however ill or well provided we may be for their reception, you shew no flutter or discomposure: That whomever you may have in your company at the time, you signify not, by the least reserved look, that the stranger is come upon you unseasonably, or at a time you wished he had not. But be facetious, kind, obliging to all; and, if to one more than another, to such as have the least reason to expect it from you, or who are most inferior at the table; for thus will you, my Pamela, cheer the doubting mind, quiet the uneasy heart, and diffuse ease, pleasure, and tranquillity, around my board. (p. 393)

Richardson's notion of largesse does not dispense with the aristocratic figure of hospitality, that is, the generous patron's table. But its content has indeed been modified along with the woman who oversees the table. To those who congregate around the table, the modern patron yields up copious sentiments rather than either the fruits of his bountiful estate or the wealth of his ample purse. In this way, Richardson transforms the patron's table from a setting that displays traditionally masculine forms of power into a therapeutic setting whose riches are distributed on a purely psychological level—through displays of militant cheerfulness. He accomplishes this simply by transforming Pamela's passive and essentially defensive virtues from nouns into verbs that "*cheer* the doubting mind, *quiet* the uneasy heart, and *diffuse ease, pleasure, and tranquillity*, around my board" (italics mine).

In virtually doing away with traditional patronage rites as the means of distributing wealth, Richardson creates a compensatory form of generosity. His notion of charity filters the economic power of the male through the sympathy of the female, and the excesses of his estate become the overflowing of her heart and trickle down in this form to needy people lower down the social ladder. Thus Pamela enjoins Mr. B to look through your poor acquaintances and neighbours, and let me have a list of such honest industrious poor, as may be true objects of charity, and have no other assistance; particularly such as are blind, lame, or sickly, with their several cases; and also such poor families and housekeepers as are reduced by misfortunes, as ours was, and where a great number of children may keep them from rising to a state of tolerable comfort: And I will choose as well as I can; for I long to be making a beginning, with the kind quarterly benevolence my dear good benefactor has bestowed upon me for such good purposes. (pp. 500–501)

We should note how Pamela defines the whole category of who should benefit from wealth that has been diverted from a patronage system into one based on the principle of charity. Only those deserve attention who are unable to provide a subsistence living for themselves, and this mobility must be due to some deficiency in themselves rather than in the conditions under which they must labor. Before they become objects of charity, these people must be listed on a case by case basis, the reason for their poverty so designated, and the amount of money distributed accordingly. This is to say that Richardson represents those who depend on the generosity of the wealthy not as a social group or faction that must be appeased, but as reckless children who require the care of responsible parents. Such a view of the distribution of wealth can make sense only if Richardson detaches the wealth from its source in inherited property, profession, and region. To do so, he again takes a page from the conduct books. To remove the wealth of the estate from the patronage system and distribute it according to the principle of charity, he has the male hand over part of his money to the female. As Mr. B explains,

God has blessed me with a very good estate, and all of it in a prosperous condition, and generally well tenanted. I lay up money every year, and have, besides, large sums in government and other securities; so that you will find, what I have hitherto promised, is very short of that proportion of my substance, which, as my dearest wife, you have a right to. (p. 387)

By means of these propositions that Mr. B offers Pamela, Richardson constructs a domestic economy that appears to be independent of the political categories maintained by an earlier patronage system.

I call attention to this economic exchange in order to demonstrate how Richardson's first novel revises the sexual contract. In addition to Mr. B's specifications for what he expects in a wife, this offer constitutes his own revision of the contract originally offered to and rejected by Pamela. As he explains in making these demands, "All that I wish, is to find my proposals agreeable to you; and if my *first* are not, my *second* shall be, if I can know what you want" (p. 386). In the course of negotiating the ideal relationship to which both parties can fully consent, Mr. B makes all the same offers that he put forth in the first contract and that would have made her his mistress. If anything, the first contract was more lucrative for Pamela than the second. We must conclude that Pamela's resistance to the first contract—resistance prompted by nothing short of the need, she implies, to preserve her very existence—was aimed only at revising the nature of the sexual contract. If Pamela is the first to find fault with the spirit in which his first proposal was made, then Mr. B is the first to explain where the source of its error lies: "We people of fortune, or such as are born to large expectations, of both sexes, are generally educated wrong." This is one of the lessons, he acknowledges, that may be gleaned from Pamela's journal: "We are so headstrong, so violent in our wills, that we very little bear control" (p. 470).

With their desires so little constrained, any relationship between a man and woman so poorly educated would be no less tempestuous than each of the parties is in and of itself. When, Mr. B continues,

> a *wife* is looked out for: convenience, or birth, or fortune, are the first motives, affection the last (if it is at all consulted): and two people thus educated, thus trained up, in a course of unnatural gratitude, and who have been headstrong torments to every one who has had a share in their education, as well as to those to whom they owe their being, are brought together; and what can be expected, but that they should pursue, and carry on, the same comfortable conduct in matrimony, and join most heartily to plague one another? (p. 471)

Given that Mr. B's second proposal resembles his first offer to Pamela, it transforms that first attempt at sexual relations between master and servant—the proposed exchange of money for pleasure—into a model for legitimate monogamy that criticizes the traditional marriage of "convenience." We see the modern notion of love emerging in the statement above, as Richardson makes "convenience," "birth," and "fortune" equivalent and puts them in a category that excludes "affection." Affection cannot coexist, this novel argues, with an economic motive for marriage, and neither fortune nor birth can therefore constitute particularly desirable features in a woman, even though they remain unqualified as such in a man. As Mr. B explains, the exchange between male and female is not primarily an economic one:

> I have ample possessions for us both; and you deserve to share them with me; and you shall do it, with as little reserve, as if you had brought me what the world reckons an equivalent: for, as to my own opinion, you

bring me what is infinitely more valuable, an experienced truth, a well-tried virtue, and a wit and behaviour more than equal to the state you will be placed in. (p. 355)

Here the exchange is one between gendered parties—a wedding of her moral authority to his particular economic practices and social place. Together they compose the same domestic world that conduct books were also intent upon making attractive to their readership.

The key to the success of this model resides in the fact that while it requires the female to submit to the male, it does not ask her to adopt the practices of the dominant class. Pamela's adamant refusal to accept the conditions of Mr. B's first offer of a contract establishes this difference, for her submission to the second proposal is as complete as her rejection of the first. The point is to distinguish the unnatural submission of a household servant to her master in an erotic adventure from the natural subordination of female to male in an ideal marriage. While it is good to obey a kind husband, it is no longer acceptable to gratify the libertine desires associated with the old aristocracy. Although the reformed country house is one where a rigid hierarchy has been restored, this principle of hierarchy opposes that which organizes the political world outside. Domestic order is not based on one's relative socioeconomic position so much as on moral qualities of mind. This principle enters into the household through the female and reforms that household by means of her writing. As if the reader did not understand the difference between the two contracts, or how the second one reorganized the whole concept of the domestic domain to situate a woman at its center, Richardson recapitulates this logic of the figure in the encounter between Pamela and Mr. B's sister, Lady Davers.

Lady Davers speaks for an archaic contract that, according to Mr. B, constitutes an economic and political alliance rather than a bond of affection. She feels that the family name has been tarnished by Pamela's claim that Mr. B did not simply take her to bed but actually married his servant. Of Mr. B's letter testifying to this marriage, Lady Davers tells Pamela, "you shewed it me, to upbraid me with his stooping to such painted dirt, to the disgrace of a family, ancient and untainted beyond most in the kingdom" (p. 417). To convince her that Pamela is not only Mr. B's wife but also the more desirable woman for a man of his station to marry requires nothing short of converting Lady Davers to a way of thinking that contradicts her own interests and very nature as a woman of the ruling class. This is something that does not take place within the pages of the novel but at some later time when Lady Davers has read

Pamela's journal. Even while testifying to the recalcitrance of this kind of woman, however, Richardson still has her acknowledge Pamela's superiority by acceding to the terms of Pamela's sentimental writing. Of her successor's entry into polite society, Lady Davers simply says, "I shall not give you my company when you make your appearance. Let your own merit make all your Bedfordshire neighbours your friends, as it has done here, by your Lincolnshire ones; and you'll have no need of my countenance, nor any body else's" (p. 466).

It is important to note that such an acknowledgment of Pamela's moral authority leaves the old categories untouched when determining the status of the male. For the acknowledgment suggests only that her possession of certain emotional qualities determines the status of the female. Even so, the change of heart on the part of Lady Davers as well as among the polite folk of Bedfordshire and Lincolnshire constitutes an important modification of prevailing kinship relations. The modification alone explains the novel's obsession with the nuances of female subjectivity. Such an obsession is demonstrated as well by the conduct books from which Richardson drew his strategies for replacing the reigning cultural ideal with another. When Lady Davers belligerently inquires where "can the difference be between a beggar's son married by a lady, or a beggar's daughter made a gentleman's wife," Mr. B provides a most concise description of the modification in which the entire body of feminine writing conspired: "Then I'll tell you, replied he; the difference is, a man ennobles the woman he takes, be she *who* she will; and adopts her into his *own* rank, be it *what* it will: but a woman, though ever so nobly born, debases herself by a mean marriage, and descends from her *own* rank to *his* she stoops to" (p. 447). This is the principle of hypergamy, or marriage "up," which both cuts the female off from the political power that might inhere in her by birth and, at the same time, enables the family to achieve higher status through her, should she marry into a higher social position. On Pamela's power to effect a marriage that moves her from the bottom of the social ladder to the top depends the conversion of the aristocracy and upper gentry to her domestic values, which is actually the formation of a new ruling class.

In addition to the other chunks of a cultural argument that for modern readers no longer needs to be waged, the last section of the novel contains several bizarre encounters between Pamela and the social world into which marriage has thrust her. As she relates to the company of polite society assembled at Lincolnshire how rudely Lady Davers had behaved towards her, the spirit of reform ripples outward in circles radiating from her center. After seeing Pamela's willing compliance to her husband's wishes, one lady allows "that it will be the interest of all the gentlemen to bring their ladies into an intimacy with one that can give them such a good example" (p. 301). But the gentlemen are also instructed by the example of her suffering; in the words of one, they "are resolved to turn over a new leaf with our wives, and *your* lord shall shew us the way" (p. 426). Furthermore, although contained within the relationship of husband and wife, reform is not without overt political ramifications. A game of cards at this gathering provides an unsubtle means of translating the change in sexual relations into political terms, and thus, one may note, a moral basis for domestic authority is extended into the realm of politics by way of thinly disguised allegory. Mr. B has this to say "in regard to the ace: . . . by the ace I have always thought the laws of the land denoted; and as the ace is above the king or queen, and wins them, I think the law should be thought so too." But this, Richardson hastens to add, does not make his reformed hero a Tory, for according to Pamela's master, "I think the distinction of *whig* and *tory* odious; and love the one or the other only as they are honest and worthy men; and never have (and never shall, hope) given a vote, but according to what I thought was for the public good, let either *whig* or *tory* propose it" (pp. 428–29). Although it has all the earmarks of offering up a mediation between contending social groups, then, the union of Pamela and Mr. B in fact does no such thing. Instead, their marriage calls into being a concept of political authority that is neither Tory nor Whig because it is other than both. Resting on the virtues of honesty and self-worth rather than on "honours," such power originates in the female from whom it spills over into the political world. This, we might say, is Richardson imagining the power of a new hegemony, which asserts the good of England in terms that somehow transcend those of social experience as he knew it to be. For his ability to imagine such an ideal political situation depends entirely on men forgetting traditional political categories and understanding all social relationships in domestic terms.

Far from making claims for this power unconsciously, Richardson seems highly aware of the politics of his rhetoric of reform. The last two hundred pages or so of his first novel indicate, if nothing else, that he is playing a sophisticated ideological game that repackages political resistance as the subjectivity of a woman. It does so in order to translate the political strategy of a decided minority into an effective rhetorical tactic. That he has this act of translation very much in mind is as clear as his revision of Mr. B's original offer of a contract to Pamela. In each case, Richardson makes the changes effected by Pamela as clear as the print on the page. Perhaps strangest of all the curious rites that he puts Pamela through in his apotheosis of the housewife is the dinner party that Mr. B stages with his friends and neighbors and the clergyman Williams. To entertain the company thus assembled, Mr. B has Williams read the "common translation" of the 137th Psalm a verse or two at a time. This is followed by Mr. B's reading of the same verses as translated in Pamela's letters. One verse, first from the Bible and then from Pamela's journal, offers a fair sample of her turn of phrase:

> IV.
> Alas! said we; who can once frame
> His heavy heart to sing
> The praises of our living God,
> Thus under a strange king?

> IV.
> Alas! said I, how can I frame
> My heavy heart to sing,
> Or tune my mind, while thus enthrall'd
> By such a wicked thing? (pp. 335–36)

If, at an earlier moment in history, the translation of the Bible into English transferred moral authority from the church to the state, then here was an equally significant shift in the structure of power in England. Pamela's verse translates the historical and political meaning of the "common translation" of a psalm into terms at once personal and universal. This is to mark symbolically a shift in moral authority from the male institutions of state to the head of household. Furthermore, although it is Mr. B who gives voice to the new language of morality, he must read Pamela's writing in order to do so. In contrast with the earlier Puritan, then, this head of household is authorized by a woman's writing rather than by the word of God. One might even go so far as to say that the Puritan revolution, which failed to seize political control through force as well as polemical writing, in fact succeeded in the eighteenth century sentimental fiction that delegates control to the female.

Such a shift in gender designates a change not only in the locus of political power but also—and just as profoundly—in its strategic target and procedures. The shift in Pamela's verse to the first-person pronoun transfers moral authority from a domestic framework to the framework of female subjectivity, which is surely to wrest such authority from the male institutions of church and state. This is not only to signal the birth of a new ideology whereby power arises from within the individual. It is also to suggest that such power operates by reconstituting the subject out of words. But to have such political power—as is also made clear by

Pamela's act of translation—words must conceal it. They must conceal all signs of operating in the name of a particular interest group and take on the features of the individual. They must work by an example that is at once highly personal, in other words, and yet applicable to virtually everyone. All this Richardson understood perfectly well, and if we deny him such knowledge, it is only because the tradition of literary criticism has not discovered what someone so ordinary as Richardson already knew by reading and writing during the period when this power was emerging but had not yet become the dominant form of social control.

The Self Contained: *Emma*

In turning from *Pamela* to *Emma*, we turn from the expansive and heavily littered domain that Richardson carves out of the culture to the clean line of Austen's minimalist art. Even though it conforms far more closely to what we consider "the art of the novel," however, Austen's fiction is no less political for achieving the self-enclosure that Richardson's writing lacks. It is clear that by Austen's time, the female subject could step forth as an object of knowledge. Unlike Richardson, who had to modify both fiction and conduct-book language to establish a category for domestic fiction, Austen was able to develop finely nuanced differences within a stable framework of domestic relations. Indeed, her novels bring to culmination a tradition of ladies fiction that concentrated on the finer points of conduct necessary to secure a good marriage—that is, on the minor indiscretions and good manners of respectable people—rather than on the will and cunning it took to preserve one's chastity from impending rape. Richardson used rape as the figure for an earlier class sexuality. He contained it within his fiction where rape identified a self that could not be violated. And by so doing, he used this woman to figure out a new form of political resistance. Writing that posits such a distinctively modern notion of the self—Pamela's own record of the assaults on her sensibility—spells out the historical dilemma Richardson confronted as well. His writing required the authorization of readers before it could lay claim to truth. As if this authorization were one of the rites sanctifying Pamela's marriage into the gentry, Richardson has her walk among her husband's polite circle of friends in the bizarre habit of a domestic saint. Bearing the letters that tell the tale of her perseverance under the domination of a libertine master, she seeks public recognition as such a figure. Without it, the implication is that her writing is nothing more than a record of subjective experience, a thinly veiled wish (as indeed Fielding saw it) rather than an example that one should use in negotiating reality. The woman is bound to her writing in a mutually authorizing relationship that awkwardly displays its circular nature in the concluding episodes of the novel.

Much to Fielding's dismay, however, Richardson successfully introduced into fiction the highly fictional proposition that a prosperous man desired nothing so much as the woman who embodied domestic virtue. By Austen's time, this proposition had acquired the status of truth. It had usurped the body of rules as invoked by Mrs. Jewkes when rebuking Pamela for denying the master's natural dominion over the body of his servant girl. On this basis, it is fair to say that a novel like *Pride and Prejudice* began where *Pamela* ended, historically speaking, by opening with "a truth universally acknowledged, that a single man, in possession of a good fortune, must be in want of a wife." In representing the "wife" as a category that wanted to be filled rather than as a category of desire yet to be opened, fiction by definition no longer opposed truth, nor did it have to perform elaborate rites of self-authorization. For Austen obviously wrote to an audience who willingly granted fiction the status of a specialized kind of truth. The key to such authority was self-enclosure. Like Burney and the other lady novelists, Austen appeared more than willing to leave the rest of the world alone and deal only with matters of courtship and marriage. While Richardson introduced conduct-book materials into the novel as a strategy of conversion, then, novels of manners settled on various strategies of containment. They did not appear to work from inside the household to produce a text capable of revolutionizing its context. But by distinguishing her polite English from the linguistic materials that she inherited from earlier novelists, Austen's fiction achieved the same political objective even more effectively than Richardson's did.

Her novels deal with a closed community of polite country people who tend to be undistinguished by either great fortune or title. In such a community, social relations appear to be virtually the same thing as domestic relations. The community can therefore be represented in terms of a household and of a relationship among households in much the same manner as the graphic representation of various households offered by *The Compleat Servant*, a book of domestic economy written around the same time Austen was writing *Emma*.[43] As in the conduct books, the problems to be confronted in the world Austen depicts all have to do with the management of leisure time. Austen invariably resolves these problems by marrying off the eligible members within that community, which is to fix them to a role within a household among households, thereby stabilizing the community. She does this, furthermore, according to rules that are at least as rigorous, by psychological standards, as were the matters of dowry and family connections in determining marriages of convenience. She developed an intricately precise language for sexual relationships from the speech and behavior of polite country gentlefolk and did so, we should note, during the same period when the great migration to the cities was occurring. Thus it is a curious twist of cultural history that such a language as hers would help to create a standard for polite English that would be shared by the newly empowered groups who read novels. Only this specialized language, it appears, could set their particular kind of literacy apart from those above and below them on the social ladder and, at the same time, identify the particular interests of this class of people with those of the entire society. If one grants that Richardson's novel established a new role for literacy to play in constituting the individual, then we must see Austen's novels striving to empower a new class of people— not powerful people, but normal people—whose ability to interpret human behavior qualifies them to regulate the conduct of daily life and reproduce their form of individuality in and through writing.

In a manner unique to Richardson and the lady novelists of the late eighteenth century, Austen used fiction to create a community free of all traces of the regional, religious, social, or factional dialects that marked other kinds of writing.[44] At the beginning of the eighteenth century, Raymond Williams explains, the educational institutions for men were a very mixed lot, more so perhaps than at any other single moment in history. At the higher secondary or university-level schools established by Nonconformists after the Restoration, says Williams, "the curriculum begins to take its modern shape, with the addition of mathematics, geography, modern languages, and crucially, the physical sciences."[45] Of the nine grammar schools, "seven of them boarding institutions," he continues, all "kept mainly to the traditional curriculum of the classics, and, while less socially exclusive than they were to become, tended on the whole to serve the aristocracy and the squirarchy, on a national basis."[46] In addition to these schools, the upper classes observed the practice of tutoring at home, which was often followed by the Grand Tour of the Continent. According to Brian Simon, it was the mark of a gentleman "not to acquire any specialist knowledge; the aim was rather, acquaintance with polite literature through study of the classics."[47] The endowed grammar schools apparently varied according to locality, those in the urban areas showing some broadening of the curriculum toward practical disciplines under the influence of men in business and trade. "Of the three old professions, the clergy was still mainly served by the universities, while law and medicine were chiefly outside of them. Of the new professions, particularly in science, engineering, and arts," Williams concludes, "a majority of entrants were training outside the university as were most of the merchants and manufacturers."[48] Despite the signs of an increasingly practical curriculum at many levels of instruction and in different locales, the education of the middle ranks of early modern society appears to have comprised an extraordinarily heterogeneous field of learning. But what might strike us as a veritable babble of writing styles was probably, to the historically attuned ear, something more on the order of a finely graduated hierarchy of specialized languages.

These men were as distinguished from those who had a polite education as they were from the illiterate masses. At the same time, however, their learning served to mark differences among them rather than to create a coherent social character. If, as Williams claims, the point of educational institutions is always to train "the members of a group to the 'social character' or 'pattern of culture' which is dominant in the group or by which the group lives," then only the aristocracy and squirarchy could be said to possess such a character.[49] Through the eighteenth century and well into the nineteenth, the rest of the male population were not only set apart from the privileged group by what they knew, spoke, and wrote. They were set apart from one another as well. The language one used would have instantly identified him as a member of the Church of England or a Nonconformist, a student of the classical tradition of education as opposed to the practical curricula, or as part of the elite group of people who used polite English rather than some non-prestige dialect.

Austen follows the path cut through this tangle of speech patterns and writing styles by the female conduct books. At the same time, it must be said that Austen carries the project of creating an alternative standard of polite writing one step further. If Richardson uses Pamela's writing to transform the speech patterns of her community, then Austen gives writing a basis in the speech of polite country people. Her own prose displaces the mix of styles that would have more accurately represented society at large. For hers is a speech community that shares proper nouns but that, curiously enough, appears to be confused as to their relative value and the relations that should obtain among them. Thus she produces a prose style capable of displaying endless individual variants within polite spoken English. By means of conversation and gossip as well as the personal letter, such writing assigns motives and feelings to social behavior and, in this way, creates a psychological basis for its meaning. Such a prose style distinguishes one member of the speech community from another. At the same time, it places one individual in relation to another in terms of subjective features that are understood by the community as a whole. If this is to found a community on little else but a common language of the self, then language itself acquires unprecedented stability as Austen uses it to point to qualities inherent in the individual rather than to the accidents of fortune and birth.[50] Thus Austen's novels equate the formation of the ideal community with the formation of a new polite standard for English.

While Austen's fiction participates with earlier domestic novels in a single cultural project, we must still distinguish her work from earlier fiction because of the degree to which she grounds her ideal community upon communication.[51] Austen's objective is not to dispute the hierarchical principle underlying the old society, but to redefine wealth and status as so many signs that must then be read and evaluated in terms of the more fundamental currency of language: how much and how accurately do they communicate?[52] One finds that the major events in her novels are all based on faulty communication: Colonel Tilney's misreading of Catherine Morland's prospects as an heiress and her misreading of him as a husband and father; Darcy's first as opposed to his second letter to Elizabeth Bennet; the dramatic entertainments at Mansfield Park; and a series of such set pieces that make questions of conduct in *Emma* almost exclusively questions of interpretation. Consider, for instance, Emma's portrait of Harriet Smith, her interpretation of Mr. Elton's charade and of letters written by the other eligible young men in the novel, the defense of her misinterpretations in the face of Knightley's criticism, and her recognition of her true feelings for him. The procedures for reading and writing extend beyond the page to the dance floor and parlor. They suggest that sexual relations are, before anything else, a linguistic contract. And inasmuch as the novel confines its theater of action within a framework where social relations are determined by sexual relations, the linguistic contract is a social contract as well.

Austen's fiction plays out the Richardsonian thematics in which a female discourse struggles with that of the male for the power to represent individual identity. The heroine once again posits a notion of identity that is founded on gender differences rather than on the political distinctions to which men adhere and on which they base their authority. But several changes have occurred between the publication of *Pamela* and the writing of *Emma*. The gap between master and servant has narrowed down considerably to an elite group of individuals who are neither aristocrats nor laborers, nor even of the mercantile and industrial classes. At the same time, a whole spectrum of fine distinctions has opened up within this politically limited field. Among these are traditional political markers that designate one's source of income, the prestige of an estate and family name, one's future prospects, and the external signs of polish and education a person of means happens to display. Such social markings invoke the late eighteenth century country gentry which the previous century of economic fluctuation had made an extremely heterogeneous group. In such a group, an individual's social identity was no doubt very difficult to read. But in Austen one finds this situation complicated further; traditional status signs have been detached from their referent in some chain of economic dependency by a local communication system—gossip—which automatically converts this information into the stuff of subjective experience. On the basis of this information, for example, Mr. Knightley can say, "'Elton is a very good sort of man, and a very respectable vicar of Highbury, but not at all likely to make an imprudent match. He knows the value of a good income as well as anybody. Elton may talk sentimentally, but he will act rationally.'"[53] Emma feels otherwise, and "more than a reasonable, becoming degree of prudence, she was very sure, did not belong to Mr. Elton" (p. 45).

Thus we see that—along with the social gap between male and female contenders—the differences in their manner of interpreting sexual behavior have dwindled considerably from those differentiating Mr. B's initial contract from Pamela's rejection and counter offer. Mr. Knightley and Emma differ only on the issue of the proportion of feeling to rationality that one should exercise in choosing a mate. Yet one feels great tension between the sexes in Austen's fiction all the same; her heroines are always seriously at odds with the men they eventually marry, and at stake in the conflict is always the basis for sexual exchange. In *Emma*, more so perhaps than in *Pride and Prejudice*, the struggle between male and female modes of representation is clearly not a struggle between two social classes. Of all the characters in this novel, Mr. Knightley and Emma are the most closely affiliated. And because they belong to the two oldest and best-propertied families in Highbury, their disagreement seems to be more a matter of personal differences—age, sex, and disposition—than one of politics. At the same time, they disagree about how individuals should find their appropriate place within the community, and their disagreement involves everyone in that community. Theirs is, in other words, precisely the issue distinguishing Tory from Whig during the eighteenth century. But when contained within a domestic framework and subjected to the outcome of courtship procedures, this political difference, as Austen imagines it, becomes one between the nineteenth century liberal and conservative positions.[54] No longer does the sexual contract constitute the terms for a conflict of classes so much as it identifies the poles of opinion within only one—literate—class. In contrast with Richardson who tends to obscure the difference between gentry and nobility, furthermore, Austens represents her elite group of country gentlefolk as one that adheres to domestic norms.

Of birth unknown and of subjective qualities as yet undecided, Harriet Smith offers the appropriate field for a debate that will determine the true signs of individual identity. The debate comprising the novel is set off, significantly, by two events that are both consequences of Emma's matchmaking. Her governess—a substitute for Emma's dead mother—takes up residence with her new husband, leaving Emma with unregulated leisure time on her hands and a supervisory position in her household to fill. The change gives her father cause to lament, "'But my dear, pray do not make any more matches, they are silly things, and break up one's family circle grievously'" (p. 7). The terms of the debate are established as Emma prematurely takes on the role of domestic supervisor and turns to more matchmaking as the means by which to occupy her idle hours. She provides herself with a companion, Harriet Smith, whom she plans to educate:

> *She* would notice her; she would improve her; she would detach her from her bad acquaintance, and introduce her into good society; she would form her opinions and her manners. It would be an interesting, and certainly a very kind undertaking; highly becoming her own situation in life, her leisure, and powers. (p. 14)

Emma believes that education can make the woman by perfecting her manners and sensibility: "'That she is a gentleman's daughter, is indubitable to me; that she associates with gentleman's daughters, no one, I apprehend, will deny'" (p. 41). Mr. Knightley evaluates Harriet according to a male system of values: "'She is the natural daughter of nobody knows whom, with probably no settled provision at all, and certainly no respectable relations'" (p. 40). Thus a struggle ensues to determine who—male or female—has the power to interpret the female accurately. Emma insists on the authority inhering in her gender: "She did not repent what she had done; she still thought herself a better judge of such a point of female right and refinement than he could be" (p. 43). In effect, she takes up the position of Pamela in arguing for Harriet's intrinsic worth, just as Knightley assumes Mr. B's role when he claims that people should marry at their own social level. He makes this claim on the basis of gender; he assumes that as a male he should establish the standard of reasonableness. When Emma questions this manly prerogative on grounds that men regard beauty and a pleasant disposition as "'the highest claims a woman could possess,'" Knightley quickly seizes the logical advantage: "'My word,

Emma, to hear you abusing the reason you have, is almost enough to make me think so too. Better be without sense, than misapply it as you do'" (p. 42).

Richardson granted full authority to the female position in this debate, which allowed him to assert a new language of the self over and against a tradition of male writing that identified individuals first on the basis of their status. Austen qualifies the power Emma claims for language to constitute individuality, but in the conflict between male and female modes of interpretation, as Austen stages it, the female does not capitulate to the male code that authorizes social status. For her, status seems to matter as much as the essential qualities of a person. As a result, signs of political distinction are transformed to point not to the object represented so much as to the person who uses the signs. This may seem an overly subtle distinction, but it is nevertheless a profound one. By creating this distinction between representation and the object represented, Austen calls into being a set of rules—a grammar—that seems to be already there. The grammar is one she creates through usage which appears to violate the rules of grammar, but which she ultimately makes those rules contain.

Emma's failure to match Harriet Smith with Mr. Elton undermines the interpretive strategies of a male who attaches identity too firmly to social status. His rejection of Harriet on grounds of unknown lineage amounts to intolerable rudeness and places Elton among the characters who rank very low on Emma's scale of politeness. All by itself, Elton's concern for social status would not condemn him to such a position. Although Mr. Knightley's impeccable manners prevent him from endorsing a mix of what he calls "levels," this same notion of politeness requires him to tolerate such violations of traditional order when they occur. But in seeking a wife who enhances his status in the community, Elton does something a truly polite person would never do. He overvalues the income a woman will bring to a marriage and thus undervalues her as a woman. Although Emma believes that Harriet's sweetness of temper and ready compliance should be sufficient for someone of Elton's stature, Harriet has no value in his eyes if a gentle disposition and pleasant appearance are indeed all she offers. In his words, "'Everyone has their level; but as for myself, I am not, I think, quite so much at a loss. I need not so totally despair of an equal alliance, as to be addressing myself to Miss Smith!'" (p. 151).

The apparent disparity between the social status and true value of an individual is no more disruptive than Emma's own abuse of language that misplaces the individual in the world of Highbury by undervaluing social status and endorsing the claims of desire over those of tradition and custom. For committing this female error of reading character, Emma must chastise herself:

> "Here have I," said she, "actually talked poor Harriet into being very much attached to this man. She might never have thought of him with hope, if I had not assured her of his attachment, for she is as modest and humble as I used to think him." (p. 155)

In this case, misreading entails a miswriting of sexual relations that misleads desire. More specifically, in representing Mr. Elton as a fit mate for Harriet, Emma has ignored their obvious social differences. As Austen was perfectly aware, this abuse of language was the vice for which novels, as well as the women who read them, were traditionally condemned. Ironically, too, it was to resist the tyranny of fixed social status signs that Richardson had Pamela steadfastly resist Mr. B's advances until he no longer lusted for her sensuous body and desired instead the qualities of mind that she displayed in her writing, writing, it should be noted, that she carefully concealed. Austen takes a critical stance toward just this kind of writing in order to produce a far more complicated situation in which representation constitutes a form of agency in its own right. In this way, she raises the question of how language may provide an accurate indication of an individual's value.

It is Emma's painting of Harriet rather than Harriet herself that attracts Mr. Elton to Emma, creating a triangulated situation where signs of the self have a seductive power independent of their author or referent. This is how Emma intends her painting to mediate relations between object and observer:

> The sitting was altogether very satisfactory; she was quite enough pleased with the first day's sketch to wish to go on. There was no want of likeness, she had been fortunate in the attitude, and as she meant to throw a little improvement into the figure, to give a little more height, and considerably more elegance, she had great confidence of its being in every way a pretty drawing at last, and of its filling its destined place with credit to them both—a standing memorial of the beauty of one, the skill of the other, and the friendship of both; with as many agreeable associations as Mr. Elton's very promising attachment was likely to add. (p. 30)

Elton values the portrait of Harriet, not because it is a portrait of Harriet, but because it embodies Emma's sense of elegant proportions, as well as her superior taste and eye. She uses representation to create the subject represented, but her power of representation gets out of control. It renders Harriet a lifeless unlikeness while attracting the gaze to Emma herself: "he [Elton] was ready at the smallest intermission of the pencil, to jump up and see the progress, and be charmed" (p. 30). But a Pygmalion she is nevertheless, for Emma's use of language creates desire where none would otherwise have existed. Matchmaking is for Austen simply another word for fiction-making.

The addition of the element of language as an agent in its own right revises the struggle between male and female that one encounters in *Pamela*. Harriet has not only been led to misconstrue Mr. Elton's feelings, thanks to Emma's representation of their relationship. Mr. Elton has been inspired to misread Emma's feelings as well. He believes that though she is above him in the social register, her emotions incline her to value him as highly as if he were on a level with her. The problem in both instances of misreading is the same. It arises in Austen's fiction whenever desire overrules the dictates of one's relative social position, whenever, that is, the female mode of interpretation works in opposition to that of the male. Indeed, it is precisely as such a contradiction of gendered interpretations that Emma understands the moment of terrible stress and embarrassment when Elton proposes to her, his social superior, instead of to Harriet: "If *she* had so misinterpreted his feelings, she had little right to wonder that *he*, with self-interest to blind him, should have mistaken hers" (p. 93). It must be noted, however, that even though Austen exposes the fallacy in Richardson's egalitarian fantasy by having such fiction as his lead her heroine astray, she still carries forth the same project in which both he and the conduct books for women are implicated. True, the problem, as Emma ponders it, is a conflict between essential qualities of the self ("feelings") and traditional social signs (what Elton believes to be in his "self-interest"). What is more, Elton has erred, not only because he thought too much like a male, but also because he fell into female strategies that legitimize feelings over and above one's social position. But Emma's fiction has, all the same, adopted these conflicting modes of interpretation and made them, as in Richardson's fiction, the basis for negotiating a contract in which gender ("his" and "hers") matters more than social signs of identity so long as social signs are designated as the domain of the male.

That Harriet Smith occasions all the semantic mismatching she does is due to the surplus of information generated by the debate over her character, which has become subject to the fictions of others. She is, like gossip itself, of anonymous origins. She has only natural beauty and a female education to recommend her. The narrator makes certain we know she comes from nowhere else but "an honest, old-fashioned boarding school, where a reasonable quantity of accomplishments were sold at a reasonable price, and where girls might be sent to be out of the way and scramble themselves into a little education, without any danger of coming back prodigies" (p. 13). In Harriet, Austen represents the woman of the conduct books whose value appears to be entirely self-generated. Like Pamela in this respect, Harriet provides the site for a mode of representation that disentangles the operations of love from relationships based on one's social station. In contrast with earlier authors of the domestic woman, however, Austen does not empower this woman to author herself. Harriet becomes the means of questioning the individual's power of writing in relation to conditions for speech that have been established by a community. She provides the means for calling attention both to the conventions that already define an individual's place in the community and to the changes that individuals may effect by making innovative use of those conventions.[55] She becomes, in other words, a way of introducing a paradox resembling the one that troubled Samuel Johnson as he pondered the relationship between grammar and usage within the speech community. Johnson claimed he was prompted to compile his *Dictionary* because English was changing so rapidly that, without some standardization of meaning, the writing of his day would be unintelligible to the next generation. But the attempt to standardize usage introduced risks of another kind. Ultimately, as Johnson conceded, the strength and longevity of a language resides in its ability to accommodate new uses in which it necessarily acquires new meaning.

Thus having raised this paradox by the insertion of extra information in the system, *Emma* proceeds to destabilize the language of the self by means of an entirely different strategy. Again, Austen disrupts communication by introducing an extra female of ambiguous status in the community. In the case of Jane Fairfax, however, it is a deficiency rather than a surplus of information that causes the problem. Jane's emotional life is contained within her impassive exterior rather than inscribed upon her appearance and behavior for others to read. It is this quality of Jane's for which "Emma could not forgive her. Wrapt up in a cloak of politeness, she seemed determined to hazard nothing. She was disgustingly, was suspiciously reserved" (p. 113). This particular imbalance in the composition of the sign produces the sense that there is much more happening beneath the surface of social identity than speech can adequately represent. This would seem to be the point of the triangulated desire of Emma, Frank Churchill, and Jane, where it is not an excess but a deprivation of signifiers that produces false desire. For sexual relations are declared by the slightest gesture or the briefest glance in such a communication situation, and the contention between the male and female modes of interpretation therefore assumes a very different form.

In the following exchange between Frank Churchill and Emma, the twin problems of suppression and disclosure overlap; there is at once too much and too little information revealed. His speech approaches the point of exposing his true feelings, whereupon hers intervenes and stifles his confession:

> He looked at her, as if wanting to read her thoughts. She hardly knew what to say. It seemed like the forerunner of something absolutely serious, which she did not wish. Forcing herself to speak, therefore, in the hope of putting it by, she calmly said. . . . (p. 265)

At this point, the problem with language in the novel, despite what Emma surmises, is not a matter of how to prevent the male in question from indiscriminate speech. The capacity to unleash asocial desire was, we should recall, the basis on which conduct books so strenuously objected to novels. It is therefore historically significant when a novel such as this no longer seeks authorization by opposing the seduction of other fiction, but calls upon fiction for a more complete representation of desire. Were Emma to let it happen in the instance cited above, the mediation of speech would provide an instrument for establishing polite relationships where they do not already exist. Where Frank Churchill is concerned, her moments of stress and embarrassment arise strictly out of her ignorance of his emotional attachment to Jane Fairfax, information that Emma suppresses by silencing him. It is as if, having condemned fiction-making as the source of unruly desire, Austen's novel can call upon fiction as a means of solving the problem that fiction itself has produced. Given its nature, this problem calls for linguistic reform.

It is worth noting how writing comes under suspicion in the process of such reform. Mr. Elton's preciously penned charade characterizes him as a man of class pretensions and mercenary concerns. To communicate love in highly figurative terms as he does is, in Austen's terms, to offer the signs of passion with a lack of emotional depth. Although Emma describes it as "'A very proper compliment!,'" she does not concur with Harriet that Elton's poem is, "'without exception, the best charade I ever read.'" Instead, she claims she "'never read one more to the purpose, certainly'" (p. 51). In saying this, Emma contradicts herself, for she also confesses that she does "'not consider its length as particularly in its favour. Such things in general cannot be too short'" (p. 52). I would like to take note of the procedures that, despite such observations, allow Emma so to misconstrue Mr. Elton's meaning, for these offer an important reversal of the sentimental translation of biblical verse I discussed in relation to *Pamela*. Emma interprets Elton's poem allegorically, creating a personal sentimental meaning to complement general political terms. Such an allegorical reading, we might recall, is perfectly in keeping with the conduct book's suggestions about the proper use of classical mythology and history within a female curriculum. But Elton's verse refuses to be nudged and coaxed into a sentimental meaning despite the fact the charade itself invites such usage. Although Emma confidently translates the first and second verses into "court" and "ship" respectively, these terms remain stubbornly affixed to a political motivation. To lend them any other meaning is to misconstrue not only the true object but also the very nature of Elton's desire:

To Miss _____.

CHARADE

My first displays the wealth and pomp of kings,
Lords of the earth! their luxury and ease.
Another view of man, my second brings,
Behold him there, the monarch of seas!

But, ah! united, what reverse we have!
Man's boasted power and freedom, all are flown;
Lord of the earth and sea, he bends a slave,
And woman, lovely woman, reigns alone. (p. 48)

As a component of this novel, the poem is the more brilliant for being composed entirely of clichés. It represents sexual relations as a power struggle, and in claiming that "woman" makes of sovereign "man" a "slave," it dramatizes a refusal of meaning to be feminized. Although Emma considers herself to be "quite mistress of the lines," her sentimental interpretaton simply conceals their meaning, which is all on the surface. Elton is hardly enthralled by the lowly Harriet but means to rise to the station of Emma herself. In the lines of this benighted man, sexual desire has not been sufficiently detached from power to be love, and no amount of interpretive ingenuity on Emma's part can make it be so.

But this sentimental misreading of Elton's poem is one part of a two-fold error that also entails her failure to understand the sincere feeling displayed in Robert Martin's letter. It is a mark of Emma's ignorance as a reader, then, that she fails to discern the superior self-worth in Robert Martin's plain style or to understand how its ability to communicate emotion so clearly to Harriet designates him as the right man for her to marry. For such writing suggests that it is Harriet herself—distinct and apart from any social identity—that he values. Again, the traditional categories of writing prove misleading, for just as men supposedly use grandiloquent expression to persuade, tradition would have it that they use the plain style for purposes of logical argument. Thus when Harriet asks if Robert's is "'a good letter? or is it too short?,'" Emma replies "rather slowly,"

"—so good a letter, Harriet, that every thing considered, I think one of his sisters must have helped him. I can hardly imagine the young man whom I saw talking with you the other day could express himself so well, if left quite to his own power, and yet it is not the style of a woman; no, certainly, it is too strong and concise; not diffuse enough for a woman. No doubt he is a sensible man, and I suppose may have a natural talent for—thinks strongly and clearly—and when he takes a pen in hand, his thoughts naturally find proper words." (p. 33)

I dwell on the analyses of style contained within Austen's novel because they are her means of raising the whole question of writing and what constitutes the polite style.

In his discussion of John Ward's lectures on rhetoric, Wilbur Howell calls attention to an interesting corruption of classical categories that occurred in many eighteenth century treatises on rhetoric. Of Ward's lectures on the plain, middle, and high styles, Howell contends, "These treatises intended the distinction to mean that different subjects require different treatments, and that true excellence in oratory consists not in cultivating the grand style at the expense of the plain but in being always able to command the three styles as the subjects demand." In borrowing the Ciceronian categories, however, rhetorical treatises such as Ward's—which grew rapidly in number along with female conduct books during the second half of the eighteenth century—adapted that "part of Latin rhetoric which gave the tropes and figures such an interminable emphasis as to discredit by implication the rhetorical function of plainness."[56] Without saying so explicitly, Howell's analysis demonstrates how the styles of oratory ranked writing according to its implicit familiarity with Latin texts; written usage of rhetoric maintained a political hierarchy, in other words, quite at odds with the classical principles of rhetoric as eighteenth century theory drew them from Cicero's *Orator*. According to Ward,

"Now each of these parts of an orator's province require [sic] a different stile. The low stile is most proper for proof and information. Because he has no other view here, but to represent things to the mind in the plainest light, as they really are in themselves, without coloring or ornament. The middle stile is most suited for pleasure and entertainment, because it consists of smooth and well turned periods, harmonious numbers, with florid and bright figures. But the sublime is necessary in order to sway and influence the passions."[57]

Thus it is highly significant that Austen should put the most admirable pen in the hand of a man of the "yeomanry," as Emma calls Robert

Martin, rather than in that of a woman, as Richardson does. By means
of Elton's charade, she declares the high style to be little more than pre-
tension by attributing it to a man "without any alliances but in trade" (p.
93). But most telling of all in Austen's subtle critique is the failure of
the high style of writing to translate into effective speech: "for with all
his good and agreeable qualities, there was a sort of parade in his speeches
which was very apt to incline her to laugh" (p. 56).

By means of Frank Churchill's letters, on the other hand, Austen introduces what Emma's former governess regards as "one of the best
gentleman's hands I ever saw" (p. 202). In this case, Mr. Knightley proves
a stern critic, however. He regards with suspicion the verbal decorum
that comes from an elite education, since the man in question does not
carry out his words in other forms of behavior. "'It is Frank Churchill's
duty to pay this attention to his father,'" Knightley argues, "'He knows
it to be so, by his promises and messages; but if he wished to do it, it
might be done'" (p. 99). On another occasion, Knightley compares the
gentleman's hand to "woman's writing," and only when Churchill's letter
arrives to confess finally the extent of his involvement with Jane Fairfax
does this suspicion give way to qualified approbation. Knightley feels that
at least the young man has begun to subordinate style to truth in his writing: "'Mystery; Finesse—how they pervert the understanding! My Emma,
does not every thing serve to prove more and more the beauty of truth
and sincerity in all our dealings with each other?'" (p. 307). Writing has
truth value in Knightley's critique only when it proves consistent with
the other modes of an individual's behavior—particulary speech—rather
than with the class that individual comes from or aspires to. Because
Austen has introduced all this writing into *Emma* as an agent of social
disruption, we must regard such critical commentary as central to the
strategic intention of the novel. The novel contains other writing than
fiction, I am suggesting, to establish the novel as a new standard for
writing. The preferred style of writing has its source in common English
and derives its value from its capacity to communicate the author's feelings without inflating or concealing them; it has all the advantages of a
stable currency. In terms of the reigning system of values, however, Martin's writing ranks below the styles of both Elton and Churchill. It ranks
below theirs because male writing bears the mark of the author's political
position and indicates that Martin occupies a lower place in the social
world than either Elton or Churchill.

It is no wonder, then, that Austen turns away from writing and from
the materials of a male education in order to produce the linguistic reforms that will eventually authorize Robert Martin's style of writing. Nor

is it any wonder that she turns to gossip and conversation, which are speech modes identified with the female, when she wants to put forth a kind of writing that reveals the true qualities of the individual. It is important to mention that, in addition to making fiction, Emma is less than conscientious in observing the strictures of female education. As a girl, she drew up "'a great many lists . . . at various times of books that she meant to read regularly through—and very good lists they were,'" according to Knightley, "'very well chosen, and very neatly arranged— sometimes alphabetically, and sometimes by some other rule'" (p. 23). Like her inability to complete a painting, her failure to read may be initially regarded as a flaw, but because of Austen's apparently critical attitude toward written culture, Emma's lack of diligence in this respect proves a virtue, a refusal to be written by culture.[58]

By the end of the novel, literacy is no longer represented in such (conduct-book) terms. It is not acquired from writing at all but through mastery of the rules for polite speech. In renouncing the figures of fiction that invariably generate desire where none should be, Emma's speech acquires a kind of politeness that represents emotional truth more accurately than writing presumably ever could. The model for this kind of speech is none other than that which unfolds with the novel's first asseveration: "Emma Woodhouse, handsome, clever, and rich, with a comfortable house and happy disposition, seemed to unite some of the best blessings of existence; and had lived nearly twenty-one years in the world with very little to distress or vex her." Such a statement appears to constitute writing that derives from speech rather than from writing. The speech is the speech of the parlor where behavior is observed and regulated, and the writing derived from that speech is a form of writing that uses gossip with all the force and precision of a diagnostic instrument. The novel's second major pronouncement on Emma's situation illustrates such use of this language: "The *real* evils indeed of Emma's situation were the power of having *rather too much* her own way, and a disposition to think *a little too well* of herself; these were disadvantages which threatened to alloy her many enjoyments" (p. 1, italics mine). How different these fine anomalies in an otherwise comfortable life are from the perils to body and soul which Pamela has to encounter.

If the hierarchy among styles of masculine writing creates a gap between writing and speech in this novel, then the hierarchy among styles of feminine speech effaces these differences between speech and writing. The writing that is closest to speech places an author low in a hierarchy of writing, but it is precisely the kind of English modeled on speech that identifies the well-educated woman. We might say that Austen attaches gender to writing in order to create a disjunction between writing and speech. Such disjunction always constitutes a serious crisis in the organization of her fictive communities. Producing this crisis allows her not only to valorize a new kind of writing based on polite speech, but also, and more importantly, it enables her to situate speech logically prior to writing. In this way, she uses speech to authorize her preferred style of writing on grounds that the source of speech, unlike that of writing, resides in the individual. And as she establishes this as the basis for the truth value of writing, Austen also grants priority to the verbal practices of women, women who may never carry out programs of reading literature, but who are nevertheless essential to maintaining polite relationships within the community.

To have the authority of language that comes straight from the heart, however, women's speech must be purified of all traces of writing. Thus it is early on in the novel that Austen has Emma renounce her novelistic practices:

> It was foolish, it was wrong to take so active a part in bringing any two people together. It was adventuring too far, assuming too much, making light of what ought to be serious, a trick of what ought to be simple. She [Emma] was quite concerned and ashamed, and resolved to do such things no more. (p. 83)

There is a special element of irony in this statement. For even as she has Emma renounce the strategies of fiction-making, Austen condemns her heroine to think out social relationships over and over again in terms of imaginary narratives. It is by this process that Emma develops a language that will enable her not only to express but also to know her own feelings, and such knowledge is the precondition for avoiding the pitfalls entailed in misrepresenting the feelings of others. Thus the novel produces a reliable language of the self by the curiously backward process of allowing its heroine to repeat her misreading of sexual relations until she knows her own feelings. Accordingly, Mr. Knightley recognizes two spirits in Emma, a "'vain spirit'" that prompts her fiction-making and a "'serious spirit'" that understands the violations of truth as they occur. "'If one leads you wrong, I am sure the other tells you of it,'" he explains (p. 225). It is in such a dialectic with fiction-making that the self-regulating voice is produced, a voice, paradoxically, that becomes virtually indistinguishable from the voice of the novelist by the end of the novel.

In drawing this relationship between gender and truth, I want to isolate a political move that distinguishes Austen from Richardson. Like Richardson, Austen represents the struggle between various modes of representation as a struggle between male and female, but for Austen the female requires reform at least as much as—often more than—the male. In view of the fact that this struggle is all about language, it is fair to conclude that Austen is not out to seize cultural authority, as Richardson was when he put Pamela in charge of Mr. B's country estate. Emma is already too much in charge of the house when the novel opens. Left with too much leisure time on her hands, Emma naturally inclines toward matchmaking. With the influx of the Eltons and the Churchills and the decline of the Bates, the power to regulate sexual relations, Austen suggests, is quite as complex as it is powerful, and it requires a far more subtle means of standardization than Richardson offered by means of his dialogue between male and female. In those instances when fiction is allowed to proceed unrestrained, words behave promiscuously, and the power Emma inherits as the woman of the house proves disruptive. On the other hand, whenever she renounces the power of speech to constitute desire, she acquires another form of power, which influences even Mr. Knightley. Of Emma's long-withheld approval of Harriet's engagement to Robert Martin, he remarks, "'You are materially changed since we last talked on this subject before.'" But upon Emma's admission, "'I hope so—for at that time I was a fool,'" he accedes to her former interpretation of Harriet's character: "'And I am changed also; for I am now very willing to grant you all Harriet's good qualities'" (p. 327). Thus, as in Pamela, male and female echo one another in a mutually authorizing relationship.

In *Emma*, however, the transformation is a double one whereby he acknowledges the value of an unextraordinary woman such as Harriet and she understands the uncommon value of the common man. The conflict between male and female did not require the conversion of the one to the other's system of values after all; it simply required finding the right kind of currency to represent what was in the interest of both. Knightley's speech is a renunciation of the conventional language of love: "'I cannot make speeches, Emma,'—he soon resumed; and in a tone of such sincere, decided, intelligible tenderness as was tolerably convincing.—'If I loved you less, I might be able to talk about it more. But you know what I am.—You hear nothing but truth from me'" (p. 296). However faltering the terms in which she has Knightley confess his true feelings for Emma, Austen proves yet more withholding when it is Emma's turn to reply. On this occasion, the voice of the novelist completely supplants that of the lover: "she spoke then, on being so entreated.—What did she say?—Just what she ought, of course. A lady always does. She said enough to show there need not be despair—and to invite him to say more himself" (p. 297). At this moment in the novel when there seems to be an absence of words, one has the sense of language reborn, not borrowed and used, as it emerges directly from the individuals in question, word by word, each loaded at last with real meaning, because each is fixed to a feeling that already exists before the individual finds words and occasion to pronounce it. This is the language of pure desire uncolored by any form of value other than its own. It discloses the core of the individual, at least of individuals who have such a core, and the core of the novel as well, that is, the motivations that all along have been silently shaping behavior.

Although Austen suggests that writing should imitate speech because speech comes straight from the self, the novel itself operates according to an entirely different principle. To ground desire in a self that exists prior to language, Austen has to disclose areas in the self that have not yet been spoken. To be present before it is spoken, desire has to be inscribed within the individual. That is to say, it has to be written.

As the reader first encounters her, Emma feels no sense of deficiency, even though, as the narrator says, she has "the power of having rather too much her own way, and a disposition to think a little too well of herself" (p. 1). The novelist grants Knightley authority to read the human character—authority that is nearly equal to her own—on grounds that he "was one of the few people who could see faults in Emma Woodhouse, and the only one who ever told her of them" (p. 5). But it is only the novelist who can turn Emma's self-sufficiency into a deficiency that instigates desire independent of a social origin If early on Emma speaks of herself as a most complete individual, Austen writes this speech as the lack of a lack, the absence of Emma's awareness that she is missing something as a female. Austen situates the fact of gender prior to speech by making Emma's speech reveal as writing the very truth it denies as speech. As she confesses to Harriet,.

> "I have *none* of the usual inducements of women to marry. Were I to fall in love, indeed, it would be a different thing! but I *never* have been in love; it is *not* my way, or my nature; and I do *not* think I ever shall. And, without love, I am sure I should be a fool to change such a situation as mine. Fortune *I do not want*; employment *I do not want*; consequence *I do not want*: I believe few married women are half as much mistress of their husband's house as I am of Hartfield; and so always first and always right in any man's eyes as I am in my father's." (p. 58, italics mine)

By giving her heroine such perfection through the possession of every material thing and every social prerogative that ever a polite person could want, Austen creates deficiency on another level. It is the same order of deficiency that prompts Emma to insult Miss Bates and thereby inspire Knightley's harshest indictment: "'How could you be so unfeeling to Miss Bates?'" (p. 258). In similar fashion, Austen attributes the smallest lapse in social decorum to a failure within the individual, a flaw which she identifies as a defect of gender.

When understood as such, each lapse in turn gives rise to some form of subjectivity appropriate to a female. Thus it is by linking Harriet with Mr. Knightley in her most socially outrageous act of mismatching that Emma is finally shot through with genuinely monogamous desire. Again, it is by creating an absence that her fiction, like the novel itself, calls forth a desire that is gendered and that therefore, by implication, is genuine: "Til now that she was threatened with its loss, Emma had never known how much of her happiness depended on being *first* with Mr. Knightley, first in interest and affection" (p. 285). From this awareness come the first signs of utterly genuine feeling that establish relations between Emma and Knightley, a union that magically stabilizes the community. Why this depends on the production of female desire becomes clear when we examine the impact of such feeling. Emma's desire for Knightley manifests itself in two ways. She becomes her own disciplinarian—far less indulgent than the gently ironic novelist—as she subjects herself to Mr. Knightley's standard of conduct: "She was most sorrowfully indignant; ashamed of every sensation but the one revealed to her— her affection for Mr. Knightley—Every other part of her mind was disgusting" (p. 284). As she rises in her own esteem to meet this standard, however, she also grows far more tolerant (as the novelist is) of others' failings.

It is when she turns her critical eye on herself, not when she tries to regulate the feelings of others, that Emma becomes the very figure of politeness. As the essential quality of the new aristocrat—so closely akin to charity, on the one hand, and to condescension, on the other, yet utterly unlike them in the complex of emotions from which it springs— politeness hangs in the balance in Emma's gravest crime, a nearly imperceptible act of rudeness toward the tiresome Miss Bates. As Mr. Knightley explains the nature of this crime to Emma, politeness emerges as the model for feelings, speech, and social behavior:

> "Her situation should secure your compassion. It was badly done indeed—
> You, whom she had known from an infant, whom she had seen grow up
> from a period when her notice was an honour, to have you now, in thought-
> less spirits, and the pride of the moment, laugh at her, humble her—and

before her niece, too—and before others, many of whom (certainly *some*) would be entirely guided by *your* treatment of her" (p. 257)

It is more than a little interesting to note that in order to fill the model Mr. Knightley sketches out for her, Emma must not only learn that she desires, but must also suppress the aggravation she feels towards women she cannot absolutely control. That Emma is so transformed in the course of the novel suggests that the acquisition of this form of literacy is the same as the formation of a nineteenth century individual. The individual is, by her very nature, unformed and in want of perfection.

To work this modification upon the Richardsonian model is to put a double edge to the power of example. If to be real is to deviate from the type, then to perfect oneself is to modify the type in aspiring to fulfill it. For one can observe the shift in Austen's emphasis away from natural virtue as the quality a woman exemplifies to a more complex understanding of subjectivity and the part example plays in shaping it. Emma's problem, as the narrator notes in the second statement of the novel, originates in her absent mother. Because her "mother had died too long ago for her to have more than an indistinct remembrance of her caresses," she was raised by a woman who "had fallen little short of a mother in affection," but who allowed Emma to have "rather too much her own way" and "to think a little too well of herself" (p. 1). While there is no lack of nurturant figures in her world (if anything, there are too many), it is the self-regulatory function missing along with the mother that is significant, and it is this which Emma acquires in learning that she loves Mr. Knightley. It is also in taking on this particular feature of gender that her example will maintain polite relations within the community rather than breed disrespect and induce mutability.

Austen's novel castigates behavior that has been prompted by social motivation—Emma's low regard for Martin, Knightley's for Harriet, Elton's for Harriet, as well as Emma's for Miss Bates. It makes such motivation, which dominates the behavior of the new Mrs. Elton, into the distinctive feature of the nouveaux riches and a false basis, therefore, for genteel behavior. By allowing the linguistic surface of relationships to be misread on repeated occasions, however, the novel inscribes the traditional signs of status within a domestic framework where they obey a new principle of political economy. That is, both men and women acquire status within an economy of conduct in which verbal behavior—their use of these signs—is paramount. The more prolifically they spend words, the less concealed and thus the less misinterpreted their feelings become, which is to say that the true nature of the self becomes more exposed.

This is as true of Augusta Elton as it is of Harriet Smith and Miss Bates, even though the latter two ladies expose a self more benign and genial. Yet despite the sense of innocence generated by Miss Bates's redundancy, she is all on the surface, her meaning too readily apparent. That she leaves nothing for one to interpret is confirmed by a glance through any edition of *Emma*, which identifies the places seamlessly filled with her speech as pages one can afford to skim over quickly. The relative value of signified to signifier is just the reverse in the case of Jane Fairfax whose self-containment requires elaborate strategies of reading. On her behavior in respect to Frank Churchill, for example, Mr. Knightley muses,

> He could not understand it; but there were symptoms of intelligence between them—he thought so at least—symptoms of admiration on his side, which, having once observed, he could not persuade himself to think entirely void of meaning, however he might wish to escape any of Emma's errors of imagination. (p. 234)

For all the aesthetic value that seems to accompany the withholding of feelings, however, Jane's manner of conduct no more represents the ideal than Miss Bates's. "'Jane Fairfax has feeling,' said Mr. Knightley—'I do not accuse her of want of feeling. Her sensibilities, I suspect, are strong—and her temper excellent in its power of . . . self control; but it wants openness'" (p. 195). Just because her true feelings are barely discernible, Jane, like Harriet, gives rise to impolite fictions. These narrative possibilities indeed break into the novel and destabilize the exchange of information that constitutes social relations themselves. Polite speech is not simply a psychological function—that point where candor meets discretion—but a medium of exchange, a form of currency that alone ensures a stable community.

I use these terms in an effort to lend the novel's self-enclosure a materiality it cannot achieve within conventional literary classifications. I use the notion of economic exchange to suggest that this novel dramatizes a linguistic exchange which it reproduces outside the framework of fiction as the conditions for reading the novel. Austen uses the traditional signs of social status to show how they wreak havoc among the members of her community if they have the power to define individuals. But communication is confused and the community disrupted just as surely when status signs are ignored. In this way, Austen demonstrates that these signs do not operate effectively within traditional rhetorical categories or within the reigning grammar of social identity. She slips signs of status into a new system of meaning, and by such usage, detaches them from a context. Through a plot consisting of repeated errors to the one (male) side and the other (female), Austen creates rules based on her usage. This grammar falls into place as such with the perfection of communication between Knightley and Emma:

> While he spoke, Emma's mind was most busy, and, with all the wonderful velocity of thought, had been able—and yet without losing a word—to catch and comprehend the exact truth of the whole; to see that Harriet's hopes had been entirely groundless, a mistake, a delusion, as complete a delusion as any of her own—that Harriet was nothing; that she was everything herself; that what she had been saying relative to Harriet had been all taken as the language of her own feelings. (p. 296)

Thus, one can argue, Austen allies herself more with Jeremy Bentham than with Samuel Johnson.

By saying this, I mean to refute the idea that Austen was an ardent little Tory who sought to make fiction justify a traditional notion of rank and status. But in opposing this position, I do not subscribe to the view of Austen as a proto-feminist rebel who thrashed against the constraints that bound an author of her sex unwillingly to convention. These, I would rather argue, are alternatives by which literary criticism rewrites the past because they are alternatives that authors such as Austen wrote into fiction, making it possible for fiction to do the work of modern culture. I have drawn upon the distinction between grammar and usage to represent the thematic opposition of personal desire to social constraint that criticism uses to figure out Austen's politics, and I have used the notion of economy, too, in an effort to lend Austen's writing a materiality it tends to lose in critical discussion. If nothing else, this chapter has attempted to demonstrate that writing, for Austen, was a form of power in its own right, which could displace the material body of the subject and the value of those objects constituting the household. In helping to establish the semiotic organization of nineteenth century England, in other words, the novel helped to create the conditions theorized by Bentham—a world largely written, one in which even the difference between words and things was ultimately a function of discourse.

My reading of *Emma* shows the degree to which Austen understood the power of usage to modify grammar or the rules governing usage. In this, her thinking resembles not only that of Samuel Johnson but that of Samuel Richardson as well. (What else is the last section of *Pamela* if not a demonstration of precisely this principle?) But unlike the eighteenth century intellectual, Austen also understood the principle underlying Bentham's theory of signs—that is, the degree to which words constitute the objects they represent. In putting forth his "entirely new system of logic," with its linguistic orientation rising out of the analysis and classification of fictions, Bentham insists on a certain economy of communication grounded in objects:

Yonder stands a certain portion of matter. By that portion of matter feelings of a certain sort are produced in your mind: by that same portion of matter feelings of a sort, if not exactly the same, at least with reference to the purpose in question near enough to being the same, are produced at the same time in my mind. Here then is the channel of communication, and the only one. Of that channel language takes possession and employs it.[59]

Much the same communication model organizes the scene in which Emma paints Harriet's portrait. We could say, on the one hand, it is also possible to argue that the portrait, in Bentham's terms, transmits Emma's meaning quite effectively. Its attempt to enhance Harriet's figure bespeaks the lack of elegance Emma sees there. Austen not only understands the power of usage to transform the rules for usage, I am arguing, she also understands that real entities, when taken up by language, exist on a more or less equal footing with fictitious ones. Language constitutes a material reality in its own right as it displaces the world of things. In Bentham's words,

as often as any object has been considered in the character of a subject of or for exposition, that object has been a word—the immediate subject of exposition has been a word; whatsoever else may have been brought to view, the signification of a *word*—of the word in question—has been brought to view: the word is not only a subject, but the only physically sensible subject, upon and in relation to which the *operation* called exposition has been performed. (p. 77)

Understanding full well the power of the word, Bentham asserts, in the chapter entitled "The Fiction of an Original Contract," that "the season of *Fiction* is now over: insomuch that what formerly might have been tolerated and countenanced under the name, would, if now attempted to be set on foot, be censured and stigmatized under the harsher appellations of *encroachment* or *imposture*" (p. 122). To put an end to the fictions on which he believed monarchy rested, however, required a new epoch of realism and a new language of truth, which did not so easily reveal its figurative power. His can be regarded as an early attempt in the great nineteenth century project to make language identical with truth, which did in fact initiate a new empire of signs.

With a kind of self-awareness rivaled, in my opinion, only by Jeremy Bentham, Austen proposes a form of authority—a form of political authority—that works through literacy rather than through traditional juridical means to maintain social relations. If, by Austen's time, sexual relations are assumed to be the specialized knowledge of the female, and if it is in female writing that the terms of such relationships are figured out, then fiction fulfills its discursive function by exemplifying the conduct of relationships between men and women. Novels do not have to launch elaborate self-defenses anymore, for they have appropriated the strategies of conduct books to such a degree that fiction—instead of conduct books—can claim the authority to regulate reading. More often than not, those conduct books that do not aim their wisdom specifically at children or members of the aspiring social groups turn a critical eye on the genre and deplore the limitations of educational programs meant only for women. I am suggesting that with Austen, if not with Burney before her, the novel supplants the conduct book as that writing which declares an alternative, female standard of polite writing.

Rather than perform the psychologizing function that conduct books by now presumed to be the purpose of female education, Austen's fiction set out to discover those same truths as the private reality underlying *all* social behavior, even that which belonged to the domain of the public and masculine, i.e., political, world. As architects of the new educational curriculum were also in the process of deciding, it was not enough to cultivate the hearts of women alone. It was now time to consider how social institutions might be changed. In the words of the Edgeworths:

> without depreciating or destroying the magnificence or establishments of universities, may not their institutions be improved? May not their splendid halls echo with other sounds than the exploded metaphysics of the schools; and may not learning be as much rewarded and esteemed as pure *latinity*.[60]

So, too, on the fictional front, where the battle for representing the woman had already been won, one can see the entire matter of relative social position—or in other words, the ranking of men—undergoing translation into linguistic features. The Edgeworths' question of whether an aristocratic education provided the entire basis for male knowledge is simply recast to consider which style of writing best represented the relative value of men. No longer, by implication, was the aristocratic tradition of letters, or "latinity," necessarily privileged in this regard. To say this would seem to contradict the argument that identifies Austen's place in history with her formulation of strategies of containment.

To read *Emma*, we must not only equate language with power. We must also equate the language of power with prose that imitates the word spoken by an elite minority of country gentlefolk quite removed from the centers of power. And if it seems dangerous to make the first equation because it empowers the Eltons and the Churchills of the world and introduces a certain fluidity into the closed and stratified world of Austen's fiction, then the second of these equations offers a way of limiting the destabilizing effects of the first. This peculiar capability on the part of her communities to be both permeable and restrictive is one that also characterized the English country gentry at the turn of the century. How the fluidity of its membership, as described in my discussion of *Pamela*, translated into a question of language is explained in Lawrence and Jeanne Fawtier Stone's *An Open Elite? England 1540–1880*. The fact that for a century the gentry was a rank to which people belonging to different social groups could ascend and from which individuals could as easily decline was inscribed upon the English countryside:

> In the eighteenth century, upwardly mobile purchasers might change the old name of a seat, because they found it insufficiently genteel or imposing to suit their aspirations. In Hertfordshire, Pricketts became Greenhill Grove, Tillers End became Coles Park, and Cokenhatch, at least for a time, became Earlsbury Park. Such name-changing of houses is an indication of the very real degree of identification between an owner and his seat: the latter's name was meant to enhance the status of the former, which is why so many houses in the eighteenth century were called 'Park' instead of the older, less grandiose, 'Hall'. By the nineteenth century, the close identi- fication of the *nouveau-riche* with his small villa was an aping, lower down the social scale, of this form of proprietorial imperialism. (p. 71)

In quite literally effacing the history of the house, the turnover of country property destabilized the signs of personal identity, a historical process recorded most obviously in *Mansfield Park* but resonating throughout all of Austen's fiction. "Since continuity of the 'house'—meaning the pa- trilinear family line—was the fundamental organizing principle to which these families subscribed," the Stones continue, "the prime object was to keep together the . . . component elements which made it up." Among these were not only the land, the family name, and a title, if there hap- pened to be one, but also—and of equal importance—the household ob- jects which preserved the family's history, "especially valuable relics such as the family archives, including the deeds and patents of nobility, por- traits of ancestors, family plate and jewels, and personal gifts from kings and queens" (p. 72). If it was primarily nostalgia for the iconicity of such household objects that animated her representation of a community in crisis, we would have to place Austen with the liberal Tories of her day. But this, I feel, would be to adopt too simplistic a view of her under- standing of the medium in which she thought out the dynamism of the ideal community. I am quite certain that Austen understood as well as anyone could the power of fiction to constitute things, truth, and reality.

It was not the country gentry and their specific interests that she promoted as the best life for everyone to live. The ways of the town and the city and their connection with commerce abroad always hover at the borders of the elite community to remind and reassure us of its limitations. It was not this particular segment of society that she idealized, then, but rather the language that constituted the nuances of emotion and the ethical refinements that seemed to arise from within to modify the political meaning of signs, a new language of kinship relations capable of reproducing this privileged community on a personal scale within society at large. It is in this respect that Austen's writing implies the presence of a new linguistic community, a class that was neither gentry nor nobility as the eighteenth century knew them, yet one that was clearly a leisure class and thus a paradoxical configuration that can only be called a middle-class aristocracy.

4

History in the House of Culture

For each new class which puts itself in the place of the one before it, is compelled, simply in order to achieve its aims, to represent its interest as the common interest of all members of society, i.e., employing an ideal formula to give its ideas the form of universally valid ones.

KARL MARX, *The German Ideology*

It is a great truth, that you cannot extinguish violence by violence. You may put it down for a time; but while you are crowing over your imaginary success, see if it does not return with seven devils worse than its former self!

ELIZABETH GASKELL, *Mary Barton*

Most literary historical accounts of domestic fiction endeavor to make a continuous narrative out of material that actually proceeds in fits and starts. This chapter will argue that the gaps in any such narrative are important. They tell us when this fiction could not deal with the important issues of the day, just as its reappearance in startlingly new forms suggests that it was engaging a particular moment in history. In other words, the sporadic production of domestic fiction implies that discontinuities were a function of fiction's place in a much larger process of meaning. Such a history also implies that the work of organizing and interpreting reality continued in other symbolic modes when fictions of courtship and marriage did not serve this purpose particularly well. This chapter will show why the period of time intervening between Austen's fiction and that of the Brontës was indeed a gap essential to understanding their respective places in history.[1]

In considering what happened to fiction during the years between 1818 and 1848, however, one encounters a problem, for the novel-reading public was preoccupied with an issue that appears to have had little to do with matters of courtship and kinship. Historians show that many people within the middle classes as well as most of those within the landowning and laboring classes were pouring their intellectual energy into a struggle to curtail industrial expansion.[2] In the aftermath of the French Revolution, diverse groups of people blamed mechanization for practically every problem troubling England. Few, if any, could ignore the poverty, food shortages, bouts of inflation, crippling illiteracy, demographic dislocation, and unrest among the laboring poor. As the supposed cause for such social disruption, the machine became so unpopular that violence against it was tolerated, if not openly condoned. The assaults on machinery seemed to be for the good of the whole society, while mechanization appeared to serve only the interests of the ruthless few.

"By all the rules of intellectual warfare," remarks Harold Perkin, "the aristocratic ideal should have won the battle for the mind. The aristocracy was the army in possession, defending a prepared position, and in control of the most powerful organs of opinion and most of the institutions of education."[3] Yet each attempt to resist mechanization ultimately strengthened the industrialists' position. They won the intellectual war—a war to determine the definition of culture itself—as the literate public began regarding resistance to machinery as more dangerous than machinery itself. The triumph of the new middle classes depended not only on the fact of an organized proletariat but also on the appearance of new modes of writing to represent it.[4] Against the gathering political opposition, middle-class intellectuals pitted representations of working-class culture as lacking culture. Their gathering in pubs, for example, was attributed to the workers' failure to enjoy a stable and sustaining domestic life. In similar terms, political resistance was portrayed as primitive and self-destructive, if not criminal and a threat to order itself. Within such a discursive framework, any form of resistance strengthened the rhetorical position of middle-class intellectuals and reformers. It proved that factories and schools were necessary. It is important to recall that the historical circumstances that made machinery a cause of debate existed before and continued well after the moment when the problems caused by industrialization were formulated in this way. But those who had long proclaimed the benefits of machinery suddenly gained such support for their position that, despite the fact that the evils of industrialism would loom still larger during the course of the nineteenth century, by the 1840s people were no longer debating whether or not machines should exist. Instead, a new set of political affiliations had formed on the basis of how best to curtail the ill effects of mechanization and so reap the benefits.

It is significant that few, if any, major domestic novels appeared during the 1820s and 1830s to take sides in the controversy over industrialization. We can only assume that the relationship between the domestic world and the world in which it was nested—a conflict that Austen did not have to deal with—was undergoing a major revision. For it is certain that the eighteenth century strategies for reforming the manor house would no longer do. It was not until the 1840s, when the intellectual battle appeared to be over, that the writing of noteworthy domestic fiction resumed. As it regained its position as a major feature of the cultural scene, fiction maintained the old equation between sexual and social relations, but the source of disruption and target of reform had definitely changed. Marriage no longer provided the antidote to restrictive and arbitrary status distinctions, and therefore it no longer softened the boundary that enclosed the dominant culture. Instead, it became commonplace to use marriage as a way of drawing a line around culture in order to preserve it in the face of a competitive marketplace. At issue in the novels of the 1840s was, in other words, the nature of the problem that marriage was supposed to resolve.

While they did not directly address the machinery question, these novels revised the entire concept of sexual desire that organized earlier domestic fiction. Instead of constituting a form of resistance, desire became a strategy for dealing with the problem posed by the machine, the problem of political resistance. In the hands of Gaskell and Dickens in particular, domestic fiction carried the process of suppressing political resistance into the domain of popular literature, where it charted new domains of aberrance requiring domestication. In discussing the political behavior of the kind of fiction that emerged during the 1840s, I want to stress the ways in which certain rhetorical strategies became techniques of social control. Richardson imagined writing as a power that could reclassify individuals on the basis of subjective qualities that appeared to have little to do with their social status. He represented the household as a space maintained by a female supervisor. But he also endowed female writing—namely, Pamela's letters—with a power that extended beyond the household to convert others to her way of knowing themselves. It is fair to say that Austen further displaced the political signs of human identity by renouncing the Richardsonian impulse to convert. In *Emma*, for example, she contains wayward interpretations of the self within the self in order to tease out far more elaborate procedures of self-discovery. Desire and self-perfection are realized as her heroine amends these fictions to form a truth at once psychological and social. But such truth, in Austen's work, does not depend on modifying political reality as such. If Richardson defines the household as that place where the rights of the individual can be realized, Austen writes the mechanism of self-regulation into that individual. Her notion of politeness hinges on this. Emma renounces Pamela's power of conversion in order to take on a superior power of example that depends on self-control. Through her perception of her own errors, she abandons the careless promptings of culture that would throw her into the arms of Frank Churchill and learns to listen to a desire all her own.

In the decades after Austen, I will explain, it is as if these strategies of spatial representation, individuation, and self-interrogation took on a life apart from the Enlightenment project that laid claim to certain powers on behalf of the individual. These strategies provided techniques for making the individual a specific object of knowledge to himself, and they did so on a mass basis.[5] Along with the conduct books, domestic fiction represented forms of female subjectivity that posited a basis for the self prior to any social identity. It rooted subjectivity in sexual desire and in one's ability to channel such desire toward socialized goals. It made the welfare of the social group depend, before anything else, on the regulation of the individual's desire. Along with other kinds of writing characteristic of the nineteenth century, domestic fiction transformed this fantasy of self-production into the procedures designed to produce men and women fit to occupy the institutions of an industrialized society.

Viewed from this perspective, the machinery question had everything to do with the history of the novel. It was in large part responsible for the changes that marked fiction as Victorian. It was also responsible for the prestige granted to novels that displayed these changes. Thus I have found it necessary to pursue a circuitous route to account for the rebirth of domestic fiction that ushered in the high Victorian period. I will deal briefly with the fiction in question. But while, in making a history of fiction, I discuss materials other than fiction, I do not consider these procedures digressive. I will be examining a field of information where accident intruded upon history, where discourse confronted the multifarious practices of a culture, and where one mode of truth contested another to determine which would define social reality. By examining this field, one can understand how new forms of information came into being and why others receded into the background. I hope to explain why, for example, the resolutions to this body of fiction tended to reduce and confine the family into a space that resembled a prison, as well as why novelists began to pour their creative energy into scenes of violence, hallucination, and chaos that characteristically displayed a madwoman at their center. More specifically, this chapter attempts to explain why deranged women suddenly came into vogue with the great domestic novels of the late 1840s.

It was as if the production of this new Victorian fiction depended on bringing forth some monstrous woman to punish and then banish from the text, as regularly happened in novels by the Brontës, Gaskell, Dickens, and Thackeray. Their manner of disclosing these women stripped away all social identity from the female. It represented the loss of such identity as the loss of gender distinctions.

Such well-known studies as Nina Auerbach's *The Woman and the Demon* and Gilbert and Gubar's *The Madwoman in the Attic* chart the literary manifestations of this figure. Finding no precedent for this woman in earlier fiction, and recognizing the power of the figure, Auerbach attributes the appearance of the demonic woman to a myth that peopled the Victorian world with female demons and angels, while Gilbert and Gubar locate the source of the madwoman in the female author whose imagination was necessarily thwarted by a limiting repertoire of conventions for her self-expression.[6] According to the many critics who work within a similar understanding of Victorian sexuality, monstrous women represent aspects of the female that exist outside of social institutions because these aspects constitute a form of resistance that social institutions control. Such criticism may, like Auerbach's, view these monsters of desire as positive figures. And with this position my own is basically compatible, given one qualification. In assuming that sexuality is only about sexuality, one accedes to the Victorian view that essential aspects of the female could not find a positive outlet within the constraints of middle-class life. Underlying the rhetoric of nineteenth century literary realism is the assumption that middle-class respectability doomed the woman to a kind of half-life within society because by definition respectability required her sexual repression. In approaching the novels in question, I would like to reverse this entire notion of cause and effect. I would like to suggest that novels themselves generated our modern conviction that social conventions systematically suppressed forms of sexuality which existed prior to those conventions and made them necessary. In place of the theory of repression, as I have already explained, I will assume that these extrasocial depths in the self were themselves products of Victorian culture. I will also assume they were produced largely in writing. Proceeding on such theoretical ground, we may consider the possibility that such deviant forms of desire were actually composed of cultural material having a history. Granting all this, it seems to me that in translating this material into psychosexual terms, Victorian novels effectively concealed the political power they exercised in so transforming cultural information. As they produced the monstrous women for which we remember them, I am suggesting, novels offered one means of producing the modern political unconscious. The argument of this chapter considers the figure of the monstrous woman as one step in a series of displacements that eventually relegated a whole realm of social practices to the status of disruption and deviance requiring containment and discipline.

The Rhetoric of Violence: 1819

We might begin to recover the history of these Victorian monsters at the opening of the nineteenth century when the term "combination" was first applied on a regular basis to many long-tolerated practices of the laboring classes. This disparaging word for organized forms of popular resistance had survived from the sixteenth century without being put to much use. Throughout the eighteenth century, most rioting observed a traditional formula that did not appear particularly threatening; rioting continued to observe the ritual pattern that contained popular uprisings within an encompassing symbolic system rather than allowing them to disrupt in such a system.[7] According to the unwritten law of agrarian England, E. P. Thompson explains, landowners felt they had a right to demand the labor they required for maintaining their estates, and laborers felt they had a right to a subsistence living in return. When their standard of living fell below a certain level, it was not uncommon for the laboring poor to stage a riot. The riots operated "within a popular consensus as to what were legitimate and what were illegitimate economic practices," a consensus that "can be said to constitute the moral economy of the crowd."[8] Rather than spontaneous disruptions of civil order, in other words, the riots were forms of symbolic behavior in which landowner and laborer played well-defined and predictable roles. In the words of Eric Hobsbawm and George Rudé, these were "the ritual occasions when the customary order of social relations was briefly stood on its head."[9] It was not uncommon to find women leading a riot or publicly accosting a grain dealer to demand better prices. Such a violation of the sexual hierarchy apparently offered another way of indicating that power relations were being overturned. Political rhetoric could be invoked in much the same way. For example, the gentlemen of one village were warned to prepare "'for a Mob of a Sivel war'" which would "'pull George from his throne and beat down the hous of rougs and destroy sets of the Lawmakers.'"[10] Those involved understood that such elaborate parodies of legitimate power served a conservative purpose as they appealed to the landowner for a remedy to the situation. The response to these riots confirms their conservative nature, for the eighteenth century landowner generally preferred to satisfy the demands of the laborers rather than call in the military.[11]

The violence characterizing the early decades of the nineteenth century leaves no doubt that one is passing into new historical territory. The Luddite rebellions in particular redefined both the scene and the objective of violence. Comprising the elite among textile workers, the Luddites saw their status disappearing with the encroachment of machinery on specialized areas of production. Their assaults upon machinery were first viewed as riots similar to those that had been practiced with minimal disruption by the eighteenth century crowd.[12] Some of the features of ritual violence remained—the issuance of warning notices, threats of mass insurrection, the use of female costumes—but the attacks against machinery were organized according to military principles. The Luddites sometimes bore real weapons as well as symbolic ones. They even impressed troops on the way to the scene of a riot. And they communicated by means of an underground network that had its own elaborate codes. More importantly, the Luddite rebellion went beyond the confines of a local riot as weavers and croppers in various parts of England claimed to be marching under the legendary leadership of General Ludd. The geographic distribution of machine-breaking incidents was so widespread that no local group of landowners could hope to bring them under control.

As Thompson argues, the Luddites simply meant to restore the finely graded social order in which they held relatively advantageous positions; even landowners and magistrates at first saw their uprising in this conservative light.[13] During the years following the French Revolution, however, the tolerance for such violence vanished. Aristocratic paranoia apparently converged with the economic interests of the industrial classes to suppress all such political activism. In this atmosphere, the first of the Combination Acts became law: "The aristocracy were interested in repressing the Jacobin 'conspiracies' of the people, the manufacturers were interested in defeating their 'conspiracies' to increase wages."[14] The novelty of the new law was in prohibiting all forms of combination, even those forms of political organization in which the artisan classes had been participating since the beginning of the eighteenth century. Particularly suspect for harboring seditious intent were not only the trade unions, but also the increasing numbers of vagrants who wandered the countryside in search of a livelihood, the households that extended beyond the immediate family, and the people who gathered in pubs. There were, in Thompson's words, "two cultures in England," one designed to resist "the intrusion of the magistrate, the employer, the parson, or the spy" into working-class life, the other aimed at containing and supervising the inherently disruptive practices of the people.[15] The conflict between these two interpretations of violence—as ritual protest or political subversion—was clearly dramatized in the Peterloo Massacre.

In their 1819 march to Manchester, representatives of a displaced and impoverished artisan class challenged the modern redefinition of ritual protest. Because their use of the figures of festival led to the Peterloo Massacre, however, it showed how drastically the meaning of ritual protest had changed. The diary of one of the leaders, Samuel Bamford, records the essentially conservative motive for calling a meeting that drew workers from all the great towns in England. Bamford writes:

> It was deemed expedient that this meeting should be as morally effective as possible, and, that it should exhibit a spectacle such as had never before been witnessed in England. We had frequently been taunted by the press, with our ragged, dirty appearance, at these assemblages; with the confusion of our proceedings, and the mob-like crowds in which our numbers were mustered; and we determined that, for once at least, these reflections should not be deserved,—that we would disarm the bitterness of our political opponents by a display of cleanliness, sobriety, and decorum, such as we never before had exhibited.[16]

The marchers observed one cultural imperative when they appeared well scrubbed and sober, but they observed quite another one when they decked themselves out for the march in headbands, carried mock weapons and embroidered banners, and used a contingent of "our handsomest girls" to lead the way. The government officials in charge completely misread the signs of ritual protest. They saw the mob "come in a threatening manner—they came under banners of death, thereby showing they meant to overthrow the government."[17] But if the workers made a mistake in mixing signs of domesticity with those of festival, the military committed a more serious violation of the traditional rhetoric of violence.

The conflict can be said to have marked a turning point in the history of violence. The march on Manchester carried the practices of ritual protest onto a political field where interpreting them in terms of an earlier moral economy proved very difficult. By winning a military victory that left some five hundred unarmed workers wounded and another eleven dead, the government suffered a political defeat. The liberal press joined with the radical organs in portraying the use of military force as more threatening to the nation than the practice of combination, or organized protest. Samuel Bamford's diary provides a clear indication of the terms in which government force was perceived in the aftermath of Peterloo:

> In ten minutes . . . the field was an open and almost deserted space. . . . The husting remained, with a few broken and hewed flagstaves erect, and a torn and gashed banner or two drooping; whilst over the whole field were strewed caps, bonnets, hats, shawls, and shoes, and other parts of male and female dress, trampled, torn, and bloody.[18]

These scattered fragments of domestic life describe a people who have been raped and pillaged, a people rather than a scene to which order has been restored. So described, the battlefield spells out a dilemma for which there was really no historical precedent. The government came under extremely harsh criticism, and workers were turned into objects of indignation and pity, for government, not the workers, seemed to represent a threat to the family.

The Rhetoric of Disorder: 1832

At this point, my history of the figure of combination diverges from the histories by Thompson and by Hobsbawm and Rudé, both of which represent the working class from its formation to the collapse of Chartism in 1848. My study shifts away from the theater of political events, as we usually define them, to that of writing and the human sciences, which took up the figure during the great cholera epidemic of 1832—at the very time when the disastrous anti-combination legislation was being repealed. New forms of writing appeared as if in response to the need to redefine the terms of class conflict so that some remedy other than force could be imagined. Commissioned by the Irish government in the late 1830s to tour the rapidly industrializing Lancashire countryside and report what he saw there, W. Cooke Taylor was one of many authors who felt compelled to update the metaphors used for describing the people. His survey provides a convenient encapsulation of the changes that combination had undergone in the writing that developed around the great project of describing "the condition of the working class" which gave rise to the human sciences. Taylor contends that one can no longer think of the people in terms "of sudden convulsions, tempestuous seas, or furious hurricanes, but as the slow swelling of an ocean which must, at some future and no distant time, bear all the elements of society aloft upon its bosom, and float them—Heaven knows whither."[19] As he translates the crowd into natural metaphors, it is not the crowd's potential to riot but the fact of its collective identity that seems to trouble this author. No longer can this popular force be either tolerated or crushed in the manner of the eighteenth century crowd. Power appears nonetheless ominous for assuming a female position in relation to the dominant culture. Its presence is not only all pervasive and necessary to life but essentially beyond the power of culture to comprehend it. Understood in these terms, the crowd calls for an entirely new means of control.

Taylor insists that the amassing of workers has made the use of force obsolete:

There are mighty energies slumbering in those masses: had our ancestors witnessed the assemblage of such a multitude as is poured out of Union Street, magistrates would have assembled, special constables would have been sworn, the riot act read, the military called out, and most probably some fatal collision would have taken place. The crowd now scarcely attracts the attention of a passing policeman, but it is, nevertheless, a crowd, and therefore susceptible of the passions which may animate a multitude.[20]

Once such a multitude would have posed an immediate threat to the state, but in this representation, it has grown less cunning and less conscious of itself as a political force. Taylor implies that it is best to see the crowd as mindlessly passionate, more like women, servants, or children. Having so drained the problem of its political content, Taylor arrives at the following solution during the same factory tour:

In fact, all the persons engaged in a mill are subject to the control of a power able to mediate between them with equal fairness and authority. . . . The steam engine is the most impartial of arbitrators: it is impassive to bribes, it is insensible to flattery, and it is the common assistant and friend to all.[21]

Representing the machine as such a rational force enables Taylor to identify it as the ideal form of male authority. Thus the machine affords the solution to the very problem it had presumably caused, namely, the amassing of workers.

Taylor's rethinking of the combination problem metaphorically translated the problem into gender differences that urban sociology was just then refining into an analytical tool. During the 1830s, numerous writers took on the task of mapping those regions of society that fostered political resistance. For example, in his book *The Moral and Physical Condition of the Working Classes Employed in the Cotton Manufacture in Manchester,* James Kay Shuttleworth marshalled all the tropes of Enlightenment discourse, especially those linking power to observation.[22] "One must descend to the abodes of poverty," he argues, "one must frequent the close alleys, the crowded courts, the overpeopled habitations of wretchedness, where pauperism and disease congregate round the source of social discontent and political disorder in the centre of our large towns, and behold with alarm, ills that fester in secret, at the very heart of society."[23] Shuttleworth's observations bring the plague-infested city to light with a gesture that unfolds both the problem and its solution. It transforms the signs of combination from those of an opposing political organization into those of a degenerate culture. Such an ethnographic gesture locates the practices associated with combination outside of culture proper and yet within the sphere of the social where they can be observed and analytically mastered.

Shuttleworth first represents working-class culture as a space lacking certain boundaries. These boundaries would form the categories that must be present, according to the Enlightenment definition, in order for culture to exist.[24] But the absence of such boundaries does not mean that, according to this figure of thought, one is in the presence of nature. Rather, it represents a culture so degenerate it can only be described in terms of dissolution and filth. Shuttleworth proceeds to supply a statistical summary of information concerning the condition of streets in the poorer sections of Manchester: "among 438 streets inspected, 214 were altogether unpaved—32 partially paved—63 ill ventilated—and 259 contained heaps of refuse, deep ruts, stagnant pools, ordure, etc." To this he adds a second set of what he calls "equally remarkable results." He itemizes the houses in need of repair, lists the number that require whitewashing, and counts those that are damp, poorly ventilated, or in need of a privy (p. 31). From there, the tabulating eye of the author moves steadily inward to discover that a similar degeneration of boundaries characterizes interior space. What I would like to stress in reproducing this information is the logic of explanation it observes. It should be noted how once the author begins to think in spatial terms, all combination—no matter how traditional—appears limited, liminal, primitive, dirty, and at the same time, subject, as the eighteenth century crowd never was, to certain forms of acculturation.

Let us note in particular what happens to the figure of combination as Shuttleworth uses it to represent conditions in the very heart of the industrial city. For this early sociologist, significantly, that heart is the bedroom, and there, in his words, one beholds "with alarm" that "a whole family is often accommodated on a single bed, and sometimes a *heap* of filthy straw and a covering of old sacking hide them in one indistinguishable *heap*" (p. 33, italics mine). This horror at the heaping and intermixing of bodies—fast becoming the characteristic way of thinking about combination—converts politically charged material into a sexual scandal. The sense of horror deepens with the discovery that two or more families may crowd into one small hovel or that a basement room often houses an entire family. Dissolution then radiates outward from the center where sociology stages the primal scene, as Shuttleworth voyeuristically peers into basement rooms that pigs cohabit with their masters, into the lodging houses where people sleep in shifts "without distinction of age or sex," and into open privies that may service as many as two hundred people (p. 33).

At the heart of the industrial city, then, the middle-class intellectual finds a mess. Here, the family appears as a heap of debris barely indistinguishable from the dirt beneath it. To assign this scene a cause, Shuttleworth takes great pains to correlate the deterioration visible in the streets and homes of impoverished neighborhoods with the number of pubs, and these in turn with the number of crimes against property. Those people who were disposed to drink and to steal were also those most easily incited to riot, Shuttleworth concludes, but this does not suggest a political cause for social upheaval. The neighborhoods where physical deterioration was particularly evident had the greatest number of pubs as well as the highest crime rate because they were where one found "a prevalence of sensuality" (pp. 62–63). Once Shuttleworth sees the physical condition of the working class in terms of gender and generation, he is able to consider the sexuality or, in other words, the moral condition of the worker to be the cause of his economic condition.

Shuttleworth explains that he gathered this data "Whilst engaged with the very intelligent members of the Board of Health, established at Manchester, in devising, and urging into operation, plans for the relief of persons suffering from Cholera" (p. 3). Whether or not the great cholera epidemics of the 1830s were what actually inspired the government officials to collect this information on the poor is not in question. For my purposes, what matters is that sanitary procedures provided the government with a model for controlling the urban masses. Foucault's *Discipline and Punish* describes the modern symbiosis of disease and power in this way: "the image of the plague stands for all forms of confusion and disorder." It is

> met by order; its function is to sort out every possible confusion: that of disease, which is transmitted when bodies are mixed together; that of evil, which is increased when fear and death overcome prohibitions. It lays down for each individual his place, his body, his disease and his death, his well-being, by means of an omnipresent and omniscient power that subdivides itself in a regular, uninterrupted way even to the ultimate determination of the individual, of what characterizes him. Against the plague, which is a mixture, discipline brings into play its power, which is one of analysis.[25]

In committing their observations to writing, the first sociologists enclosed a problem of class relations and national proportions within a discrete space divided by streets, homes, and bedrooms. As it translated a political scandal into a sexual one, such writing apparently began to exercise a form of political power in its own right.

In writing *Artisans and Machinery*, Peter Gaskell set out to take issue with Shuttleworth's conclusions. Gaskell saw England's industrial productivity increasing at the expense of an artisan class that seemed considerably better off in a pre-industrial society. Artisans are not at all given to violence, he contends, but are family men who have been torn against their wills from their wives and children by the factory system. Thus he initially represents the problem in terms that point the finger of blame at industrialization. But while Gaskell means to take issue with Shuttleworth on the cause of the problem, he draws upon Shuttleworth's data. These data do not allow him to examine for long any political cause, but direct him to look instead for a cause in the personal degradation that results from industrialization. Gaskell begins by insisting that the deplorable condition of the artisans arises "from the separation of families, the breakup of households, the disruption of all those ties which link man's heart to the better position of his nature,—viz., his instincts and social affection."[26] Although he means to blame the factory system for destroying the artisan's traditional way of life, Gaskell comes around full circle to identify that way of life as the problem. He describes the artisan's household as lacking divisions that *ought* to organize personal life. As he notes, "the promiscuous way in which families herd together,—a way that prevents all privacy, and which, by bringing into open day things which delicacy commands should be shrouded from observation, destroys all notions of sexual decency and domestic chastity" (p. 89). Despite the author's initial intention, then, he still uses the tropes of division to designate order and those of combination to represent disorder.

In the following passage from Gaskell's study, one can observe his logic turning around to enclose within the artisan's household all the problems causing the disruption of that household:

> A household thus constituted, in which all the decencies and moral observance of domestic life are constantly violated, reduces its inmates to a condition little elevated above that of the savage. Recklessness, improvidence, and unnecessary poverty, starvation, disobedience, neglect of conjugal rights, absence of maternal love, destruction of brotherly and sisterly affection, are often its constituents, and the results of such a *combination* are moral degradation, ruin of domestic enjoyments, and social misery. (p. 89, italics mine)

I would like to note how, once the language of primitivism appears, it takes a simple step for this cultural logic to move interchangeably back and forth between terms representing the physical condition of the poor ("poverty" and "starvation") and those representing their moral degeneracy ("recklessness," "improvidence," "disobedience") until cause and consequence are completely reversed. "Moral degradation, ruin of domestic enjoyments, and social misery" are all "the results of such a combination." In this context, the term "combination," never a neutral word, carries overtones of sexual impropriety or illicit mixing, even as it refers to the scattering of family members. Whether intentionally or not, Gaskell posits a shadowy sexual cause for the disruption of the traditional family.

Wanting to rescue the family rather than cast blame on the artisan, Gaskell laments the passing of a time when families were, as he says,

> bound together by the strong link of affection, each member in its turn, as it attained an age fitted for the loom, joined its labour to the general stock, its earning forming part of a fund, the whole of which was placed at the disposal of the father or the mother, as the case may be; and each individual looked to him or to her for the adequate supply of its wants. (p. 60)

But a project that begins by lamenting the divisive effects of the factory system upon family, village, and class ultimately relocates the problem within a domestic framework. So contained, it takes the form of sexual behavior that violates the most basic familial principles. Thus when he imagines the solution to this problem in terms of a family reunion, Gaskell represents the family in terms that cancel out the original family.[27] In marked contrast with the traditional artisan as he was previously described, the rehabilitated man

> is now stationary, has lost his predatory habits, and has assumed his rank as a social and moral being; that in his further advances he still improves his habitation, builds his house in a more durable manner, and with better materials; divides it into distinct compartments, and separates the sexes; that his wife is no longer an instrument of his labour, but depends upon him for support; that promiscuous intercourse between the sexes is condemned and prohibited as injurious to the marriage contract; and that thus, step after step, he goes on to the maximum of civilisation and exellence of social confederation. (p. 77)

True, Gaskell initially sets the traditional family against the inhumanely mechanistic organization of the factory. But as his study progresses, one sees the family change. The household is subjected to the same spatial, compartmental, and gendered perception that organized factory space.

While sociology redefined political resistance as the lack of order within the private world of the individual, another kind of writing attempted to humanize the factory. Not as prolific as the new sociology perhaps, but certainly copious enough to warrant our attention, this writing represented the factory as having precisely the boundaries in which working-class culture was being found so deficient. The philosophy of manufacturing, as it called itself, began by stripping machinery of the unpleasant features it had acquired in previous decades. Blake's "dark Satanic mills," Carlyle's "huge demonic machine," Southey's "fungeous excresence from the body politic," or the tyrannical King of Steam who belches his way through political cartoons and working-class ballads provide us with some sense of the monstrous images this new kind of writing had to overcome.

One of the more influential attempts at representing the machine as a rational system, Charles Babbage's treatise *On the Economy of Machinery and Manufacturers* illustrates how the machine became both the instrument and figure of social order itself. Babbage shows that even though the motion of the machine originates in an explosive surge of power, such power is essentially unproductive. It manifests all the irregularities of human labor in a dangerously intensified form. The corrective effects of the machine are set in motion as the flywheel translates this violent and intermittent force into a continuously productive one. A "governor" or thermostat then guarantees both uniformity of product and steadiness of production. Babbage's description couples the principle of uniformity with that of division to differentiate individuals according to function. A conveyor belt allows individuals to remain fixed within a space where the productivity of each can be carefully monitored.[28] It is obvious that Babbage is doing much more than designing a factory. He has stumbled upon a new way of thinking about political power.

In his description, one finds that the machine is no longer in opposition to nature but rather the extension and perfection of it. Andrew Ure, an equally influential author on the subject, developed this notion into an even more idealized representation of machinery. In Ure's account, the virtues of the factory system become apparent when one sees that system as "a vast autonmaton, composed of various mechanical and intellectual organs, acting in uninterrupted concert for the production of a common object, all of them being subordinated to a self-regulated moving force."[29] Such an image mingles the languages of technology and medicine to make one mode of analysis for mechanical and natural objects alike. This is to endow organic life with mechanical properties, on the one hand, for natural objects are represented as rationally comprehensible systems. On the other hand, the machine acquires qualities of the modern individual. It becomes an autonomous being with rational intelligence of its own. When all the systems of any such mechanism "are in harmony," according to Ure, "they form a body qualified to discharge manifold functions by an intrinsic self-governing agency, like those of organic life" (p. 55). This mediation of man and machine constitutes what Ure, in one of his chapter titles, calls "The Moral Economy of the Factory System," replacing what Thompson referred to as the "moral economy of the eighteenth-century crowd" as the organizational principle for political relations. It is revealing, I think, that just as the forces of nature empower Babbage's machine, so nature and mechanism comprise mutually dependent concepts in Ure's figure. I am suggesting that these representations of the factory as a rational order assumed this form as they sought imaginatively to overcome the problem of political resistance.

Ure claims that the factory offers a haven of civilization to workers whose abuse of machinery is a sign of their primitive condition. "When the wandering savage becomes a citizen," Ure explains, "he renounces many of his dangerous pleasures in return for tranquility and protection" (p. 278). The author thus uses the social contract in rethinking the relation between owner and workers according to the relationship he has just established between machinery and nature; the factory offers workers "continous labor of a lighter kind with steadier wages" in exchange for their renunciation of violence (p. 278). And the socializing effects of the factory do not end there. The factory also feminizes the female, whose body grows more slim and erect as she tends a mechanical loom. Contrary to opinion, factory life improves her appearance in other ways. As Ure notes, "Many of them have adopted the tasteful modes of wearing neat handkerchiefs on their heads, and altogether not a little of the Grecian style of beauty" (p. 350). Moreover, maidenly virtue has not been compromised by the mingling of sexes that supposedly occurs in the factory, for as Ure remembers, "One of them whose cheeks had a fine rosy hue, being asked how long she had been at factory work, said nine years, and blushed from bashfulness at being so slightly spoken to" (p. 351). The salutory effects of the place also extend to children, who are kept after work, segregated according to sex, cleaned up, and then given "instruction in reading, writing, and arithmetic" (p. 351). Once threatened by the factory, family life, in Ure's view, is now wedded to the mechanistic principle. His factory provides precisely that order which the artisan's household lacks but which is necessary to an individual's "normal" development. For purposes of my argument, it is particularly important to notice what Ure's use of domestic space has in common with Shuttleworth's: Both use domestic space to represent a form of power that has no privileged locus, that is neither repressive nor dogmatic, and whose efficacy resides in a capacity to distribute, classify, analyze, and provide spatial individuality for any object.

The Politics of Domestic Fiction: 1848

Having made this detour through extraliterary territory, let me return now to the matter with which I began, the domestic fiction that appeared in

1848. During the thirty-year period when the figure of combination was politically hot, it was commonly used to represent social disorder as a sexual scandal. During the same period, almost no domestic novels were written. Gone were the heroines of Richardson, Burney, and Austen who seemed to challenge the boundaries of family, status, and role. In the later fiction, marriages that changed people's social status never led to personal happiness. Most often they led to personal disaster, especially for women. Meanwhile, the household became a place for restoring the boundaries that had been obscured by exactly this socially ambitious form of desire. Although the domestic fiction written after 1848, like the fiction written before 1818, still dealt with problems of misguided desire and still resolved them in marriage, it nevertheless had to figure out these problems differently. For there was another political target for novels to domesticate and feminize.

The novels of 1848 begin with violent scenes of punishment and exclusion: Hindley's brutal denigration of Heathcliff in *Wuthering Heights;* Jane Eyre's night of torment in the red-room; Joseph Sedley's abrupt rejection of Becky in *Vanity Fair;* the gratuitous suffering that workers endure at the hands of Bounderby and Carson in novels by Dickens and Elizabeth Gaskell. And each of these scenes of unjustified punishment generates tremendous outrage on behalf of the powerless. To begin with, the violence itself seems to have an external cause. In one form or another, history has intruded upon the household and disrupted its traditional order. The Napoleonic wars in *Vanity Fair* destroy Amelia's traditional hopes for happiness and foster Becky's reckless ambitions. History in the form of archaic inheritance laws and British colonialism similarly disrupts conventional romance in *Jane Eyre* when Rochester's house is found to contain an extra chamber hiding a wife he married for her fortune and brought home from the East Indies years before. In contrast with the manor houses of Richardson and Austen, Brontë's Thornfield Hall cannot contain its historical materials, and she feels compelled to destroy the house before she allows Jane and Rochester to marry. The ruthless operations of capitalism enacted by Heathcliff dismantle the families that organize *Wuthering Heights,* as he supplants the legal heir to the Earnshaw estate and then proceeds to overturn every traditional relationship in the novel. The introduction of new historical material is yet more conspicuous in *Mary Barton* where domestic relationships must somehow be rescued out of the stuff of the new sociology.

It is curious that when Mrs. Gaskell represents the problem in explicitly political terms—

> Living in Manchester, but with a deep relish and fond admiration for the country, my first thought was to find a frame-work for my story in some

rural scene; and I had already made a little progress in a tale, the period of which was more than a century ago, and the place on the borders of Yorkshire, when I bethought me how deep might be the romance in the lives of some of those who elbowed me daily in the busy streets of the town in which I resided. I had always felt a deep sympathy with the care-worn men, who looked as if doomed to struggle through their lives in strange alternations between work and want; tossed to and fro by circum-stances, apparently even in greater degree than other men.[30]

—the disruption of violence appears to have no political cause. Although *Mary Barton* begins by lamenting the ever-widening gap between classes, Gaskell soon devotes all her rhetorical ingenuity to outlawing the practice of combination. In contrast with Shuttleworth and the many others who wrote about conditions in the city, she writes as a novelist and thus as a woman. As such, she can claim to "know nothing of Political Economy, or of the theories of trade" (p.38). For a historical study, however, the strategies that Gaskell's fiction actually shares with the writing of Shut-tleworth and others are more important than the ways in which her fiction differs from their empirical data.

The conventions of sociology are just as important as sentimental con-vention in determining how the problem of the workers' condition came to be understood. The two modes of writing work hand in hand to confine political disruption within an apolitical framework. Although Mrs. Gas-kell includes political material in its most topical form, history virtually disappears from her novel as class conflict comes to be represented as a matter of sexual misconduct and a family scandal.[31] The other novels I am considering similarly uncover a sexual scandal as the source of dis-turbances that tear a family apart. The bond linking Catherine to Heath-cliff—across time and space and in violation of marriage laws—causes her ghost to disrupt Lockwood's slumber. This compels him in turn to solicit the history of sexual relations that identifies the bond between Catherine and Heathcliff as the secret cause of all the disruptive events in the novel. Such illicit desire is also the ultimate truth we discover in *Jane Eyre*. Beneath all the sexual adventures comprising Rochester's his-tory, Jane uncovers the far greater scandal of a marriage based solely on money and lust that preclude a companionate relationship. And what else creates change in *Vanity Fair* if not Becky's subversive sexual behavior? It is she who deprives Amelia of a loving husband well before Thackeray has him killed off on the battlefield at Waterloo.

Which returns us, then, to the question of the monstrous women for whom this fiction is remembered: What role did they play in the historical process I have been sketching? As I have explained in earlier chapters, the eighteenth century was concerned with representing the legitimate alliance of the sexes. But by the high Victorian period, that alliance had to displace and resolve a very different political conflict. As Foucault notes in *The History of Sexuality*, there came a point during the nineteenth century when "the legitimate couple, with its regular sexuality, had a right to more discretion. It tended to function as a norm, one that was stricter" than an earlier notion of sexuality, but one that was less subject to representation as well.[32] *Pamela* fails to be a good novel in present-day terms largely because Richardson goes on, after Mr. B acknowledges Pamela's desirability as a wife, to describe their state of perfect matrimony. But even at that he stops short of describing the perfect wedding night he claims is theirs at last to enjoy. Foucault reminds us, however, that during the nineteenth century,

> what came under scrutiny was the sexuality of children, mad men and women, and criminals; the sensuality of those who did not like the opposite sex; reveries, obsessions, petty manias, or great transports of rage. It was time for all these figures, scarcely noticed in the past, to step forward and speak, to make the difficult confession of what they were. (pp. 38–39)

Such figures overshadow the normal characters in the novels of the late 1840s, but perhaps nowhere so obviously as in work of the Brontës.

No reader forgets Rochester's "bad, mad, and embruted" wife as she is represented here:

> In the deep shade, at the further end of the room, a figure ran backwards and forwards. What it was, whether beast or human being, one could not, at first sight tell: it grovelled, seemingly, on all fours; it snatched and growled like some strange wild animal; but it was covered with clothing; and a quantity of dark, grizzled hair, wild as a man, hid its head and face.[33]

Or consider the last view we receive of the woman who drives Heathcliff to commit crimes against the family in *Wuthering Heights*. As he recounts it, "'I got the sexton to remove the earth off her coffin lid, and opened it. I thought once, I would have stayed there, when I saw her face again—it is hers yet—he had hard work to stir me; but he said it would change, if the air blew on it.'"[34] Representing the last of the earlier generation of Earnshaws and embodying their pre-individualistic notion of identity, the same woman lives on into the present as a ghostly child. In this form, she enters the sleep of the utterly modern individual who has invaded her bedroom and peered into the books that bear traces of her personal history. In a scene where Brontë deliberately neglects to draw distinctions between subjective and objective experience, this ghostly woman grasps Lockwood, the intrusive narrator, with "a little ice-cold hand." Such encroachment by a female upon the male consciousness turns the room into something resembling the scene of rape, only here the features of aggressor and victim are grotesquely confused along with the features of gender. As the narrator describes, "I pulled its wrist on to the broken pane, and rubbed it to and fro till the blood ran down and soaked the bedclothes; still it wailed, 'let me in!' and maintained its tenacious grip, almost maddening me with fear" (p. 30). Unlike the desire that threatened to take forms of rape or adultery in earlier fiction, this material cannot be domesticated by marriage. It is definitely outside of culture.

Thackeray uses a similar figure of boundary dissolution to represent certain human desires that cannot be included within the novel, at least not in any literal way or realistic mode of description. On discovering Becky's infidelity, her husband tears up their household, reducing it to "a *heap* of tumbled vanities lying in a wreck," and sends her back to the streets from which she came (italics mine).[35] It is significant that once outside the bounds of polite society, Becky loses her sharp socioeconomic delineation. To represent what a woman in this state becomes, Thackeray resorts to a literary figure, the sirens of classical mythology. Apparently they "look pretty enough when they sit upon a rock and beckon you to come," but, the narrator warns, when they sink into their own element—in this case, the city—"those mermaids are about no good, and we had best not examine the fiendish marine cannibals, feasting on their pickled victims" (p. 617). As the classical figure for misdirected desire is rewritten for a Victorian audience, we should note, it loses its aesthetic features and takes on those of a savage. No matter how closely Becky may resemble the people of polite society, that resemblance is at best superficial. Her sexual behavior reveals her origins in another class.

Henry Mayhew's famous classification system for criminal behavior in *London Labour and London Poor* (1862) can be viewed as a blatant attempt by a middle-class intellectual to tranform the problem of an impoverished working class by translating this social dilemma into sexual terms.[36] In constructing his system of all the criminal types populating London, Mayhew cut through the political categories—distinctions based on one's source of income and place within a competitive economy—that had been isolated and refined in the earlier writing on political economy. For Mayhew, the first and most basic social distinction among men was the profound gulf between those who worked and those who did not. Among those who *would* not work were all criminal types, according to Mayhew. Such a view toward the vast number of unemployed that characterized Victorian England may help to explain how capitalism became relatively stable by the mid-nineteenth century despite continuing fluctuations in the economy. As Thomas Laqueur reminds us:

The great divisions in early nineteenth century society were not between the middle and the working classes but between the idle and the non-idle classes, between the rough and the respectable, between the religious and the non-religious. All of these divisions ran across class lines. The puritan ethic was therefore not the monopoly of the owners of capital; it was the ideology of those who worked against those who did not.[37]

While this binary opposition was forged in the sociological descriptions of the 1830s and 1840s, the second half of the nineteenth century would make such categories impervious to interrogation. In *London Labour and London Poor*, Mayhew begins straightforwardly enough to map out the various kinds of crime that comprise London lowlife, but his description abruptly swerves away from crimes against property. It departs from the world of male deviance and singles out prostitution as the figure for virtually all other forms of criminal behavior:

> Literally construed, prostitution is the putting of anything to vile use; in this sense perjury is a species of prostitution, being an unworthy use of the faculty of speech; so again, bribery is a prostitution of the right of voting; while prostitution, specially so called, is the using of her charms by a woman for immoral purposes. . . . Be the cause, however, what it may, the act remains the same, and consists in the base perversion of a woman's charms—the surrendering of her virtue to criminal indulgence. (p. 35)

We should note the reflex that makes the woman into the agent of her own prostitution ("the using of her charms by a woman," "the surrendering of her virtue"). It is worth pausing over this curious tendency to view prostitution as the only crime that seems to be its own cause. The role that prostitution plays in Mayhew's classification system as a whole is also worth noting. In his description, prostitution is at first only one category among the many kinds of crime committed by people who will not work. But eventually the category balloons into an elaboration comprising half the entire volume and becomes both the figure for crime in general and the implicit source of all crime. Not only does sexual conduct provide the basis for Mayhew's entire catalogue of urban criminal types, but the theme of prostitution provides him with a means of comparing all modern cultures and those of earlier periods as well. In short, Mayhew's description of London advances a notion of deviance that aims at the laboring poor but that can be extended to other cultures. His urban sociology therefore provides the general basis for anthropological procedures.

After his exhaustive study of prostitution throughout time and geographical location, Mayhew begins the section entitled "Thieves and Swindlers" by offering an analogy for the curious structure of his project:

"In tracing the geography of a river it is interesting to go to its source.
. . . We proceed in a similar manner to treat of the thieves and swindlers
of the metropolis" (p. 273). At the source of urban criminal culture, he
discovers a female who is precisely what the domestic woman is not, and
he describes her in the same terms as he described the prostitute:

> Thousands of our felons are trained from their infancy in the bosom of
> crime. . . . Many of them are often carried to the beershop or gin palace
> on the breast of worthless drunken mothers, while others, clothed in rags,
> run at their heels or hang by the skirts of their petticoats. (p. 273)

By way of this reference to Mayhew, I want to call attention to the importance of the prostitute in nineteenth century political thought, which
uses this figure to evaluate people in terms that have nothing to do with
their economic circumstances or political position.[38] Yet sexual conduct
is clearly a political language. It places both individuals and cultures on
a moral continuum that declares any sexual behavior other than legitimate
monogamy as perverse and criminal. Mayhew not only specifies an elaborate system of normal desires and a standard for the conduct of private
life. He also uses that historically specific model of sexuality as a universal and timeless one.

In turning now to the fictional use of the prostitute, we find that she
is also the figure underlying all the monstrous women under consideration. An early Victorian novel and not yet Dickens' full-blown treatment
of the relationship between money and love, the two halves of the Victorian world, *Oliver Twist* (1837) provides one of the clearest illustrations
of the rhetorical purpose of the prostitute's almost obligatory appearance
in fiction. Dickens' characterization of Nancy, the good-hearted prostitute, demonstrates how a uniquely Victorian logic was formulated out of
the materials of an earlier moment in history. In her, the dangerous elements that must be abolished in the prostitute is clearly present as such
rather than, as in later novels, dispersed among the features of her less
obvious avatars. Nancy is the figure of illicit sexuality; her behavior confuses money with sex. But if Nancy commits the crime of prostitution
and—worse yet—delivers Oliver over to Fagin, her devotion to her man
Sikes surpasses any other affiliation in the novel, and she ultimately is
the one who returns Oliver to polite society by divulging the secret of his
pedigree. Paradoxically, then, Nancy is the antithesis of the absent mother
and an alternative source of nurturance as well as a surrogate for that
mother. It has to be the mixing of illicit sexual features with the attributes
of the good mother that makes her body the site of sexual violence. More
than any other scene in the Dickens repertoire, including even the death

of little Nell, the scene in which Sikes bludgeons his prostitute-lover to death both fascinated and appalled the audiences who flocked to hear Dickens' reading performances.[39] The power of the scene has everything to do with the fact that Nancy is the representation of another class sexuality as well as a positive figure. Her mutilated body expresses intense hostility toward the working classes, even though Dickens represents them as victims who need to be rescued. One could say this body provided a field where two notions of the family confronted one another and the old gave way to the new.

Having noted the habit of Victorian culture to sexualize all combination, that is, to render all collective forms of social organization as sexual violations, one still must ask what the novel did differently. The dramatic reappearance of domestic fiction during the late 1840s suggests that these novels had their own role to play. They not only contained disorder within the household, but they also gave it female form. In other words, coming between Shuttleworth in the 1830s and Mayhew in the 1860s, novels further displaced the conflict between competing social formations as they turned combination into a female who lacked femininity. It is no accident that all the monstrous women in question have other than middle-class origins. Resembling Bahktin's figure of the grotesque body in several ways, this kind of female body is open, permeable, and ambiguously gendered. In her, other sexual behaviors linger on as archaic forms that are both powerless and terrible. And as these cultural materials are contained within the body of a deranged woman, all threats of social disruption suddenly lose their political meaning and are just as suddenly quelled.

With the murder of Nancy, the collective ethos of the urban underworld in *Oliver Twist* is demoralized and the characters scattered. The transformation of the prostitute's body into a battered corpse instantly criminalizes the merry gang of thieves who rescue Oliver from certain starvation. But the murder of Nancy also provides a way of containing this alternative form of social organization within a figure of combination and a way of transforming that figure into one that can be subjected to middle-class authority. Nancy appears in several forms throughout the novel, but the one that most closely resembles the monstrous women of the Brontës' fiction is not the woman who has been reduced to a pool of gore, though indeed, in the narrator's words, "it was a ghastly figure to look upon" (p. 323). Instead, she assumes truly Gothic proportions only after her murder and as she lives on in the mind of her killer.[40] It is not as a material body at all that she exercises her power, then, but as a psychological one:

For now, a vision came before him, as constant and more terrible than that from which he had escaped. Those widely staring eyes, so lustreless and so glassy, that he had better born to see them than to think upon them, appeared in the midst of darkness: light in themselves, but giving light to nothing. There were but two, but they were everywhere. If he shut out the sight, there came the room with every well-known object—some, indeed, that he would have forgotten, if he had gone over its contents from memory—each in its accustomed place. (pp. 327–28)

As she comes back to haunt the criminal, we should note, the figure of the prostitute works on the side of legitimate authority. She exercises a panoptical power that sees deep into the hearts of men and from whose gaze they cannot hope to escape, it is so all encompassing. This power is a form of social control in its own right and is in fact required to bring the novel to a successful conclusion. As her figure is contained within the framework of Sikes' subjectivity, it turns his body against him, makes him visible wherever he goes, and drives him finally to serve as his own executioner:

"The eyes again!" he cried, in an unearthly screetch.

Staggering as if struck by lightning, he lost his balance and tumbled over the parapet. The noose was at his neck. It ran up with his weight, tight as a bow-string, and swift as the arrow it speeds. (p. 347)

It is certainly a significant event when a novel represents an execution that is not performed by the state but by the criminal himself. And it is even more significant when the power of the state is enhanced simply by knowledge of the crime, as if such knowledge were in itself a remedy. Coming after the murder of Nancy and performed by Sikes' own conscience, his execution is staged in a manner that makes no demands on liberal sympathies. In contrast with the state execution of Fagin, the execution of Sikes is arranged so that readers can simply enjoy the extinction of a professed class enemy. His death is not only a public execution, but also a scene on the scaffold that he stages for himself.

Like sociology, the novel represents the disruption of domestic order in terms of combination; the destruction of boundaries between nature and culture reveals itself in a mixture of genders and generations and associates the scene of such dissolution with filth and disease. These qualities would be exaggerated in the cities of slightly later novels such as *Bleak House* and *Our Mutual Friend,* but the novels of the 1840s already observe the figurative logic of sociological description. They use scenes of discipline to restore the household disrupted by aberrant forms of desire. By way of a remedy, each novel offers up a static tableau that represents the family in a highly idealized and decidedly modern form. One glimpses such a scene through the window of Wuthering Heights as the Earnshaw family history ends. Here the household encloses a new generation of lovers within a radically exclusive space that is divided according to sex and to function. Thus we see the young Catherine deliberately departing from earlier sentimental heroines as she educates Hareton for a gentleman's role:

> He was a young man respectably dressed, and seated at a table, having a book before him. His handsome features glowed with pleasure, and his eyes kept impatiently wandering from the page to a small white hand over his shoulder, which recalled him by a smart slap on the cheek whenever its owner detected such signs of inattention. (p. 243)

A similar scene of rehabilitation also concludes the courtship of Jane Eyre and Rochester. Tucked away from the world with an invalid husband, Jane describes their relationship in terms that endow her with all the panoptical powers we observed both in Dickens' Nancy and in the second Catherine of *Wuthering Heights:*

> Literally, I was (what he often called me) the apple of his eye. He saw nature—he saw books through me; and never did I weary of gazing for his behalf, and of putting into words the effect of field, tree, town, river, cloud, sunbeam—of the landscape before us; of the weather around us— and impressing by sound on his ear what light could no longer stamp on his eye. (p. 397)

It is in the use of disciplinary strategies that *Vanity Fair* resembles the other great novels of its day, as Thackeray leaves us in a world he imagines as a joyless bazaar partitioned off into booths. Such women as Becky Sharp pose no threat to us in this highly individuated world. And because they each have revealed some slightly twisted desire, these characters suddenly become more alike than different, and marriage among them resembles nothing so much as a prison.

I would like to suggest that these novels were making history as they turned scenes of punishment into those that represented order in terms resembling representations of the factory, prison, and schoolroom. Novels incorporated new political material and sexualized it in such a manner that only one resolution would do: a partitioned and hierarchical space under a woman's surveillance. Because it is the earliest and least psychological of the novels I have been considering in this chapter, *Oliver Twist* again offers the most revealing display of social redemption through the domestication of desire. After scattering the underworld characters and purging them from his novel, Dickens encloses Oliver himself within a household and places him with a cousin who is neither mother, nor sister, nor lover, but who has displaced all of these roles. In this way, the reconstituted family recalls the death of the original family that the novel had originally sought to restore. The novel ends with a scene that also marks the death of an earlier mode of fiction. No matter how much the present resembles the past homologically, an abyss opens between them when Oliver's true mother reappears as a name for which there can never be a referent. Even more so than Nancy, the prostitute, Agnes, the true mother, becomes a disembodied woman:

> Within the altar of the old village church, there stands a white marble tablet, which bears as yet but one word,—"Agnes!" There is no coffin in that tomb; and may it be many, many years, before another name is placed above it! But, if the spirits of the Dead ever come back to earth, to visit spots hallowed by the love—the love beyond the grave—of those whom they knew in life, I believe that the shade of Agnes sometimes hovers round that solemn nook. I believe it none the less because that nook is in a Church, and she was weak and erring. (p. 368)

Like Emily Brontë, Dickens leaves us with the ghosts of fiction past, figures of desire that have no place to occupy within the social order but, for that very reason, all the more important a role to play in constituting the household.[41]

Figures of Desire: The Brontës

On my way to the annual Brontë conference at the University of Leeds in 1981, I decided to test a hypothesis. The conference that year was concerned with the Brontës' relationship to their historical context. In writing my own paper for the event, I had already grown dissatisfied with answers that posed the question of context and text in terms of the conventional model of base and superstructure. Ready to be convinced that the Brontës were somehow part of the history of England rather than self-enclosed neurotics or socially aware writers who addressed topical issues, I tried an experiment. I asked my cab driver what he considered to be the most important event of 1848. With an air of absolute certainty, he told me, "The death of Emily Brontë."[42] He could respond in this way without hesitation, yet after more than a century's worth of literary criticism, we have no way of explaining why two women writers from a remote region of Yorkshire should occupy a place of such prominence in the British cultural consciousness. I am convinced there is a direct relationship between the historical importance of their fiction and the difficulty we have historicizing the Brontës; they had more to do with formulating universal forms of subjectivity than any other novelists. If today their writing seems unrelated to history, it is because they perfected tropes to distinguish fiction from historically bound writing. These tropes translated all kinds of political information into psychological terms. As they displaced the facts and figures of social history, the Brontës began producing new figures of desire that detached the desiring self from place, time, and material cause. Never mind that Heathcliff comes from the streets of Liverpool and that Brontë sets the date of his appearance in the novel around the time of the provincial hunger riots (1766). By the end of *Wuthering Heights* he has become a phantasm of unfulfilled sexual desire.

As if to testify to the success of the Brontës' fables of desire, literary criticism has compulsively read these novels according to the same psychologizing tropes they formulated. Indeed, contemporary criticism has turned the Brontës' novels into sublimating strategies that conceal forbidden desires, including incest, which is generally considered the most plausible key to the novels.[43] Critics still seem to be asking what else, if not such desire, could have motivated the elaborate sequences of substitutions that finally allow both *Wuthering Heights* and *Jane Eyre* to end with satisfactory marriages. The Brontës still entice us to extend their own aesthetic process to inscribe, finally, all their historical material within figures of desire. So powerful is the hermeneutic circle that makes their language of the self into its own basis for meaning that the noblest efforts to evade this trap are ensnared themselves as critics inevitably adopt a modern psychological vocabulary to interpret the Brontës' fiction. Traditional interpretations look at the Brontës' distortion of domestic convention and say their fiction dramatizes the necessity of adhering to the conventions of middle-class subjectivity.[44] They posit a meaning, or depth, that actually exists on the surface in the manipulation of signifiers. Psychoanalytically oriented criticism has turned this tautology inside out to argue that in ultimately conforming to the conventional notion of love, the Brontës displaced and denied their true desires; their fiction consequently records a process of sublimation and repression.[45] Feminist criticism has added a further twist to the argument by turning the model of repression around once again to dispute the premise that these novels conceal desires which the Brontës could not consciously acknowledge. For the feminist critic, figures of desire generally point to forms of feeling that the authors could not unleash without violating what it meant then to be a woman. By setting language in opposition to emotion, one can then argue that the Brontës distorted the conventions of love as an expres-

sion of their frustration and rage at being women writers within a patriarchal society.[46]

But contentious as this field may appear, Brontë criticism has in fact
agreed to disagree on a relatively minor question, namely, how willingly
and consciously did these authors resist or submit to Victorian conventions of love? All Brontë criticism grants a priori that desire and language
are opposed. Both the degree of aesthetic perfection that the Brontës
achieved in their writing and the degree of emotional health that we can
discern in their work depend on the nature of the opposition between
desire and language and on the author's ability to achieve mediation. In
perpetuating a tradition that opposes language to emotion, however, Brontë
criticism has agreed not to dispute the primary assumptions that (1) meaning is grounded in the emotional life of the authors, and (2) in being so
autobiographical, their language refers back to a family dynamic which
exists prior to its representation in fiction. To be sure, criticism often
credits the Brontës with being among the first to represent certain—still
psychologically valid—states of mind. But Brontë criticism also accepts
the fundamentally modern assumption that such representations were motivated by states of mind that the authors actually experienced but whose
meaning they distorted for lack of modern analytic techniques. Because
the Brontës could not finally articulate what they repressed, the argument
goes, it is the critic's job to provide the psychological insight and thereby
complete the hermeneutic circle.

I must hasten to qualify these generalizations by acknowledging the
few critics who have undertaken the work of explaining why such fantasies of desire emerged during the mid-nineteenth century and spoke to
the interests of the literate classes. Attempts to answer this question generally proceed on the assumption that, as Terry Eagleton argues, the Brontës'
"ideological structure arises from the *real history* of the West riding in
the first half of the nineteenth century; and it is . . . imaginatively grasped
and transposed in the production of the Brontës' fiction."[47] Thus sociological criticism tends to understand "ideology" as something that comes
from outside of fiction, outside of language per se. Arising in the masculine domain of economics and politics where history occurs, ideology
is subsequently taken into the household through the private world of
individual consciousness, and from there it becomes the stuff of fiction.
The household, the family, and the material body of the subject remain
unchanged despite the fact that political information has come in and gone
out of the house through the individual mind. The Brontës' fiction constitutes a mediation between female subject and the masculine world of
objects, a mediation that, according to Eagleton, represents "the isolation

of all men in an individualistic world" (p. 4). Having thus distinguished fictional text from historical context, this mode of criticism can read the Brontës' fiction as "the opaque but decipherable signs" of events that occur in a world of material objects outside of language and outside of any particular human consciousness. In such a sociological model, it seems, fictions of female subjectivity acquire historical meaning as they are translated into an allegory for economic change. Underlying such criticism is the unquestioned assumption that while, as Eagleton puts it, "the sisters would certainly have seen a good deal of destitution on their own doorstep," history in effect stopped there (p. 13). It is as if history, by definition, could not enter into the household.[48]

But let us assume such emphasis on the behavior of male institutions is not what the Brontës were challenging. I do not think they felt that power existed exclusively in such institutions. It is more likely they were still in touch with a time when people knew better. The true dynamic of history was largely invisible, one can imagine Charlotte observing, and those favored by the tradition of letters—the fashionable writers—were hardly the ones to possess historical knowledge and put it in writing. At some point in her life, it is very possible she saw the advantage she possessed in having experienced so much of the world only in and through language—the written materials that flowed through the Brontë household. For her and her siblings, more than for most other people, this writing was not merely the record of experience but one and the same thing as experience itself. Writing provided the Brontës with the means to create themselves rather than simply to represent individuals who already existed as such beforehand. Biographical evidence provides us no grounds for the assumption that the Brontë sisters found writing a repressive mechanism. In fact, all of the evidence suggests that from a remarkably early age they thought of personal fulfillment in terms of writing, and consequently they prepared themselves to be novelists the way other women supposedly prepared themselves to be wives and mothers.[49] To say this is to call into question the main presupposition on which most Brontë criticism rests, namely, the curiously tenacious belief that writing and desire are ontologically different and ideologically opposed.

Yet it does not require any great stretch of imagination to think that these women knew the power of language to constitute subjectivity and knew as well that such power was easily available to women. In Charlotte's biographical sketch that followed her preface to the 1850 edition of *Wuthering Heights,* there is nothing to suggest that she resents the family's rude origins and intellectually isolated condition. Quite the contrary, there is everything to suggest she sees distinct advantages in her position. To those who might reject Emily's novel on the grounds that its writing lacked polish and self-restraint, Charlotte writes:

> Men and women who, perhaps, naturally very calm, and with feelings moderate in degree, and little marked in kind, have been trained from their cradle to observe the utmost evenness of manner and guardedness of language, will hardly know what to make of the rough, strong utterance, the harshly manifested passions, the unbridled aversions, and headlong partialities of unlettered moorland hinds and rugged moorland squires, who have grown up untaught and unchecked, except by mentors as harsh as themselves. (p. 9)

The family's removal from the centers of political power and fashionable intellectual life does not brand Emily as ignorant except in the most superficial way. In fact, Charlotte suggests, her sister's position in life allowed her to experience the emotions more completely and to understand their mysterious workings. In contrast, the typical novel reader has been educated to behave and speak in polite terms and to understand others accordingly. But such an education leaves one ill prepared to understand emotion as anything but an idealized and therefore standardized surface that necessarily conceals the individual self. A novelist reared in the rugged north country actually possesses self-knowledge that her refined southern counterpart lacks, or so Charlotte implies, and therefore, the differences between the author of *Wuthering Heights* and her readership arise not from the ignorance of the author, but from that of polite readers. In other words, their marginal relationship to the tradition of letters gave the Brontës access to an entirely different body of knowledge that by its very nature disrupted the life of the parlor. It was doubtless for this reason that both Charlotte and Emily used conspicuously marginal narrators in their most successful fiction.

Let us suppose for a moment that Foucault was right, then, and there really was a moment in political history when power became knowledge and worked mainly through discourse to create a subject ideally suited to inhabit a modern institutional culture. Let us suppose, further, that the whole middle-class enterprise depended on making that subject known to himself or herself as one who could be analyzed, evaluated, developed, improved, and judged happy and/or successful in comparison with others, even with those of other places and times. Such a form of consciousness would have depended on a language that detached its object of knowledge from the vicissitudes of history. To put it another way, this consciousness would have depended on a language that defined history as the exclusive history of male institutions—the history of the economy, church, law, and other procedures of state. So delimited, history could not reveal the history of subjectivity—the history of desire, pleasure, care of the body, normal behavior, use of leisure time, gender differences, and family relations. These are assumed to be in the domain of nature or else in a domain of culture that is outside of history. Even Lévi-Strauss concurs with traditional history writing which assumes that sexuality had to exist before male institutions could arise, because sexuality provided the basis of all economic exchange.[50] But in saying this, we create a historically specific form of subjectivity that automatically distinguishes male from female and designates the male as the motivating force of history. And because this particular form of consciousness was so important to the stability of a capitalist society, I contend, writing that constituted the self as such an object of knowledge was a primary agent of history. For such writing to work as effectively as it did, however, it had to conceal its own power to create forms of desire.

It is because the Brontës have encouraged readers to seek out the meaning of fiction in a recognizably modern form of consciousness that their novels have played an important part in British history. If one gives any credence to the notion of a history of subjectivity and to the priority of writing in constituting subjectivity as an object of knowledge, then it is a relatively simple step to see the Brontës as agents of history. We can assume their fiction produced—and continues with each act of interpretation to produce—figures of modern desire. These techniques have suppressed the political identity along with the knowledge of oneself as such. The production of the political unconscious has accompanied the production of the sexual subject, I believe, and in this way has constituted the repressive power actually exercised by a polite tradition of writing.

The Brontës indeed saw their work as a reaction against the tradition of domestic fiction exemplified by Jane Austen. Charlotte's correspondence explains that they regarded Austen's as an aesthetics of the surface. Charlotte allowed that Austen "does her business of delineating the surface of the lives of genteel English people curiously well," but Charlotte rejected her predecessor's notion of polite writing on grounds that it was deficient in a particular kind of knowledge, the knowledge of genuine emotion. In Charlotte's view, an aesthetics founded on polite behavior prevented "even a speaking acquaintance" with the passions. Charlotte opposed Austen's polite behavior to a new language of motivation, creating, as she did so, the relation of surface to depth between their two different modes of writing: "What sees keenly, speaks aptly, moves flexibly, it suits her to study, but what throbs fast and full, though hidden, what the blood rushes through, what is the unseen seat of life and sentient target of death—*this* Miss Austen ignores." The new territories of the self that the Brontës sought to represent were the unseen desires of women. To represent the passions they claimed Austen had failed to reveal, the Brontës borrowed supernatural figures from fairy tale and figures of passion from romance; they made these materials represent the unseen but very real emotional power of women. If they designated certain forms of female desire as outside of culture, they did so in order to make these forms represent a new basis in nature for the self, thus a new human nature. And so Charlotte's critique of Austen concludes with the famous statement that establishes such forms of sexuality as the basis for the aesthetics of fiction: "Jane Austen was a complete and most sensible lady, but a very incomplete, and rather insensible (not senseless), woman."[51]

To make the language of social behavior reveal the ordinary self at its truest and deepest, the Brontës had to dismantle that language. Austen had fine-tuned the language to such a degree that there appeared to be no gap whatsoever between the behavior of characters and their motivations by the end of each one of her novels. Such a language of the self presented itself as an accurate statement of one person's relation to another. Her marriages, for example, make statements that are at once perfectly personal and perfectly political. The wedding scene that concludes *Emma* illustrates the precision which conventional social behavior achieved in both senses. Thus the scene testifies to the ability of language to mediate the gap between a woman's personal desire and her social behavior:

> The wedding was much like other weddings, where the parties have no taste for finery or parade; and Mrs. Elton, from the particulars detailed by her husband, thought it all extremely shabby, and very inferior to her own. . . . But, in spite of these deficiencies, the wishes, the hopes, the confidence, the predictions of the small band of true friends who witnessed the ceremony, were fully answered in the perfect happiness of the union.[52]

Austen's heroines marry as soon as their desire has been correctly aimed and accurately communicated. But the Brontës broke up this congruity of personal and social experience by endowing their heroines with desire for the one object they could not possess, namely, Heathcliff and Rochester as first encountered in the novels. These males are historically obsolete. This frustration of conventional novelistic closure does not, however, repress some desire that exists prior to its figuration as writing, but provides a strategy by which to expand the semiotic space for representing personal desire. At this moment in cultural history, I am suggesting, desire suddenly became the metonymic exploration and discovery of more or less adequate substitutes for the original object of desire. Substitutes also played an important role in Austen's fiction, to be sure. As Chapter 3's discussion of Harriet Smith demonstrates, substitutes in *Emma* offer a way of discovering the one true object of desire. When one discovers what one wants in an Austen novel, then, the story is almost over. But when one discovers what one wants in the Brontës' novels, the story has just gotten underway. Their heroines typically desire the one man whom society forbids them to marry, giving rise to the notion that social conventions are, in an essential way, opposed to individual desire. That such a rhetorical opposition provides the necessary precondition for a modern theory of repression will become clearer upon examination of what Charlotte Brontë does to the conventional wedding scene in *Jane Eyre*. And how sexual repression obscures the fact of social oppression will reiterate the general thrust of this chapter and provide its conclusion.

Charlotte Brontë first refers to such a conventional wedding scene as the one from *Emma* in the famous parlor game in which Rochester forces Jane to watch him court the haughty Blanche Ingram:

> Then appeared the magnificent figure of Miss Ingram, clad in white, a long veil on her hand, and a wreath of roses round her brow; by her side walked Mr. Rochester, and together they drew near the table. . . . A ceremony followed, in dumb show, in which it was easy to recognize the pantomime of a marriage. (p. 160)

Those witnessing this scene believe the charade discloses Mr. Rochester's true feelings for Miss Ingram. But Rochester fully dispels the most conventional meaning of the charade when he tells Jane that he had substituted Miss Ingram for Jane herself in order to arouse Jane's desire for the very role her rival appeared to occupy:

> "I would not—I could not—marry Miss Ingram. You—you strange, you almost unearthly thing!—I love you as my own flesh. You—poor and obscure, and small and plain as you are—I entreat you to accept me as a husband." (p. 283)

Brontë thus displaces the most conventional meaning of the pantomimed wedding with this profession of feelings, which makes Blanche into a mere substitute for Jane, and Jane, in turn, into the original object of desire. This triangulation of desire accomplishes two goals at once. It constitutes another level of events that social conventions concealed and falsified. It also determines that such events can only make themselves known through disturbance and rupture.

That Jane is the true object of Rochester's desire is no longer in doubt once she is represented as the very antithesis of the traditionally desirable woman. "Strange," "unearthly," "poor and obscure," "small and plain" as she is, Jane represents a desire so highly personalized that it can be understood only through the force it exerts on the social surface of experience. It defies explanation in terms of any rational and worldly motive. Rochester's profession of feelings would in fact make a fine sentimental conclusion to the game, but the scene of marriage has several more transformations to undergo before Brontë will permit that to happen. A few days before their wedding, Jane awakes to behold a strange figure—another substitute—trying on her wedding veil:

> presently she took my veil from its place: she held it up, gazed at it long, and then, she threw it over her own head, and turned to the mirror. At that moment I saw the reflection of the visage and features quite distinctly in the dark oblong glass. (p. 311)

In a moment of extraordinary self-alienation, Jane sees her own image in the mirror just before the wedding ceremony is supposed to begin, and she describes her image as if it belonged to the intruder she saw earlier in her bedroom: "I saw a robed and veiled figure, so unlike my usual self that it seemed almost the image of a stranger" (p. 315). Again she sees herself as a substitute for a substitute. By so distorting the traditional figure of the bride, Brontë produces an ominous discontinuity between the social form and personal content of desire. These symbolic reenactments of the wedding ceremony accumulate to constitute a mode of representation that is neither fantastic nor real in any conventional sense. They make the past into something that resembles what Freud would later call day-residue material in order to represent a purely psychological experience.

Separating such self-explanatory social gestures from their traditional content, as demonstrated in the wedding scenes in *Jane Eyre,* is a strategy that characterizes both *Jane Eyre* and *Wuthering Heights.* Both novels make the conventions for representing sexual relations point to a new domain of meaning that exists prior and in opposition to conventions which had, in Austen's work, appeared to represent an individual's most genuine desires. Jane's marriage to Rochester begins in the family vault only to be disrupted by the disclosure of his "bad, mad, and embruted" wife, a disruption which requires the reader to understand Rochester's courtship of Jane, like his courtship of Blanche, in an entirely different light. Gestures now carry a hidden but truer meaning that refers back to a secret history of sexual relationships. With the disclosure of the madwoman, furthermore, the heroine/narrator herself suddenly acquires a more modern psychological dimension. Believing that Jane's night of madness as a prisoner in the red-room links her to the madwoman, many readers do not see Jane as Rochester does. To him, she is the embodiment of every virtue that his monstrous wife lacks. But many readers see the two women as more and less sublimated versions of the same kind of sexual desire— an intense ambivalence toward traditional male-female relationships that has its source in Brontë herself. I will go no further than this in explaining how such an intrusion of historically earlier forms of sexuality upon domestic relations changes the way we read a novel. One could of course make a similar case for the disclosure of the ghostly nun's true identity in *Villette* and how that changes the way we read Lucy Snowe's character. The same holds true in every Dickens novel when we discover the secret web of family relationships responsible for all the sinister turns of plot. I will simply claim that, with the disclosure of the madwoman, a whole set of possibilities for reading female desire opens up within the world of writing so that we can never take sexual relations at face value again. They have to be understood as part of a suppressed personal history.

Emily Brontë's novel provides an even more obvious example of tropes that recast history in a psychological light. In *Wuthering Heights,* the narrator encounters a totally illegible social surface upon his entry into the household under Heathcliff's control. Still, Lockwood believes he understands the working of human relationships. That he particularly fancies himself to be an acute reader of the female character is revealed when Brontë has him recall an experience from his recent past:

> While enjoying a month of fine weather at the sea-coast, I was thrown into the company of a most fascinating creature, a real goddess in my eyes, as long as she took no notice of me . . . if looks have language, the merest idiot might have guessed I was over head and ears: she understood me at last, and looked a return—the sweetest of all imaginable looks. And what did I do? I confess it with shame—shrunk icily into myself, like a snail. (p. 19)

Lockwood brings to his understanding of human relationships a notion of sexuality that designates the female as an object of desire. What spoils her beauty are signs of her desire for him; she does some looking of her own.

This way of knowing that looks only at the surface proves terribly inadequate when Lockwood attempts to understand the relationships contained within *Wuthering Heights.* He links the young Catherine to Heathcliff simply because Heathcliff bears outward and visible signs of gentility. In addition, he fails to see the possibility of a bond forming between Catherine and Hareton Earnshaw because the true heir has been reared in a servant's position. Thus Lockwood relies on the same polite conventions that fail to acknowledge the passionate force linking this woman's mother to Heathcliff because such a bond would have to extend between two extremes within the social order. But Brontë does not merely have us watch Lockwood stumble along so ill equipped by the knowledge of sexual relations that the polite world allows. Rather, she dramatizes his lack of knowledge in a scene that recalls his earlier encounter with a desirable woman and that identifies the characteristic failure of his perception. Here are his thoughts as he watches young Catherine:

> now, I had a distinct view of her whole figure and countenance. She was slender, and apparently scarcely past girlhood: an admirable form, and the most exquisite little face that I have ever had the pleasure of beholding: small features, very fair; flaxen ringlets, or rather golden, hanging loose on her delicate neck; and eyes—had they been agreeable in expression, they would have been irresistible. (p. 19)

Again, the problem of the gaze. The woman does not behave like the docile object of the gaze, but returns the gaze in a manner—this time not sweetly, but with scorn and desperation—that displays the presence of subjectivity. Her eyes violate his aesthetically grounded notion of desire as they become the signs of an active female self.

At the center of Lockwood's confusion is the identity of Catherine Linton Heathcliff, soon to become Earnshaw. She and her mother reveal the limits of the polite conventions on which he has relied exclusively for understanding social experience. The two Catherines, besides bearing the same name themselves, have acquired virtually all the family names in the book—some more than once. The disjunction of their social identities marks the shifting trajectory of female desire. The first Catherine marries Edgar Linton because she loves only Heathcliff and wants to "'get him out from under my brother's power'" (p. 73). The second Catherine, daughter to the first, spends her wedding night closeted with Heathcliff's dying son Linton in a scene that resembles others in the novel where monogamous desire is linked with both incest and necrophilia. Under these circumstances, marriage quite literally ceases to embody desire, or rather, it embodies desire only to the degree that desire has brutally misshapen the social conventions that seek to suppress and contain it. In this way, the novel locates desire elsewhere, in an extrasocial dimension of human experience.

The intrusion of Catherine's ghost into Lockwood's dream serves the same purpose as the disclosure of Rochester's mad wife in *Jane Eyre*. This rupture confuses genders and generations, calling into question what is inside as opposed to outside the individual. Consequently, such confusion redraws the lines circumscribing individual identity but defines them according to a new principle of difference. In righting the order of social relations, then, the Brontës reconstitute the individual as a particular field of knowledge whose identity is neither socially nor genealogically determined because its fate or "development" is propelled by female desires.

Under such circumstances, the possibilities and prerogatives of female subjectivity seem to expand immensely, as the discovery of the first Catherine accounts for much of Heathcliff's ferocity, much as the discovery of Bertha Mason explains Rochester's surliness. It is important to note that in the process of handing over such powers of motivation to the female, fiction does something to history. Understanding the configuration of social relationships which concludes both *Wuthering Heights* and *Jane Eyre* requires another order of history that is no longer considered history at all. It is a tale told by a woman. It is a history of sexuality.

Thus the Brontës have come to be known for a literary language that allows emotion to overpower convention and become a value in its own right, blotting out all features of political person, place, and event. Their language of the self mixes sacred—often Miltonic—figures with the worst sort of Gothic claptrap to recast those figures in grotesquely somatic forms. Their novels hinge on affiliations that soar across the social gulf between a Gypsy and the daughter of an old landowning family or between an unattractive governess and her master. In the face of the essential incompatibility of the social roles they attempt to couple, the Brontës endow their lovers with absolute identity on an entirely different ontological plane. So Catherine Earnshaw proclaims, "'Nelly, I am Heathcliff—he's always, always in my mind—not as a pleasure, any more than I am a pleasure to myself—but as my own being'" (p. 77). Heathcliff also speaks of the two as comprising a single body, though certainly not a material body, and Brontë allows the lovers to share a kind of half-life until their bodies have decayed into one another in a common grave.

And lest we consider Charlotte Brontë less extravagant in her manner of literalizing the figures of passion, we should recall the moment when Jane Eyre implores God to help her resist St. John Rivers' coercive proposal of marriage. At that moment, Jane hears her name miraculously repeated three times by "a known, loved, well-remembered voice—that of Edward Fairfax Rochester; and it spoke in pain and woe wildly, eerily, urgently" (p. 369). Responding to his voice, Jane finds Rochester missing his right eye and hand, and the dialogue of the lovers' reunion paints this singularly grisly scene:

> "On this arm I have neither hand nor nails," he said, drawing the mutilated limb from his breast, and showing it to me. "It is a mere stump—a ghastly sight! Don't you think so, Jane?"

"It is a pity to see it; and a pity to see your eyes—and the scar of fire
on your forehead: and the worst of it is, one is in danger of loving you
too well for all this; and making too much of you." (p. 384)

Even without the irony of the final clause, this is a rather original statement of love. Again, social conventions are remade to suggest a totally
new psychological content as Brontë ruptures the continuity between motivation and behavior, thereby implying that no two individuals' desires
are the same.

When the Brontës infuse their heroines with desire for the one male
who cannot possess them, everyone within the field of social possibilities
becomes a mere substitute for the original, and socially mediated forms
of desire never again provide anything approximating *complete* gratification—to wit, Rochester's missing parts. This eternal deferral of gratification might appear to set desire forever in the realm of romance and
therefore forever at odds with reality, but such is not the case.[53] As the
Brontës represent it, desire acquires a reality in its own right, a reality
equivalent to, though often in conflict with, the reality principle. If anything, desire wins out over the reality principle, as these novels progressively reorganize disparate elements of the socioeconomic field into an
artificial unity—that of the narrative consciousness. Not only social signs,
but anatomical elements, biological functions, behaviors, sensations, and
pleasures all become signs of male or female desire. And as they do so,
the principle reorganizing the object world into this gender formation takes
on the proportions of a causal principle and a universal meaning to be
discovered.

Domestic novels had once aspired to respectability, like Pamela herself, by remaining free of any taint of erotic desire. With the Brontës,
however, the history of the novel took a contrary turn. In their hands,
domestic fiction began playing out a fierce struggle to socialize desires
whose origin and vicissitudes comprised one's true identity as well as his
or her possibilities for growth. This event in the writing of desire achieved
its most extreme form in the sensation novels of the 1860s and in the
poetics of sexuality that grew up around such controversial fiction as a
way of domesticating it.[54] A statement by Blanche A. Crackenthorpe in
her 1895 article, "Sex in Modern Literature," shows how firmly Charlotte
Brontë's revision of Austen had taken hold by that time:

> the mystery of sex, no matter how much or how often it is ignored or
> misinterpreted, remains, and will continue to remain, the most beautiful
> *motif* for all creative work in every department of Art. It is the most pow-
> erful and the most convincing factor in life. It is the prompter alike of the
> finest and of the basest actions. It is the very atmosphere of life itself.[55]

I would like to note how radically universalized Brontë's aesthetic manifesto on behalf of the individual's desire has become in the hands of a traditional critic. It is also worth noting that sexuality has, by 1895, become the instrument of, and not the resistance to, conventional morality. It was inevitable that it should do so, for in disputing the political categories of the industrializing world, the Brontës represented sexual desires as more primary than and distinct from political categories.

I will conclude by providing an example or two of another language of sexuality that coexisted with the Brontës'. Martha Vicinus's *The Industrial Muse* preserves the written record of an oral tradition that rarely finds its way into literary discussion because it lost out in the struggle for literacy, even though versions of it persist in the culture to this day. Here, for example, are verses from "The Bury New Loom," which Vicinus calls "one of the most popular poems celebrating the life of a joiner" and which was first published as a broadside in 1804:[56]

> I said: my dear lassie, believe me, I am a good joiner by trade,
> And many a good loom and shuttle before me in my time I have made.
> Your short lams and jacks and long lams I quickly can put in tune.
> My rule is in good order to get up and square a new loom.
>
> She took me and showed me her loom, the down on her wrap did appear.
> The lams, jacks and healds put in motion, I levelled her loom to a hair.
> My shuttle ran well in her lathe, my treadle it worked up and down,
> My level stood close to her breast-bone, the time I was riving her loom.

We might note, in comparison with Andrew Ure's mechanized organicism, how differently these verses understand the relationship between the machine and those who work it. The verses obviously celebrate an artisan household that by the early 1800s had come to be viewed as essentially hostile to the middle-class household and to the woman at its center. It was this form of sexuality that Shuttleworth made the figure and cause of the impoverishment and demoralization of the artisan class. It was also this form of sexuality that the factory sought to change by fixing workers within a totally individuated and functional space.

But such is not how novels represent the struggle to determine what form of literacy the people would have. To illustrate how novels use the gendered body to contain and displace materials expressing other politial viewpoints, I have selected a brief but telling example from *Jane Eyre*. This is a scene in which the reader is supposed to feel all the rage of the politically oppressed rise up and inspire Jane's speech as Mr. Brocklehurst puts her through a catechism:

> "No sight so sad as that of a naughty child," he began, "especially a naughty little girl. Do you know where the wicked go after death?"

"They go to hell," was my ready and orthodox answer.

"And what is hell? Can you tell me that?"

"A pit full of fire."

"And should you like to fall into that pit, and to be burning there for ever?"

"No, sir."

"What must you do to avoid it?"

I deliberated a moment; my answer when it did come, was objectionable: "I must keep in good health and not die." (p. 27)

As in Mr. Gradgrind's interrogation of girl number 20 in the opening of Dickens' *Hard Times*, Jane's schoolgirl rebellion translates a political struggle for the control of meaning into a struggle between genders and generations. It is significant that instead of having to talk their way out of the lascivious embrace of an aristocrat as their historically earlier counterparts did, these Victorian heroines battle against the linguistic domination of a middle-class bureaucrat and father figure. The cultural stage has been set, one might say, for Dora's dialogue with Freud, as described in Chapter 5. More important for purposes of the present chapter, however, is the way in which the struggle between gender and generations domesticates the larger political struggle for literacy. As gratifying as Jane's verbal aggression against institutional language may seem politically, Brontë is not offering resistance in the face of political oppression when she has Jane distort the catechism. Like virtually every other novelist who is well known today, she displaces class conflict onto sexual relations and inscribes them within a modern institutional culture. Thus contained, they come to represent two poles within middle-class discourse rather than the hegemonic struggle between that discourse and cultural voices capable of speaking another political truth. Appearing during the coal miners' strike of 1844, the "Miner's Catechism" demonstrates how the catechism was used as a means of political contestation:[57]

1 Ques. What is your name?

Ans. PETER POVERTY

2 Q. Who gave you that name?

A. My godfathers and godmothers in my baptism, wherein I was made a member of the Black Coal Pit, a child of Slavery, and an inheritor of the sunless mine.

3 Q. What did your godfathers and godmothers then do for you?

A. They did promise and vow three things in my name. First, that I should renounce all opposition to my master's will. Secondly, That I should believe that every Word and Action of the Viewers was said and done

for my benefit. Thirdly, That I should obey them in every thing, work
for their benefit alone, and live in poverty and want all the days of my
life.

The Victorian novel's transformation of household space into an instrument that can be used to classify any social group and keep it under
observation does not make the novel simply one more instance of the
relation of representation to power. The sudden appearance in the 1840s
of novels that turned political information into a language of the modern
self adds something to the theory of power. The prominence of domestic
fiction suggests the degree to which such power did not in fact rely on
overtly juridical or economic means so much as on cultural hegemony,
that is, on the notion of the family, norms of sexual behavior, the polite
use of language, the regulation of leisure time, and all those microtech-
niques that constitute the modern subject. The monstrous female becomes
intelligible within the history of this subject as she marks a site where
political resistance was gendered and neutralized. In this figure, I have
argued, combination comes forth to reveal itself as aberrant sexual desire.
It appears that in performing this act of displacement, some novels ceased
to be considered dangerous to the emotional stability of women, children,
and servants. Indeed, some fiction gained respectability and eventual literary status insofar as it provided an appropriate means of disciplining
the impressionable mind, a means, in other words, of limiting the ways
in which individuals could imagine their relation to the political reality.

But those novels that did so contain the process by which political
differences came to be seen as degraded forms of sexuality were still
potentially dangerous. In order to displace political resistance onto the
primitive and criminal, novels had to contain "other" cultural materials,
the traces of other political practices and other class sexualities. True,
such materials were debased as they were sexed and set in opposition to
the family. But as these recalcitrant elements are contained in and banished from the novel, one feels the text flattening; in giving its materials
over to pure ideology, domestic fiction sticks the reader with a paler version of love, a narrower idea of sexuality. Think, for example, of the
second Catherine in *Wuthering Heights,* the Jane Eyre who returns to
Thornfield a second time to become Rochester's wife, the second wife
Rawdon Crawley takes in Becky Sharp's place, the Mary Barton who
recovers her health but not her sensuality as she looks forward to marriage, or Dickens' substitution of Sissy Jupe for Louisa Gradgrind. In
each case, the limits of normalcy seem to narrow as the novel includes
only those elements that make ever more fine distinctions between gen-

ders and generations. Thus it was not enough to represent combination as savagery and diseased desire. It was also necessary to establish a tradition of reading that would universalize modern desire in order to implant it within every individual as the very thing that makes him or her human.

The Brontës, in particular, represent a moment in the history of sexuality when one can observe this connection. First received as the work of Ellis Bell, an author of uncertain gender and an obvious affiliation with an earlier moment in cultural history, *Wuthering Heights* troubled its readers. But Charlotte Brontë knew just how to make her sister's novel more readable. She attached a "biographical notice" to the 1850 edition, allowing people to read the novel as the product of a fatally ill, mentally disturbed, and culturally primitive female. In the preface that accompanies the biographical notice, Charlotte transforms these features into those of a creative genius who is bisexual, at once ancient and childlike, possessed of demonic energy, yet mortally flawed and doomed to live on as a literary object.[58] If *Wuthering Heights* strikes us as a self-enclosed text with a curiously private system of meaning, this is not due to the author's estrangement, we may assume, but rather to a tradition of reading that compulsively repeats Charlotte's initial gesture of textual enclosure.

5

Seduction and the Scene of Reading

"I was walking about in a town which I did not know. I saw streets and squares which were strange to me. Then I came into a house where I lived, went to my room, and found a letter from Mother lying there. She wrote saying that as I had left home without my parents' knowledge she had not wished to write to me to say that Father was ill. 'Now he is dead, and if you like you can come.'"

SIGMUND FREUD, *Fragment of an Analysis of a Case of Hysteria*

One day, a boy arranged such a "feminine" scene, with wild animals as intruders, and I felt that uneasiness which I assume often betrays to an experimenter what his innermost expectations are. And, indeed, on departure and already at the door, the boy exclaimed, "There is something wrong here," came back, and with an air of relief arranged the animals along a tangent to the circle of furniture.

ERIK H. ERIKSON, *Childhood and Society*

It may be with some regret that we feel the passion depart as the first generation of lovers dies out of *Wuthering Heights* or when a much subdued Rochester reappears in *Jane Eyre* without his hand, eye, and lunatic wife, but there is no question that these figures of desire have become obsolete. The circumstances in which we find them at the end of these novels tells us that such manifestations of sensuality may be regarded with nostalgia but not wished back into being. For the kinship rules of an earlier culture reside on a different plane from social experience and the language that represents it. But even though they exist in the memories of certain individuals strictly as symbolic phenomena, the lovers are no less real. Each is at once the fact and figure of otherwise nonexistent and inexplicable experiences such as Lockwood's dream, Jane's night in the red-room, the eerie circumstances of Heathcliff's death, and the preternatural voice that calls Jane back to Rochester. In each case, past family relations reappear as uncanny phenomena that make some unintelligible claim upon the present. Detached from their moment in history, these figures appear to represent the desires of the individual before whom they appear. Thus the Brontës call up the ghosts of the history of sexuality to represent a domain of passion that seems to well up in opposition to the contemporary conventions of courtship and kinship relations. To be internalized and made safe for polite readers, historically earlier sexual practices are discovered in dreams, hallucinations, and unfulfilled wishes that conflict with the conduct of sexual relationships in the present. In the hands of the Brontës and other sensation novelists, the history of sexuality becomes the stuff of individual neuroses.

Repression in the Brontës' fiction operates, I am suggesting, as a trope for turning the materials of history into a representation of consciousness, specifically the history of sexuality, so that fiction may transform earlier sexual relations into forms of subjectivity that are ever so much more comprehensive and complex. And if, as I believe is the case, the novel contains the history of sexuality within it, then its own history—the history of fiction—is displaced along with that "other" history. Given the omnivorous behavior I am attributing to the novel, there is very little cultural material that cannot be included within the feminine domain. Consequently, there is very little political information that cannot be transformed into psychological information. This chapter will discuss the implications of the embedding of history within subjectivity as first enacted in fiction and then passed on into the modern institutions responsible for reifying that notion of subjectivity which women were supposed to possess and which novels were supposed to disseminate.

This chapter will suggest how the trope of repression creates conditions for communication that maintain a certain form of social contract. As the individual reads what is outside, he or she appears to be revealing what is inside and receiving, in turn, some liberating or therapeutic benefit. This is even true of Jane's experience in the red-room which can be taken as the unleashing of rage at her aunt and the cause for her subsequently being sent away to school. Communication in this event is not so much an encounter between self and other as it is a self-confrontation. I will argue that the political relations governing the scene of reading as imagined in the Brontës' fiction are the very same political relations that govern the scene of seduction as it was defined by Richardson and reproduced wherever political relations may be figured out as a sexual contract.

The communication situation established by seduction is one where the female subject desires to be what the other desires her to be. To relinquish the power of self-definition is the whole objective of seduction, as *Pamela* demonstrates. But if the woman relinquishes the power to discover a self that she believes society considers to be her true self, then the distinction between seduction and education is rhetorical. If seduction becomes, once again, the strategy that the dominant class sets to work through its institutions, and if these institutions speak with moral as well as political authority, then Pamela's resistance can no longer be virtuous; it becomes, by definition, neurotic. On this basis, I will argue that a therapeutic contract underlies all modern institutions and particularly those institutions most responsible for domesticating culture, that is, the psychotherapeutic and literary institutions that actively maintain a hermeneutics of the gendered self over their respective domains of behavior and writing.

The Woman's Museum: *Jane Eyre*

Before turning to the relationship between gender and power in a modern information-based culture, I would like to linger for a moment over a few scenes in *Jane Eyre*. These scenes identify for readers the nature of the text they are encountering. Such self-reflexivity always identifies the female as the one with the power to determine the meaning of words and things, a power capable in certain instances of changing the nature of the words and things themselves. In one scene, Jane enters Thornfield Hall for the first time to repeat the same gesture of cultural "penetration" that Richardson enacts through Pamela. When Pamela enters an aristocratic manor house—although, to be sure, a middle-class version of an aristocratic manor house—she exposes the secrets of another class sexuality to moral examination. But it is definitely a different order of country house that Jane Eyre enters a century later. Jane initially encounters

> A snug, small room; a round table by a cheerful fire; an armchair high-backed and old-fashioned, wherein sat the neatest imaginable little elderly lady, in widow's cap, black silk gown, and snowy muslin apron . . . ; nothing in short was wanting to complete the beau ideal of domestic comfort. A more reassuring introduction for a new governess could scarcely be conceived: there was no grandeur to overwhelm, no stateliness to embarrass; and then, as I entered, the old lady got up, and promptly and kindly came forward to meet me.[1]

Thus Jane finds the inside of the house to be thoroughly lettered. It is a place that has already been colonized by the conduct books as well as by novels like those Austen wrote. What is this, in fact, if not a scene from one of those novels: enclosed, familiar, "reassuring," where "nothing in short was wanting"?

In writing *Northanger Abbey*, Austen appears to have put the past safely in the past. She teaches the heroine of her first novel to understand the excesses of patriarchal culture as a feature of fiction and as the undisciplined imaginations of women, not as a social reality. Her heroine learns, to her great embarrassment, that manor houses where libertine lords might control the bodies of women no longer have any place in the social reality of England:

> Remember the country and age in which we live. Remember that we are English, that we are Christians. Consult your own understanding, your own sense of the probable, your own observation of what is passing around you—Does our education prepare us for such atrocities? Could they be perpetrated without being known, in a country like this, where social and literary intercourse is on such a footing; where every man is surrounded by a neighborhood of voluntary spies, and where roads and papers lay everything open? Dearest Miss Morland, what ideas have you been admitting.[2]

The terrors of aristocratic power have given way to ones that are less terrible and more effective, as Austen represents a social world regulated by surveillance or, in her words, "voluntary spies." What Brontë does in the pages following Jane's arrival at Thornfield, then, is to reopen the paranoid spaces within an earlier manor house that Austen had panelled over with the modern version of English common sense. Brontë's use of such material is not at all like Richardson's use, however. She brings this archaic material back into fiction precisely because it is archaic. As such, it cannot represent the actual public and social conditions of Brontë's time. It can only represent a private and psychological reality. Although infused with the demonic power that Richardson and Radcliffe had attributed to aristocratic culture, the rooms in Rochester's house are nevertheless "of proportions not vast, though considerable; a gentleman's manorhouse, not a nobleman's seat" (p. 86). The rooms therefore hold the materials for a drama that is not only highly individual but also utterly commonplace.

A century before, conduct books for women turned the objects and personnel of the household into the signs and symbols of the woman who oversaw them and whose taste and sense of duty they could not help but communicate. The conduct books also created a curriculum of texts— bits and pieces of the native English cultural past—held together by certain textualizing strategies alone. Only such an antiquarian array of texts, we should recall, and only an array that was cast in psychological terms by specific procedures of interpretation, could ensure the production of a female sensibility. But where the conduct books of the eighteenth century constructed a gendered ideal of normalcy, the Brontës' fiction supplements the standardized body of female knowledge with strange and occult information. This information implies a self that is deeper than and essentially different from the self that has already been written. Each room within Thornfield Hall is a familiar site to readers of fiction, and each is a different citation; all the rooms are brought together in a single house of fiction by no principle other than that of Jane's textualizing eye. There is "the long and matted gallery" that concludes in "slippery steps of oak," a library whose "volumes of light literature, poetry, biography, travels, a few romances" seem to promise "an abundant harvest of entertainment and information" (p. 90), a dining room "with purple chairs and curtains, a Turkey carpet, walnut-panelled walls, one vast window rich in stained glass, and a lofty ceiling, nobly moulded," and a drawing room whose exotic appointments strike Jane as those of "a fairy place." It was, she says, "a very pretty drawing room, and within it a boudoir, both spread with white carpets" (p. 91). Rooms seem to open into rooms within rooms to suggest a capability for infinite interior expansion.

In fact, it is fair to say that Brontë composes Jane's autobiography out of a series of such rooms. Consequently, she bonds domestic space to the woman who inhabits it in a way that had never been so represented before. The Brontës' novels deal in a variety of spaces—rooms within mansions—that do not in fact belong together in the same text. This is not because they are, like the various places in a novel such as *Mansfield Park,* incompatible in socioeconomic terms. Rather, they represent historically discontinuous households. For every Thrushcross Grange, there is a Wuthering Heights. When Monsieur Paul purchases a thoroughly domesticated space for himself and Lucy Snowe, the forbidding chambers of Madame Walravens spring into view. The tenant of Wildfell Hall has a regency manor house in her past and one that is thoroughly purged of the past in her future. When we encounter Mrs. Fairfax snugly ensconced as if in an Austen parlor, then, we ought to know that she is in but one room in a house of many mansions that open up within one another to incorporate new cultural materials within the private world.

The Brontës use these rooms to represent undiscovered territories within the self that antedate the known and novelistically represented. Thus well before she discovers the attic room that emprisons Rochester's first wife,

Jane discovers places in the house that no longer provide a setting for the practices of daily life. She finds "some of the third-story rooms, though dark and low, were interesting from their air of antiquity." In all these rooms are the materials of other writing, deliberately excluded from the parlor world by Austen, but taken back into the novel by Brontë and put to new purposes:

> The furniture once appropriated to the lower apartments had from time to time been removed here, as fashions changed; and the imperfect light entering by their narrow casements showed bedsteads of a hundred years old; chests in oak or walnut, looking, with their strange carvings of palm branches and cherubs' heads, like types of the Hebrew ark; rows of venerable chairs, high-backed and narrow; stools still more antiquated, on whose cushioned tops were yet apparent traces of half-effaced embroideries, wrought by fingers that for two generations had been coffin-dust. All these relics gave to the third story of Thornfield Hall the aspect of a home of the past: a shrine of memory. (p. 92)

These "relics" constitute a kind of residue of daily life—and of the novel— that history renders obsolete, but for which women and novelists eventually find new uses. Later in this chapter, for example, I will show how this material is used to represent the repressed consciousness of hysterical women. Thus containing the debris of culture, domestic culture as Brontë represents it has all the qualities of a museum.

I have in mind such a museum as the Victoria and Albert where objects are quite deliberately arranged according to the strangest mix of categories, not unlike the hodgepodge of periods, genres, modes, motifs, materials, themes, and schools that characterized the female curricula of the eighteenth century, and not unlike our modern literary histories, which sort out and assemble a canon according to a similar principle. Within this particular museum, the march of history is nowhere so visible as in a series of rooms—mainly parlors and bedrooms—where the furniture has been collected from the various periods of British history. The museum effectively conceals the human effects of the Empire within the very structure organized by its acquisitive stategies, much as the apparent randomness of Dickens' junk shops conceals the individual lives that lie in fragments there. The establishment of such museums in England was, as Francis Sheppard points out, a practice peculiar to the nineteenth century: "This was the age of the foundation of the National Gallery in 1824 (in Pall Mall, until its removal to Trafalgar Square in 1837), of the National Portrait Gallery in 1856 and of the South Kensington Museum in 1857, from which later developed the Science Museum and the Victoria and

Albert Museum."[3] These museums, Raymond Williams explains, were among the many institutions "representing a critical phase in the commercial organization of popular culture."[4] Indeed, the mid-1800s saw a number of institutional developments. In addition to the beginning of public museums in 1845, there were limited provisions in 1850 for public libraries and public parks. According to Williams, "The fierce controversy surrounding these innovations (from the charges of extravagance to the anxious pleas that the working people must be 'civilized') tends to drop away, in our minds, according to subsequent interpretations." The underlying cause for this act of forgetting is what Williams calls "the selective tradition," which effects changes in the way the past is recalled by breaking up "a single story, though one of great complexity and conflict," into separate histories with different principles of causality.[5]

If one of the most persuasive arguments for the official institutions of culture was, as Williams claims, launched on the grounds that culture was an effective means of civilizing the working class, it is terribly ironic that, as Sheppard notes, "few if any of these places were open on Sundays—the British Museum, for example, not until 1896." "Their use," Sheppard continues, "was therefore restricted to persons of leisure, or (to quote the regulations of the British Museum in 1810) to 'persons of decent appearance.'"[6] But containment and reorganization of culture for purposes of public display were probably not meant to have the effect of stratifying people according to their access to culture. It is more likely that the intent behind the containment of culture was not so much to exclude anyone in particular as to recontextualize certain areas of culture. Even today these museums are places where the relics of the historical past have become as so many household objects, detached from their economic origins and fit to keep only the most polite company. It is in this respect that I find Charlotte Brontë's house of culture particularly interesting.

In the third story of Thornfield Hall, the past is used to fill several rooms that, having no apparent domestic utility, seem superfluous. Jane asks, "'Do the servants sleep in these rooms?'" To which the obliging Mrs. Fairfax replies, "'No; they occupy a range of smaller apartments to the back; no one ever sleeps here'" (p. 93). In these rooms, one encounters neither physical nor even metaphysical nature, neither body nor soul. According to Brontë, what one finds in these rooms is a cultural past that—like Freud's "uncanny"—refuses to stay in the past. Thus we find Jane Eyre musing on the stuff in these rooms as on a "shrine of memory":

I liked the hush, the gloom, the quaintness of these retreats in the day; but I by no means coveted a night's repose on one of those wide and heavy beds: shut in, some of them, with doors of oak; shaded, portraying effigies of strange flowers, and stranger birds, and strangest human beings,—all which would have looked strange, indeed, by the pallid gleam of moonlight. (p. 92)

Resembling the room where Lockwood encounters the ghost of Catherine Earnshaw in *Wuthering Heights*, the rooms in the third story provide the site where the day and night of conscious experience may be distinguished. Here, Fuseli-like figures that can originate in art alone challenge the distinctions between vegetable, animal, and human categories by defamiliarizing each of them. But this obsolete and grotesque art, in challenging nature's most basic distinctions, does not point to some supernatural presence. Although Mrs. Fairfax explains, "'one would almost say that, if there were a ghost at Thornfield Hall, this would be its haunt,'" it is likely that Brontë only raises the possibility of an intrusive supernaturalism in order to cancel it out: "'So I think: you have no ghost, then,'" Jane replies. And it is just as likely that in cancelling out such use of historically earlier material, Brontë erases its history. For when Mrs. Fairfax confirms that no ghost is known to inhabit the rooms in question, Jane inquires further, "'Nor any traditions of one? no legends or ghost stories?'," and Mrs. Fairfax replies in terms that call attention to the absence of history: "'I believe not. And yet it is said the Rochesters have been rather a violent than a quiet race in their time: perhaps, though, that is the reason they rest tranquilly in their graves now'" (p. 93).

I have described at length Jane's encounter with the various rooms in Thornfield Hall because they not only provide a model of the novel itself but also express the link between the history of sexuality and that of literature. Brontë uses the third-story rooms in particular to tell the reader precisely what has been done to the past to make a Victorian novel; her description of these rooms explains what the novel had to do to enter the domain of literature; and it records a change in the notion of what literature was, a change effected by the novel that in turn enabled the novel to enter that cultural domain. Brontë's fiction represents writing as a reality in its own right. She deliberately brings alien cultural materials within a domestic framework and destroys their cultural otherness, making it impossible for one to use them to imagine another period in time and another political reality. As the author of this world of relics, Brontë sets herself in the position of the bricoleur, a trashman of sorts, who embodies the power to break down a cultural text into components that can be used to construct a whole new system of relationships. In this way, the "extra" rooms in Thornfield resemble an attic whose decontextualized objects await usage that will miraculously endow them with value. Such a space within culture allows change; it allows old information to permeate a self-enclosed text and become new information. Over such a space in middle-class cultures the woman is symbolically in charge, since she is the one who supervises the objects of the household. Presumably she is also the one who determines what things have value. The antique acquires its value as it is dusted off and restored to the household where it retains some of what Walter Benjamin calls "cult value." If, as he says of early photographs, "the cult of remembrance of loved ones, absent or dead, offers a last refuge for the cult value of the picture," then the cult of remembrance of the old manor house offers such a refuge for the cult of the old aristocracy. Some of the mystery of the old aristocracy clings onto the cultural debris one finds in the rooms of Thornfield Hall and makes the objects of the past appear all the more mysterious because they cannot be reproduced in a middle-class world.[7]

Jane has had this power to transform cultural objects and to give them new life since the beginning of the novel. In the first chapter, such a transformation begins when she reads *Bewick's History of British Birds*. Self-conscious of the process, she describes the plates portraying arctic birds: "Of these death-white realms I formed an idea of my own: shadowy, like all the half-comprehended notions that float through children's brains, but strangely impressive" (p. 6). Of another plate Jane says, "I cannot tell what sentiment haunted the quite solitary churchyard"; in turning to another, she describes "two ships becalmed on a torpid sea" as "marine phantoms"; and as if to destabilize the referential world still further, she tells us that "each picture told a story, mysterious often to my undeveloped understanding and imperfect feelings" (p. 6). Chapters later, the material she has internalized reappears in paintings that were done "in the last two vacations I spent at Lowood, when I had no other occupation" (p. 109). Worth noting here is how different her paintings are from Emma's painting of Harriet Smith, for Jane's representations do not pretend to represent something in the world of objects at all. When Rochester asks, "'Where did you get your copies?'" she replies without hesitation, "'Out of my head'" (p. 109). As if to reinforce the nature of the transformation that her narrative is continuously making, then, Brontë has Rochester inquire further about this "head": "'Has it other furniture of the same kind within?'" (p. 110). Thus Jane proceeds to translate into words what she had translated from mind into paint:

These pictures were in water-colours. The first represented clouds low and livid, rolling over a swollen sea: all the distance was in eclipse; so, too, was the foreground; or, rather, the nearest billows, for there was no land. One gleam of light lifted into relief a half-submerged mast, on which sat a cormorant, dark and large, with wings flecked with foam: its beak held a gold bracelet, set with gems. (p. 110)

We are certainly supposed to recognize the "subjects" that Jane says had "risen vividly on my mind" as the images of *Bewick's History of British Birds* come back to life as figments of imagination rather than imitations of nature. Natural history, ostensibly observed, then written, and finally read, finds its way into Jane's psychic life and onto her canvas where it provides a language for otherwise inarticulate desires.

But these images do not observe the conventional categories of emotional life after undergoing various transformations. In borrowing content from new cultural sources, Brontë allows content to intrude—as in the paintings—and to modify form. Jane describes the very act of painting as "one of the keenest pleasures I have ever known." At the same time, she claims to have been "tormented by the contrast between my idea and my handiwork: in each case I had imagined something which I was quite powerless to realise" (p. 111). In having her heroine say this, Brontë has her lay claim to the angst of a Romantic poet, and a good deal of critical ink has been spent in demonstrating that Charlotte Brontë herself should be understood in terms of that role. But I prefer to think that Brontë inserted these verbal paintings into Jane's narrative as a way of displaying the qualities of mind that have the power to make an otherwise unattractive governess so desirable to a man like Rochester. The heightened state of mind in which pleasure and torment are blended is not that of a professional poet. It is the mental state of a schoolgirl who finds herself with "nothing else to do" (p. 111). Thus Jane begins a metacommentary on her works by saying "first, I must premise that they are nothing wonderful" (p. 110). The defamiliarized bits of culture that intrude into Jane's narrative as the images in paintings, books, and dreams detach these images from any referent in the world and endow them with another kind of meaning that partially realizes the inchoate motions of mind. Consequently, the only history that culture comes to tell in Brontë's fiction is the history of a cultural transformation from mind to visible form to words, a history of the self and of its language. Like Richardson and Austen, Brontë is interested both in the interstices between the official ceremonies of life and in representing the activities of the female mind turned in upon itself during leisure hours.

But how different a mind this is from Emma's, and how different the way it behaves when it is not otherwise occupied! Emma's paintings are only partially realized too, but this is because she is too busy with words to complete a painting, not because she experiences emotions for which there is no adequate medium of expression. In Brontë's novel, on the other hand, words summon up visual images which point to territories within the self that are beyond the scope of verbal representation. These images seem to break into the textual surface maintained by Jane's unrelenting moral superiority over all other characters and over the reader as well. They indicate a lack of control on her part that invites sexually subversive interpretations.

Modern Men: *Shirley* and the Fuegians

But these images are composed of culture and ultimately serve to express deviant desires in a manner that allows Jane to contain and control such desires. Consequently, the images ultimately provide Brontë with the means of controlling the reader as well. In fact, this is a strategy that carries over from the Brontës to other Victorian authors whose narratives tend to turn into pictures as well, forming hypostatic images in which the materials of narrative—as in the genre paintings and monuments that also characterize Victorian culture—are already interpreted. That is to say, these visual images control the response to materials contained within them by shaping those materials into conventional figures that express various emotions—a careworn governess, a young woman cast out of her father's house, a dog in mourning beside his dead master's shoes, Ophelia drowned. Few materials from life or literature proved capable of resisting the emblematic strategies of Victorian art. In producing what is called a "popular culture," I am suggesting, such art developed ways of suppressing the explanatory logic of English cultural competence—Austen's common sense—as it was spoken and written by people with ordinary literacy. This art developed an iconography of subjectivity that could be transported from one text to another and extended across media. Considered in relation to these other uses of the visual, the images in *Jane Eyre* appear, not as the primary process thinking they are sometimes taken to be, but as metalanguage or strategies of textuality that control the very framework in which reading takes place. They control the identity of the reader by making one an object of knowledge to oneself in startling new ways.

Written in 1849 only two years after *Jane Eyre*, *Shirley* is known as Charlotte Brontë's most explicitly political novel and one of several less than successful attempts on the part of later novelists to write historical fiction in the tradition of Walter Scott. The story is situated in an industrializing area of the north of England during the time of the Luddite rebellions. It records the shift of power from the old landowning families to a new cast of bureaucrats, represented by the two Moore brothers, a factory owner and a tutor who is soon to be magistrate of Briarfield Parish. It also records the shift from one form of kinship relations, which are rooted in a landowning culture, its laws of inheritance and family alliances, to mating rules that conform to a modern notion of love and produce what is known as the nuclear family. To tell the story of an institutional culture—where power comes to reside, not in fathers, but in factories, charitable organizations, and schools—the novel internalizes conflict and the operations of political power. Beginning with a conflict between groups of men who represent competing economic interests, ethnic identities, and religious sects, the novel produces a homogeneous community comprising only two different kinds of individual—men and women, parents and children—all of whom can be paired off according to gender and generational bonds. The process of breaking down a social identity into individual identities nucleates the family, and as the social text decomposes, the inherent conflicts within it disappear. This process is accomplished through the agency of a woman. For this to occur, the woman in authority, the landowning Shirley Keeldar, must relinquish her masculine qualities and grow to resemble the unextraordinary Caroline Helstone, a relatively unattractive orphan who has been adopted by the local minister. In all these respects, including the presence of such historically doubled heroines, the novel resembles the Brontës' earlier fiction.

But what makes *Shirley* clearly a later novel than *Jane Eyre*—and the historical element I particularly want to stress—is the role it attributes to literature in effecting certain historical changes. Early on in *Shirley* there is a scene of reading that both initiates the historical transformations characterizing Victorian literature and represents a model of the communication situation in which such transformations occur. The scene provides a paradigm for the power of reading that is particularly germane to the purpose of this chapter. In the scene, *Coriolanus* is read aloud and commented upon, as if to give the reader procedures for reading not only such an openly political text as Shakespeare's but the fictional narrative to follow as well. In doing so, the scene demonstrates the strategies that would actually be used to appropriate Shakespeare for middle-class culture; it also reveals the very real political interests that this way of reading literature served. My description of the scene will identify the connection between those procedures for reading that were developed in the curricula for women during the eighteenth century and those interpretive procedures that modern secondary and college curricula promote in the United States and England. In showing the rationale by which the second half of the nineteenth century extended these procedures to male education, however, I also want to mark an important difference between Charlotte Brontë's understanding of this process and our own. I do not believe we are as conscious of the politics of literary interpretation as she was.

That she understood the politics of encountering Shakespeare, not as public theater, but as a work of literature is immediately apparent. It is perhaps not surprising that Caroline Helstone, in one of her notably few acts of self-assertion, reads Shakespeare as a way of passing leisure hours with her cousin Robert Moore. They consider such games as chess, draughts, and backgammon only to reject them as "silent games that only keep one's hands employed."[8] More interesting still is the fact they also reject gossip because they are not "sufficiently interested in anybody to take pleasure in pulling their character to pieces" (p. 114). Having eliminated the pastimes such a pair might have enjoyed in earlier fiction, Caroline makes this curious proposal:

"though we don't want to think of the present existing world, it would be pleasant to go back to the past; to hear people that have slept for generations in graves that are perhaps no longer graves now, but gardens and fields, speak to us and tell their thoughts, and impart their ideas." (p. 113)

All other forms of leisure activity are passed over for reading, which consequently enables writing to mediate the relationship between male and female. This, one should recall, is the only moment of intimacy between Caroline and Robert until she visits his sickbed near the end of the novel and, in so doing, cements their relationship. Thus it is fair to say that *Shirley* begins where *Jane Eyre* and *Wuthering Heights* end. The figure of a woman with a book has already come to represent the sexual contract: "He placed it between them, reposed his arm on the back of Caroline's chair, and thus began to read" (p. 116).

Far more detailed than similar exchanges of an earlier period, this scene of reading indicates an acute awareness of the power of literacy. Brontë gives the power far more clarity than the vaguely civilizing force that women in earlier fiction could exercise over aristocratic men by way of the written word. Robert Moore is half Belgian, half English. It is through reading English literature, according to Caroline, that he "shall be entirely English" (p. 114). Robert is socialized as he acquires this specialized language, for as she explains, "'Your French forefathers don't speak so sweetly, nor so solemnly, nor so impressively as your English ancestors, Robert'" (p. 114). Nor does being English refer to one's political iden- tity—as Shakespeare would have understood it—so much as to the most basic qualities of human nature. Caroline has selected for Robert to read aloud a passage that, in her words,

> "is toned with something in you. It shall waken your nature, fill your mind with music, it shall pass like a skillful hand over your heart. . . . Let glorious William come near and touch it; you will see how he will draw the English power and melody out of its chords" (p. 114).

Just as Robert is Anglicized by reading Shakespeare, the Bard is trans- formed by the domestic setting in which he is read. Rather than estranged and culturally other, the Renaissance text is received as the voice of Rob- ert's ancestor (even though Robert was born and reared a Belgian!). This resurrected relative proves capable of speaking to him across time and cultural boundaries. Brought to life as it is read in this setting, then, the written Shakespeare takes on the subjectivity of an early nineteenth cen- tury factory owner who was reared in Belgium. To endow the text with these qualities is to transform Shakespeare into a work of literature in the modern sense of the term. It is entirely accurate to say that as we observe Shakespeare becoming the nineteenth century man, we also witness an early version of our own literary training. For here, extending through the female to the male and acquiring universal application through him, are the interpretive procedures that translate historical material into mod- ern psychological terms.

But as in every other representation of the sexual exchange that we have examined, to constitute one party is also to constitute the other. Even as it constitutes Shakespearean drama as a written text, then, this scene of reading turns writing into the record of and basis for speech. The written Shakespeare has taken the place of gossip. More important than that, the written word, when spoken, becomes the direct expression of emotions that exist prior to any speech act and that arise, so it appears, from pre-verbal sources within the self. Brought to life as a modern form of subjectivity, Shakespeare becomes the means of reproducing the same form of subjectivity within the reader. Reading such texts as *Coriolanus* "'is to stir you'," Caroline explains, "'to give you new sensations. It is to make you feel your life strongly, not only your virtues, but your vi- cious, perverse points. Discover by the feeling the reading will give you at once how high and how low you are'" (p. 115). If Shakespeare loses all those features of thought that identify him with his moment in history, then Robert loses features of a similar kind. In a stroke, reading Shakespeare takes the extremely controversial attitudes characterizing an owner intent on mechanizing his factory and translates them into terms which locate him within a hierarchy of emotions that all men are theoretically capable of feeling. The "English power" that Robert acquires by virtue of the exchange enacted through reading is simply the power of knowing himself in modern terms. For this is how Brontë describes the transformation Robert experiences as he reads Shakespeare under the loving tutelage of Caroline Helstone: "stepping out of the narrow line of private prejudices, he began to revel in the large picture of human nature, to feel the reality stamped upon the characters who were speaking from that page before him" (p. 116).

In effect, Caroline asks Robert to renounce one mode of power—which she associates with the imperiously patriarchal nature of Coriolanus—and to adopt another—which she identifies as a benevolent form of paternalism. She is effectively suppressing the political content of *Coriolanus* to make a Renaissance text represent a new form of political authority. This appears *not* to be a form of authority at all because it models itself upon family relationships and operates in and through subjectivity. As it is read by a woman and used to mediate a sexual exchange, *Coriolanus* becomes the means by which a historical change is brought about, the means, that is, by which authority is internalized and subjectivity itself becomes a self-regulating mechanism. Thus Caroline provides a moral for Robert to "'tack to the play: . . . you must not be proud to your workpeople; you must not neglect chances of soothing them, and you must not be of an inflexible nature, uttering a request as austerely as if it were a command'" (p. 114).

Brontë was not being the least bit ironic in having her heroine say this. She obviously understood the power of reading literature far better than we do. Indeed, the entire episode is designed to show that because Caroline is well trained as a female reader she will therefore make Robert a wonderful wife. If we can now assume that the process of socialization begins at home under the supervision of the mother, Brontë's novel records a time when it did not, when such a reproducible family unit existed mainly as fiction. Through fiction, it appears, this kind of household first acquired its power to reproduce a particular form of social relations rooted in gender. Thus Brontë's scene goes to some lengths to differentiate the roles played by male and female in the exchange mediated by Shakespeare. To Robert go the masculine emotions that allow him to participate in the spirit of a Roman emperor:

The very first scene in *Coriolanus* came with smart relish to his intellectual palate, and still as he read he warmed. He delivered the haughty speech of Caius Marcius to the starving citizens with unction: he did not say he thought his irrational pride right, but he seemed to feel it so. (p. 116)

But Moore also differs from his earlier counterpart, for the play's "war-like portions did not rouse him much," Robert claimed; "he said all that was out of date, or should be; the spirit displayed was barbarous" (p. 116). Imperious words still suit him while violent displays of force leave him cold, but this is when Caroline's domesticating strategies come into play. Having established Robert's nature as male by virtue of his response to the aggressive elements of Shakespeare, Brontë demonstrates how his nature may be improved—made suitable for a modern England—through the female. She has Caroline look "up at him with a singular smile" and deliver a critique of his character, which is revealed and subjected to remediation through the act of reading: "'There's a vicious point hit already,' she said; 'you sympathize with that proud patrician who does not sympathize with his famished fellow-men, and insults them'" (p. 116). Then there are scenes in the play that Robert cannot read so well because, as comic scenes, they are more suited to the female reader. As if by a natural principle the pair divide the labor of reading, "and Caroline, taking the book out of his hand, read these parts for him" (p. 116). By these and other strategies Brontë's scene of reading accomplishes what it describes. It transforms a historical text into one that speaks subjective truths in a way that distinguishes male nature from female according to a new cultural logic. But just as Shakespeare is taken up and contained within the consciousness of these readers, the readers themselves are sexed by the text as they perform it: "all scenes made of condensed truth and strength, came on in succession, and carried with them in their deep, fast flow, the heart and mind of reader and listener" (p. 117).

If nothing else, this scene reveals how historical materials are appropriated for a modern humanist discourse. The reader in this contract, namely Robert, is asked to give a performance of the written text, a reading that subjects all his Belgian traits to feminization and Robert himself to assimilation. Brontë is less than subtle in dramatizing the process by which reading rids him of the foreign devil; she seems to know exactly what political objectives the reading of Shakespeare accomplishes as it inscribes Robert's desire within the ethos of the new middle classes. Brontë also puts the woman in charge of this change even as she has Caroline read the less important passages in Shakespeare. But although there is no question that Brontë understands the power of reading, the teacher's investment in this relationship is never interrogated. Retiring, feminine, and thoroughly benevolent, Caroline's power is hardly acknowledged. Yet she is the one who declares that reading certain texts "'is to stir you; to give you new sensations. It is to make you feel your life strongly, not only your virtues, but your vicious, perverse points'" (p. 115). And when Robert concludes his reading, she is the one to catechize him, "'Now, have you felt Shakespeare?'" (p. 117). She deliberately suppresses all that is political in *Coriolanus* as so much noise in her effort to bring to the foreground the grand current of human emotions. She also establishes the framework for reading the text oppositionally, as the difference between what is truly English and what is not. The framework is designed to turn everything other (in this case "French") into a lack, a lack of the English language, which is also a lack of humane feelings. Thus in guiding his reading with her smiles and admonitions, Caroline disseminates a specialized language, a set of procedures capable of defining all cultural materials psychologically and thereby transforming them into works of high culture.

It is important to note what happens to the poetic tradition as the production of high culture becomes a feminine and feminizing process. It is noteworthy that one finds Brontë's most explicit discussion of poetry in her most openly political novel, a fact that can only encourage us to question the relationship between politics and poetics in this novel. It is also important to note that, again, the novel establishes the relationship in terms of the sexual contract. In addition to the relationship that Robert and Caroline conduct through the reading of Shakespeare, another relationship that literature mediates is the one between Shirley and Sir Philip Nunnely, who represent the old ruling class much as it had been represented in a Walter Scott novel. Nothing like his libertine counterpart that used to haunt domestic fiction, this aristocratic male pleases the woman he courts: "She liked him because she found him kind and modest, and was charmed to feel *she had the power to amuse him*" (p. 446, italics mine). Brontë considers the ability to amuse to be a female power and attributes such power to both Shirley and Caroline by virtue of the fact they are both women, despite the vast difference in their social origins. Although Shirley sees in Caroline's appearance and demeanor nothing "out of the common way in mind and attainments," the "more did she wonder to discover the self-won knowledge" her mild-mannered companion possesses. Still more important, "Caroline's instinct of taste, too, was like her own" (p. 231). In further specifying the "knowledge" that makes the orphaned Caroline an equal to Shirley, Brontë insists that their authority on literary matters identifies both of them as women of the new ruling classes:

> Few, Shirley conceived, men or women have the right taste in poetry: the
> right sense for discriminating between what is real and what is false. She
> had again and again heard very clever people pronounce this or that pas-
> sage, in this or that versifier, altogether admirable, which, when she read,
> her soul refused to acknowledge as anything by cant, flourish, and tinsel,
> or at the best, elaborate wordiness. (p. 231)

This passage alone indicates how far historically the poetics of the plain
style has come since its appearance in Robert Martin's letter of proposal
to Harriet Smith in *Emma*. In relation to the others I have selected from
Shirley, this passage suggests a multidimensional change in the history
of female subjectivity. Women are still the interpreters and evaluators of
emotional life, but the critical activity they perform now endows this novelistic standard of taste with cultural authority superior to that of the poet.

To display the features of an elite male education debilitates one in the
cultural environment defined by this novel. However pleased Shirley may
be with Sir Philip's attention, she still finds this aristocratic male to be
an unacceptable mate on the grounds that he rudely usurps the woman's
prerogative to control leisure time:

> One slight drawback there was—where is the friendship without it?—Sir
> Philip had a literary turn: he wrote poetry, sonnets, stanzas, ballads. Per-
> haps Miss Keeldar thought him *a little too fond of reading and reciting
> these compositions;* perhaps she wished the rhyme had possessed more ac-
> curacy—the measure more music—the tropes more freshness—the inspi-
> ration more fire; at any rate, she always winced when he recurred to the
> subject of his poems, and usually *did her best to divert the conversation
> into another channel.* (p. 446, italics mine)

Thus we find Sir Philip—certainly an irreverent allusion to Sir Philip
Sidney—notably impotent in effecting a sexual relationship because he
uses the wrong kind of language. "And when he had her all to himself,"
Brontë explains, "and the sea lay before them, and the scented shade of
gardens spread round, and the tall shelter of cliffs rose behind them, he
would pull out his last batch of sonnets, and read them in a voice trem-
ulous with emotion" (pp. 446–47).

According to Brontë, both prose and poetry proceed best when least
rhetorical. While including Shakespeare within the domain of humane
letters, she excludes the aristocratic tradition of poetry. In its place, she
introduces the sentimental verses from Chénier's "La Jeune Captive."
Caroline recites the verse in French as her half of the evening's exchange
with Robert Moore, as if to say that poetry—in its place—represents the
feminine feelings tolerably well. If reading certain parts of Shakespeare
and being corrected by Caroline prepare him to govern the sphere of men,
then reading poetry prepares her emotionally to be a factory owner's wife.

For as she recites the verse in French, the face of this generally listless woman becomes more "animated, interested, touched—she might be called beautiful." "Such a face," continues Brontë, "was calculated to awaken not only the calm sentiment of esteem, the distant one of admiration; but some feeling more tender, genial, intimate: friendship, perhaps—affection, interest" (p. 119). If earlier literature was designed to display one's status along with one's education, then poetry when included in Brontë's novel provides the occasion for self-display of a different kind. Like the novel, it becomes a theater for displaying the individual's psychological features. Brontë represents Robert Moore as a more desirable mate than Sir Philip Nunnely on grounds that he does not attempt to write his emotions but allows them to be written. He exposes his otherwise inarticulate passions through reading so that Caroline may in turn soften him into an amiable mate. Although Sir Philip is already amiable in precisely this way, Robert is the more desirable for possessing something male within himself that requires taming. For it is clearly he who makes a world in which women have a place and function. If this basis for granting the Belgian industrialist superiority over the aristocratic poet has lost plausibility for the modern reader, one need only recall how similarly Darwin represented relations between the sexes in *The Descent of Man, and Natural Selection in Relation to Sex*, another Victorian text:

> The sexual struggle is of two kinds; in the one it is between individuals of the same sex, generally the males, in order to drive away or kill their rivals, the females remaining passive, whilst in the other, the struggle is likewise between individuals of the same sex, in order to excite or charm those of the opposite sex, generally the females, which no longer remain passive, but select the more agreeable partners.[9]

But it is surely not to install the female as the means of socialization that Darwin factors gender differences into his theory of evolution. More to the point, Darwin's narrative domesticates history itself as he describes the domesticating influence of the female upon natural history. The competitive struggle among different species flattens out in this later piece of writing as modern man comes into natural dominance with the domestication of his aggressive instincts. As it represents culture as man's triumph over his own desire, Darwin's afterthought to the *Origin of the Species* transforms natural history into a narrative that justifies repression and exalts sublimation.

The role played by art in such a history is especially significant. In concluding his *Natural Selection in Relation to Sex*, Darwin uses a psychoaesthetic principle to explain the development of all qualities of mind (e.g., "courage" and "perseverance"), cultural accomplishments (from "weapons" to "musical organs, both vocal and instrumental"), as well as natural features (such as "strength and size," "colours, stripes and marks, and ornamental appendages"). All these features—and what else is there?—have been "indirectly gained by the one sex or the other," he contends, "through the influence of love and jealousy, through the appreciation of the beautiful in sound, colour or form, and through the exertion of a choice; and these powers of the mind manifestly depend on the development of the cerebral system" (p. 402). His comparative study of primitive cultures acknowledges the degree to which human desire, like that of any other species, appears to be triggered by certain forms and figures, chief among which are features connoting gender. These, he notes further, vary greatly from culture to culture. Having posited a biological basis for differentiating the roles of the sexes, then, Darwin's theory turns around on itself and roots sexuality entirely in culture.

The logic of sexual selection that binds politics to poetics becomes clear once we consider what happens to Darwin's notion of domestication. This notion is, for purposes of my argument, simply another name for feminization, the form that political power assumes in all the fiction I have been discussing. In selecting "the more agreeable partners," the female of the species quite literally creates the male in the image of her desires; kinship rules arise from a nearly unconscious aesthetic principle. As Darwin explains it, the principle of sexual selection "is closely analogous to that which man unintentionally, yet effectually, brings to bear on his domesticated productions, when he continues for a long time choosing the most pleasing or useful individuals, without any wish to modify the breed" (p. 398). Every time Darwin mentions sexual selection, in fact, he demonstrates this curious need to ally the principle governing kinship relations as closely to a natural process as possible. Such is the reason why he ascribes the function of sexual selection to the female or else to the least rational operations of the male cerebral system. Thus in rephrasing the eugenic principle of animal husbandry to describe that principle by which man selects his own mate, Darwin contradicts his earlier statement which describes the selective power operating through women: "Man scans with scrupulous care the character and pedigree of his horses, cattle, and dogs before he matches them; but when he comes to his own marriage he rarely, or never, takes any such care" (p. 402). Darwin goes on to argue that while man is "impelled by nearly the same motives as are the lower animals when left to their own free choice," he is nevertheless so far superior to them that he highly "values mental charms and virtues" (pp. 402–403). An aesthetic capacity in man that attracts him to the woman of virtue is both closer to nature and more civilized than that faculty by which man calculates how to serve his own interests. In theory, then, man is superior to the beast only insofar as he observes the model of sexual relations developed in conduct books and domestic fiction. For these represent a man as desiring a woman who applies the same aesthetic principles he practices in domesticating animals. "On the other hand," Darwin concedes, "he is strongly attracted by mere wealth or rank" (p. 403)..

In arriving at this tortured conclusion, Darwin's attempt to work sexuality into his theory of natural history keeps threatening to contradict his effort to celebrate as culture that specialized area of culture where sex is detached from power. By using, as the yardstick of human development, man's ability to appreciate beauty, Darwin finds himself caught in a curious paradox in which his anthropology—based, it would seem, on the power of beauty—openly contradicts a natural history that is propelled by innate competitive desire. His study concludes by painting a scene in which the implications of his earlier theory come back to haunt him. Darwin stands horror-struck as this vision of cultural history revives itself in his memory:

> The astonishment which I felt on first seeing the Fuegians on a wild and broken shore will never be forgotten by me, for the reflection at once rushed into my mind—such were our ancestors. These men were absolutely naked and bedaubed by paint, their long hair was tangled, their mouths frothed with excitment, and their expression was wild, startled, and distrustful. They possessed hardly any arts, and like wild animals lived on what they could catch; they had no government, and were merciless to every one not of their own small tribe. He who has seen a savage in his native land will not feel much shame, if forced to acknowledge that the blood of some more humble creature flows in his veins. As for my own part I would rather be descended from that heroic little monkey, who braved his dreaded enemy in order to save the life of his keeper; or from that old baboon, who, descending from the mountains, carried away in triumph his young comrade from a crowd of astonished dogs—as from a savage who delights to torture his enemies, offers up bloody sacrifices, practises infanticide without remorse, treats his wives like slaves, knows no decency, and is haunted by the grossest superstitions. (pp. 404–405)

As this scene of perverted family relationships returns to haunt him, it should recall for us the form that primitive conditions assumed for such men as Shuttleworth who explored the dark alleyways of urban culture earlier in the nineteenth century. In regard to this, we should note that—despite the resemblance between primitive man and "wild animals"—it is not nature that Darwin opposes to culture in factoring sexual selection into his theory. It is another culture, where the aesthetic principle is over-ruled by a form of male rivalry that renders the female powerless.

It is strangely appropriate that Darwin should disavow his entire theory of evolution by containing it within a disturbing memory. In representing nature as a sexual exchange rather than as the competition among different species for dominance, this later study suppresses the traces of historical struggle he once saw in natural objects and makes them speak only of sexual differences. To maintain the superiority of the middle-class male within such a system, however, Darwin feels compelled to cancel out force as the natural basis for superiority within the species. He turns to precisely the logic of exchange that Brontë formulates in *Shirley*. To stabilize a competitive world, her model requires that desire be differentiated according to gender; men must desire a woman capable of domesticating them, just as women must desire the competitive male. At the moment when Darwin finally divides the entire natural universe according to this principle, the image of primitive culture intrudes. And it is then that Darwin strikes an emotional identification with his natural ancestors outside the species, rather than see himself as the product of cultural history.

I would like to call particular attention to the fact that he represents primitive culture as not a culture at all because it suppresses female authority. The male acts out desires that, in marked contrast with the instincts of natural species, destroy all social affiliations. Darwin's nightmare consequently implies a model of culture that depends not so much on the competitive prowess of the male as on the female's ability to domesticate him. And thus he represents a situation that encourages readers to invest their political interests in a woman who devotes herself entirely to attracting and then domesticating a man's desire, a situation where for her to desire anything else contradicts her essential nature as a female. More serious still is the implication that a female's failure to desire a male will put civilization itself at the mercy of the male's unregulated competitive instincts. Darwin's revision of the theory of natural selection raises the question that would preoccupy modernist authors so diverse as Yeats, Lawrence, Joyce, Woolf, and Freud: the question of what women desire.

Modern Women: Dora and Mrs. Brown

I am convinced that the turn-of-the-century preoccupation with the unconscious arose in response to the question of what women want. The discovery of hysteria simply refined the question by directing it to the matter of whether or not the daughters of good middle-class fathers really wanted to be seduced. Modernist authors would decide that in fact women desired exactly what they, as the culture's appointed guardians of courtship and kinship, had declared impermissible. Women either desired the forbidden or else they were unnatural and perverse. Their forbidden desire comprised an earlier culture's tolerated sexual practices against which the emergent class once asserted its moral authority. In other words, practices that appeared to have no place within middle-class culture were in fact necessary to maintain the authority of the middle classes. These practices were the privileged form of the "other," the darkness requiring enlightenment, the lack requiring remediation, the perversion requiring reform. In taking up their argument with the dominant class, the modernist novels that remain most important to us now are those that laid claims to new authority for fiction—that of high culture—by opening up areas of female subjectivity which seemed to challenge the dominant class sexuality as formulated by Mayhew, Darwin, and others. But, I will argue, all these efforts to write female desire one way or another cooperated in a larger effort that enclosed certain cultural materials within a structure of consciousness that would further decontextualize and remove these materials from history. In accepting the primacy of sexual distinctions, authors were endorsing the same basis for human identity, regardless of whether they wrote about traditional monogamy or sexual transgression. To do so was to prescribe a set of alternatives that, in political terms, did not offer alternatives at all.

To bring the history of female subjectivity into the twentieth century, I would like to isolate a number of strategies that novels used to revise the nineteenth century language of the self and formulate the twentieth century language of consciousness. With the early studies on hysteria, we are clearly entering historical territory where using the word "subjectivity" no longer seems appropriate. For by the end of the nineteenth century the word had apparently achieved palpability to the degree that people no longer asked whether it was the basis for identity. Nor did they seem inclined to challenge the fact that subjectivity was essentially sexual in nature. Rather, they disputed the materials that might be contained within this framework, discovering, among other things, that women could contain within themselves much that was male and vice versa. They disputed the matter of how to classify these materials—for example, as preconscious or unconscious. They also disputed the way in which value should be distributed among these categories, and argued that value should be determined either according to an individual's ability to perform traditional roles or according to a notion of health and normalcy that was oriented more toward the individual's needs. With the development of a discourse of "consciousness," the strategies by which historical materials had been written into those composing an interior space underwent a quantum leap and began to behave as a "text" in our modern understanding of the word. They behaved as if they all issued from a central consciousness whose vicissitudes they consequently dramatized. The gender distinctions between home and marketplace, which organized the surface of social experience, were replicated as male and female desires, which cohabited interior space and contended for control of the individual's fantasy life. It was within the space of a single consciousness that, in theory, the conflict between Pamela and Mr. B was carried on, the outcome of which was to determine who had authority to define female desire. Within the theater of consciousness, however, the historical ground acquired by the female was lost as the male regained authority to write the emotions and determined what women wanted.

It should be noted that, while the male still spoke the language of the dominant class, it was language of an entirely different class than the one represented by the seducer in Richardsonian narratives. By the late nineteenth century, the language of power belonged, not to the old aristocracy, but to a professional class of doctors, teachers, lawyers, men and women in the service professions, and bureaucrats of all kinds. This was the class of people who a century earlier had been responsible for representing society as economically competing classes, on the one hand, and as a universal set of family relationships on the other. To their three-part model in which landowner contended with industrialist and industrialist with worker, Harold Perkin contends, we must add another category designating the intellectuals and professional classes who formulated the narratives in which social reality had come to be understood. It was they who declared the agents and determined the issues on which the other groups were opposed. Such men and women constituted "the forgotten middle class, in short, because," according to Perkin, "they forgot themselves. Except when postulating a place for their idealized selves in other classes' ideal societies, they generally left themselves out of their social analysis."[10] But the idea behind the panoptical strategy used by experts or specialists is to constitute a field of knowledge as if they are not part of it, thus freeing them to play the role of disinterested viewer. Where this power of surveillance is the operative form of political power— namely, within institutional cultures—the one who appears to be most disinterested has the most to gain by assuming such a relationship to the thing being observed.

It is not difficult to imagine how, during the nineteenth century, the novelist's position became problematic in relation to these other writers. Because the novel—in England at least—was written in the language of women, novelists could not really be considered among the professional people and intellectuals. This was true despite the fact it was indeed possible for women to enter certain professions. For the novel uttered emotional truths that were responsible for establishing a specific order of kinship relations as normal and desirable. But when the modernist novel set fiction in opposition to the languages of a bureaucratic society, a struggle commenced that transformed the formal strategies of fiction along with its political objective. The outcome of this phase of fiction's ongoing dialectic with itself ensured that fiction would be authorized no longer by common sense—the body of female knowledge—but by way of reference to the specialized language of literature. The body of knowledge that had belonged to the mother and housewife came under professional scrutiny and was discovered to be a web of deceptions and "tales." Within a relatively short period of time, then, the language of kinship was no longer the woman's domain. It became instead the domain of the counselor and the therapist. At the same time, nationality ceased to provide the "natural" framework for conducting a study such as mine. A new principle other than nation, class, or even gender apparently organized communication and thus bestowed upon writing a modern identity. The age that, according to Woolf, began in 1910 was an age of writers who were alienated from both nation and class. It was the age of androgynous and sexually experimental writers as well. Yet within this field of writing, one's manner of opposing sexuality to nation and class produced highly individual styles of writing. Such forms of individuality emerged, as I see it, through new and ever more sophisticated representations of female subjectivity.

To lay out a background against which this assertion may appear reasonable, I will begin with what I consider the prototype of the modernist text, Freud's *Fragment of an Analysis of a Case of Hysteria*. It is perfectly possible to read the story of Dora as a return to Richardson's narrative dialectic of fiction within fiction. Rather than writing the female as an object of male desire, Freud strikes out against the sexuality of the dominant class in this historically groundbreaking study. He works against novelistic displacements of sexuality as he helps Dora to peel back the layers of fiction by which she denies the genital basis of her desire. In this respect, it can be argued that the creation of analytic discourse marks the return of Mr. B and revaluates his undisplaced sexuality as liberation rather than libertinism. One can indeed claim, as Freud did, that he works against a century of prudery to create a more flexible notion of normalcy than that which confines sexual desire to legitimate monogamy. It is Freud's daring conviction that we must understand perversion, not in opposition to middle-class norms, but as a less developed stage of normal sexual development:

> Each one of us in his own sexual life transgresses to a slight extent—now in this direction, now in that—the narrow lines imposed upon him as the standard of normality. The perversions are neither bestial nor degenerate in the emotional sense of the word. They are a development of germs all of which are contained in the undifferentiated sexual pre-disposition of the child, and which, by being suppressed or by being diverted to higher, asexual aims—by being *sublimated*—are destined to provide the energy for a great number of our cultural achievements. When, therefore, any one has *become* a gross and manifest pervert, it would be more correct to say that he has *remained* one, for he exhibits a certain stage of *inhibited development*.[11]

At crucial places in Freud's writing, then, one may note the nineteenth century figure of illicit combinations appearing to ask for tolerance and a place within culture: "perversions are neither bestial nor degenerate in the emotional sense of the word." The question I would like to pose, from a strictly historical viewpoint, is this: in forgiving the pervert, does this notion of sexuality identify a different politics than, say, James Kay Shuttleworth's or Charles Darwin's?

There is no question that Freud's "Dora," along with the earlier case studies on hysteria, constitutes a new moment in the history of sexuality. But it is, I think, a new chapter in the discourse of sexuality rather than the beginning of a paradigmatically new book on the human subject. The passage quoted above illustrates that this chapter is governed by the same figures of culture as Shuttleworth's, Mayhew's, or Darwin's. If anything, one finds the nineteenth century strategies of interiorization carried much further in Freud's early case histories, all of which are histories of female subjectivity. For here, Freud makes gender the essential component of consciousness by locating the origin of all conscious development in genital sexuality. He overturns the traditional exchange in which the entire female body is the object of desire; he identifies the phallus as the basis for desire; and he defines all other forms of desire as deceptions that operate as "defenses" against acknowledging desire for the phallus as the single most basic human reality. With this strategy, Freud develops a professional language of the self capable of redefining any resistance to that notion of the self as a symptom of repression and denial. Defining the problem in this way, he can write stories of female desire in which, like Rousseau's individual, the individual becomes more herself—healthy, complete, and functional. When he finds that the stories told by women conceal the true nature of sexual desire, Freud revises their narratives in a way that proposes to liberate and heal.

The studies on hysteria translate a female language of subjectivity into a language that Freud himself likens to those of both "gynaecologist" and "archaeologist." It is significant that he represents his work in these capacities by means of the Enlightenment trope of "bringing to light." Here is one of those instances when he conceptualizes his role in relation to the patient:

> In the face of the incompleteness of my analytic results, I had no choice but to follow the example of those discoverers whose good fortune it is to bring to the light of day after their long burial the priceless though mutilated relics of antiquity. I have restored what is missing, taking the best models known to me from other analyses; but like a conscientious archaeologist I have not omitted to mention in each case where the authentic parts end and my constructions begin. (p. 12)

One should note the recurring presence of "relics." In this and other respects, Freud understands the materials with which he works in terms of the same museum-like structure in which the Brontës had first carved out new territories of female subjectivity. They broke down the stuff of an earlier historical moment in order to create the operative psychological categories of modern culture. The same house of culture organizes the early studies on hysteria, but Freud encloses the whole domain of earlier sexual practices within the woman. In these case studies, as opposed to the sensational fiction of the Victorian period, the stuff of cultural history represents a dissolution of domestic categories within the self (i.e., "the undifferentiated sexual pre-disposition of the child") and thus sets the stage for further penetration, mapping, and control of the individual.

It is worth noting, however, that Freud's sense of "good fortune" is not mitigated in the least by the fact that these "relics" of the past within the self are "mutilated." His analytic procedures presuppose an absence that needs to be filled. They establish the role of analysis, then, as supplying the missing parts. Upon encountering such a self-representation, the canny reader must expect "analyses" to supplement the voice of the "authentic" subject, which in turn becomes a voice fraught with forms of self-deception, denials, or defenses.[12] One can expect this with some degree of certainty because the subject's speech in Freud's communication model has all the features of the female body itself: those of a disfigured or "mutilated" male, essentially regressive, but at the same time, containing the secrets that authorize male discourse. This body provides both the verification and the substance of Freud's writing. Even as he transforms the body into an incomplete thing forever desiring the missing part that will complete it, he endows the female with the power, paradoxically, to empower the male.

As Freud's archeological model suggests, the male requires the female to complete him. As such, the contractual model still exists. When maleness and femaleness were understood as economic and emotional power respectively, as they generally were during the eighteenth and nineteenth centuries, the semiotic operations of the contract were relatively clear; the contract translated money into love and converted the competitive operations of the marketplace into family relations. With Freud, however, the places of the family provide the ultimate explanation for all power relations. In contrast with the Puritan treatise on marriage, which thought of the natural father as a "governor," the psychological case study considers all political superiors as "father figures." Furthermore, the father himself comes to be represented as a partial figure, the penis. Reducing all the features of gender to the genitals allows Freud to think of sexual relations as a relationship of presence to absence, but his rhetorical strategy is not particularly effective in controlling the female. If it were, there would be no need for his elaborate attempts to represent what women want. The absence he wants to create, and which allows him to measure all things by the male, implies a presence that cannot be acknowledged. It is there in the unzoned female body that one finds a kind of desire not controlled by the phallus. Such desire is older and, like the desire embodied in the Brontës' female protagonists, can dissolve the boundaries differentiating parent from child and male from female consciousness. Before Freud can devote himself to the question of oedipal rivalry, he apparently feels compelled to put this desire to rest. To do so, he attempts to invalidate a whole tradition of thinking in which such desire was the ultimate cause of historical change. I am speaking of the tradition of domestic fiction and the history of sexuality it records.

In their effort to overturn this tradition, Freud's narratives arrive at a successful conclusion when the woman confronts the fact that she desires only her father, that all her fears of seduction are simply strategies for denying the fact of her forbidden desire. By means of a game of semantic mismatching in which all objects ultimately refer to the penis, this kind of narrative transforms into figures of the father those objects designated as objects of desire and fear. But in the project to constitute female subjectivity the penis is only a penis unless and until it is desired by the mother. Where there appears to be only one source of power, namely, the male, there are actually two, on the male and in the female. The penis goes in as just another penis, but it comes out of the mother as a phallus. By recasting the sexual contract in such somatic terms, this theory offers the ultimate mystification of middle-class power. The nature of the exchange that distinguishes genders and situates them in a mutually authorizing relationship cannot be perceived. And because the exchange is no longer perceptible, gender seems to rest on the one-sided fact of the male's biological nature.[13]

But before his analysis of Dora can get off the ground, Freud must identify gaps in Dora's narrative, for gaps imply there is another truth, a buried context, a missing framework to be exposed. His identification of gaps turns Dora's text into a string of metaphors for her otherwise inarticulate desires. Thus Freud writes, "Even during the course of their story patients will repeatedly correct a particular or a date, and then perhaps, after wavering for some time, return to their first version" (p. 17). Upon discovering hesitancies and corrections on the part of a storyteller, the analyst proceeds to revise the damaged speech. In doing so, he authorizes a narrative that is not only written but also highly specialized, scientific, and male:

> The patients' inability to give an ordered history of their life in so far as it coincides with the history of their illness is not merely characteristic of the neurosis. It also possesses theoretical significance. For this inability has the following grounds. In the first place, patients consciously and intentionally keep back part of what they ought to tell—things that are perfectly well known to them—because they have not got over their feelings of timidity and shame (or discretion, where what they say concerns other people): this is the share taken by conscious disingenuousness. (p. 17)

It is important to note how the strategy of gap-making is also a strategy for representing the storyteller's text as a set of pathological symptoms. This strategy creates both a space in which analysis can insert itself and a pathology that requires analysis as a cure. To identify a gap in the story is to produce a need in the woman for a new language of the self. Each form of resistance Freud encounters speaks of such a need and calls forth a communicative strategy to address it. There are, for example, those obstructions to his pursuit of knowledge that arise from standards of politeness or personal loyalty, or simply from the sense of how personal information should be rendered in narrative form. Thus Freud identifies an "unconscious disingenuousness," which arises when information that patients can recall at other times "disappears when they are actually telling their story, but without their making any deliberate reservations" (p. 17). But information which is not accessible to the patient at all is finally that which colors the other narrative transformations of this multileveled model. This point of origin is the part of the self that is outside of language and also the reference point of language, as Freud represents it: "there are invariably true amnesias—gaps in the memory into which not only old recollections but even quite recent ones have fallen—and paramnesias, formed secondarily so as to fill in those gaps" (p. 17). Quite paradoxically, then, there are gaps inside of gaps, and there are also gaps where there appear to be none, for the logic of repression presupposes that if there are few mistakes in the patient's narrative, "a falsification of memory has occurred" to obscure the loss of true memory (p. 17).

The production of gaps thus conspires with tropes of inversion to reveal the repressed materials of subjectivity. Again, Freud will claim that "from the nature of the facts which form the material of psychoanalysis," it follows "that we are obliged to pay much attention in our case histories to the purely human and social circumstances of our patients as to the somatic data and symptoms of the disorder." Although, as he says, "our interest will be directed towards their family circumstances," the case history in fact regularly effects semantic inversions that establish psychological truth in a contradictory relationship to the "family circumstances" surrounding the patient (p. 17). These strategies again are those of the formalist text, which cuts itself off from a "context" as an independent, if interdependent, form of truth; it maintains an absolute difference between inside and outside, a form of alienation that does not appear political because it occurs at a pre-social, sexual level.

Feminist criticism has already made us aware of Freud's gross insensitivity in presuming that unlike Dora, "a healthy girl in such circumstances, having no prior sexual experience," would have certainly felt "a genital sensation" upon being forcibly embraced and kissed on the mouth by Herr K., a longtime friend of her father and husband of her father's mistress. Precisely because Dora resists this idea with such conviction, Freud persists in the idea that a normal woman would not only feel but would also want to feel this "genital sensation." On this basis alone, he declares, "I should without question consider a person hysterical in whom an occasion for sexual excitement elicited feelings that were preponderantly or exclusively unpleasurable; and I should do so whether or no the person were capable of producing somatic symptoms" (p. 44). By making such a declaration as a medical diagnosis, Freud hits upon a strategy of professionalism that challenges the tradition of representation going back to *Pamela* and questions the form of authority that depends chiefly on resisting seduction. Only insofar as she could say "no" did Pamela possess any power of self-definition. But in a communication situation where strategies of reversal rule meaning, her "no" actually means "yes," and signs of disgust therefore disguise pleasure. In this respect, we can regard Freud's dialogue with Dora as an elaborate reenactment of the earlier struggle between Pamela and Mr. B. In reenacting the struggle to identify what is female in the woman, however, Freud's narrative inverts and displaces the Richardsonian idealization of the woman.

Within the clinical setting, Freud enters into a dialectic with fiction and with the body of female knowledge that authorizes it. Regarding fiction's depths as a surface that conceals the truth of human sexuality, he discovers new depths in the female that represent all human relationships as genital engagement and make pathological the woman's lack of desire for the male organ:

> I have formed in my own mind the following reconstruction of the scene. I believe that during the man's passionate embrace she felt not merely his kiss upon her lips but also the pressure of his erect member against her body. This perception was revolting to her; it was dismissed from her memory, repressed, and replaced by the innocent sensation of pressure upon her thorax, which in turn derived an excessive intensity from its repressed source. Once more, therefore, we find a displacement from the lower part of the body to the upper. (p. 29)

All these transformations of Dora's story of her unpleasant encounter with Herr K. have a clear objective in mind, as do Freud's other attempts to write Dora. Her case history can be read as a rewriting of domestic fiction that translates its "virtues" into pathological "symptoms" in order to reveal the secrets of female consciousness. The inversion this brings about in the ideal relationships of an earlier age is clear enough. Rather than empowering her to read the emotions of others, Dora's account of Herr K.'s advances, as well as of her father's own scandalous behavior, all reveal to Freud her deepest and unacknowledged wish—to possesss her own father. Where Dora denounces others for violating kinship relations, Freud reads her own incestuous desire.

Freud came to understand this case as one in which he failed to interpret a negative transference relationship and thereby to establish a positive transference. He could not read Dora's relationship to her significant other— always the father—in terms of the relationship she conducted with her analyst. He concluded that any successful analysis depends on establishing such a positive relationship between analyst and analysand. But instead she walked out on him—as an act of "revenge," he contended— never to confront her true feelings for her father, for Herr K., or for the other principal involved in her story, Frau K., her father's mistress. In a postscript to his narrative, Freud later reached the conclusion that he himself had failed to understand the nature of the transference relationship. In actuality, he determined, Dora had established a relationship with him that allowed her to act out revenge toward Herr K. rather than love for her father. Later still, in a footnote to his postscript, he decided that the case did not resolve itself satisfactorily because he had failed to recognize "the importance of the homosexual current of feeling in psychoneurotics" (p. 120). Nowhere, in all his various interpretations of the lack of a positive transference between himself and Dora, is there room in Freud's model for the most obvious logical possibility, namely, that she never did at some level desire her father.

Freud persisted in constituting the communication situation as a double bind created by a genital notion of desire, according to which the female is either in love with her father and essentially normal or else not in love with her father and a lesbian. Rather than working within the limits posed by these alternatives, I would like to suppose for a moment that Dora was right to understand her options differently. Behind her lay a tradition of writing about courtship and kinship, after all, that aimed at making her resist seduction. It predisposed her to resist even those forms of seduction condoned by her father, who she felt had been encouraging Herr K.'s advances toward her in exchange for allowing the open affair between her father and Frau K. to continue. Against the father's ancient prerogative to exchange his daughter's body in marriage, Dora consequently positioned her own authority as a post-Enlightenment woman who was culturally empowered to say which sexual relations were forbidden or approved. At first, even Freud admitted that "it was easy to see her reproaches were justified":

> When she was feeling embittered she used to be overcome by the idea that she had been handed over to Herr K. as the price of his tolerating the relations between her father and his wife; and her rage at her father's making such a use of her was visible behind her affection for him. (p. 34)

Dora had evidently described her household as if it came from a sensational novel in which earlier sexual practices intruded upon domestic order and violated the cultural boundaries separating genders and generations. Although its sensationalism diminishes considerably as her story is contained within analytic discourse, it nevertheless achieves a nightmarish effect. But even at this early point in his narrative, Freud finds it necessary to destabilize Dora's authority. Dropping suggestions that "she was feeling embittered" and "overcome by the idea" of her father's flagrant adultery and abuse of paternal authority, Freud lays the seeds of meaning that will be discovered as another narrative concealed beneath and more authentic than her own.

The curious thing is how quickly Freud overturns this sordid tale and uses it to mount a defense of the father that invalidates the story-telling strategies of the woman: "The two men had of course never made a formal agreement in which she was treated as an object for barter; her father in particular would have been horrified at any such suggestion" (p. 34). Soon he turns Dora's reproaches against her: "A string of reproaches against other people leads one to suspect the existence of a string of self-reproaches with the same content. All that need be done is to turn back each single reproach on to the speaker himself" (p. 35). Having overturned the literal meaning and the reference point of her accusations, Freud then proceeds to locate the violation of kinship relations in Dora herself:

> She had made herself an accomplice in the affair, and had dismissed from her mind every sign which tended to show its true character. It was not until after her adventure by the lake [when Herr K. forced himself upon her] that she began to apply such a severe standard to her father. (p. 36)

By a swift sequence of tropes, then, Dora finds herself in the role of panderer just where she had situated her father. By an equally swift sequence of tropes, all the women in this story, with the exception of Frau K., are found deficient in their desire for men and therefore complicit in one way or another in the father's illicit relationship. One cannot help but wonder why the rhetoric of analysis works with such dexterity to cast Dora, her mother, and her governess in a pathological light, all the while exculpating the syphilitic father who carries on an affair with Frau K.

It is worth noting that the symptoms of psychological disease are the very same features denoting qualities of depth and value in the domestic woman. Pamela's power of self-definition began with her power to say "no." By means of this power, she withheld her body from a system of exchange in which women were currency among men. But by this initial act of negation, she authorized an exchange based on mutual consent between male and female. She relinquished her economic and social identity in this exchange and acquired the power to oversee domestic economy and sexual relations. She also relinquished her body in order to diffuse herself into the objects and personnel of the household. For two centuries, a woman's desire had been so narrowly focused on becoming such a woman. Indeed, her very survival had been taught to her in these terms. And so, it must have come as a shock to be told that all this was a mechanism of repression, that the real depths of the female did not reside in her maternal instincts, her affection for female friends, her domestic duties, or her concern for the weak and the poor.

In the name of her health and liberation, Freud views the mother's domesticity as an unhealthy sign and installs an eternally desirous woman in her place. His ideal is a woman who feels herself lacking as such and, in order to fill the lack, desires nothing so much as the male organ. The prerogative that enables Pamela to say "no" to all of Mr. B's advances is not available to Dora whose "no" may be at any time taken to mean "yes": "If this 'no,' instead of being regarded as the expression of an impartial judgement (of which, indeed, the patient is incapable), is ignored, and if work is continued, the first evidence soon begins to appear that in such a case 'no' signifies the desired 'yes'" (pp. 58–59).[14] More than that, her persistent "no's" indicate an inability to say yes, a flaw in her sexuality. Freud observes the following rules in interpreting Dora's refusal of Herr K.'s advances: "The 'no' uttered by a patient after a repressed thought has been presented to his conscious perception for the first time does no more than register the existence of a repression and its severity" (p. 58). Either she cannot admit the degree to which she desires Herr K. because to do so would mean acknowledging her desire for her father and for Freud himself, or else—the conclusion he finally reaches—she is deeply angry with men.

The case history of Dora does not stop with identifying the flaw in her desire, but goes on to analyze the other women in Dora's world whom Freud considers defective as well because they withhold themselves from men. Using accounts from both Dora and her father, Freud constructs a version of the domestic woman that strips her of the kind of authority with which Richardson had invested Pamela. Of Dora's mother, Freud writes:

> I was led to imagine her as an uncultivated woman and above all as a foolish one, who concentrated all her interests upon domestic affairs, especially since her husband's illness and the estrangement to which it led. She presented the picture, in fact, of what might be called the "housewife's psychosis." (p. 20)[15]

Freud diagnoses Dora's governess as equally pathological, even though she seems the very antithesis of the mother in all the important ways: she is cultivated and desires Dora's father. In her case, Freud does not invert but simply draws upon Victorian convention. She, Freud explains, is "an unmarried woman, no longer young, . . . well-read and of advanced views" (p. 36). This woman, in other words, possesses many of the features of Nelly Dean, Emily Brontë's narrator, but they acquire a different meaning in the modernist text. Rather than possess the kind of knowledge required to understand the conflicting currents of desire that shape the family history, this woman corrupts desire to produce conflict between father and daughter. At this point in his version of the case, Freud identifies the governess as the source of Dora's "secret knowledge" of adult sexual practices and the one who calls Dora's attention to her father's relationship with Frau K. But in adopting this stereotype of the governess, we should note, Freud conveniently deflects criticism that might fall on his own shoulders. Lest his readers consider him capable of putting improper ideas in a young girl's head, he explains:

> There is never any danger of corrupting an inexperienced girl. For where there is no knowledge of sexual processes even in the unconscious, no hysterical symptom will arise; and where hysteria is found there can no longer be any question of "innocence of mind" in the sense in which parents and educators use the phrase. (p. 49)

That Freud already detects hysterical symptoms in Dora means that she is already corrupted. And rather than attribute any of the girl's knowledge of adult sexuality to a father who carried on an affair with his friend's wife in a outrageously open manner, Freud sees fit to attribute her sexual awareness to the proverbial teller of tales and corrupter of youth, the governess. Although sexually inactive herself, this woman "used to read every sort of book on sexual and similar subjects, and talked to the girl about them" (p. 36).

If we consider Freud's relationship with Dora as the struggle between two modes of representation for the power to define the desirable female, there is only one conclusion we can draw. This is a struggle between male and female modes of representation for the authority to define female desire. But the comparison between psychoanalytic discourse and domestic fiction is informative in another respect. Although Freud insists that Dora's "no" means "yes"—that she does desire the father—she refuses to authorize his inversion of meaning. Just as she resisted her father's attempts to give her to Herr K. in exchange for Frau K., she again exercises the traditional female prerogative to refuse the exchange that gives rise to Freud's interpretation of what she desires. She plays Pamela to the end, leaving Freud without a successful conclusion to his case history.

If we extend the parallel between Freud and Richardson further, we see that in creating a communication situation with Dora that revises female desire, Freud reenacts the scene of seduction. "What are transferences?" he asks, only to reply: "They are new editions or facsimiles of the tendencies and fantasies which are aroused and made conscious during the progress of analysis" (p. 116). In the case of women, transference relationships are always reenactments of the desire for the father. Acceptance of this framework for communication is necessary for a successful analysis, according to Freud, "since it is only after the transference has been resolved that a patient arrives at a sense of conviction of the validity of the connections which have been constructed during the analysis" (p. 116–17).[16] His theory of desire requires that Dora acknowledge her desire not only for her father but also for Herr K. and ultimately for Freud himself. It is also important that she regard other women as rivals for the father's affection, for the genital logic of his theory depends on "connections" that define the various members of the household according to differences that arise from male and female desire.

With this in mind, it is interesting to note how Freud resolves his narrative when Dora rejects the framework of seduction and walks out on him. What results is a sequence of endings that, in keeping with modernist fiction, create formal closure without effecting semantic closure.[17] On the one hand, he entertains the possibility that he was deficient in displaying his love:

> Might I perhaps have kept the girl under my treatment if I myself had acted a part, if I had exaggerated the importance to me of her staying on, and which, even after allowing for my position as her physician, would have provided her with a substitute for the affection she longed for? (p. 109)

On the other hand, still representing his plight as one might a failed love affair, he accuses Dora of "thus bringing those hopes to nothing—this was an unmistakable act of vengeance on her part" (p. 109). He initially concludes that Dora has rejected him for the very reasons she rejected Herr K. and turned against her father, because he, like them, was what she desired. Of the neurotic in general he says, "If what they long for the most intensely in their phantasies is presented to them in reality, they none the less flee from it" (p. 110). But this simple inversion evidently does not satisfy Freud's requirements for a narrative, for he continues to cast about for a resolution. And when he hits upon it, it comes in a form that fills in two gaps in his narrative which have persisted in troubling him.

There is the question of Dora's knowledge of adult sexuality, the source of which she apparently forgets, but which Freud attributes to her governess. This question remains to the end a challenge to a theory that understands sexuality as the most essential component of the individual. If desire is supposed to be rooted in genital sexuality, then it originates within the individual as instincts that must be socialized. Any possibility that desire comes from a source outside the individual undermines the whole theory of repression and, with it, the authority of a language of the self that proposes to bring the deepest and most primitive areas of consciousness to light. In his essay, "The 'Uncanny,'" Freud confronts this problem head on. Having identified the fear of something uncanny as the return of repressed material, he acknowledges certain uncanny experiences that do not necessarily arise from any individual act of repression. It is possible for experiences of "the omnipotence of thoughts, instantaneous wish fulfillments, secret power to do harm and the return of the dead" to occur when cultural history refuses to stay in the past and overlaps with present-day reality:

> We—or our primitive forefathers—once believed in the possibility of these things and were convinced that they really happened. Nowadays we no longer believe in them, we have *surmounted* such ways of thought; but we do not feel quite sure of our new set of beliefs, and the old ones still exist within us ready to seize upon any confirmation. As soon as something actually happens in our lives which seems to support the old, discarded beliefs, we get a feeling of the uncanny.[18]

From this cultural phenomenon, Freud distinguishes another form of uncanny experience that occurs only when such infantile complexes as fear of castration and womb fantasies—materials of the individual's history harbored within the unconscious—emerge to disrupt one's adult perception of reality. The "distinction between the two" kinds of uncanny experience is, according to Freud, "theoretically very important" ("The 'Uncanny,'" p. 249). But the more he attempts to distinguish the two, it appears, the more he in fact undermines the distinction between the psychological and the historical: "We might say that in the one case what had been repressed was a particular ideational content and in the other the belief in its physical existence" ("The 'Uncanny,'" p. 55). His reasoning on the "return of the repressed" thus concludes by questioning the whole notion of repression, as Freud, to his credit, acknowledges: "But this last way of putting it no doubt strains the term 'repression' beyond its legitimate meaning" ("The 'Uncanny,'" p. 55). The question of Dora's sexual knowledge is the same one posed by the dual sources of "uncanny" materials. They question the validity of Freud's distinction between desires that are "inside" the individual and those that have arisen from the knowledge passed from one woman to another.

Related to the question of Dora's knowledge is another question—just as nagging—concerning what Dora does want if she does not want these men. Thus Freud feels his narrative is complete when he strikes upon this answer decidedly after the fact of his dialogues with Dora. Quite abruptly, however, Freud seems to abandon his basic assumptions that the governess was the source of Dora's forbidden knowledge and that Dora's rejection of men was a way of denying her desire for her father, and he arrives at this resolution to all the enigmas of Dora's case:

> I failed to discover in time and to inform the patient that her homosexual (gynaecophilic) love for Frau K. was the strongest unconscious current in her mental life. I ought to have guessed that the main source of her knowledge of sexual matters could have been no one but Frau K.—the very person who later on charged her with being interested in those same subjects. Her knowing all about such things and, at the same time, she always pretending not to know where her knowledge came from was really too remarkable. (p. 120)

He is troubled, then, by women's knowledge. He is downright suspicious of knowledge that women pass from one to another, for this knowledge seems to obstruct his own attempts to write Dora's desires, and he identifies that knowledge with the ontogenesis of diseased desire, the source of which he thus locates in the female.

That a power struggle of some significance takes place in this case history is apparent in Freud's changing representatons of Dora, the woman who refuses to be seduced. At first, he finds her "engaging" (p. 23). A short time later, however, she becomes "pitilessly sharp" (p. 32). This slippage continues along the same trajectory as Freud renames her "sharp sighted" Dora (p. 34). Soon she is "the little thumb sucker" (p. 94) and, finally, a "vengeful" woman (p. 119). Freud's name calling records openly his own growing antagonism toward the girl as she pits her knowledge of sexuality against his and persists in an alternative representation of herself. Particularly noteworthy is his dissociation of the female's power of surveillance ("sight") from her maternal qualities. Rather than sympathetic, soft, and tender, Dora is associated with the unfemale word "sharp"—"pitilessly sharp" and "sharp sighted." And even though Herr K. and his wife later admit Dora's accusations are true when, after losing faith in the benefits of analysis, she confronts them outright with her narrative, Freud does not concede her the right either to declare her own feelings or to pass judgement upon the sordid business taking place in her household. It is not that he wants to write Dora, I think, so much as that he refuses to abandon the hermeneutic procedures which stand to win him professional status. He feels compelled to defend these procedures throughout his account of Dora's treatment, as if she threatened to betray his theory to his competitors.

That Freud should insist upon Dora's lesbian desires in the face of the outcome of her narrative is peculiar indeed: "Years have gone by since her visit. In the meantime the girl has married" (p. 122). But even supposing her personal history does not in fact converge with a domestic novel as, according to Freud's notion of health, it eventually must, it is still necessary to ask why he regards lesbianism as the answer to all the questions that trouble him most in her case. Those who are quick to note Freud's groundbreaking tolerance for male homosexuality would do well to remember how intolerant he is of bonds among women, of female masturbation, or for that matter, of simple indifference on the part of a woman toward men. To put it crudely, male homosexuality affirms the desirability of the penis while female homosexuality does not.

I draw all these inferences from Dora's speech as Freud has written it. I have examined only Freud's side of the contract, the side that he is analyzing in terms of the transference relationship between patient and analyst. It is only fair, then, to examine the kind of material that comprises Dora's side of the communicative exchange, since the transference relationship they enact is supposed to have originated in her. It is the patient who establishes this framework for communication with the analyst by enacting relationships real and imagined, and it is the transference relationship she establishes with the doctor that provides him with information about her.[19] As Freud declares, "Psychoanalytic treatment does not *create* transferences, it merely brings them to light" (p. 117). In the course of analysis, Dora's side of the relationship yields two dreams which are supposed to reveal desires that cannot be openly stated. Here is the first dream Dora reports to Freud:

"A house was on fire. My father was standing beside my bed and woke me up. I dressed myself quickly. Mother wanted to stop and save her jewel-case; but Father said: 'I refuse to let myself and my two children be burnt for the sake of your jewel-case.' We hurried downstairs, and as soon as I was outside I woke up." (p. 64)

The second dream is the epigraph to this chapter. The dreamwork in both instances is shaped by a figure that should be utterly familiar to fiction readers—that of the house. This house is associated in the first dream with the mother's body and in the second with writing, that is, with the mother's letter ("Then I came into a house where I lived, went to my room, and found a letter from Mother lying there."). It is a female territory from which, in the first dream, she is evicted by the father's phobia and, into which, in the second dream, she is peacefully readmitted upon the father's death ("She wrote saying that as I had left home without my parents' knowledge she had not wished to write to me to say that Father was ill. 'Now he is dead, and if you like you can come'" [p.94]).

If Freud could compare his work to that of an archeologist and Herr K. could feel justified in making a pass at Dora because "'I get nothing out of my wife,'" it was because these men shared the same way of thinking about sexuality, even though as individuals they used it quite differently to think out their positions in the modern world. They invoke the figure of the house as a woman's body that contains something they need. In Herr K.'s case, presumably the woman contains his maleness, while in Freud's more sophisticated version of the figure, she contains knowledge. But whether it is the woman's desire for his penis that he requires or her knowledge of such desire, it is the woman who empowers the man. It appears that the same figure of the house as a woman's body that contains knowledge came to serve as a model for culture itself at the opening of the modern period. Having shown how this figure underlies and authorizes the psychoanalytic fables of desire, I would like to turn to an author of fiction to explore the political implications of the figure.

Less than thirty years after Dora abandoned her analysis with Freud, Virginia Woolf made her famous trip to the British Museum and looked up the books written on the subject of "woman" only to discover that she was "perhaps, the most discussed animal in the universe."[20] This led to Woolf's famous address to the Arts Society at Newnham, an address that was later expanded in the published essay with the suggestive title, *A Room of One's Own.* The question that prompts this essay's musings upon culture is one that any study of the English novel must eventually broach. Examining the titles listed under "women" in the subject catalogue of the British Museum, Woolf asks, "Why are women, judging from this catalogue, so much more interesting to men than men are to women?" All the museum's books explaining "that women have less hair on their bodies than men, or that the age of puberty among the South Sea Islanders is nine" did not answer this question, she complains, and so did not help her to compose a lecture about "Women and Fiction" (p. 30). These books were empty.

In discussing this period in the history of the novel, I find Woolf particularly useful for reasons that have little to do with her being a woman by nature and far more to do with her understanding of what it means to be a woman in relation to culture. In *A Room of One's Own,* Woolf composed, for the first time, a history of women's literature. Her narrative begins with a question: If Shakespeare had had a sister, and if she had been as talented and ambitious as he, what would she have produced? Nothing, concludes Woolf; the circumstances would not have allowed it. The category represented by Shakespeare's sister remains largely imaginary until the end of the eighteenth century: "Thus towards the end of the eighteenth century a change came about which, if I were rewriting history, I should describe more fully and think of greater importance than the Crusades or the Wars of the Roses. The middle-class woman began to write" (p. 69). It is Woolf's contention that women possess a different kind of knowledge than men: "For women have sat indoors all these millions of years, so that by this time the very walls are permeated by their creative force, which has, indeed, so overcharged the capacity of bricks and mortar that it must needs harness itself to pens and brushes and business and politics" (p. 91). As women, individuals therefore possess a different form of power, which Woolf represents in the images of empty rooms, houses, and enclosures that reappear throughout her writing.

It is not my intention to interpret these as sexual images and thereby to arrive at a sexual mythology that authorizes Woolf over Freud on the basis of gender. What I do want to discuss is Woolf's ability to step outside of the framework in which Freud had fixed Dora. Woolf defines a position for herself as a writer that allows her to infuse the modern communication situation with some of its historical ramifications. She understands precisely the one advantage that comes from having been excluded from the male institutions of state, and she refuses to romanticize her marginal status. The advantage she has is one that Freud had not yet discovered when he treated Dora: the power of countertransference. As his theory developed, this power would become the provenance of the analyst's specialized training, the kind of knowledge analysands never know even as they come to understand the nature of the transference relationship. Countertransference is much more than the transference of the analyst, a transference that, having been analyzed, the analyst recognizes as such. And it cannot be acquired simply by inverting the relationship between analyst and patient. Countertransference is the understanding of what is truly other about the other. Such understanding allows one to recognize instantly when and where resistance to the analysis of transference sets in, and knowing the nature of resistance is everything in a culture where power ultimately resides in writing. For once it is known, resistance can be professionally interrogated and redefined. In this respect, countertransference is institutional power par excellence.

Such power, Woolf suggests, is the answer to the question of what men want out of women. It is significant that she identifies her power in a kind of reverie that deliberately draws on the very forms of cognitive power that middle-class culture had found dangerous in women and had developed a female curriculum to curtail. The answer comes in part by way of a representation that both invokes and mocks the analytic setting. In musing over the question of why men are so interested in defining women, she doodles. She draws a picture of the kind of individual who must have written the unhelpful books listed in the museum's catalogue and finds that she has depicted an angry professor. Reflecting upon her own drawing, she arrives at a truth:

> Yet it is in our idleness, in our dreams, that the submerged truth sometimes comes to the top. A very elementary exercise in psychology, not to be dignified by the name of psycho-analysis, showed me, on looking at my notebook, that the sketch of the angry professor had been made in anger. (p. 32).

It is at the moment when she grasps the entire communication situation as such that she understands two things: She understands the "other," and she understands his need to write women. At such moments as this in her fiction, one becomes aware that Woolf is shifting to a level of meaning where the images of fluidity and enclosure for which she is known stop referring to anything outside of themselves, and the text consequently provides its own metalanguage. In addition to knowing the other and his need to write about women, then, she also demonstrates that what is inside the woman is nothing if it is not writing.

I mean this, not in any cleverly post-modernist sense, but quite literally: There are several stylistic involutions in her writing that demonstrate an acute awareness of the degree to which consciousness itself has been written and much of it written by women. Her radically fanciful biography of Orlando can be considered a history of gender differences and of the forms of subjectivity these differences engender, as well as a history of fashion. As a modern writer, she writes such a history self-consciously as a novel, knowing full well the degree to which novels have shaped the way one knows both oneself and others. She goes so far as to suggest that novels are equivalent in some very real way to individuals. The preface to *Orlando* begins by acknowledging something to this effect: "Many friends have helped me in writing this book. Some are dead and so illustrious that I scarcely dare name them, yet no one can read or write without being perpetually in the debt of Defoe, Sir Thomas Browne, Sterne, Sir Walter Scott, Lord Macaulay, Emily Brontë, De Quincey, and Walter Pater—to name the first that come to mind."[21]

If *Orlando* demonstrates that the relationship between fiction and consciousness is clearly a historical one, then Woolf's well-known essay, "Mr. Bennett and Mrs. Brown," explains the politics of writing modernist fiction. To live in a modern society requires everyone to have a specific knowledge of character, according to Woolf: "Our marriages, our friendships depend on it; our business largely depends on it; every day questions arise which can only be solved by its help."[22] But in contrast with other people, novelists "do not cease to be interested in character when they have learnt enough about it for practical purposes" (p. 189). Just as representing individuals constitutes the work of the novelist, so the novel provides the specialized language of character. The novelist has the authority to determine how people read people. Woolf claims for the novel, in effect, the status of a metalanguage or theory of character. But as a theory, Woolf feels, the traditional novel has suddenly become obsolete. In explaining what she finds lacking in the great Edwardian fiction writers, Wells, Galsworthy, and Bennett, Woolf conjures up the familiar figure of the house and—in a highly self-conscious manner—works a modernist variation upon it. Her purpose in comparing Bennett's strategies of representing the woman with her own strategies is to display the historical limitations of "character" as the previous century understood it. Mocking how Bennett characterizes the heroine of Hilda Lessways by describing everything except Hilda herself, Woolf writes: "Heaven be praised, we cry! At last we are coming to Hilda herself. But not so fast. Hilda may have been this, that, and the other; but Hilda not only looked at houses, and thought of houses; Hilda lived in a house. And what sort of house did Hilda live in? Mr. Bennett proceeds . . . " (p. 198). By taking us on an extended critical tour of Bennett's "houses," Woolf demonstrates that he represents only the exteriors of houses and only the outside of the woman after whom he has entitled his novel. Woolf's critique of Bennett indicates her acute awareness of the body of knowledge that obstructed Freud's analysis of Dora. For in setting her own style against Bennett's, she uses the room—or in this instance, the house—to represent that knowledge housed, as it were, in the body of the woman. It is in terms of this figure, then, that she analyzes the deficiency of Edwardian novels:

> They have laid an enormous stress on the fabric of things. They have given us a house in the hope that we may be able to deduce the human beings who live there. To give them their due, they have made that house much better, worth living in. But if you hold that novels are in the first place about people, and only in the second about the houses they live in, that is the wrong way to set about it. (p. 201)

She uses the house quite deliberately to suggest that the secrets it contains are one and the same as the depths contained within the woman. What is inside the woman, she maintains, cannot be represented by authors who impose a theory of sexuality upon the individual. In exploiting the novel's power to define the individual, they totally fail to represent that individual, and the novel's power to create sexual difference is the most exploitative strategy of all:

> If you say to the public with sufficient conviction, "All women have tails,

and all men humps," it will actually learn to see women with tails and men with humps, and will think it very revolutionary and probably improper if you say, "Nonsense. Monkeys have tails and camels humps. But men and women have brains, and they have hearts." (p. 201)

If of late the novel has not been fulfilling its cultural role particularly well, the reason, according to Woolf, is because the nature of social relationships has changed and the interpretive strategies offered by fictional characters (what *she* means by character) have not changed sufficiently to make the world intelligible: "All human relations have shifted—those between masters and servants, husbands and wives, parents and children" (p. 189). While it obviously begins in the household, the novel's territory is not really confined there, for changes in the realm of private experience radiate outward. And as Woolf explains, "when human relations change there is at the same time a change in religion, conduct, politics, and literature. Let us agree to place one of these changes about the year 1910" (p. 189). That the traditional strategies for representing personal life became obsolete at that point does not, in her opinion, mean that the novel has outlived its function. To the contrary, it simply means that to preserve traditional hierarchies of the household at a time when the household is undergoing some profound structural change is to misrepresent and thereby bully people into conformity. Woolf therefore calls for an alternative way of understanding human relationships.

In this essay, Woolf demonstrates her own idea of how the exemplary individual should appear in fiction by describing a woman she encountered on a train from Richmond to Waterloo. She names this woman Mrs. Brown. While Freud gave his patient the name of Dora to protect the individual whose true identity he was about to reveal, Woolf gives her fictional character a pseudonym to signify both that she as an author does not really know the woman and that anything she writes about her is consequently fictional. The pseudonym is one way of granting the woman her otherness. Its blatant fictionality is a way, too, of reasserting the power of female knowledge over and above that which is written by men and of identifying that body of knowledge with the novel. To describe a very ordinary woman she meets on the train, Woolf sketches the bare outlines of an intricate network of relationships that involve a Mr. Smith who appears to be bullying Mrs. Brown about someone named George during their brief ride together. These bare suggestions of relationships imply both a past made of various conflicts and alliances and a future when the matter will reach some kind of resolution. But Woolf does more than to piece together bits of a plot or even to understand the desires and fears enacted in the relationship between Mr. Smith and Mrs. Brown. She also explains the relationship that she, as a spectator and author, has to her own subject matter: "I had no time to explain why I felt it somewhat tragic, heroic, yet with a dash of the flighty, and fantastic, before the train stopped, and I watched her disappear, carrying her bag, into the vast blazing station" (p. 192). This, contrary to the Edwardian approach, is what she feels a novel should do to the representation of character. Understanding a relationship—in fact, having a relationship—with another individual is virtually the same thing as writing a novel. Her representation of Mrs. Brown further describes the relationship between subject and author:

> Here is character imposing itself upon another person. Here is Mrs. Brown making someone write a novel about her. I believe that all novels begin with an old lady in the corner opposite. I believe that all novels, that is to say, deal with character, and that it is to express character—not to preach doctrines, sing songs, or celebrate the glories of the British Empire, that the form of the novel, so clumsy, so verbose, and undramatic, so rich, elastic, and alive, has been evolved. (p. 193)

This definition of the novel lays claim to authority for writing on the traditionally female grounds that novels represent the vicissitudes of consciousness linking individuals and, at the same time, isolating them from one another. The implication is that individuals alone constitute a specialized language of the self capable of representing life in its most ordinary and yet mysterious manifestations—as exemplified by Mrs. Brown.

According to Woolf's way of thinking, history does not take place where Bennett situates it, in the world outside of the house. Rather, history makes its mark on human experience in such small personal ways as when "Mrs. Brown took out her little white handkerchief and began to dab her eyes" (p. 191). Here, at the centers of little networks of human relations, occur those changes that will eventually show up in "religion, conduct, politics, and literature" (p. 189). It is for this reason that so many authors find it necessary to write about the woman and attempt to fix her identity. But in writing about women, as Woolf demonstrates by writing about Mrs. Brown, authors actually say more about themselves, about their understanding of the task of writing, and about what they think truth ought to be. The truth they represent does not already exist in the woman but is a truth produced strictly in writing. In explaining why the men who write books about women seem so angry, then, Woolf comes as close as anyone does to explaining what kind of truth is written when one tries to fill in the spaces inside of women. The following passage from *A Room*

of One's Own contains the germs of a theory of sexuality that, if somewhat whimsical, is at once historical and political:

> Women have served all these centuries as looking-glasses possessing the
> magic and delicious power of reflecting the figure of man at twice its nat-
> ural size. Without that power probably the earth would still be swamp and
> jungle. The glories of our wars would be unknown. We should still be
> scratching the outlines of deer on the remains of mutton bones and barter-
> ing flints for sheepskins or whatever simple ornament took our unsophis-
> ticated taste. Supermen and Fingers of Destiny would never have existed.
> The Czar and the Kaiser would never have worn their crowns or lost them.
> Whatever may be their use in civilised societies, mirrors are essential to
> all violent and heroic action. That is why Napoleon and Mussolini both
> insist so emphatically upon the inferiority of women, for if they were not
> inferior, they would cease to enlarge. That serves to explain in part the
> necessity that women so often are to men. And it serves to explain how
> restless they are under her criticism; how impossible it is for her to say to
> them this book is bad, this picture is feeble, or whatever it may be, without
> giving far more pain and rousing far more anger than a man would do who
> gave the same criticism. For if she begins to tell the truth, the figure in
> the looking-glass shrinks; his fitness for life is diminished. How is he to
> go on giving judgement, civilising natives, making laws, writing books,
> dressing up and speechifying at banquets, unless he can see himself at
> breakfast and at dinner at least twice the size he really is? (p. 36)

This passage suggests that sexuality is largely written and, indeed, entirely a matter of culture. What we actually uncover when we open up
the woman is that she is only words, signifiers. Insofar as this surface
truth is represented as the deepest and most essential truth of human nature—whether discovered by poet, scientist, or politician—then female
nature is the very heart of ideology. Understanding the relationship between words and things, and granting words priority over things, Woolf
can therefore use sexuality as the means of challenging traditional male
notions of history which assume that events occur separately from and
prior to their representation. Indeed, she establishes a connection between
the practices of primitive man, the political conquests of twentieth century
fascism, and the seemingly frivolous verbal activities of bureaucratic man
on grounds that in all instances men are empowered by women.

These men are all motivated by something that determines how they
become objects of knowledge to themselves and by what standard they
measure themselves in relation to others. Woolf describes the female as
a "mirror" to represent sexuality as such an intrapersonal and therefore
political construct:

The looking-glass vision is of supreme importance because it charges the vitality; it stimulates the nervous system. Take it away and man may die, like the drug fiend deprived of his cocaine. Under the spell of that illusion, I thought, looking out of the window, half the people on the pavement are striding to work. (p. 36)

I see this passage as a modernist updating of the sexual contract that controlled Darwin's thinking. Instead of the competitive urge that man inherits from his primitive forebears and that woman subdues in making him fit for family life, Woolf posits the "looking-glass vision," a purely cultural compulsion, but a compulsion nevertheless, to fulfill an image of maleness in opposition to and as different from the woman.[23] As a mythology, she suggests, sexuality combines the effect of a natural force with the addictive power of a drug that not only governs personal relationships but motivates economic life as well.

Although Dora walked out on Freud and although such a writer as Woolf dealt with psychoanalysis in a less than reverent fashion, Freud's model of sexuality ultimately won out over theirs. It won out over Dora's nineteenth century narrative of subjective experience, and it won out over Woolf's claim that the artist, rather than the physician, knew the intricacies of consciousness and understood the consequences of allowing theory to suppress the history of subjectivity. Freud took pains to protect Ida Bauer's anonymity, but the fame of his case history prompted her to adopt his pseudonym for her and allow herself to be known as Freud's Dora.[24] It is not stretching a point to say that Woolf was similarly written by Freud. The circumstances of her bohemian intellectual's life and melodramatic death, together with the irresistible way in which her writing plays with the language of consciousness, have encouraged more than one generation of readers to filter her fiction through the grid of Freudian mythology.

I would like to suggest that both Dora and Mrs. Brown were markers of historical change. They came into existence as writing at the very moment when the authority granted for over a century to the record of women's feelings was undergoing revision.[25] It is significant that, in his case history of Dora, Freud usually refers to himself as a physician, for in saying this he pits the authority of a professional (male) institution against the authority of common sense and a woman's feelings, of diagnosis against commonplace and gossip, of knowledge against self-deception. In Freud's representation of Dora, the language of secular morality to which Pamela had laid claim was transformed according to a new thematics of health and disease. These reclassified the entire field of female knowledge according to forms of desire that, as they were somatically represented, could be subjected to the physician's analysis. But such analysis only appeared to make a palpable object of the mysteries "inside" the woman. In reality, analysis created mythological figures for the metaphysics of sexuality by endowing modern desire with a biological origin and form. This mythology rendered the woman's authority over sexual desire— whether it was manifested in Dora's nineteenth century sensibility or in Woolf's self-consciously verbal displays—instantly anachronistic. In the long run, Freud's professional voice and medical mythology determined the course that the discourse of sexuality pursued during the twentieth century.

Epilogue

I am convinced that the household Richardson envisioned for Pamela has grown more powerful during the time that has passed between his day and ours. This is true not only because the self-enclosed family often conceals a host of abuses, but also because, with the emergence of the professional couple as an economic reality, gender roles have changed in significant ways. The ideal of domesticity has grown only more powerful as it has become less a matter of fact and more a matter of fiction, for the fiction of domesticity exists as a fact in its own right. It begins to exert power over our lives the moment we begin to learn what normal behavior is supposed to be. Whether or not we accept it as truth, this fiction alone enables very different individuals to sit down to dinner in entirely unfamiliar places without finding them particularly strange, to shuffle into classrooms with people they have never met and with whom they may have little else in common, and to enjoy melodramas and sitcoms produced in regions or even countries other than theirs. In this respect, the most powerful household is the one we carry around in our heads.

I feel this power keenly—the power of all the domestic clichés we have grown half ashamed to live by. And I have tried to demonstrate how this power was given to women and exercised through them. To that end, I have used certain novels to explain how a notion of the household as a specifically feminine space established the preconditions for a modern institutional culture. I have argued that, in the hands of an intellectual such as Richardson, the female was used to contest the dominant notion of kinship relations. The novel, together with all manner of printed material, helped to redefine what men were supposed to desire in women and what women, in turn, were supposed to desire to be. Sometime around the end of the eighteenth century, however, the novel took a rather different direction. In the hands of Burney and Austen, fiction could still be said to oppose the domestic woman to women of title and wealth, but a woman's behavior was even more likely to be impugned if it seemed to be motivated by desires that could also be attributed to the daughters of merchants and, later, to working-class girls. It is finally for their mercenary lust that the Bingley sisters strike us as less than desirable in Austen's *Pride and Prejudice,* and the same point is still more forcefully made in *Jane Eyre* by the acquisitive urge that attracts Blanche Ingram to Rochester and repels him from her.

With the novels of Burney and Austen, furthermore, the conduct-book ideal of womanhood provided the ideal against which novelistic representations of women asserted themselves as being more true to life. On the premise that no one really measured up to this ideal, Victorian fiction took on the task of retailoring the representation of women to indicate that each individual had slightly different desires; no two women could be right for the same man, nor any two men for the same woman. In Dickens, then, one finds that the ideal marriage is not represented as being anything more or less than a fiction. With remarkable regularity, the best possible sexual relationships to be achieved in his fiction turn out to be inferior substitutes for an original mother or father. As if to say that an idealized fiction of love had an unhealthy grip on human desire, Thackeray treats Amelia Sedley harshly for conforming to the feminine ideal and also punishes her husband Dobbin for confusing love with conformity. The novels by Dickens and Thackeray—and for that matter, all Victorian fiction—testified in one way or another to a power of sentimentality that Richardson could only imagine.

For a readership that understood the ideal woman as an imaginary construct, the fallen woman underwent a change of status as well. Every woman was, like Louisa Gradgrind, a little bit fallen. What mattered was that she never gave into her own desire but waged an unrelenting battle against it. And so, as the nineteenth century got underway, the domestic woman no longer constituted a form of political resistance. She, rather than the aristocratic woman, represented the dominant view. But while there can be little debate in this regard about the angelic woman, is it possible to say, on the other hand, that women who did not fill the cultural mold—the madwomen and prostitutes of Victorian fiction—constituted a form of resistance? In discussing the rhetorical power that was exercised through monstrous representations of women, I have argued that the very aspects of the female which supposedly resisted acculturation came to play an especially powerful role in a discourse that redefined any form of political resistance as a form of individual pathology. To define political resistance in such psychological terms was to remove it from the snarl of competing social and economic interests in which every individual was entangled. Rather than oppose the domestic woman and the principle of gender differentiation that her very presence upheld, the monstrous woman of Victorian fiction was an agent in and product of an individuating process that taught people to forget how the motives and behavior of others expressed a political identity. How these mad, bad, and embruted women represented political differences is, I think, a more interesting question than how the fictional norms of femininity kept women in line. The question of what purpose was actually served by the women who did not aspire to the feminine ideal has bearing on how we regard the history of fiction, what we see its work to be, how we understand the relationship between women and fiction, and what we use fiction to say about women today.

I have insisted that the opposition of angel and monster was just that— an opposition within the discourse of sexuality. It provided a means of suppressing other oppositions. In fact, a central purpose of my argument has been to show how the novel exercised tremendous power by producing oppositions that translated the complex and competing ways of representing human identity into a single binary opposition represented by male versus female. All the different ways in which the conflict between Pamela and Mr. B might have been conceived—political complexities that Fielding's fiction tried and failed to restore—were first reduced to the conflict between male and female, which turned out to be no conflict at all. The nineteenth century was to simplify the political opposition further. It dealt with men and women who were never so far apart in social terms as Richardson's lovers. It concentrated on conflicts within the female character, between her innate desires and the role she was destined to occupy. Contained within a field where gender assumed priority over the signs of one's region, religious sect, and political faction, the domestic woman and her demonic "other" posed a psychological opposition. In political terms, however, monster and angel worked discursively as a team to suppress other notions of sexuality—namely, those attributed to the aristocracy and laboring classes—that did not adhere to the ideal of legitimate monogamy. By thinking in such oppositions, we ourselves have come to inhabit a political world composed not of races, classes, or even genders, but of individuals who in varying degrees earn or fail to earn our personal trust and affection. As the world around us acquires psychological complexity, political conflicts tend to appear simpler still.

I am suggesting that over time the novel produced a language of increasing psychological complexity for understanding individual behavior. I am suggesting, too, that as fiction progressively uncovered the "depths" of individual identity, a complex system of political signs was displaced.

Signs of wealth, status, and religious affiliation began to define a "surface" that had no reliable connection with the self in which true motivations were buried. As the individual came to be known in this way, a modern form of power, which could not be distinguished from such knowledge, took over. People, at least the people who mattered, conceived themselves within a political reality comprising, on the one hand, an array of unique individuals and, on the other, a body of all individuals—an abstract and standardized body, rather than one that was heterogeneous and permeable.

We ourselves exercise this form of power in teaching students to read the novel as an account of a developing character, as the unfolding of historical events that take place somewhere outside of language, or else as the growth of a verbal artifact. In each instance, we make the work of fiction transparent. In each instance, we teach our students to distinguish depth from surface in a way that turns writing into a specific form of individual, into a mirror of a particular world of objects, or into an autonomous world of imagination. Seldom are we moved to acknowledge how writing creates the distinction between depth and surface, subject and object, or between these and the literary forms of representation. In suppressing the fact and agency of writing, we also suppress the historical process by which these spheres of self, society, and culture were created and held in equilibrium. We place the relationship among these spheres— and thus the political power exerted by fiction—beyond our power to question.

Feminist criticism has made significant inroads into a tradition of reading that has suppressed the political dimension of fiction. Such criticism has asked readers to acknowledge the political bias inherent in literary histories that offer only a view from the top, a view that always identifies itself as the dominant view because it professes to be politically neutral. Until feminism intruded into novel criticism, literary criticism—even of the most innovative kind—had collaborated with other kinds of history to silence women and marginalize them. Men represented women as they wished them to be, or else they showed how women failed to fulfill those wishes. And women therefore wrote despite a tradition that was hostile to their own desires and requirements for self-expression. This has been the mainline feminist argument within the literary disciplines, an argument that has made its mark on the *Norton Anthology,* on literary curricula, on professional journals and the university presses, as well as on hiring practices. Although my purpose is not to quarrel with this position, I have nevertheless stressed the ways in which modern culture has empowered middle-class women because I believe the time has come when, empowered to speak as women about writing women and to speak about women whom men have written about, we have to acknowledge the fact that our voice has exercised no little political force. Because women have been written, they have become visible as such, and writing as women has made it possible for a distinctively female voice to be heard. It is the way in which we are visible, then, and the conditions under which we are heard—and not silence—that now seem to constrain us, even though these limitations initially empowered women to write. Once we identify the historical limitations of gender, it seems to me that either we have to live within them or else we must define another position from which to speak.

The rhetoric of victimization has worked its way into the heart of literary critical theory and will remain there, I am sure, to generate rereadings of texts by, for, and about women for a number of years to come. Powerful academic women will continue to insist on the powerlessness of women, and their mentors, senior colleagues, and college deans will doubtless support women in this effort as they are supporting them now. Certainly, such an authority has come hard-earned to academic women and should not be relinquished without a struggle. But it should not prevent us from undertaking other projects that go beyond the work these women have already done. For they have done much more than inaugurate a tradition. They have not only created a market for criticism that articulates the forms of subordination in which women work, write, and live out their lives, but they have also opened the way for new areas and methods of research. If one stresses the particular power that our culture does give to middle-class women rather than the forms of subordination entailed in their exclusion from the workplace and confinement to the home—and I think both slants on modern culture are valid, if not equally timely—then there is clearly a great deal of work to do. The articulation of women's power requires many participants, no one of which can be right or complete in herself. When there is some reason to question the appropriateness of men telling the story of women's victimization, it is, I think, legitimate for men and women to do the kind of work that situates women both as objects of desire and as writing subjects within social history.

In 1928, Woolf suggested that an event of major historical proportions occurred when middle-class women began to write. Supporting this claim, as Woolf herself evidently knew, required nothing less than to rewrite history. From her perspective, the moment when "the middle-class woman began to write" had more to do with creating the modern world than the events we usually consider historically significant. For Woolf, it was an event "of greater importance than the Crusades or the Wars of the Roses" (*A Room of One's Own*, p. 69). Despite recent interest in the history of representation *qua* representation, relatively few literary scholars and critics have explored the role of representation *in* history. While we have all paid lip service to the power of literacy, we have not considered in a detailed and systematic way whether literature has played a part in political history. Indeed, it is the tendency of the disciplines in Britain and the United States to detach the writing we teach as literature from the other symbolic practices that compose history per se. Woolf's claims for the significance of women's writing suggests that this tendency has direct bearing on women. If writing is not figured into political history, then political power will continue to appear as if it resides exclusively in institutions that are largely governed by men, and the role played by women at various stages in the middle-class hegemony will remain unexamined for the political force that it was and still is today.

It is worth recalling that when middle-class women began to write, the writing of political economy took on unprecedented explanatory power. Writing itself appeared to lose political significance along with courtship procedures, marriage practices, and the organization of the household. As the inheritors of such history, we tend to identify important historical data as the products of men. I was particularly struck by this point while completing this book. At the time, I happened to attend a conference devoted to the Spanish Golden Age when a problem emerged very much like that which confronts many of us who deal with women's writing. A historian had been invited to respond to a paper concerned with the political viewpoint represented by artisan poets in sixteenth century Mexico. He appeared perplexed, skeptical about the value of such information to historians, since it yielded little in terms of what he could use as "evidence." The only truths that he could allow to be declared truths were those based, in his words, "on counting cattle and bags of grain." It is difficult to believe that this extremely narrow notion of history could claim much respect. Yet on grounds that only a specific kind of information could be considered historical data, he sought to trivialize whatever such poetry had to say about history. Not only did he understand human culture in terms of an unexamined emphasis on productive labor, he also understood work in terms of products that the modern world attributes to men. Moreover, his representation did not acknowledge its basis in representation. The historian in question never counted a single head of cattle or bag of grain. He simply privileged account books over all other forms of representation. His bias was deep.

Indeed, so fixed is the idea that political meaning derives from a source outside of writing that all manner of printed material occupies no place within the academic disciplines. The argument for this book relies in particular on women's conduct books of the eighteenth and nineteenth centuries, but there are more, many more, kinds of writing to be read and analyzed that have so far been excluded from consideration by the humanistic disciplines. All such writing provides the record of everyday life as it was supposed to be lived, and much of it was written for, by, and about women. Today anyone interested in the relationship between women and fiction can encounter a storehouse of such historical materials.

It was in contrast with Woolf's account of her trip to the British Museum, as described in *A Room of One's Own*, that I saw my visit to the Fawcett Museum. Certainly humble in comparison with the British Museum and located on the wrong side of London, this collection offers the visitor a visible sense of all the work to be done, the various kinds of history yet to be told. I was brought to the Fawcett by a conviction that such authors as Burney and Austen did not compose their characters, households, or thoughts and feelings about love from the stuff of real life, as practices other than writing are often so crudely designated. I was not looking for social or psychological equivalents for cattle and bags of grain. To develop nuances where Richardson had made proclamations, to drop just a detail where he had mapped territories, these women, I thought, had to be perfecting a craft. They had to be refining a practice that already existed as such. They had to be taking part in the history of writing. Conduct books for women, many by women, fill a significant number of shelves in the Fawcett. My plan was to mine them for the history of the kind of writing that domestic fiction aspires to reproduce and modify in keeping with the times. Had I been faithful to that plan, I would have produced a history of female feelings and domestic duties as a companion piece to those political histories that explain the formation of the proletariat and the triumph of the factory system. But I could not keep this women's history out of politics. I could not detach the issues of gender from those of class. In tracing the formation of these separate spheres, I found I could not describe one as if it were independent of the other. Nor would the humbler domestic history garnered from fiction and the holdings of the Fawcett Museum remain subservient to its masculine counterpart, namely, the traditions of political and economic history. More solid than numerical accounts of cattle and grain were the books on the shelves in the Fawcett library, and their presence told a much clearer truth than cattle or grain ever could. The historical changes visible there have governed the argument of this book.

Simply by looking at these books on the shelves and noticing how their number varied through the last two centuries or so, I observed an event of some magnitude in the history of British culture. There were conduct books for women before the eighteenth century, to be sure, but in examining the volumes to determine how the representation of women would change as the eighteenth century began, I found that their number increased many times over within just a decade or two. Thus I encountered an explosion of print all bent on telling people how to conduct themselves in the rituals of everyday life. I also observed that, with the sudden increase in the production of conduct books, there was a decisive shift in the number of those devoted to making women desirable rather than telling men how to assume a high position in life. But I was not struck by this observation alone. Another came fast on its heels that must be factored into the first: As the number of conduct books devoted to women increased, those exalting the virtues of aristocratic women abruptly fell off in popularity.

It was clear to me that a new kind of woman had come into being. I could see her rise with remarkable speed to cultural prominence over her more and less noble counterparts, and I could see how in the process she transformed the whole idea of what it meant to be noble. This woman is the one whose history I have traced in domestic novels and other kinds of writing contemporary with them. I have tried to show how certain texts represented her as uniquely equipped to set in motion a process that would inspire future generations to reproduce the modern household compulsively, as if by a natural desire. In this way, the domestic woman—who may, for all we know, have existed in representation for as long as a century before she stepped forth from the pages of books to oversee middle-class parlors—became a function of each functional individual's psychic life. By occupying a place in the mind, the household made it possible for masses of diverse individuals to coexist within modern culture.

To prove such an hypothesis to the satisfaction of those who believe that history resides in an account of cattle and grain will take many years and many more researchers. Much of the material that will provide a more adequate history of the modern period has as yet to find a place within the disciplines. It has long been kept out of sight within the unclassified space of popular culture. Conduct books for women must be viewed as just one among many forgotten kinds of information that are similarly woven into the fabric of fiction. As the sort of data that conventional histories cannot account for, most of this material has the status of junk. But for the very reason it does resemble the stuff of an attic, such material can suddenly acquire enormous power as it finds some use among the objects of knowledge. It is this kind of residual cultural information that can supplement the structures determining reality at a given moment of time. And by supplementing the structures that determine reality, this kind of information will call for a more adequate model of history that includes the history of sexuality and that accounts for ourselves as gendered selves. In such a history, writing by, for, and about women must occupy a central position.

Notes

Introduction: The Politics of Domesticating Culture, Then and Now

1. Samuel Richardson, *Pamela, or Virtue Rewarded* (New York: W.W. Norton, 1958), pp. 111. Citations of the text are to this edition.

2. Ian Watt, *The Rise of the Novel* (Berkeley: University of California Press, 1957), p. 57.

3. Sandra M. Gilbert and Susan Gubar, *The Madwoman in the Attic: The Woman Writer and the Nineteenth Century Literary Imagination* (New Haven: Yale University Press, 1979). See especially pp. 45–92.

4. By "the patriarchal model," I mean specifically the historical phenomenon that linked the political authority of the father over the household to that of the king in a mutually authorizing relationship. On this point, for example, see Gordon J. Schochet, *Patriarchalism in Political Thought* (New York: Basic Books, 1975) and Lawrence Stone, *The Family, Sex, and Marriage in England 1500–1800* (New York: Harper and Row, 1977), pp. 239–40.

5. I draw here on David Musselwhite's argument which implicitly challenges such notions of the politics of the novel as Bahktin articulates in *The Dialogic Imagination: Four Essays,* trans. Michael Holquist (Austin: University of Texas Press, 1981). Rather than view the novel as a form that—like carnival—resisted hegemony, Musselwhite argues that the novel appropriates symbolic practices that would otherwise behave as forms of resistance. I intend to suggest that the politics of the novel are determined, on the one hand, by the genre's tendency to suppress alternative forms of literacy and to produce the homogenized discourse we know as polite standard English. I will push this argument further and suggest that, on the other hand, the novel's politics depend on how we use the genre today. In writing this book, I am assuming that one may expose the operations of the hegemony by reading the novel as the history of those operations. If there is any truth in this claim, then in adopting the novel's psychologizing strategies, one only perpetuates the great nineteenth century project that suppressed political consciousness. David Musselwhite, "The Novel as Narcotic," *1848: The Sociology of Literature* (Colchester, England: University of Essex, 1978), pp. 208–209.

6. In this respect, I take issue with critics whose discussion of sexuality is grounded in nature. For example, Jeffrey Weeks, in objecting to Foucault, insists that "discourse is not the only contact with the real." *Sex, Politics, and Society: The Regulation of Sexuality since 1800* (London: Longman, 1981), pp. 10–11. To refute Foucault, however, he relies on the very strategies that Foucault identifies as constituting the discourse of sexuality. Weeks nevertheless tries to cut the Gordian knot which a Foucauldian understanding of sexuality presents: "Robert Padgug has recently *written* that 'biological sexuality is the necessary precondition for human sexuality. But biological sexuality is only a precondition, a set of potentialities which is never unmediated by human reality.' That sums up the fundamental assumption of this work" (p. 11, italics mine). Along with Padgug and others, Weeks invokes a biological basis for sexuality which is transcultural and outside of history, although, admittedly, "never unmediated by human reality." Along with Foucault, I would argue that the difference between nature and culture is always a function of culture, the construction of nature being one of culture's habitual tropes of self-authorization. And I would ask if the gendered body belongs to a nature that is beyond culture, as Weeks seems to assume, then why was it not until relatively recently that the difference between male and female came to dominate representations of the biological body. Writing about seventeenth century gynecology, for example, Audrey Eccles notes that "anatomically" it was "held there was virtually no difference between the sexes, the man's penis and testicles being exactly analogous to the uterus and ovaries." *Obstetrics and Gynaecology in Tudor and Stuart England* (London: Croom Helm, 1982), p. 26. Particularly in a culture that mythologizes sex by suppressing its political dimension, the idea of natural sex, it seems to me, poses a contradiction in terms that is without doubt the purest form of ideology.

7. Michel Foucault, *The History of Sexuality*, Vol. I, *An Introduction*, trans. Robert Hurley (New York: Pantheon, 1978), p. 8. Citations of the text are to this edition.

8. In using the term "soul," Locke invokes the metaphysics of an earlier theocentric culture, but he does so in order to decenter that metaphysics and provide a material basis for individual consciousness. "I see no reason," he claims, "to believe that the soul thinks before the senses have furnished it with ideas to think on; and as those are increased and retained, so it comes, by exercise, to improve its faculty of thinking in the several parts of it; as well as, afterwards, by compounding those ideas, and reflecting on its own operations, it increases its stock, as well as facility in remembering, imagining, reasoning, and other modes of thinking." *An Essay Concerning Human Understanding*, vol. I (New York: Dover, 1959), p. 139. Locke therefore retains the term of an earlier metaphysics, but he uses it to describe subjectivity as a mode of production exactly analogous to the development of private property. It is fair to say, further, that when "soul" is supplanted by gender as the source and supervisor of the individual's development, the whole notion of subjectivity is no less metaphysical than it is in Locke's ungendered representation. The metaphysical basis for human identity—and the role of language in self-production—is simply less apparent as such.

9. Maria Edgeworth and Robert L. Edgeworth, *Practical Education*, vol. II (London, 1801), p. ix. Citations of the text are to this edition.

10. Thomas Walter Laqueur, *Religion and Respectability: Sunday Schools and Working Class Culture 1780–1850* (New Haven: Yale University Press, 1976).

11. Laqueur, p. 229.

12. In recounting the growth of restrictive laws on alehouses and the attempts to regulate leisure time, Peter Clark has written, "In 1776 John Disney blamed the spread of popular disturbances on 'unnecessary and ill-timed' assemblies in drinking houses. The same year Oxfordshire landowners called for stern measures against vagrants and disorderly alehouses, while soon after the parish vestry at Terling in Essex proclaimed that 'alehouses are the common resort of the idle and dissolute' and went on to impose a strait-jacket of controls on the village's solitary establishment." *The English Alehouse: A Social History 1200–1830* (London: Longman, 1983), p. 254.

13. Allon White, "Hysteria and the End of Carnival: Festivity and Bourgeois Neurosis," *Semiotica*, 54 (1985), 97–111.

14. Fredric Jameson argues that it is necessary for criticism to abandon "a purely individual, or merely psychological, project of salvation," in order to "explore the multiple paths that lead to the unmasking of cultural objects as socially symbolic acts." *The Political Unconscious: Narrative as a Socially Symbolic Act* (Ithaca: Cornell University Press, 1981), p. 20. In invoking Jameson's concept from time to time, I will stress that the political unconscious is no less historical than any other cultural phenomenon. My study implicates the rise of the novel in the production of a specific form of political unconscious that suppressed the inherently political nature of kinship relations, for one thing, and of representations of women for another. Pre-Enlightenment authors seem to have been acutely aware of the politics of courtship and family relations. Removing these areas of culture from the domain of politics was a self-conscious feature of eighteenth and nineteenth century fiction. But the history of such semiotic process is one that our modern notion of literature systematically erases. For purposes of this study, I am particularly interested in how domestic fiction helped repress the politics of sexuality as it concealed its own political operations and how, in so doing, it differentiated itself from other fiction to earn literary status for fiction.

15. Jacques Donzelot, *The Policing of Families*, trans. Robert Hurley (New York: Pantheon, 1979), p. 92.

16. For a discussion of the paternalism that emerged in opposition to patriarchy in seventeenth century Puritan writing, see Leonard Tennenhouse, *Power on Display: The Politics of Shakespeare's Genres* (New York: Methuen, 1986), especially the chapter entitled "Family Rites." In describing the alternative to patriarchy that arose at the end of the seventeenth and beginning of the eighteenth century in aristocratic families, Randolph Trumbach opposes the term "patriarchy" to the term "domesticity," by which he refers to the modern household. This form of social organization is authorized by internal relations of gender and generation rather than by way of analogy to external power relations between

monarch and subject or between God and man. *The Rise of the Egalitarian Family* (New York: Academic Press, 1978), pp. 119–63.

17. Kathleen M. Davis, "The Sacred Condition of Equality—How Original were Puritan Doctrines of Marriage?" *Social History*, 5 (1977), 570. Davis quotes this list from John Dod and Robert Cleaver, *A Godly Forme of Householde Gouernment* (London, 1614).

18. See, for example, Patricia Crawford, "Women's Published Writings 1600–1700," in *Women in English Society 1500–1800*, ed. Mary Prior (London: Methuen, 1985), pp. 211–81.

19. Brian Simon, *Studies in the History of Education 1780–1870* (London: Lawrence and Wishart, 1960), pp. 1–62.

20. In elaborating the scene on the scaffold, Foucault pays close attention to the dismembered body of the criminal in the first two chapters of *Discipline and Punish: the Birth of the Prison*, trans. Alan Sheridan (New York: Vintage, 1979). However, the material body disappears once Foucault moves into the modern period and power works not upon the body so much as through the penetration and inscription of the subject as subjectivity. The body on the scaffold continues on in Foucauldian discourse as if it were another body, a body of knowledge, and that of an entirely different order of subject—the patient in the clinic. But in fact, as Laqueur has shown, the history of the material body does not end here. The position of the criminal on the scaffold in fact came to be occupied by the pauper's body that eighteenth century science required for the theater of anatomy, and that modern culture, by appropriating common burial grounds for private property, had placed on the market. See Foucault's *The Birth of the Clinic: An Archaeology of Medical Perception*, trans. A.M. Sheridan Smith (New York: Vintage, 1973) and Thomas Laqueur, "Bodies, Death, and Pauper Funerals," *Representations*, 1 (1983), 109–31.

21. Bakhtin's twin figures of the grotesque body and mass body offer a way of imagining an alternative social formation to our own. These figures have special appeal for people interested in researching political history from a viewpoint antagonistic to power, a viewpoint which privileges the history of the subject rather than that of the state, because Bakhtin himself obviously wanted to see in the past forms that resisted the joyless and fearful conditions of the totalitarian government under which he wrote. Thus he uses Rabelais to construct the figure of carnival that would idealize all those symbolic practices that resisted the exclusive political body organizing courtly romance. Mikhail Bakhtin, *Rabelais and his World*, trans. Helene Iswolsky (Cambridge: MIT Press, 1965). Allon White and Peter Stallybrass use the figure of carnival to trace the history of resistance into the modern period in *The Body Enclosed* (Ithaca: Cornell University Press, 1986). I wish to thank the authors for allowing me to see portions of their book while in manuscript.

22. In *The Long Revolution* (London: Chatto and Windus, 1961), Raymond Williams describes this process. (Especially see his discussion of the growth of a reading public and of a popular press, pp. 156–213). I have used, as the conceptual backbone of this book, his concept of a political revolution that took the

form of a cultural revolution. Unlike Williams, however, I have focused on the process of gendering that was crucial to the triumph of a form of power based on cultural control and the dissemination of information. My work is especially concerned with how writing for and about women influenced the kind of information that was produced by "the long revolution," as well as how such writing identified the targets at which such information was directed.

23. Addressing the same issue, Cora Kaplan writes: "Masculinity and femininity do not appear in cultural discourse, anymore than they do in mental life, as purely forms at play. They are always, already, ordered and broken up through other social and cultural terms, other categories of difference. Our fantasies of sexual transgression as much as our obedience to sexual regulation are expressed through these structuring hierarchies. Class and race ideologies are, conversely, steeped in and spoken through the language of sexual differentiation. Class and race meanings are not metaphors for the sexual, or vice versa. It is better, though not exact, to see them as reciprocally constituting each other through a kind of narrative invocation, a set of associative terms in a chain of meaning. To understand how gender and class—to take two categories only—are articulated together transforms our analysis of each." "Pandora's Box: Subjectivity, Class and Sexuality in Socialist Feminist Criticism," (ms. p. 3). I am indebted to the author for allowing me to consult this manuscript.

Chapter 1: The Rise of Female Authority in the Novel

1. Walter Ong, quoted by Irene Tayler and Gina Luria, "Gender and Genre: Women in British Romantic Literature," in *What Manner of Woman*, ed. Marlene Springer (New York: New York University Press, 1977), p. 100.

2. In *A Literature of Their Own* (Princeton: Princeton University Press, 1977), Elaine Showalter explains how by the 1860s, a number of prominent women authors had worked their way into editorial positions that, "like the one Dickens and Thackeray occupied at *Household Words* and the *Cornhill*, provided innumerable opportunities for the exercise of influence and power" (p. 156). The role of the critic-reviewer was not completely unknown to women even during the eighteenth century. See, for example, Elizabeth Montagu's *Dialogues of the Dead* (1760) and Anna Seward's critical essays in *Variety* (1787–88), in Ioan Williams, *Novel and Romance: 1700–1800, A Documentary Record* (New York: Barnes and Noble, 1970), pp. 222–29, 357–66.

3. Certainly with the emergence of a theory of political economy and the influential writing of the Scottish philosophers like Dugald Stewart, contract theory had all but disappeared as a model of government. On this point, see Maxine Berg, *The Machinery Question and the Making of Political Economy 1815–1848* (Cambridge: Cambridge University Press, 1980), pp. 32–42, and Stefan Collini, Donald Winch, and John Barrow, *That Noble Science of Politics: A Study in Nineteenth Century Intellectual History* (Cambridge: Cambridge University Press, 1983), p. 38.

4. Louis Althusser, *Politics and History: Montesquieu, Rousseau, Hegel, and Marx*, trans. Ben Brewster (London: NLB, 1972), p. 129. Citations of both texts are to this edition.

5. Jean-Jacques Rousseau, *The Social Contract*, in *The Social Contract and the Discourse on the Origin of Inequality*, ed. Lester G. Crocker, trans. Lester G. Crocker and Henry J. Tozer (New York: Washington Square Press, 1967), p. 21. Citations of the text are to this edition.

6. David Hume, "Of the Original Contract," in *Essays Moral, Political, and Literary*, eds. T.H. Green and T.H. Grose (Darmstadt, West Germany: Scientia Verlag Aalen, 1964; rpt. London, 1882), p. 460.

7. Hume, "That Politics May Be Reduced to a Science," in *Essays Moral, Political, and Literary*, p. 99.

8. Jeremy Bentham, *Bentham's Theory of Fictions*, ed. C.K. Ogden (New York: Harcourt, Brace and Company, 1932), p. 123. Citations to the text are to this edition.

9. Ioan Williams explains that the novel was not considered polite reading in England until the end of the eighteenth century. *The Idea of the Novel in Europe 1600–1800* (New York: New York University Press, 1979), p. 137. Lennard Davis, *Factual Fictions: The Origins of the English Novel* (New York: Columbia University Press, 1983) has shown that the novel was in fact considered dangerous because "its very theoretical and structural assumptions were in some sense criminal in nature, and that part of the nature of this criminality was specifically located with the violence and social unrest from the lower classes" (pp. 123–24). Against Richardson's proselytizing attempts to elevate fiction to a moral plane, Fielding's well-known preface to *Joseph Andrews* attempts to make the novel literary; he proposes a number of classical models that the novelist might imitate. When fiction did shake off its criminal origins, however, it did not become respectable by observing the aristocratic tradition of letters as Fielding advised, but rather by adopting the moralizing strategies that Richardson had introduced into fiction. During the nineteenth century, well after the novel had become a respectable mode, it was still not thought to be literature. This is the rationale Fredric Rowton puts forth in the preface to *The Female Poets of Great Britain* (Philadelphia, 1853; rpt. 1981): "the Author confidently hopes that the work which he here presents to the reader will justify the position he has assumed, and at least prove that the Poetical Faculty is not confined to one of the sexes" (p. xxxviii). Rowton argues that women are capable of writing literature because they have a "Poetical Faculty." As late as 1871, however, Charles Darwin insisted upon a biological basis for women's failure to write any notable literary works: "The chief distinction in the intellectual powers of the two sexes is shewn by man attaining to a higher eminence, in whatever he takes up, than woman can attain—whether requiring deep thought, reason, or imagination, or merely the use of the senses and hands. If two lists were made of the most eminent men and women in *poetry*, painting, sculpture, music . . . history, science, and philosophy, with half-a-dozen names under each subject, the two lists would not bear comparison." *The Descent of Man, and Natural Selection in Relation*

to Sex, vol. II, eds. John Tyler Bonner and Robert M. May (Princeton: Princeton University Press, 1981; rpt. 1871), p. 327 (italics mine). From evidence of this sort, then, it is fair to conclude that well into the nineteenth century literature was associated with poetry and fiction was not, because, for one reason, fiction was written by women.

10. I have gathered this and other valuable information concerning the generic definition of the novel from Homer Obed Brown's book in progress, *Institutions of the English Novel in the Eighteenth Century.* I am grateful to the author for generously allowing me to read the manuscript.

11. Brown, "The Institution of the English Novel," in *Institutions of the English Novel in the Eighteenth Century,* ms. p. 1.

12. Richardson appears to have quite self-consciously tried to establish, in his words, "a new species of writing." Reconstructing the genesis of his first novel, he explains in a letter to Aaron Hill, "at last I . . . began to recollect such subjects as I thought would be useful in such a design [that is, a book of exemplary letters, or a type of conduct book, for young women], and formed several letters accordingly. And, among the rest, I thought of giving one or two as cautions to young folks circumstanced as Pamela was. Little did I think, at first, of making one, much less two volumes of it. But, when I began to recollect what had, so many years before, been told me by my friend, I thought the story [of Pamela, supposedly a local incident], if written in an easy and natural manner, suitably to the simplicity of it, might possibly introduce a new species of writing, that might possibly turn young people into a course of reading different from the pomp and parade of romance-writing, and dismissing the improbable and marvellous, with which novels generally abound, might tend to promote the cause of religion and virtue." *Selected Letters,* ed. John Carroll (Oxford: Clarendon, 1964), p. 41.

13. John Stuart Mill, "The Subjection of Women," in *Women's Liberation and Literature,* ed. Elaine Showalter (New York: Harcourt Brace Jovanovich, 1971), p. 36. Citations to the text are to this edition.

14. Darwin, p. 398.

15. Rowton, p. xiv.

16. See, for example, Eli Zaretsky, *Capitalism, The Family and Personal Life* (New York: Harper and Row, 1976) and Anne Foreman, *Femininity as Alienation* (London: Pluto Press, 1977) for sociological explanations of the change in sex roles that accompanied the growth of an industrial society in England. In *The Feminization of American Culture* (New York: Avon Books, 1978), Ann Douglas describes a similar phenomenon in nineteenth century America. Elaine Showalter's *A Literature of Their Own* provides an invaluable description of how these changes influenced the policy of the publishing industry with respect to women writers.

17. Lawrence Stone, *Family, Sex and Marriage in England 1500–1800* (New York: Harper and Row, 1977), pp. 390–405.

18. Rowton, p. xvii. It should be noted that the same logic can be found in the more sophisticated critics of the age. Consider, for example, the close par-

allels between Rowton's poetics and this statement by George Henry Lewes: "Woman, by her greater affectionateness, her greater range and depth of emotional experience, is well fitted to give expression to the emotional facts of life, and demands a place in literature corresponding with that she occupies in society." "The Lady Novelists," in *Women's Liberation and Literature*, p. 174.

19. Jane Austen, *Pride and Prejudice*, ed. Donald J. Gray (New York: W.W. Norton, 1966), p. 1. Citations of the text are to this edition.

20. Charlotte Brontë, *Jane Eyre*, ed. Richard J. Dunn (New York: W.W. Norton, 1971), pp. 30–31. Citations of the text are to this edition.

21. George Eliot, *Middlemarch*, ed. Bert G. Hornback (New York: W.W. Norton, 1977), p. xiii. Citations of the text are to this edition.

22. George H. Ford, *Dickens and His Readers: Aspects of Novel Criticism Since 1836* (New York: W.W. Norton, 1965), p. 81.

23. Mary W. Shelley, *Frankenstein, or The Modern Prometheus*, ed. M.K. Joseph (New York: Oxford University Press, 1971), p. 10.

24. Elizabeth Gaskell, *Mary Barton, A Tale of Manchester Life*, ed. Stephen Gill (Harmondsworth: Penguin, 1970), p. 38. Citations of the text are to this edition.

25. Charlotte Brontë, letter to W.A. Williams in 1859, in *The Brontës: Their Friendships, Lives and Correspondence*, vol. III, eds. T.J. Wise and J.A. Symington (London: Oxford University Press, 1932), p. 99.

26. Charlotte Brontë, "Biographical Notice of Ellis and Acton Bell," in Emily Bronte, *Wuthering Heights*, ed. William M. Sale, Jr. (New York: W.W. Norton, 1972), p. 8. Citations of the text are to this edition.

27. William Sale prefaces his selection of the early reviews of *Wuthering Heights* with this assessment: "The critical reception of *Wuthering Heights* has been generally assumed to have been unsympathetic, and so of course it seems in the light of the extraordinary tributes that have been later paid to the novel. But if we compare what Charlotte herself said of the novel in her "Preface" with what many of the early critics had said, we should perhaps conclude that both Charlotte and the critics were finding it difficult to come to terms with a strangely different piece of fiction." In Emily Brontë, *Wuthering Heights*, p. 227.

28. J. Hillis Miller, *The Disappearance of God* (New York: Shocken, 1965), p. 157.

29. The term "counterimage" comes from Herbert Marcuse's "The Affirmative Character of Culture," in *Negations* (Boston: Beacon Press, 1968), pp. 88–133.

30. Ian Watt, *The Rise of the Novel* (Berkeley: University of California Press, 1957). Watt sees the novel as a "mirror" of class conflict rather than a struggle in its own right to seize hold of certain strategically powerful signs, symbols, and practices. For this reason, he has trouble explaining not only the phenomenon of Austen's fiction, but also Richardson's success. That is, he cannot account for the fact that Richardson, puritanical as he was, "should have signalized his entry into the history of literature by a work which gave a more detailed account of a single intrigue than had even been produced before" (p. 172).

31. As Dorothy Thompson points out, the name of the People's Charter "defined it as a working class radical movement" and distinguished it from a middle-class political enterprise. *The Chartists: Popular Politics in the Industrial Revolution* (New York: Pantheon, 1984), p. 57.

32. On this point, see Nancy Armstrong, "Emily Brontë In and Out of Her Time," *Genre,* 15 (1982), 243–64.

33. Showalter, *A Literature of Their Own,* p. 182 ff.

34. Virginia Woolf, *Mrs. Dalloway* (New York: Harcourt Brace Jovanovich, 1953), p. 14.

35. Woolf, *Orlando: A Biography* (New York: Signet, 1960), p. 117.

36. Jean Rhys, *Wide Sargasso Sea* (New York: W.W. Norton, 1966).

Chapter 2: The Rise of the Domestic Woman

1. There have been conduct books ever since the Middle Ages. From medieval to modern example, they most always imply a readership who desires self-improvement and for whom self-improvement promises an elevation of social position. For a collection of essays that discuss the wide variety of conduct books from the Middle Ages to the present day, see *The Ideology of Conduct: Essays in Literature and the History of Sexuality,* eds. Nancy Armstrong and Leonard Tennenhouse (New York: Methuen, 1987). For a discussion of conduct books in the Middle Ages, see Kathleen Ashley, "Medieval Courtesy Literature and Dramatic Mirrors for Female Conduct," in *The Ideology of Conduct.* See Ann R. Jones, "Nets and Bridles: Conduct Books for Women 1416–1643," in *The Ideology of Conduct,* for a discussion of conduct literature in Renaissance England and Italy. Also see Suzanne M. Hull, *Chaste Silent & Obedient: English Books for Women 1475–1640* (San Marino, Calif.: Huntington Library, 1982); Ruth Kelso, *The Doctrine for the Lady of the Renaissance* (Urbana, Ill.: University of Illinois Press, 1956); Louis B. Wright, *Middle-Class Culture in Elizabethan England* (Ithaca, N.Y.: Cornell University Press, 1935), pp. 121–227; and John E. Mason, *Gentlefolk in the Making: Studies in the History of English Courtesy Literature and Related Topics from 1531 to 1774* (Philadelphia: University of Pennsylvania Press, 1935). The eighteenth century conduct book has been discussed by Joyce Hemlow, "Fanny Burney and the Courtesy Books," *PMLA,* 65 (1950), 732–61; Marilyn Butler, *Maria Edgeworth: A Literary Biography* (Oxford: Clarendon, 1972); and Mary Poovey, *The Proper Lady and the Woman Writer: Ideology as Style in the Works of Mary Wollstonecraft, Mary Shelley, and Jane Austen* (Chicago: University of Chicago Press, 1984), pp. 3–47.

2. Frank Whigham, *Ambition and Privilege: The Social Tropes of Elizabethan Courtesy Theory* (Berkeley: University of California Press, 1984); John L. Lievsay, *Stefano Guazzo and the English Renaissance, 1575–1675* (Chapel Hill: University of North Carolina Press, 1961); and Ruth Kelso, *The Doctrine of the English Gentleman in the Sixteenth Century.* Vol. 14, *University of Illinois Studies in Language and Literature* (1929).

3. See, for example, Hull, pp. 31–70.

4. For a discussion of such writing produced by women during the seventeenth century, see Patricia Crawford, "Women's Published Writings 1600–1700," in *Women in English Society 1500–1800*, ed. Mary Prior (New York: Methuen, 1985), pp. 211–81.

5. Bathsua Makin, *an essay to revive the antient education of gentlewomen* (1673), cited by Crawford, p. 229.

6. Hemlow, "Fanny Burney and the Courtesy Books," p. 732.

7. See Crawford's Appendix 2, pp. 265–71.

8. Commenting on a later surge in the publication of conduct books, Mary Poovey claims that "Conduct material of all kinds increased in volume and popularity after the 1740s," p. 15.

9. Raymond Williams notes that the failure to renew the licensing act in 1695 resulted directly in the growth of the press, *The Long Revolution* (London: Chatto and Windus, 1961), pp. 180–81.

10. Mason, *Gentlefolk in the Making*, p. 208. *The Whole Duty of a Woman . . . Written by a Lady* (1695) should not be confused with the later *The Whole Duty of Woman* (1753) written by William Kendrick.

11. Harold Perkin, *The Origins of Modern English Society 1780–1880* (London: Routledge and Kegan Paul, 1969), p. 24. Citations of the text are to this edition. Perkin follows a line of argument similar to Peter Laslett, *The World We Have Lost: England Before the Industrial Age*, 2nd ed. (New York: Charles Scribner's, 1971), pp. 23–54. R.S. Neal has faulted Perkin and Laslett for offering a historical representation of society that does not reveal the makings of a class conflict, *Class in English History 1680–1850* (Totowa, N.J.: Barnes and Noble Books, 1981), pp. 68–99. See as well E.P. Thompson, "Eighteenth-Century English Society: Class Struggle Without Class?" *Social History*, 3 (1978), 133–65. Perkin responds to Thompson in "The Condescension of Posterity: Middle-Class Intellectuals and the History of the Working Class," in *The Structured Crowd: Essays in English Social History* (Sussex: The Harvester Press, 1981), pp. 168–85. Both Perkin and Laslett rely heavily on the manner in which social relations were represented to formulate histories of those relations. In citing Perkin for certain kinds of information, I am not interested so much in how he says things really were as I am in the representations he uses. I am interested in the struggle among such representations to define a social reality. It is in relation to the data that modern historians consider as history that I position "female" information, which represents, in my opinion, this nascent capitalist thinking.

12. Ian Watt, *The Rise of the Novel* (Berkeley: University of California Press, 1957) and Richard D. Altick, *The English Common Reader: A Social history of the Mass Reading Public 1800–1900* (Chicago: University of Chicago Press, 1957).

13. Timothy Rogers, *The Character of a Good Woman, both in a Single and Married State* (London, 1697), p. 3. Citations of the text are to this edition.

14. *The Young Ladies Companion or, Beauty's Looking-Glass* (London, 1740). Citations of the text are to this edition.

15. E. Smith, *The Compleat Housewife or, Accomplished Gentlewoman's Companion* (London, 1734), p. 2. Citations of the text are to this edition.

16. T.S. Arthur, *Advice to Young Ladies on their Duties and Conduct in Life* (London, 1853), pp. 12. Citations of the text are to this edition. Although this is an American conduct book, its inclusion in the Fawcett Museum collection—whose other holdings in this area are British—suggests that it was among the few that were popular in England as well as abroad. It is possible that the more active duties required of New England women at this time were deemed appropriate for English women of the lower middle classes.

17. Thomas Broadhurst, *Advice to Young Ladies on the Improvement of the Mind and Conduct of Life* (London, 1810), pp. 4–5.

18. Jacques Donzelot writes that "wealth was produced to provide for the munificence of states. It was their [the aristocracy's] sumptuary activity, the multiplication and refinement of the needs of the central authority, that was conducive to production. Hence wealth was in the manifest power that permitted levies by the state for the benefit of a minority." *The Policing of Families,* trans. Robert Hurley (New York: Pantheon, 1979), p. 13. In this manner, the display of wealth as ornamentation of the body was a sign of social rank that could be read by one and all.

19. For a discussion of the country-house poem, see G.R. Hibbard, "The Country House Poem of the Seventeenth Century," *Journal of the Warburg and Courtauld Institutes,* 19 (1956), 159–74; Charles Molesworth, "Property and Virtue: the Genre of the Country-House Poem in the Seventeenth Century," *Genre,* 1 (1968), 141–57; William Alexander McClung, *The Country House in English Renaissance Poetry* (Berkeley: University of California Press, 1977); Don E. Wayne, *Penshurst: The Semiotics of Place and the Poetics of History* (Madison: University of Wisconsin Press, 1984); and Virginia C. Kinny, *The Country-House Ethos in English Literature 1688–1750: Themes of Personal Retreat and National Expansion* (Sussex: The Harvester Press, 1985). Don E. Wayne argues that it was nostalgia for the ideals of the old but now vanished aristocracy that the new country house was always supposed to summon up; even today the surviving country homes retain, in his words, "a vestige" of "the theater for the enactment of a certain concept of 'home'" (p. 11).

20. *Tudor Royal Proclamations, The Later Tudors: 1588–1603,* vol. III, eds. Paul L. Hughes and James F. Larkin (New Haven: Yale University Press, 1969), p.175. Citations of the text are to this edition.

21. Leah S. Marcus, "'Present Occasions' and the Shaping of Ben Jonson's Masques," *ELH,* 45 (1978), 201–25.

22. *The Political Works of James I,* ed. C.H. McIlwain (Cambridge: Harvard University Press, 1918), p. 343. Citations of the text are to this edition.

23. Harry Payne, "Elite *vs* Popular Mentality in the Eighteenth Century," *Studies in Eighteenth Century Culture,* 8 (1979), 110.

24. *The Complete Servant, Being a Practical Guide to the Peculiar Duties and Business of all Descriptions of Servants* (London, 1825), p. 4.

25. Mark Girouard, *Life in the English Country House: A Social and Architectural History* (New Haven: Yale University Press, 1978), p. 270.

26. Broadhurst, p. 8.

27. Broadhurst, pp. 12–13.

28. Broadhurst, p. 18.

29. Broadhurst, p. 18.

30. Elizabeth Hamilton, *Letters: Addressed to the Daughter of a Nobleman on the Formation of Religious and Moral Principle* (London, 1806), p. 109. Citations of the text are to this edition.

31. On this point, see M. Jeanne Peterson, "The Victorian Governess: Status Incongruence in Family and Society," in *Suffer and Be Still: Women in the Victorian Age*, ed. Martha Vicinus (Bloomington: Indiana University Press, 1972), pp. 3–19.

32. *The Young Woman's Companion (Being a Guide to Every Acquirement Essential in Forming the Character of Female Servants, Containing Moral and Religious Letters, Essays and Tales, also Valuable Receipts and Directions, Relating to Domestic Economy)* (London, 1830), p. 32.

33. Mrs. Pullan, *Maternal Counsels to a Daughter: Designed to Aid Her in the Care of Her Health, Improvement of Her Mind, and Cultivation of Her Heart* (London, 1861), p. 227.

34. Erasmus Darwin, *A Plan for the Conduct of Female Education in Boarding Schools* (Dublin, 1798), p. 3. Citations of the text are to this edition.

35. The Countess Dowager of Carlisle, *Thoughts in the Form of Maxims Addressed to Young Ladies on their First Establishment in the World* (London, 1789), p. 4.

36. Mrs. Taylor, *Practical Hints to Young Females on the Duties of a Wife, a Mother, and a Mistress to a Family,* (London, 1818), p. 18.

37. Broadhurst, p. 5.

38. T.S. Arthur, p. 191.

39. *The Compleat Servant*, p. 1.

40. *The Compleat Servant*, p. 4.

41. *The Compleat Servant*, p. 270.

42. Jane Austen, *Emma*, ed. Stephen M. Parrish (New York: W.W. Norton, 1972), p. 335.

43. Elizabeth Gaskell, *Mary Barton, A Tale of Manchester Life*, ed. Stephen Gill (Harmondsworth: Penguin, 1970), p. 49.

44. Claude Lévi-Strauss, *The Savage Mind,* (Chicago: University of Chicago Press, 1973), p. 150.

45. Dorothy Van Ghent, for example, writes: "This general principle of reciprocal changes, by which things have become as it were daemonically animated and people have been reduced to thing-like characteristics—as if, by a law of conservation of energy, the humanity of which people have become incapable had leaked out into the external environment—may work symbolically in the association of some object with a person so that the object assumes his essence and his meaning. . . . This device of association is a familiar one in fiction; what distinguishes Dickens' use of it is the associated object acts not merely to *illustrate* a person's qualities symbolically—as novelists usually use it—but that it has a necessary metaphysical function in Dickens' universe: in this universe

objects actually usurp human essences; beginning as fetishes, they tend to—and sometimes quite literally do—devour and take over the powers of the fetish worshipper." *The English Novel: Form and Function* (New York: Harper and Row, 1961), pp. 130–31.

46. Charles Dickens, *Our Mutual Friend,* ed. Monroe Engel (New York: Random House, 1960), p. 136.

47. Rogers, p. 3.

48. Hannah More, *Strictures on the Modern System of Female Education, The Works of Hannah More,* vol. I (New York, 1848), p. 313.

49. Dr. John Gregory, *A Father's Legacy to his Daughters* (London, 1808), p. 47.

50. *The New Female Instructor or, Young Woman's Guide to Domestic Happiness* (London, 1822), p. 2.

51. I am indebted on this point to Thomas Laqueur's discussion of the Sunday schools as an instrument of social control by virtue of their ability to appropriate leisure time. *Religion and Respectability: Sunday Schools and Working Class Culture 1780–1850* (New Haven: Yale University Press, 1976), pp. 227–39. For a different account of the use of leisure time in the nineteenth century, see Hugh Cunningham, *Leisure in the Industrial Revolution, 1780–1880* (New York: Croom Helm, 1980).

52. Arthur, p. 76.

53. Concerning the popularity of Samuel Smiles' *Self-Help* (1859), a book that represented self-regulation as the key to success in the business world, historian Asa Briggs notes that 20,000 copies were sold within a year of its first appearance. *The Age of Improvement 1783–1867* (London: Longman's, 1959), p. 431.

54. Erasmus Darwin, p. 63.

55. Martha Vicinus, *Independent Women: Work and Community for Single Women 1850–1920* (Chicago: University of Chicago Press, 1985), p. 15. Citations of the text are to this edition.

56. Madame de Walend, *Practical Hints on the Moral, Mental and Physical Training of Girls at School* (London, 1847), p. 64.

Chapter 3: The Rise of the Novel

1. For an account of the early eighteenth century tradition that linked the novel with lowlife, see Lennard Davis, *Factual Fictions: The Origins of the English Novel* (New York: Columbia University Press, 1983), pp. 123–37. For the objection to the novel because of its quasi-erotic appeal, see John Richetti, *Popular Fiction Before Richardson's Narrative Patterns 1700–1734* (Oxford: Clarendon, 1969). In an issue of Addison and Steele's *Spectator,* for example, Mr. Spectator warns readers about the perils of May, advising that women "be in a particular Manner how they meddle with Romances, Chocolates, Novels, and the like Inflamers, which I look upon to be very dangerous to be made use of during this great Carnival of Nature," quoted in *Four Before Richardson: Selected English*

Novels 1720–1727, ed. William H. McBurney (Lincoln: University of Nebraska Press, 1963), p. xi. The novel was considered a use of language—often written by women—that was designed to inflame the passions. Modern readers have noted this quality in the language of many of the novels written by women in the first half of the eighteenth century. Patricia Meyer Spacks thus describes several works by Eliza Hayward and Mary Manley as "semi-pornographic novels," in "Every Woman is at Heart a Rake," *Eighteenth Century Studies*, 8 (1974–75), 32. It was the pornographic element in some of their language that led William Forsyth in 1871 to refrain from quoting examples of pre-Richardsonian fiction for his book *The Novels and Novelists of the Eighteenth Century in Illustration of the Manners and Morals of the Age* (Port Washington, New York: Kennikat, 1971; rpt. 1871). He claims that he cannot cite examples of the coarse manners of women novelists before Richardson: "Necessarily I cannot give quotation to show this for in doing so I should myself offend" (p. 162). See also Jean B. Kear, "The Fallen Woman from the Perspective of Five Early Eighteenth Century Women Novelists," *Studies in Eighteenth-Century Culture*, 10 (1981), 457–68, and Ruth Perry, *Women, Letters, and the Novel* (New York: AMS Press, 1980). For a list of what were considered novels before the category was redefined, see William H. McBurney, *A Checklist of English Prose Fiction 1700–1739* (Cambridge: Harvard University Press, 1960).

2. Thomas Broadhurst, *Advice to Young Ladies on the Improvement of the Mind and Conduct of Life* (London, 1810), p. 53.

3. Terry Eagleton has discussed the role of Richardson's fiction in seizing hold of the signs and symbols of the dominant culture and putting them to use on behalf of another set of socioeconomic interests. *The Rape of Clarissa* (Minneapolis: University of Minnesota Press, 1982), pp. 30–39. Ann Douglas has shown how feminization operated as a middle-class strategy within a Protestant culture. *The Feminization of American Culture* (New York: Avon, 1978).

4. Thomas Gisborne, *Enquiry into the Duties of the Female Sex* (London, 1789), p. 54.

5. Harriet Martineau foresaw a serious social problem arising from a program of education that prepared women to be nothing more than wives: "Their charge of their own maintenance is thrown upon large numbers of women, without the requisite variety of employments having been opened to them, or the needful education imparted. A natural consequence of this is, that women are educated to consider marriage the one object in life, and therefore to be extremely impatient to secure it." *How to Observe: Morals and Manners* (London, 1838), p. 176. Mrs. Pullan is less overt in challenging middle-class notions of love than Martineau. Thus she dramatizes the general acceptance—by the end of the century—of Martineau's position that women should be better equipped for survival in the economic world than a specialized female education generally made them: "and let no English woman in selecting her occupation forget that the pride and boast of her country is its *commerce*. That all the great institutions of our land, its schools, its hospitals, its libraries, its wealth at home, and the civilization it has diffused abroad, it owes to its merchants and its trade. In remembering all

this, she will cease to think it a degradation to be turned a tradeswoman." *Maternal Counsels to a Daughter: Designed to Aid Her in the Care of Her Health, Improvement of Her Mind, and Cultivation of Her Heart* (London, 1861), p. 148.

6. Erasmus Darwin, *A Plan for the Conduct of Female Education in Boarding Schools* (Dublin, 1798), p. 25.

7. The tendency to educate women simply so that they could display that fact drew criticism from many sources. In every one of Austen's novels, for example, there is an explicit attack on female education. In *Mansfield Park*, Lady Bertram has brought Mrs. Norris in to educate her daughters and Fanny. It is apparent, however, that their education is supposed to be as exclusive as the one that distinguishes males according to classes. We learn that in contrast to Fanny the "Miss Bertrams" know some French, can play duets, are able to recite the kings of England in chronological order "with the dates of their accession, and most of the principal events of their reigns . . . and of the Roman emperors as low Severus; besides a great deal of the Heathen Mythology, and all the Metals, Semi-Metals, Planets, and distinguished Philosophers." To which Austen adds, "it is not very wonderful that with all their promising talents and early information, they should be entirely deficient in the less common acquirements of self-knowledge, generosity and humility." (New York: Signet, 1964), pp. 17–18. A half-century later in her testimony before the Schools Inquiry Commission in 1865, Frances Mary Buss criticized the state of education for girls in similar terms. But even though she was arguing for equal education for girls, her charges, unlike boys, were expected to have "accomplishments," including music, painting, and needlework. *Victorian Women: A Documentary Account of Women's Lives in Nineteenth Century England, France, and the United States*, eds. Erna Olafson Hellerstein, Leslie Parker Hume, and Karen M. Offen (Stanford: Stanford University Press, 1981), pp. 76–80. See also Emily Faithfull, *How Shall I Educate My Daughter?* (London, 1863); Josephine Kamm, *Hope Deferred: Girls' Education in English History* (London: Methuen, 1965); Joan N. Burstyn, *Victorian Education and the Ideal of Womanhood* (London: Croom Helm, 1980); and Martha Vicinus, *Independent Woman: Work and Community for Single Women 1850–1920* (Chicago: University of Chicago Press, 1985), pp. 163–210.

8. Jacques DuBoscq, *The Accomplish'd Woman* (London, 1753), p. 17.

9. Madame de Walend, *Practical Hints on the Moral, Mental, and Physical Training of Girls at School* (London, 1847), p. 62.

10. DuBoscq, p. 21.

11. In *Purity and Danger: An Analysis of Pollution and Taboo* (London: Routledge and Kegan Paul, 1966), Mary Douglas identifies various ways in which the body can be used to define the boundaries of a community (p. 122). Her notion of social pollution is germane to my argument, which pursues the idea that the new middle classes acquired their first group identity as such by redefining the female body, its external boundaries, the internal lines of its system, and certain contradictions that could be contained within it.

12. DuBoscq, p. 4.

13. *The Young Woman's Companion (Being a Guide to Every Acquirement*

Essential in Forming the Character of Female Servants, Containing Moral and Religious Letters, Essays, and Tales, also Valuable Receipts and Directions, Relating to Domestic Economy) (London, 1830), p. 146.

14. DuBoscq, p. 17.

15. *The Young Lady's Friend* (Boston, 1837), p. 81.

16. *The Young Lady's Friend*, p. 427.

17. Broadhurst, p. 49.

18. Madame de Walend, p. 79.

19. *The Young Lady's Friend*, p. 245.

20. Elizabeth Hamilton, *Letters: Addressed to the Daughters of a Nobleman on the Formation of Religious and Moral Principle* (London, 1806), p. 212.

21. Hamilton, p. 212.

22. Erasmus Darwin, pp. 32–33.

23. From the conduct book called *The Ladies Library*, Ruth Perry cites a warning to parents about the seductive effects of reading novels. The passions "'are apt to insinuate themselves into unwary readers, and by an unhappy Inversion a copy shall produce an Original. . . . Indeed 'tis very difficult to imagine what vast Mischief is done to the World by the False Notions and Images of Things . . . represented in these Mirrors.'" *Women, Letters, and the Novel*, p. 155.

24. *The Young Ladies Conduct: or, Rules for Education*, (London, 1722), p. 130.

25. Erasmus Darwin, p. 44.

26. Erasmus Darwin, p. 37.

27. Erasmus Darwin, p. 39.

28. Mrs. Pullan, p. 51.

29. Mrs. Taylor, *Practical Hints to Young Females on the Duties of a Wife, a Mother, and a Mistress to a Family* (London, 1818), p. 41.

30. Sarah Tyler, *Papers for Thoughtful Girls, with Illustrative Sketches of Some Girls' Lives* (London, 1863), p. 23.

31. For a definitive study of modern mothering as the reproduction of gender distinctions, see Nancy Chodorow, *The Reproduction of Mothering, Psychoanalysis and the Sociology of Gender* (Berkeley: University of California Press, 1976).

32. *The Young Woman's Companion*, p. 161.

33. For a discussion of the immediate popularity of *Pamela*, see T.C. Duncan Eaves and Ben D. Kimpel, *Samuel Richardson: A Biography* (Oxford: Clarendon, 1971), pp. 119–53.

34. Kathleen M. Davis, "The Sacred Condition of Equality—How Original were Puritan Doctrines of Marriage?" *Social History*, 5 (1977), 570. Davis quotes this list from John Dod and Robert Cleaver, *A Godly Forme of Householde Gouernment* (London, 1614).

35. Robert Cleaver, *A Godly Forme of Householde Gouernment* (London, 1598), p. 4.

36. Samuel Richardson, *Pamela, or Virtue Rewarded* (New York: W.W. Norton, 1958), pp. 198–99. Citations of the text are to this edition.

37. For this understanding of Richardson's political role, I am indebted to Terry Eagleton's discussion of Richardson as a middle-class intellectual. Borrowing Gramsci's notion of the "organic intellectual," Eagleton argues convincingly that Richardson's novels "are not mere images of conflicts fought out on another terrain, representations of a history which happens elsewhere; they are themselves a material part of those struggles, pitched standards around which battle is joined, instruments which help to constitute social interests rather than lenses which reflect them. These novels are an agent, rather than an account, of the English bourgeoisie's attempt to wrest a degree of ideological hegemony from the aristocracy in the decades which follow the political settlement of 1688." *The Rape of Clarissa*, p. 4.

38. Lawrence Stone and Jeanne C. Fawtier Stone's *An Open Elite? England 1540–1880* (Oxford: Clarendon, 1984) grants this issue all the complexity it deserves. The gentry was an extremely fluid socioeconomic group, they explain, from which one could decline by necessity to the status of a merchant, and to which tradesmen, on the other hand, could rise given sufficient prosperity. In 1710, Steele apparently claimed, "as did many others before and after him, that 'the best of our peers have often joined themselves to the daughter of very ordinary tradesmen upon . . . valuable considerations'" (p. 20). The Stones isolate three factors contributing to this unstable social situation: "The first was the alleged fact, that merchants were busy buying landed estates, building seats, and turning themselves into squires or nobles. The second was another alleged fact, that the declining gentry often restored their fortunes by putting their sons, especially their younger sons, into trade. The third was an alleged social attitude, the relatively easy acceptance of self-made men, as companions or marriage partners, by persons of genteel birth and elite status" (p. 20). Later citations of the text are to this edition.

39. On the relation between writing and the "will" in *Clarissa*, Tony Tanner observes that "the isolated writer is secure within her writing, whereas the speaker/ listener has to negotiate in (Clarissa's case) the always possible dangers of physical propinquity. Thus part of her final triumph is to *write* her *will* (not just the document of bequest, but *will* in all senses of the word), since, physically speaking, she could never live it. *This* will, with all its positives and imperatives, cannot be negated or gainsaid." *Adultery in the Novel: Contract and Transgression* (Baltimore: Johns Hopkins University Press, 1979), p. 111.

40. Of the various attempts to possess Pamela's writing, Lennard Davis notes, "Pamela-the-heroine becomes replaced by Pamela-the-linguistic simulcrum." *Factual Fictions*, p. 184.

41. Eaves and Kimpel's *Samuel Richardson: A Biography* documents both his contacts with people of higher station and his many friendships with women. See William Beatty Warner, *Reading Clarissa: The Struggles of Interpretation* (New Haven: Yale University Press, 1979), pp. 143–218, for an ingenious account of the games Richardson played in making revisions that would tantalize readers.

42. Voyeurism had long been a standard feature of the kind of novel Richardson claimed he was not writing. By shifting the voyeuristic gaze from Pa-

mela's body to her writing, Richardson is quite literally shifting Mr. B out of the narrative world from which he comes and into what Richardson claims is "a new species of writing." The shift of the gaze from male to female, as I see it, changes the very nature of the gaze from voyeurism to supervision and, with it, the role of the novel from semi-scandalous tale-telling to demonstrations of exemplary behavior. For discussion of the voyeurism in novels before Richardson, see Ruth Perry, *Women, Letters, and the Novel*, pp. 157–67. "A new species of writing" is Richardson's phrase in a letter to Aaron Hill, *Selected Letters*, ed. John Carroll (Oxford: Clarendon, 1964), p. 41. On the meaning of the phrase itself, see William Park, "What was new about the 'New Species of Writing'?" Studies in the Novel, 2 (1970), 112–30, and his "Romance and the 'New' Novels of Richardson, Fielding, and Smollett," *Studies in English Literature*, 16 (1976), 437–50.

43. See my discussion in Chapter 2 of *The Compleat Servant, Being a Practical Guide to the Peculiar Duties and Business of all Descriptions of Servants* (London, 1825).

44. The nature of that community has been the point of a well-known disagreement. See, for example, Lionel Trilling, *"Emma," Encounter*, 8 (1957), 45–59, and John Bayley, "The 'Irresponsibility' of Jane Austen," *Critical Essays on Jane Austen*, ed. B.C. Southam (New York: Barnes and Noble, 1969), pp. 9–14.

45. Raymond Williams, *The Long Revolution*, (London: Chatto and Windus, 1961), p. 134.

46. Williams, p. 134.

47. Brian Simon, *Studies in the History of Education 1780–1870* (London: Lawrence and Wishart, 1960), p. 23.

48. Williams, p. 134.

49. Williams, p. 126.

50. It is testimony to her power to create the impression of a separate, yet familiar and unique, speech community that several critics discuss Jane Austen's work on the basis of some kind of linguistic analysis. See, for example, K.C. Phillips, *Jane Austen's English* (London: Andre Deutsch, 1970); Norman Page, *The Language of Jane Austen* (Oxford: Basil Blackwell, 1972); and Mary Varanna Taylor, "The Grammar of Conduct: Speech Act Theory and the Education of Emma Woodhouse," *Style*, 12 (1978), 357–71.

51. For a discussion of Austen as "the mother" of the nineteenth century novel, see Clifford Siskin, "A Formal Development: Austen, the Novel, and Romanticism," *The Centennial Review*, 28/29 (1984–85), 1–28.

52. Daniel Cottom, "The Novels of Jane Austen: Attachments and Supplantments," *Novel*, 14 (1981) 152–67, has discussed the power of society in terms of the power over conditions of communication in Austen's novels.

53. Jane Austen, *Emma*, ed. Stephen M. Parrish (New York: W.W. Norton, 1972), p. 44. Citations of the text are to this edition.

54. To classify Austen's politics, Marilyn Butler places her within eighteenth century categories: "in eighteenth-century terms, she is a Tory rather than a Whig."

Jane Austen and the War of Ideas, (Oxford: Clarendon, 1975), p. 2. In nineteenth century political terms, I am arguing, the eighteenth century distinction between Tory and Whig no longer appears to have defined the important difference between one person's political viewpoint and another's.

55. While I would take issue with Tony Tanner's general model, which presupposes more categories—nature, culture, male, female—than it questions for historical purposes, my own understanding of the operation of language in *Emma* bears striking affinities, I think, with the relationship between community and communication that Tanner describes in his introduction: "Thus the energies of the family are ideally aimed at countering any slippage or shifting in the status quo, at resisting change, supplying lacks, filling up gaps, and denying unacceptable kinds of difference. . . . But language itself introduces gaps and lacks into conscious being, as we have seen, and as a phenomenon, it is rooted in difference, change, and shifting. Thus there is a potential paradox between the speaker who is an owner (in the bourgeois sense), for speaking presages desire and change, while ownership succumbs to the logic of inertia and permanence." *Adultery in the Novel*, p. 115.

56. Wilbur Samuel Howell, *Eighteenth-Century British Logic and Rhetoric* (Princeton: Princeton University Press, 1971), p. 115.

57. Howell, p. 115.

58. Kim Sloan, "Drawing—A 'Polite Recreation' in Eighteenth-Century England," Studies in Eighteenth-Century Culture, 11 (1982), notes that when drawing and painting began to be taken up by the aristocracy and the upper middle-class practitioners to fill up their leisure time, mastering the rudiments of drawing and painting was considered a virtue. When, however, they became practical skills for naval personnel and tradespeople, painting and drawing had to be distinguished as leisure-time activities. It was necessary to indicate the very amateur quality of the rendering and to point out other signs that suggested this female artistic activity was not to be confused with the work of those who needed the skill for their occupation. By the end of the eighteenth century, Sloan writes, "women amateurs concerned themselves less with the ability to draw and were turning to easier artistic accomplishments" (p. 234).

59. Jeremy Bentham, *Bentham's Theory of Fictions*, ed. C.K. Ogden (New York: Harcourt, Brace and Company, 1932), p. 64. Citations of the text are to this edition.

60. Maria Edgeworth and Robert L. Edgeworth, *Practical Education*, vol. II (London, 1801), pp. 383–84.

Chapter 4: History in the House of Culture

1. This observation is not unique, of course. It is noted as well in a number of well-known literary historical studies including such standard works as Ernest Baker's exhaustive ten-volume *The History of the English Novel* (London: H.F. and G. Witherby, 1924–39) (see especially volumes VI, VII, and VIII); Walter

Allen's chapter, "The Early Victorians," in *The English Novel: A Short Criticaı History* (New York: Dutton, 1954); Lionel Stevenson's *The English Novel: A Panorama* (Boston: Houghton Mifflin, 1976); and T.B. Tomlinson's *The English Middle Class Novel* (London: Macmillan, 1976). Although bent on giving less prestigious (in our modern terms) fiction its due, Tomlinson reiterates what the other studies more or less consciously imply: "To put it with more historical accuracy: what seems to me to have happened was that writers from Jane Austen onwards picked up leads developed in the main by Richardson, whose heroines grasp unconsciously perhaps but very accurately, the mixture of personal and economic factors surrounding them, and then went on to develop the middle class and bourgeois interests that he had distilled as at least one of the novel's main concerns. There are breaks in the history of the novel between Austen's death in 1817 and the early Dickens (most of the concerns of Scott's novels are rather different from those in the English novel), but certainly by the mid-century a hundred years after Richardson, there is no doubt about the status and function of the English novel: it is very much a middle class enterprise" (p. 12). See also volume III of the *Cambridge Bibliography of English Literature 1800–1900*, ed. George Watson (Cambridge: Cambridge University Press, 1969), which shows for the period between 1818 and 1847 a proliferation of minor fictional genres, including historical narratives in the manner of Scott, romances in the manner of Radcliffe and Walpole, so-called "silver fork novels," novels of local color, particularly Irish and Scottish, jest books, diaries, and albums of fashionable people, as well as the beginning of the working-class novel tradition. On this last category, see also Martha Vicinus, *The Industrial Muse: A Study of Nineteenth Century British Working-Class Literature* (New York: Barnes and Noble, 1974), pp. 113–35. There is, however, a remarkable absence of novels exhibiting the characteristic behavior of domestic fiction. Andrew Block's *The English Novel, 1740–1850* (London: Grafton & Company, 1939), a checklist of all novels published during the years from 1818 to 1847, offers no indication that a cache of domestic fiction has been buried away under some other heading.

2. Between the years 1815 and 1848, argues Maxine Berg, "mechanization presented a distinctively ambiguous face to contemporaries. It was far from clear whether it was a portent of inevitable economic revolution or but one course of development among several, which might be adopted or rejected, in whole or in part, depending upon the nation's goals and priorities." During this period of radical uncertainty, people representing the whole economic spectrum apparently took a stand on this issue, most of them—at least initially—in opposition to the unchecked spread of factories. "The machinery question," Berg writes, "became in fact the hinge which connected the new economic relations of production with the wider culture and consciousness of the new bourgeoisie and working classes." As Berg convincingly demonstrates, "With perhaps greater clarity than any other contemporary issue the machinery question defined the lines of division between these classes." *The Machinery Question and the Making of Political Economy* (Cambridge: Cambridge University Press, 1980), p. 2.

3. Harold Perkin, *The Origins of Modern English Society 1780–1880* (London: Routledge and Kegan Paul, 1969), p. 290.

4. In pre-industrial societies, as Maurice Godelier explains, "relations of production, or economics, do not occupy the same locus and consequently do not take on the same forms nor is their mode of development the same, and hence they do not have the same effects upon the reproduction of society, and of history. There was a moment," he contends, "when economic production, for the first time, enabled humanity to perceive more clearly the role of economics and the material conditions of production upon the evolution of society, and of history." "The Ideal in the Real," in *Culture, Ideology and Politics,* eds. Raphael Samuel and Gareth Stedman Jones (London: Routledge and Kegan Paul, 1982), p. 31. By facing off theories of economic take-off against census figures indicating that by 1850 agriculture and domestic service were still by far the most important occupations, Berg disputes the belief that economic causality alone explains the rapid economic and technical transformations characterizing the 1820s and 1830s (Berg, p. 3). She demonstrates that it was not until then that people came to understand history in terms of the operations of an economy that was distinct from both theology and kinship relations. If we grant her thesis any validity at all, we must consider the industrial revolution, as it came to be called, as the triumph of a new way of representing industrial growth. The industrial revolution was a matter of representation as much as one of money and goods, in other words, for representation granted autonomy to the marketplace and privileged its operations in any explanation of historical change.

5. On the use of these strategies, see Michel de Certeau, *The Practice of Everyday Life,* trans. Steven D. Rendall (Berkeley: University of California Press, 1984).

6. Nina Auerbach, *The Woman and the Demon: The Life of a Victorian Myth* (Camridge: Harvard University Press, 1982) and Sandra M. Gilbert and Susan Gubar, *The Madwoman in the Attic: The Woman Writer and the Nineteenth Century Literary Imagination* (New Haven: Yale University Press, 1979).

7. E.P. Thompson, "The Moral Economy of the English Crowd in the Eighteenth Century," *Past and Present,* 50 (1971), 78–79.

8. Thompson, "The Moral Economy of the English Crowd in the Eighteenth Century," p. 79.

9. Eric Hobsbawm and George Rudé, *Captain Swing* (New York: W.W. Norton, 1968), p. 61.

10. Thompson, "The Moral Economy of the English Crowd in the Eighteenth Century," p. 127.

11. Thompson, "The Moral Economy of the English Crowd in the Eighteenth Century," p. 127.

12. E.P. Thompson, *The Making of the English Working Class* (New York: Random House, 1966), pp. 543–52.

13. Thompson, *The Making of the English Working Class,* pp. 543–52.

14. Thompson, *The Making of the English Working Class,* p. 198.

15. Thompson, *The Making of the English Working Class*, p. 198.

16. Samuel Bamford, *Passages in the Life of a Radical*, vol. II (London: Frank Cass, 1967; rpt. 1839–41), pp. 176–77.

17. Thompson, *The Making of the English Working Class*, p. 681.

18. Bamford, p. 208.

19. W. Cooke Taylor, *Notes of a Tour in the Manufacturing Districts of Lancashire* (London: Frank Case, 1968; rpt. 1841), p. 6.

20. W. Cooke Taylor, p. 7.

21. W. Cooke Taylor, pp. 120–21.

22. I am drawing here and elsewhere in this chapter on Michel Foucault's *Discipline and Punish: The Birth of the Prison*, trans. Alan Sheridan (New York: Vintage, 1979). Particularly important is the idea that discursive strategies replace the use of force as the approved means of social control. In borrowing Foucault's narrative of cultural change to organize my own observations and data, however, my purpose is to emphasize what was at stake in making the idea of a "mechanism," as he frequently refers to these strategies, provide moral justification for industrial growth. I also want to stress the degree to which discourse, in becoming the means of social control, did not assume this role by virtue of a power inherent within it. Although forms of resistance to the institutionalization of culture play a crucial role in Foucault's model, it is not in preserving an earlier notion of order that they do so, nor is it the process of dismantling other cultural formations that he dramatizes. His story of power therefore often describes what seems to be the inexorable unfolding of order.

23. James Phillips Kay Shuttleworth, *The Moral and Physical Condition of the Working Classes Employed in the Cotton Manufacture in Manchester* (London: Frank Cass, 1970; rpt. 1832), p. 8. Citations of the text are to this edition.

24. In describing the travel writers and proto-anthropologists of the period 1650–1750, J.M. Coetzee explains how they sought to banish the edenic ideal of culture and fixed culture instead to the idea of work. "Anthropology and the Hottentots," *Semiotica*, 54 (1985), 91. Certain categories such as dress, diet, medicine, habitation, law, and trade follow from this, according to Coetzee: "These categories have at all costs to be kept apart. For the collapse of categories into one another threatens a collapse of systematic discourse into what the traveller started with: a set of sightings and observations selected from sense-data only on the grounds that they are striking, remarkable; that is to say, into mere *narrative* rather than comprehensive *description* (p. 89).

25. Foucault, *Discipline and Punish*, p. 197.

26. Peter Gaskell, *Artisans and Machinery: The Moral and Physical Condition of the Manufacturing Population Considered with Reference to Mechanical Substitutes for Human Labor* (London: Frank Cass, 1968; rpt. 1836), p. 6. Citations of the text are to this edition.

27. On the artisan family, see Hans Medick, "The Proto-Industrial Family Economy," in *Industrialization before Industrialization*, trans. Beate Schempp, eds. Peter Kreidte, Hans Medick, and Jurgen Schlumbohm (Cambridge: Cambridge University Press, 1981), pp. 21–29.

28. Charles Babbage, *On the Economy of Machinery and Manufacturers* (London, 1835), pp. 38–73.

29. Andrew Ure, *The Philosophy of Manufacture: or, An Exposition of the Scientific, Moral, and Commerical Economy of Great Britain* (London, 1835), p. 13. Citations of the text are to this edition.

30. Elizabeth Gaskell, *Mary Barton, A Tale of Manchester Life*, ed. Stephen Gill (Harmondsworth: Penguin, 1970), p. 37. Citations of the text are to this edition.

31. For a discussion of the relationship between courtship and politics in mid-Victorian novels, see Ruth Yeazell, "Why Political Novels Have Heroines: *Sybil, Mary Barton*, and *Felix Holt*," *Novel*, 18 (1985), 126–44.

32. Michel Foucault, *The History of Sexuality*, Vol. I, *An Introduction*, trans. Robert Hurley (New York: Pantheon, 1978), p. 38. Citations of the text are to this edition.

33. Charlotte Brontë, *Jane Eyre*, ed. Richard J. Dunn (New York: W.W. Norton, 1971), p. 257–58. Citations of the text are to this edition.

34. Emily Brontë, *Wuthering Heights*, ed. William M. Sale, Jr. (New York: W.W. Norton, 1972), p. 228. Citations of the text are to this edition.

35. William Makepeace Thackeray, *Vanity Fair*, eds. Geoffrey and Kathleen Tillotson (Boston: Houghton Mifflin, 1963), p. 516. Citations of the text are to this edition.

36. Henry Mayhew, *London Labour and London Poor*, vol. IV (New York: Dover, 1968; rpt. 1862), p. 35. Citations of the text are to this edition.

37. Thomas Walter Laqueur, *Religion and Respectability: Sunday Schools and Working Class Culture 1780–1850* (New Haven: Yale University Press, 1976), p. 239.

38. For a discussion of the prostitute in Victorian England, see Judith R. Walkowitz, *Prostitution and Victorian Society: Women, Class, and the State* (Cambridge: Cambridge University Press, 1980).

39. Dickens began to write *Oliver Twist* when *Pickwick Papers* was first appearing in serial form. Throughout his career, he included excerpts entitled "Sikes and Nancy" in his public reading performances. The death of Nancy remained a set piece in his repertoire despite the fact his doctors had warned him that reading this particular episode severely overexcited him and endangered his life. The same strategies for dealing with the culture of poverty that appear in this novel shape John Forster's *The Life of Charles Dickens* (London: Chapman and Hall, 1872) as well as every novel Dickens subsequently wrote. On this point, see J.S. Schwarzbach, *Dickens and the City* (London: Athlone, 1979), p. 12. But the novel's wide reception, however mixed it was at first, suggests that in bringing the city back into fiction, *Oliver Twist* offered a form of narrative thinking in which the political fantasies of a new generation of readers, as well as the scars of Dickens' traumatic childhood, were inscribed. In the winter of 1838, to cite a notable instance from Kathleen Tillotson's commentary in the Clarendon edition of *Oliver Twist*, the young Queen Victoria was finding the novel "'excessively interesting'" reading, even while an earlier generation of readers, rep-

resented by her mother and Lord Melbourne, admonished Victoria for " 'reading light books' " and expressed their distaste for this one's "low, debasing style." *Oliver Twist,* ed. Kathleen Tillotson (Oxford: Clarendon, 1966), p. 600. Citations of the text are to this edition.

40. On the notion of the "new Gothic," see Robert B. Heilman, "Charlotte Brontë's 'New' Gothic," *The Victorian Novel: Modern Essays in Criticism,* ed. Ian Watt (New York: Oxford University Press, 1971), pp. 166–67.

41. I have discussed this point in "Emily Brontë In and Out of Her Time," *Genre,* 15 (1982), 243–64.

42. The paper I read at this conference eventually became "Emily Brontë In and Out of Her Time." But it must be acknowledged that the idea to ask a cabbie about the importance of the year 1848 was directly inspired by Patsy Stoneham's article for a conference at Essex devoted to the year 1848. Stoneham begins her article—"The Brontës and Death: Alternatives to Revolution," in *1848: The Sociology of Literature,* eds. Francis Barker et al. (Colchester: University of Essex, 1978)—with an account of how her upcoming attendance at the Essex conference was received by two friends, both educated, though not specialists in the literary disciplines. One asked of the year 1848, "Did something special happen then?" Although neither had any recollection of the events that have made that year so important to historians, Stoneham notes, they were perfectly aware of the fact that 1848 had something to do with "the Brontës and death" (p. 79).

43. In his creation of a great tradition of the novel, F.R. Leavis cannot find a place for the Brontës and thus relegates them to the status of eccentrics deserving only a note, "Note: 'The Brontës,' " in *The Great Tradition* (New York: New York University Press, 1967), p. 27. Leavis is not alone in declaring that the Brontës cannot be placed within a tradition and must therefore be understood as psychological anomalies. The common practice among literary historians is to assume that the Brontës wrote a transparent language of the self that reveals their unconscious—and generally unhealthy—wishes. This practice can be seen in Rosamond Langbridge, *Charlotte Brontë: A Psychological Study* (London: Victor Gollancz, 1973); Helene Moglen, *Charlotte Brontë: The Self Conceived* (New York: W.W. Norton, 1976); and Barbara Hill Rigney, *Madness and Sexual Politics in the Feminist Novel: Studies in Bronte, Woolf, Lessing, and Atwood* (Madison: University of Wisconsin Press, 1978). More recently, John Maynard has attempted to modify this tradition by demonstrating that Charlotte Brontë was not pathological in our terms or in those of her own day, but that her novels were in fact a working through of problems that constitute normal sexual development. *Charlotte Brontë and Sexuality* (Cambridge: Cambridge University Press, 1984).

44. For example, in *Eros and Psyche: The Representation of Personality in Charlotte Brontë, Charles Dickens, George Eliot* (New York: Methuen, 1984), p. 63, Karen Chase does to *Jane Eyre* what Dorothy Van Ghent did to *Wuthering Heights,* in *The English Novel: Form and Function* (New York: Harper and Row, 1961), pp. 154–70. I consider these to be among the very best traditional (formalist) analyses of the Brontës because each isolates historically significant aes-

thetic patterns within the text. But while these reading procedures might lead, in the case of other novelists, to questions about how and why reification of a particular pattern was occurring in the middle of the nineteenth century in England, such historical questions tend to be forclosed in discussions of the Brontës. Thus Van Ghent concludes with a murky psychological speculation about why Emily Brontë wanted to overcome the barriers organizing *Wuthering Heights*: "Perhaps the dark powers that exist within the soul, as well as in the outer elemental world, would have assumed the language of consciousness, or consciousness would have bravely entered into companionship with those dark powers and transliterated their language into its own" (p. 170). After an expert consideration of the use of space in *Jane Eyre*, Chase similarly turns that text inward to produce a radically ahistorical form of truth: "But now we need to ask whether these spatial images express only Jane's instabilities or whether they allow for the expression of emotional harmony" (p. 85). I use these examples to illustrate the tendency of formalist studies to pose alternatives for meaning that are not true alternatives at all. Because both authors ultimately reify forms of modern consciousness, they cannot explain how and why the novel transformed its historical materials to create a double bind where meaning resides in one of two conditions for consciousness.

45. Using different strategies, for example, Helene Moglen produces essentially the same kind of psychological truth: "To the extent that it dramatizes the conflict of larger social and psychological forces, it offers also the larger truth of myth. But what is extraordinary is that this novel, born of repression and frustration, of limited experience and less hope, should have offered an insight into psychosexual relationships that was visionary in its own time and remains active in ours." *Charlotte Brontë: The Self Conceived*, p. 145.

46. This, in terribly oversimplified terms, is the well-known argument of Gilbert and Gubar's *The Madwoman in the Attic*.

47. Terry Eagleton, *Myths of Power: A Marxist Study of the Brontës* (New York: Barnes and Noble, 1975), p. 4. Citations of the text are to this edition.

48. In writing the biographical sketch of her sister for the second edition of *Wuthering Heights*, Charlotte Brontë used the same figure to separate her sister's novel from political controversy when she claimed that history stopped, magically, at Emily's doorstep as if something prevented it from crossing the threshold: "Where delineation of human character is concerned, the case is different. I am bound to avow that she had scarcely more practical knowledge of the peasantry amongst whom she lived, than a nun has of the country people who sometimes pass her convent gate. My sister's disposition was not naturally gregarious; circumstances favoured and fostered her tendency to seclusion; except to go to church or take a walk on the hills, she rarely crossed the threshold of home." "Biographical Notice of Ellis and Acton Bell," in *Wuthering Heights*, p. 10.

49. I am not only referring to the collective fictions of Angria and Gondol in which the Brontës literally repackaged all their learning for inclusion within a novelistic narrative that took the form of a fictional history of kinship relations. I have also in mind the care with which they rehearsed the process of actually

producing a novel complete with illustrations. For example, the title page of Charlotte's youthful *The Search After Hapiness* reads, "A Tale by Charlotte Brontë, presented by herself and sold by nobody, August the seventeenth eighteen hundred and twenty nine." (New York: Simon and Schuster, 1969).

50. Claude Lévi-Strauss, *The Elementary Structures of Kinship*, trans. James Harle Bell and John Richard von Sturmer, ed. Rodney Needham (Boston: Beacon Press, 1969). See also Tony Tanner, *Adultery in the Novel: Contract and Transgression* (Baltimore: Johns Hopkins University Press, 1979), pp. 83-87.

51. Brontë's references to Jane Austen's fiction are from a letter to W.A. Williams in 1859, in *The Brontës: Their Friendships, Lives, and Correspondence*, vol. III, eds. T.J. Wise and J.A. Symington (London: Oxford University Press, 1932), p. 99.

52. Jane Austen, *Emma*, ed. Stephen M. Parrish (New York: W.W. Norton, 1972), pp. 334-35.

53. This is one of several points in this chapter for which I should acknowledge my debt to John Kucich for generously allowing me to consult portions of the manuscript of his book *Repression in Victorian Fiction*, forthcoming in 1987 from the University of California Press. His views are expressed in different terms than mine, but our work nevertheless converges on the point I am discussing here, namely, the productive aspect of Victorian repression. Kucich regards his work on Charlotte Brontë as "an attempt to redefine behavior in certain novels that has been tied to fear and guilt as, instead, a nineteenth-century strategy for exalting interiority" (ms. p. 5).

54. Winifred Hughes, *The Maniac in the Cellar* (Princeton: Princeton University Press, 1980), pp. 38-72, and Elaine Showalter, *A Literature of Their Own* (Princeton: Princeton University Press, 1977), pp. 153-81.

55. Blanche A. Crackenthorpe, "Sex in Modern Literature," *Nineteenth Century*, 37 (1895), 607-16.

56. "The Bury New Loom," in Vicinus, *The Industrial Muse*, p. 40.

57. "Miner's Catechism," in Vicinus, *The Industrial Muse*, p. 75.

58. Charlotte's testimony to her sister's genius was, I think, no less calculated than genuinely felt. Describing Emily's condition during the period when *Wuthering Heights* was composed, Charlotte uses these characteristically Victorian terms: "Stronger than a man, simpler than a child, her nature stood alone. The awful point was, that, while full of ruth for others, on herself she had no pity; the spirit was inexorable to the flesh." "Biographical Notice of Ellis and Acton Bell," in *Wuthering Heights*, pp. 7–8. It seems to me that the same peculiar cultural logic, which contians female creativity and gives it pathological causes and consequences, still underlies characterizations of the female artist and intellectual today.

Chapter 5: Seduction and the Scene of Reading

1. Charlotte Brontë, *Jane Eyre*, ed. Richard J. Dunn (New York: W.W. Norton, 1971), p. 83. Citations of the text are to this edition.

2. Jane Austen, *Northanger Abbey*, ed. Anne Henry Ehrenpreis (Harmondsworth: Penguin, 1972). pp. 199–200.

3. Francis Sheppard, *London 1808–1870: The Infernal Fen* (Berkeley: University of California Press, 1971), p. 361.

4. Raymond Williams, *The Long Revolution* (London: Chatto and Windus, 1961), p. 57.

5. Williams, p. 57.

6. Sheppard, p. 362.

7. Walter Benjamin, "The Work of Art in the Age of Mechanical Reproduction," in *Illuminations*, ed. Hannah Arendt (New York: Schocken, 1969), p. 226.

8. Charlotte Brontë, *Shirley*, ed. Andrew and Judith Hook (Harmondsworth: Penguin, 1974), p. 114. Citations of the text are to this edition.

9. Charles Darwin, *The Descent of Man, and Natural Selection in Relation to Sex*, vol. II, eds. John Tyler Bonner and Robert M. May (Princeton: Princeton University Press, 1981; rpt. 1871), p. 398. Citations of the text are to this edition.

10. Harold Perkin, *The Origins of Modern English Society 1780–1880* (London: Routledge and Kegan Paul, 1969), pp. 257–58.

11. Sigmund Freud, *Fragment of an Analysis of a Case of Hysteria*, in *The Standard Edition of The Complete Psychological Works of Sigmund Freud*, vol. III, trans. James Strachey (London: The Hogarth Press, 1953), p. 50. Citations of the text are to this edition.

12. Toril Moi has discussed Freud's use of the figure of the relic, in "Representations of Patriarchy: Sexuality and Epistemology in Freud's Dora," *In Dora's Case: Freud-Hysteria-Feminism*, eds. Charles Bernheimer and Claire Kahane (New York: Columbia University Press, 1985), pp. 186–87.

13. In his critique of the reigning critical theories that do not deal with ideology, Don E. Wayne isolates a problem inherent in those that do. Writing of Macherey and De Man, and referring to Tony Wilden, Althusser and Lacan as well, Wayne argues that they share "an epistemology in which negation is confused with absence, difference with opposition, and relationship with identity." This observation can help us understand why the oppositional strategies of Freudian discourse have remained relatively unshaken by literary critical procedures. It seems to me that most literary criticism allows the "absence" of maleness to remain confused with the "negation" of femaleness. Genitalizing the mother's body allows Freud to confuse the negation of that body with the simple absence of the penis. But the myth of the phallus just as clearly uses the mother's body as a transforming agency, or "constitutive presence which remains hidden because it cannot be articulated." "*Gnosis* without *Praxis*: On the Dissemination of European Criticism and Theory in the United States," *Helios*, 7 (1979–80), 15.

14. For a related discussion of Dora's "no," see Madelon Sprengnether, "Enforcing Oedipus: Freud and Dora," *In Dora's Case*, pp. 261–67.

15. Evidence for the mother's so-called "housewife's psychosis" rests exclusively on her strict adherence to middle-class codes. Before this moment in history, no one was called ill—let along psychotic—for being too clean. It thus has

to be an important moment when, for the first time in history, a woman is considered pathological for her cleanliness while her syphilitic husband is considered more or less normal for carrying on an affair in the midst of the household.

16. So important is the scene of seduction to the transference situation that Freud would later advise a lesbian patient to be treated by a female analyst. "The Psychogenesis of a Case of Homosexuality in a Woman," in *Standard Edition*, vol. XVIII, pp. 145–72. See also Suzanne Gearhart, "The Scene of Psychoanalysis: The Unanswered Questions of Dora," *In Dora's Case*, pp. 116–19, and Jacqueline Rose, "Dora: A Fragment of an Analysis," *In Dora's Case*, pp. 134–35. In his "Observations on Transference-Love," Freud describes the styles of women who either refuse to be seduced or are too easily seduced, in *Standard Edition*, vol. XII, pp. 157–71.

17. Steven Marcus has discussed some of the features this case shares with modernist fiction in "Freud and Dora: Story, History, Case History," in *Representations* (New York: Random House, 1975), pp. 247–309.

18. Freud, "The 'Uncanny,'" *Standard Edition*, vol. XVII, pp. 247–48. Citations of the text are to this edition.

19. Freud's views on the nature and the importance of transference changed over time. For a discussion of the history of transference and its place in the analytic process, see Merton M. Gill, *Analysis of Transference,*" Vol. I, *Theory and Technique* (New York: International Universities Press, 1982), as well as H. Muslin and Merton M. Gill, "Transference in the Dora Case," *Journal of the American Psychoanalytic Association*, 26 (1978), 311–28.

20. Virginia Woolf, *A Room of One's Own*, (New York: Harcourt, Brace and World, 1975), p. 26.

21. Woolf, *Orlando: A Biography* (New York: Signet, 1960), p. 5.

22. Woolf, "Mr. Bennett and Mrs. Brown," in *Approaches to the Novel*, ed. Robert Scholes (Scranton, Pa.: Chandler, 1961), p. 188. Citations of the text are to this edition.

23. It is interesting to note that about this time Freud was revising the triadic model of desire that underlies his entire theory of culture. He sought to account for the importance of the mother as something other than an object for which father and son competed. As he revised the model of the mind, beginning with his paper "On Narcissism" about fifteen years after Dora's case and continuing with his fully developed model in *The Ego and the Id* (1923), he not only altered his conception of mental processes, he also gave greater emphasis to the preoedipal stages of development and therefore to the central importance of the mother in the dyadic relationship with the child of either sex. In this way, he provided a place for the mother in the development of culture that later psychoanalytic theorists would elaborate. It might also be noted that, at this time, Leonard Woolf was publishing English translations of all of Freud's writings and also all the publications of the British Psychoanalytic Institute. In addition, of course, many people close to Virginia Woolf were deeply involved in the psychoanalytic movement and followed closely its most subtle changes, including those brought about

by the work of Melanie Klein and her claims for the singular importance of preoedipal experiences in the formation of the individual. My point here is not to argue a cause-and-effect relationship between Freud's revision of his model and Woolf's emphasis on mirroring. I would, however, like to suggest that the efforts of Freud, Woolf, and other modernist writers to rediscover the importance of mirroring as one of the functions of the domestic woman certainly indicate that a battle was being waged for the kind of knowledge such women were supposed to possess.

24. Twenty years after she broke off her meetings with Freud, Ida Bauer introduced herself to Felix Deutsch as Freud's Dora. Deutsch, "A Footnote to Freud's 'Fragment of an Analysis of a Case of Hysteria,'" *In Dora's Case*, pp. 35–43.

25. For a discussion of Woolf's style as part of a general revision of authorial strategies that accompanied the rise of modernism, see Nancy Armstrong, "A Language of One's Own: Communication-Modeling Systems in Woolf's *Mrs. Dalloway*," *Language and Style*, 16 (1983), 343–60.

Index